When should I travel to get the best airfare?
Where do I go for answers to my travel questions?
What's the best and easiest way to plan and book my trip?

frommers.travelocity.com

Frommer's, the travel guide leader, has teamed up with **Travelocity.com**, the leader in online travel, to bring you an in-depth, easy-to-use resource designed to help you plan and book your trip online.

At **frommers.travelocity.com**, you'll find free online updates about your destination from the experts at Frommer's plus the outstanding travel planning and purchasing features of Travelocity.com. Travelocity.com provides reservations capabilities for 95 percent of all airline seats sold, more than 47,000 hotels, and over 50 car rental companies. In addition, Travelocity.com offers more than 2,000 exciting vacation and cruise packages. Travelocity.com puts you in complete control of your travel planning with these and other great features:

Expert travel guidance from Frommer's - over 150 writers reporting from around the world!

Best Fare Finder - an interactive calendar tells you when to travel to get the best airfare

Fare Watcher - we'll track airfare changes to your favorite destinations

Dream Maps - a mapping feature that suggests travel opportunities based on your budget

Shop Safe Guarantee - 24 hours a day / 7 days a week live customer service, and more!

Whether traveling on a tight budget, looking for a quick weekend getaway, or planning the trip of a lifetime, Frommer's guides and Travelocity.com will make your travel dreams a reality. You've bought the book, now book the trip!

Other Great Guides for Your Trip:

Frommer's Irreverent Guide to Amsterdam

Frommer's Belgium, Holland & Luxembourg

Frommer's Europe

Frommer's Europe from $70 a Day

Frommer's Gay & Lesbian Europe

Hanging Out in Europe

Europe For Dummies

Here's what the critics say about Frommer's:

"Amazingly easy to use. Very portable, very complete."
—*Booklist*

♦

"The only mainstream guide to list specific prices. The Walter Cronkite of guidebooks—with all that implies."
—*Travel & Leisure*

♦

"Complete, concise, and filled with useful information."
—*New York Daily News*

♦

"Hotel information is close to encyclopedic."
—*Des Moines Sunday Register*

♦

"Detailed, accurate and easy-to-read information for all price ranges."
—*Glamour Magazine*

Amsterdam

11th Edition

by George McDonald

Hungry Minds, Inc.
An International Data Group Company
Foster City, CA • Chicago, IL • Indianapolis, IN • New York, NY

About the Author

George McDonald is a former deputy editor of and currently contributing writer for *Holland Herald,* the in-flight magazine of KLM Royal Dutch Airlines. He has written extensively about Amsterdam and the Netherlands for international magazines and travel books such as *Frommer's Belgium, Holland & Luxembourg; Frommer's Europe;* and *Frommer's Europe from $70 a Day.*

Published by:

Hungry Minds, Inc.

909 Third Ave.
New York, NY 10022

Find us online at **www.frommers.com**

ISBN 0-7645-6264-9
ISSN 0899-3181

Editor: Matthew Garcia
Production Editor: Stephanie Lucas
Photo Editor: Richard Fox
Design by Michele Laseau
Staff Cartographer: Roberta Stockwell
Production by Hungry Minds Indianapolis Production Department

Special Sales

For general information on Hungry Minds' products and services please contact our Consumer Care department; within the U.S. at 800-762-2974, outside the U.S. at 317-572-3993 or fax 317-572-4002. For sales inquiries and reseller information, including discounts, bulk sales, customized editions, and premium sales, please contact our Customer Care department at 800-434-3422.Manufactured in the United States of America.

5   4   3   2   1

Contents

6 Exploring Amsterdam   122

7 Strolling & Biking in Amsterdam   158

8 Shopping   177

9 Amsterdam After Dark   197

List of Maps

AN INVITATION TO THE READER

In researching this book, we discovered many wonderful places—hotels, restaurants, shops, and more. We're sure you'll find others. Please tell us about them, so we can share the information with your fellow travelers in upcoming editions. If you were disappointed with a recommendation, we'd love to know that too. Please write to:

Frommer's Amsterdam, 11th Edition
Hungry Minds, Inc.
909 Third Avenue
New York, NY 10022

AN ADDITIONAL NOTE

Please be advised that travel information is subject to change at any time—and this is especially true of prices. We therefore suggest that you write or call ahead for confirmation when making your travel plans. The authors, editors, and publisher cannot be held responsible for the experiences of readers while traveling. Your safety is important to us, however, so we encourage you to stay alert and be aware of your surroundings. Keep a close eye on cameras, purses, and wallets, all favorite targets of thieves and pickpockets.

WHAT THE SYMBOLS MEAN

✪ Frommer's Favorites

Our favorite places and experiences—outstanding for quality, value, or both.

The following abbreviations are used for credit cards:

AE	American Express	ER	EnRoute
CB	Carte Blanche	EC	Eurocard
DC	Diners Club	MC	MasterCard
DISC	Discover	V	Visa

FIND FROMMER'S ONLINE

www.frommers.com offers up-to-the-minute listings on almost 200 cities around the globe—including the latest bargains and candid, personal articles updated daily by Arthur Frommer himself. No other Web site offers such comprehensive and timely coverage of the world of travel.

Introducing Amsterdam

Live and let live, easygoing, liberal, and tolerant are some of the labels most often applied to Amsterdam—and with good reason. In the 1960s Amsterdam became the hippie capital of Europe; in the 1990s the city and Holland have taken leading roles in liberalizing laws regarding homosexuality, even sanctioning gay marriages. Similar attitudes help explain the existence of Amsterdam's Red Light District, which is as much a city tourist attraction as the Rijksmuseum or the Stedelijk Museum.

It's surprising, though, just how many people today still think of Amsterdam as being caught in some rose-tinted time warp of free love, free drugs, and free everything. The heady heyday of the '60s and '70s—if it ever really existed to the extent that legend and the soft-focus afterglow of memory would have us believe—has given way to new millennium realities. A tour of the burgeoning suburban business zones, whose award-winning modern architecture is light-years away from Golden Age gables, is evidence enough of Amsterdam's new priorities. The city government has worked assiduously to transform Amsterdam from a hippie haven to a cosmopolitan international business center, and there seems little doubt that it is succeeding.

Fortunately, it has not been completely successful. Amsterdam is still "different." Its citizens, bubbling along happily in their multiracial melting pot, are not so easily poured into the restrictive molds of trade and industry. Not only do free thinking and free living still have their place here, they are the watchwords by which Amsterdam lives its collective life. Don't kid yourself though. Holland's standard of living is among the highest in the world, and Amsterdam's "free living" is fueled not so much by clouds of hashish smoke as by the wealth generated by a successful economy.

A side effect of the city's concern with economics is that all you youthful backpackers out there who don't wash much, who stay in hostels or cheap hotels, and who think "coffeeshops" are the high point of the city's cultural life are no longer quite as welcome as you used to be. You don't spend enough money, you see, and you contribute to the city's image problem. When you come back in 10 years with a salary that lets you stay in a good hotel, buy tickets for the Concertgebouw and the Muziektheater, eat in a Japanese restaurant, and pick up a diamond or two, why then, everything will be different.

Don't be offended: It's nothing personal, just business—there isn't a tourist zone on earth that wouldn't rather have more money than less.

Amsterdam Orientation

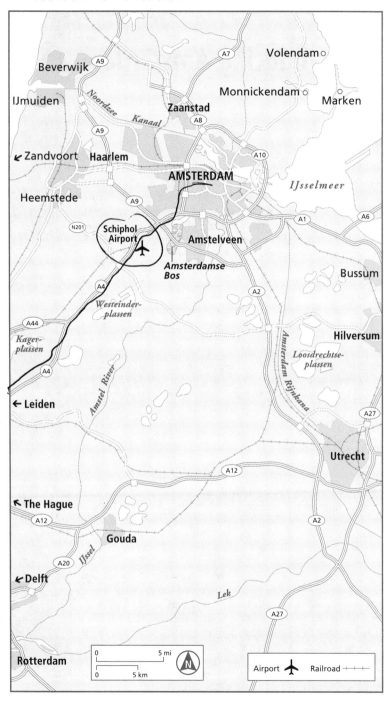

Beverwijk · A9 · A7 · Volendam ○

IJmuiden

Noordzee Kanaal

Zaanstad · A8

Monnickendam ○ · Marken ○

A9

A10

Zandvoort · Haarlem

AMSTERDAM

IJsselmeer

Heemstede · A9

Schiphol Airport

Amstelveen

A1 · A6

N201

Amsterdamse Bos

Bussum

A4

Westeinderplassen

A2

Amsterdam Rijnkanaal

A44

Kagerplassen

Hilversum

Loosdrechtseplassen

A4

Leiden

Amstel River

A27

Utrecht

A12

The Hague

A12 · A2

Gouda

A20 · IJssel

Delft

Lek

A27

Rotterdam

| 0 | 5 mi |
| 0 | 5 km |

Airport ✈ · Railroad ┼┼┼┼

Still, all is far from lost: You can smoke hash to your heart's content if that's what you want. More important, you can still enjoy Amsterdam, its culture, history, and beauty, without stretching the limits of your credit cards.

The city will quickly capture you in its spell—especially at night, when the more than 1,200 bridges spanning the nearly 200 canals are lit with a zillion tiny lights that give them a fairy-tale appearance, or in the morning, when the cityscape slowly unfolds through a mysterious mist to reveal its treasures. Besides the many canals and bridges, Amsterdam offers such delights as the Vincent van Gogh Museum, the Rembrandthuis Museum, the Artis Zoo, the Albert Cuyp flea market, the floating flower market, antiquarian bookstores, brown cafes and tasting houses, and chic cafes and nightclubs.

Amsterdam, the kind of place that's comfortable in a domestic way, is perhaps best summed up in Henry James's description of the city as "perfect prose." The city has been drawn to a human scale. Few skyscrapers mar the clarity of the sky; instead, narrow brick houses topped with plain or ornamental gables and keystones line the streets and canals. The populace mostly walks or bicycles from place to place.

Perhaps the city's greatest asset is its inhabitants. Every Dutch person seems to speak at least three languages—many speak English fluently—and virtually all are friendly to visitors—plop yourself down in a brown cafe (the Dutch equivalent of a neighborhood bar) with nicotine-stained walls to enjoy a beer or a *jenever* (gin), you soon find yourself chatting with an amiable Amsterdammer.

Both the city and its people will make your trip to Amsterdam a memorable and extraordinary experience.

1 Frommer's Favorite Amsterdam Experiences

- **Cruising the Canals:** Hop aboard a glass-topped canal boat for a cruise through Amsterdam's beautiful canals, where you get the best possible view of all those gabled Golden Age merchants' houses—and ignore anyone who tells you it's a tourist trap.
- **Seeing the Old Masters:** Stand in front of Rembrandt's *The Night Watch* at the Rijksmuseum, where 200-plus rooms display works by Dutch and other European masters.
- **Visiting with Vincent:** Visit the Vincent van Gogh Museum, where you can trace the artistic and psychological development of this great, unfortunate painter. Then head next door to the always challenging Stedelijk Museum of Modern Art.
- **Remembering Anne Frank:** Spend a reflective moment in the tragic world of Anne Frank, amid the surroundings of her family's World War II hideaway, now the Anne Frankhuis, where she wrote her famous diary.
- **Treating Your Ears:** Take in a classical music concert at the Concertgebouw, one of the most acoustically perfect halls in the world (the musicians are quite good too).
- **Taking a Tiptoe Through the Tulips:** Pick up a bunch of tulips at the floating Flower Market on the Singel, if only to brighten up your hotel room.
- **Hunting for Antiques:** Four hundred years of Amsterdam history, including a piece of the city's Golden Age, is there for the taking in the Nieuwe Spiegelstraat antiques quarter. All you need is a (big) fistful of guilders.
- **Shopping for a Steal:** Pick up bargains at the Waterlooplein Flea Market and the Albert Cuyp Markt.

- **Cycling the City:** Rent a bicycle and join the flow of cyclists for one of the classic Amsterdam experiences—but go carefully.
- **Riding a Canal Bike:** Amsterdammers scoff at this. Let them. Peddle yourself through the water for an hour or two on your own private boat and tour the canals in style (not much style, I admit).
- **Skating the Canals:** Strap on long-bladed *Noren* skates and join Amsterdammers in their favorite winter outdoor activity.
- **Crossing Bridges:** Cross over as many of the city's 1,200 canal-spanning bridges as you can. The views are great.
- **Going American:** Join *tout* Amsterdam for coffee, tea, and *gâteau* in the stunning art nouveau ambience of the Café Américain in the American Hotel.
- **Beaching About Zandvoort:** Come rain, hail, or shine, take the train for the short hop to Amsterdam's brassy seaside resort and let the bracing North Sea air blow you away.
- **Popping a Herring:** Okay, raw herring is an acquired taste. But the only way to acquire the taste for it is to try, and the only way to eat it is whole, holding the fish by the tail with your face to the wide Dutch sky.
- **Eating a *Rijsttafel* (Rice Table):** Anything from 15 to 30 little Indonesian dishes, some of them as fiery as a Space Shuttle launch.
- **Sinking a *Jenever* (Gin):** Spend a leisurely evening in a brown cafe, the traditional Amsterdam watering hole. Your first sip of *jenever* must be a "look, no hands" effort, leaning over the bar.
- **Boosting Ajax:** Shout yourself hoarse for Amsterdam's soccer hotshots, Ajax, at their high-tech new stadium in the suburbs.
- **Walking on the Wild Side:** Stroll through the Red Light District to examine the quaint gabled architecture along its narrow 16th-century canals—oh, yes, and you might also notice certain ladies watching the world go by through their red-fringed windows.
- **Visiting a "Coffeeshop":** Yes it's true—smoking marijuana is officially tolerated in Amsterdam's very special "smoking coffeeshops." These places aren't your neighborhood cafes, and they're not for everyone, but they're an established part of Amsterdam's alternative tradition. You'll be able to buy and smoke marijuana inside, and no law-enforcement agency is going to hassle you.

2 Best Hotel Bets

For the full details on these hotels, see chapter 4.

- **Best Value:** Taking all factors into account—price, location, facilities, hospitality, Dutchness, and that indefinable something that makes a stay memorable—the **Estheréa,** Singel 303–309 (☎ **020/624-5146**), is the best value in town.
- **Best Location:** Just off Leidseplein, the city's most lively square, close to theaters, cinemas, the casino, heaps of shops and restaurants, canal boats, street performers, trams, and general gusto, you find the **American Hotel,** Leidsekade 97 (☎ **020/ 624-5322**). It's a great location all on its own, and its art deco Café Américain is a city institution.
- **Best for Canal-Side Luxury:** No fewer than 24 old canal houses along the Prinsengracht were converted to create the **Pulitzer ITT Sheraton,** Prinsengracht 315–331 (☎ **020/523-5235**)—which would ordinarily be considered a serious loss, except that the Pulitzer is a genuine prizewinner.

- **Best for Tradition: Die Port van Cleve,** Nieuwezijds Voorburgwal 178–180 (☎ **020/624-4860**), is one of the city's oldest hotels, but has entirely modernized rooms, so you can celebrate the 17th century in 20th-century comfort.
- **Best for Families:** The **Crowne Plaza Amsterdam City Centre,** Nieuwezijds Voorburgwal 5 (☎ **020/620-0500**), provides reliable accommodations and service in a family-friendly environment close to Centraal Station and the main transport links. You also get an indoor swimming pool.
- **Best for Business Travelers:** The **Golden Tulip Barbizon Palace,** Prins Hendrikkade 59–72 (☎ **020/556-4564**), is modern, luxurious, stylish, and efficient, and has an excellent location—opposite Centraal Station—and a full range of business facilities.
- **Best for Prestige:** Prestige isn't everything, of course, but the opulent **Amstel Inter-Continental Amsterdam,** Professor Tulpplein 1 (☎ **020/622-6060**), has it in abundance and offers much more, including one of the city's best restaurants and a superb location beside the River Amstel. This is the first choice of visiting celebrities, so don't be surprised if you see some famous faces.
- **Best Unknown Hotel in Amsterdam:** A combination of location, decor, personal service, enthusiastic owners, and general all-round quality wins the small and little-known **Seven Bridges,** Reguliersgracht 31 (☎ **020/623-1329**), this accolade.
- **Best Budget Hotel:** Many cheap hotels leave something to be desired in the cleanliness department. Not so with the **Van de Kasteelen,** Frans van Mierisstraat 34 (☎ **020/679-8995**), a simple, clean, and friendly hotel whose owners hail from Indonesia.
- **Best American Welcome:** T. Boddy, American owner of the **Amsterdam Wiechmann,** Prinsengracht 328–330 (☎ **020/626-3321**), got his introduction to Europe courtesy of Uncle Sam during the Second World War. He's still enjoying the fruits of victory at his command post on the Prinsengracht, and extends a warm welcome to visiting compatriots.

3 Best Dining Bets

For the full details on these restaurants, see chapter 5.

- **Best for Opulence:** Royalty eat at **La Rive,** in the Amstel Intercontinental Hotel, Professor Tulpplein 1 (☎ **020/622-6060**), as do movie stars, rock stars, opera stars, tennis stars, and even ordinary folks with well-padded pocketbooks. It's luxuriously opulent, the location is great, and the food is outstanding.
- **Best Value:** It breaks my heart to write this, because I know it will only make it harder to find a seat at **De Prins,** Prinsengracht 124 (☎ **020/624-9382**). But duty calls. When you eat in this handsome, friendly, cozy, warm—in a Dutch word, *gezellig*—brown cafe-restaurant, you'll wonder why you paid twice as much for food half as good in that other place the evening before.
- **Best Decor: Café Américain,** in the American Hotel, Leidsekade 97 (☎ **020/ 624-5322**), really ought to be on UNESCO's World Cultural Heritage list. We're talking Américain the beautiful; the Dutch jugendstil and art deco elegance includes magnificent chandeliers and velvet upholstery. In the past, *tout* Amsterdam liked to be seen here (and some of it still does), but now it's mostly for tourists. Don't let that worry you, though: It's still great.
- **Best Al Fresco Dining: Kort,** Amstelveld 12 (☎ **020/626-1199**), has a big, wide terrace beside the Prinsengracht, set back from the water (and the traffic)

and shaded by trees—and you can even reserve terrace tables on warm summer evenings when such places are worth their weight in your favorite currency. But even the wonderful setting pales in comparison to the food.

- **Best Romantic Meal:** Ignore all those whose lips curl into a sneer at such a suggestion— *"Why, the very idea!"*—and clamber aboard an **Amsterdam Dinner Cruise,** run by Holland International (☎ **020/622-7788**). I won't go so far as to say you'll never eat better, but you have the music, the candlelight, the canals, and maybe the moon over the water, too.

- **Best Ambience:** Short of smuggling french fries into a performance, you can't eat closer to the Concertgebouw than at **Bodega Keyzer,** Van Baerlestraat 96 (☎ **020/671-1441**). Keyzer has some great stories, some great customers, some great looks, and some great food.

- **Best Grand Cafe:** It's not just because of its balcony overlooking Rembrandtplein, or its youthful palm court orchestra, or its breezy Caribbean atmosphere that somehow mixes happily with its continental look, or even just because of its excellent food, that **Royal Café de Kroon,** Rembrandtplein 17 (☎ **020/ 625-2011**), is the best grand cafe in town. It's because of all these things, and because it really is rather grand.

- **Best Traditional Dutch:** It sounds contradictory to say that **Restaurant d'Vijff Vlieghen** ("The Five Flies"), Spuistraat 294–302 (☎ **020/624-8369**), is a tad touristy and still traditional Dutch. But somehow it manages to be both.

- **Best American:** Well, Tex-Mex anyway. **Rose's Cantina,** Reguliersdwarsstraat 38–40 (☎ **020/625-9797**), is more of a popular institution than a truly great eatery, though the food can be quite good. You'll probably have to wait a while for a table, during which time Rose's deploys its secret weapon—marvelous margaritas—which is why it's sometimes hard to say how the food tastes.

- **Best Steak:** They've been selling and counting steaks at **De Poort,** Nieuwezijds Voorburgwal 176–180 (☎ **020/624-0047**), for well over a century. Maybe you'll be the lucky one who gets number 6,000,000.

- **Best Vegetarian: Bolhoed,** Prinsengracht 64 (☎ **020/626-1803**), takes this title for its joie de vivre, romantic atmosphere, and excellent and imaginative vegetarian cooking.

- **Best Fast Getaway:** You wouldn't expect that a restaurant on a train station platform would be a good place to eat, but **1e Klas,** Centraal Station (☎ **020/ 627-3306**), is just about worth missing your train for. It offers plenty of good choices and standards that go far enough above the usual run of train station buffets.

- **Best Sandwich:** The only problem with **Sal Meijer,** Scheldestraat 45 (☎ **020/ 673-1313**), is that it's a bit removed from the action. You can have them deliver, but their delicious authentic kosher sandwiches are well worth a tram ride.

- **Best Indonesian:** Amsterdammers seem to think they own Indonesian food (though not as much as denizens of The Hague do), and everyone has his or her own favorite place. With so many Indonesian restaurants in the city, it's hard to pick just one. Still, **Kantjil en de Tijger,** Spuistraat 291 (☎ **020/620-0994**), has a restrained, refined character and consistently good food.

- **Best Brunch:** At **Café Luxembourg,** Spuistraat 24 (☎ **020/620-6264**), you can read the international newspapers provided for you while drinking coffee that actually tastes like coffee and munching your way through an extensive range of snacks.

- **Best Business Lunch:** If it's just a casual affair, many Amsterdam businesspeople will be perfectly happy with a snack from a seafood stall, but if you aim to impress, try the **Mangerie de Kersentuin,** in the Garden Hotel, Dijsselhof-plantsoen 7 (☎ **020/664-2121**). The cuisine is the perfect counterpart to the elegant, refined, yet unstuffy surroundings.

- **Best View:** The big picture windows at the **Excelsior,** in the Hôtel de l'Europe, Nieuwe Doelenstraat 2–8 (☎ **020/531-1777**), provide an unsurpassed view of the Amstel River and Muntplein.
- **Best Kids' Spot:** For small diners with big appetites, there can be no better experience than the **KinderKookKafé,** Oudezijds Achterburgwal 193 (☎ **020/625-3527**), where kids even get to cook their own meals (carefully supervised).
- **Best Pretheater Dinner:** A lot depends on what theater you're going to, of course, as proximity can be a virtue in itself. If you are bound for opera or dance at the Muziektheater, make it **Breitner,** Amstel 212 (☎ **020/627-7879**), which has lots of practice at getting theater-goers fed and watered in style without adding to the stress factor.
- **Best Late-Night Dinner:** You can't help feeling a little sorry for the staff at **De Knijp,** Van Baerlestraat 134 (☎ **020/671-4248**), when you saunter in round about midnight. They've been going hard for hours, but are ready, willing, and just about able to do it one more time.

2

Planning Your Trip: The Basics

Amsterdam isn't hard to come to grips with even if you arrive there cold (in the preparedness sense). The local tourist organization, **VVV Amsterdam,** prides itself on being able to answer any conceivable travel question that any conceivable traveler might have—excepting only those that are illegal or of seriously doubtful moral worth. The city is foreign, of course, but not impossibly so, one reason being that so many Dutch speak English.

Of course, any trip to a foreign destination can become an ordeal if not at least minimally planned. Although in the last couple of years the dollar has moved up strongly against the guilder, that might change, and the Netherlands remains an expensive country, which for most travelers adds financial force to the wisdom of planning.

To really put your best foot forward, you want to know how much everything will cost; how you're going to get there; what documents, clothing, and other travel necessities you should bring along; and when you should go to best take advantage of special events in the city. In this chapter you'll find all the information you need to help you plan your trip before you leave home.

1 Visitor Information

TOURIST OFFICES

Before leaving for the Netherlands, you can obtain information on the country and its travel facilities by contacting the **Netherlands Board of Tourism (NBT),** which maintains offices in countries around the world. In the **United States,** you can reach them at: 355 Lexington Ave., 21st Floor, New York, NY 10017 (☎ **212/370-7360;** fax 212/370-9507); 9841 Airport Blvd., Suite 103, Los Angeles, CA 90045 (☎ **310/348-9339;** fax 310/348-9344); 225 N. Michigan Ave., Suite 1854, Chicago, IL 60601 (☎ **312/819-1636;** fax 312/819-1740).

In **Britain** (covering **Ireland** also), NBT is at: 18 Buckingham Gate, London SW1E 6LB (☎ **020/7828-7900;** fax 020/7828-7941); in **Canada:** 25 Adelaide St. East, Suite 710, Toronto, ON M5C 1Y2 (☎ **416/363-1577;** fax 416/363-1470).

You can also contact the umbrella organization for the country's many local tourist information organizations (see Visitor Information under "Orientation" in chapter 3): **Netherlands Board of Tourism (NBT),** Vlietweg 15, Postbus 458, 2260 MG Leidschendam (☎ **070/371-5705;** fax 070/320-1654).

Passengers traveling to the Netherlands on KLM should have a look inside the airline's in-flight magazine *Holland Herald,* which is written in English and has an "Out in Amsterdam" section that covers events, exhibits, restaurants, shopping, and nightlife.

AMSTERDAM ON THE WEB

The official site from the Netherlands Board of Tourism, **www.visitholland.com**, is awkwardly designed (expanding your browser to its full size helps), but it does have useful advice. The most comprehensive site is VVV Amsterdam's **www.visitamsterdam.nl**. For a tighter focus on places to see and be seen, try **www.amsterdamhotspots.nl**. If you're interested in an American expat's experiences in the city, go to **www.homepage-amsterdam.com**. You'll love the clear images at **www.channels.nl**, one of the best virtual tours on the Net; you can direct your own tour and chat with others about Amsterdam. The cleanly designed **www.go-amsterdam. org** includes an extensive "A–Z Index" with listings for museums, hotels, transportation, and other categories.

2   Entry Requirements & Customs

DOCUMENTS

U.S., Canadian, Australian, New Zealand, and South African citizens need only a valid passport for a visit to the Netherlands for stays of less than 3 months. British and Irish citizens, like all other citizens of the European Union (EU), need only an identity card—but as neither country has an official identity card it makes sense to carry the passport. If you're a citizen of another country, be sure to check the travel regulations before you leave. If you are planning to stay longer than 3 months, you should contact the **Bureau Vreemdelingenpolitie** (Foreigner Police Office) at Johan Huizingalaan 757 (☎ **020/559-6300**) in Amsterdam for further information. No health and vaccination certificates are required, and drivers need only produce a valid driver's license from their home country.

CUSTOMS

ENTERING THE NETHERLANDS   Visitors 17 years and older arriving from countries that are not members of the European Union may bring into Holland duty-free 400 cigarettes or 100 cigars or 500 grams of tobacco; 1 liter of alcohol over 22 proof or 2 liters of alcohol under 22 proof or 2 liters of liqueur plus 2 liters of wine; and 50 centiliters of perfume. Other goods must not exceed a value of Dfl 500 ($212.75). Duty-free shopping was abolished in all EU countries on January 1, 1999. Therefore, standard allowances do not apply to goods bought in another EU country and brought into the Netherlands.

There are no limitations on the amount of foreign currency you can bring into the country.

At your port of entry you enter either the EU Citizens or Non-EU Citizens section at Passport Control, and then one of two Customs clearance aisles, red or green, depending on whether or not you have "goods to declare."

If you're carrying valuables with you, take the receipts along. When you return home, these receipts will be proof that you owned such items before your trip to Amsterdam, and thus will protect you against any unwarranted duty charges. Also, keep receipts for current foreign purchases together and accessible to show Customs officials when returning home.

RETURNING HOME   If you have been away for at least 48 hours, you can bring back into the **United States,** every 30 days, up to $400 worth of goods per person duty-free. There are a few restrictions on amounts: 1 liter of alcohol (you must be over 21), 200 cigarettes, 100 non-Cuban cigars, and one bottle of perfume that is also trademarked in the United States. Special restrictions apply for military personnel and to the importation of antiques, works of art, automobiles, and motorcycles, as well as anything you mail home. Once per day, you can mail yourself $200 worth of goods duty-free; mark them "for personal use." You can also mail to other people up to $100 worth of goods per person, per day; label each as "unsolicited gift." Any package must have on its exterior a description of the contents and their values. You cannot mail alcohol, perfume (it contains alcohol), or tobacco products.

You pay a flat 10% duty on the first $1,000 worth of goods over $400, and 12% for everything over $1,400. Beyond that, it works on an item-by-item basis. For more information on regulations, check out the **U.S. Customs Service** Web site at **www. customs.ustreas.gov** or write to them at Box 1301, Constitution Avenue, Washington, DC 20044, to request the free *Know Before You Go* pamphlet.

To prevent the spread of diseases, you can't bring any plants, soil, fruits, vegetables, meats, or other foodstuffs into the U.S. This includes even cured meats like salami (no matter what the shopkeeper in Europe says). You may bring in the following: bakery goods, all but the softest cheeses (the rule is vague, but if the cheese is at all spreadable, don't risk confiscation), candies, roasted coffee beans and dried tea, fish (packaged salmon is okay), seeds for veggies and flowers (but not for trees), and mushrooms. Flower bulbs must have an official phyto-sanitary certificate on the package. Check out the USDA's Web site at **www.aphis.usda.gov/oa/travel.html** for more information.

For **Canadian** citizens and residents: All valuables that you take with you should be declared on the Y-38 form before your departure from Canada, including serial numbers of valuables you already own, such as expensive foreign cameras. Duty-free allowances are limited to $500 once a year, after an absence of 7 days, and a maximum of 200 cigarettes, 50 cigars, 1kg (2.2 pounds) of tobacco, and 40 imperial ounces of liquor. Gifts mailed from abroad, at a maximum rate of $60 a day, should be plainly marked "Unsolicited Gift, Value Under $60." For a clear summary of Canadian rules, write for the booklet *I Declare,* issued by **Revenue Canada,** 2265 St. Laurent Blvd., Ottawa, ON K1G 4KE (☎ **613/993-0534;** www.canada.gc.ca).

For citizens and residents of **Britain, Ireland,** and other European Union countries: Duty-free shopping was abolished in all EU countries on January 1, 1999. Therefore, standard allowances do not apply to goods bought in an EU country and brought back home to another EU country. British and Irish currencies do not carry import or export restrictions. For more information, contact **Her Majesty's Customs and Excise,** Passenger Enquiry Point, 2nd Floor, Wayfarer House, Great South West Road, Feltham, Middlesex, TW14 8NP (☎ **020/8910-3744;** www.open.gov.uk).

For **South Africa,** Customs allowances are 400 cigarettes, 50 cigars, 250 grams of tobacco, 1 liter of spirits, 2 liters of wine, 50 ml perfume, 250 ml eau de toilette. Also gifts, souvenirs, and all other goods to the value of R500; thereafter, duty is levied at 20%.

The duty-free allowance in Australia is A$400, or for those under age 18, A$200. Personal property mailed back from Holland should be marked "Australian goods returned," to avoid payment of duty. On returning to Australia, citizens and residents can bring in 250 cigarettes or 250 grams of loose tobacco, and 1.125ml of alcohol. If you're returning with valuable goods you already own, such as foreign-made cameras, you should file form B263. A helpful brochure *Know Before You Go,* is available from Australian consulates or Customs offices. Australian currency does not carry import or export restrictions. For more information, contact **Australian Customs Services,** GPO Box 8, Sydney NSW 2001 (☎ **02/9213-2000**).

The duty-free allowance for **New Zealand** is NZ$700. Citizens and residents over age 18 can bring in 200 cigarettes, or 50 cigars, or 250 grams of tobacco (or a mixture of all three if their combined weight does not exceed 250 grams); plus 4.5 liters of wine and beer or 1.125 liters of liquor. Fill out a certificate of export, listing the valuables you are taking out of the country; that way you can bring them back without paying duty. New Zealand currency does not carry import or export restrictions. Most questions are answered in a free pamphlet, *Customs Guide for Travellers (Notice no. 4)*, available at New Zealand consulates and Customs offices. For more information, contact **New Zealand Customs,** 50 Anzac Ave., PO Box 29, Auckland (☎ **09/ 359-6655**).

3 Money

GUILDERS & CENTS

The **guilder** (*gulden*), officially abbreviated NLG (for Netherlands guilder), is the basic unit of currency in the Netherlands; however, the abbreviation preceding prices that you actually see in the country will probably be *Dfl* (for Dutch florin; the form used in this book), *Hfl* (for Holland florin), *fl*, or the symbol *f;* all holdovers from earlier days when the florin was coin of the realm. Just ignore the written symbol and read all prices as guilders.

There are 100 cents to each guilder. Six **coins** are currently in circulation: Dfl .05 (*stuivertje*), Dfl .10 (*dubbeltje*), Dfl .25 (*kwartje*), Dfl 1 (*gulden*), Dfl 2.50 (*rijksdaalder*), and Dfl 5 (*beatrix*). The 1 cent coin is no longer in circulation and though single cents are used in some prices (in supermarkets, for example), the final bill will always be rounded off to the nearest 5 cents. The six **banknotes** come in different colors: Dfl 10 (blue), Dfl 25 (red), Dfl 50 (orange/yellow), Dfl 100 (brown), Dfl 250 (purple), and Dfl 1,000 (green). Each note has a bumpy patch on one corner; this is the bill's denomination in Braille. The price conversions in this book are based on an exchange rate of Dfl 2.35 = US$1. Bear in mind that exchange rates fluctuate daily.

Dutch currency is based on the decimal system, but the Netherlands uses the continental numbering system in which a comma replaces the decimal point. Consequently, you will not see prices written in the familiar format of 1.95, 3.50, 5.00, and so on, but as 1,95; 3,50; 5,00; and so on. The continental numbering system also places a point where we would place a comma, so that bigger numbers will be seen as 1.250,55; 2.327,95; instead of as 1,250.55; 2,327.95; and so on. Just remember to reverse the system you're used to: comma in place of point; point in place of comma.

For details on **currency exchange,** see "Fast Facts: Amsterdam" in chapter 3. You might want to have some guilders with you to take care of expenses incurred upon arrival, when you may be too rushed, or arrive too late at night, to change money.

THE EURO

During the lifetime of this book, the new European currency, the **euro** (symbol: €; official abbreviation: EUR), will move from being virtually a theoretical unit of money, used only for noncash transactions using check, credit card, or some other bank-related system, to being a cash-in-your-hand reality. On January 1, 2002, euro banknotes and coins will be introduced. Over a 6-month transition period, guilder banknotes and coins will be withdrawn from circulation and replaced with euros. At the end of this period the guilder will disappear and the euro will be the sole currency of the Netherlands and the 10 other European Union nations.

I've continued to list prices in guilders in this edition (with the exception of those establishments that now list their prices in euros) because the guilder will be legal

The Dutch Guilder, the U.S. Dollar & the British Pound

For American Readers   At this writing, $1 was approximately Dfl 2.35 (or Dfl 1 = 45¢), and this was the rate of exchange used to calculate the dollar values given in this chapter (rounded to the nearest dollar).

For British Readers   At this writing, £1 was approximately Dfl 3.60 (or Dfl 1 = 30p), and this was the rate of exchange used to calculate the pound values in the table below.

Note: Exchange rates fluctuate from time to time and may not be the same when you travel to Holland.

DFL	U.S.$	U.K.£	DFL	U.S.$	U.K.£
1	0.45	0.34	10	4.45	3.45
2	.90	0.69	20	8.90	6.90
3	1.35	1.03	30	13.50	10.34
4	1.80	1.38	40	18.00	13.79
5	2.25	1.72	50	22.50	17.24
6	2.70	2.07	75	33.75	25.86
7	3.15	2.41	100	45.00	34.48
8	3.60	2.76	125	56.25	43.10
9	4.05	3.10	150	67.50	51.72

tender until mid-2002. If experience since the euro's January 1, 1999, introduction is anything to go by, the Dutch will hang on to their beloved—and beautifully designed—guilder bills and coins until the last possible moment. But you're likely to see more and more prices at hotels, restaurants, attractions, shops, and nightlife venues listed in both guilders and euros or even in euros alone. For comparison purposes, €1 = Dfl 2.2, and that rate is fixed.

There are 100 euro cents to each euro. Eight euro **coins** will be in circulation: €.01, €.02, €.05, €.10, €.20, €.50, €1, and €2. The seven euro **banknotes** will be: €5, €10, €20, €50, €100, €200, and €500.

Note: At the time of writing, $1 was worth €1.07. This was close enough to parity to make the simple mental math of $1 = €1 worthwhile for a general comparison of prices between dollars and euros—but still far enough off the exact figure to cause significant inaccuracy where large amounts are concerned. The dollar/euro rate is sure to fluctuate, but so long as it remains close to 1 for 1, this should make calculation easier for American visitors.

ATMS

You can withdraw guilders from bank automated-teller machines (ATMs) at many locations in the city (see "Fast Facts: Amsterdam" in chapter 3 for more details) using ATM cards and credit cards. Although banks charge a transaction fee, usually 4%, for the service, withdrawing cash from an ATM will probably secure you the most favorable rate of exchange. You find ATMs at Schiphol Airport, Centraal Station and other main railway stations, and throughout the city. **Plus** (☎ **800/843-7587;** www.visa.com/atms) and **Cirrus** (☎ **800/424-7787;** www.mastercard.com/atm) are the two most popular networks; check the back of your ATM card to see which network your bank belongs to, then call or ask your bank for the Visa Plus ATM Locator Guide or MasterCard's ATM Travel Directory. Check also with your bank to find out if you need a new personal ID number (PIN) to use in ATMs abroad.

CREDIT CARDS

Visa and **MasterCard** (also known as **EuroCard** in Europe) are the most widely used cards in the Netherlands. **American Express** is often accepted, mostly in the middle- and upper-bracket category. **Diners Club** is not as commonly accepted as American Express. Credit cards are not so commonly accepted in Holland as in the United States and Britain. Many restaurants and shops, and some hotels, don't accept them at all, and others add a 5% surcharge for card payment. You can use these cards to withdraw cash from many ATM machines (see above).

If you make a purchase with a credit card, remember that credit-card companies compute the exchange rate on the date the charge is posted, not on the date you actually made the transaction. The exchange rate is among the best you can get, but you have to allow for a foreign-exchange transaction charge, usually 2½%. It can still pay you to make purchases with your credit card, as long as you remember to pay your balance in full when the credit-card bill comes, to avoid losing money on interest charges.

See "Fast Facts: Amsterdam; Useful Telephone Numbers" for local numbers to call if your credit card is lost or stolen.

TRAVELER'S CHECKS

These are becoming something of an anachronism from the days before 24-hour ATMs made cash accessible at any time. However, traveler's checks are as reliable as currency and can be replaced if lost or stolen. It's a good idea, for safety's sake, to carry most of your money in traveler's checks instead of cash. Besides, an ATM may be out of service just when you need it most, or won't accept your PIN number, or because your bank balance has fallen below the magic threshold it gives you a message that adds up to, "Sorry, I guess you'll have to starve." Banks and GWK exchange offices give a better rate of exchange than shops and hotels. Be sure to keep a record of the numbers of your traveler's checks in a separate place; replacing lost checks will then be a simple matter.

Traveler's checks are available at almost any bank, **American Express** office (☎ **800/221-7282**), and most AAA offices. You can use your **Visa, MasterCard, American Express,** and **Diners Club** cards to buy them. Service charges range from 1% to 4%.

4 When to Go

In-season in Amsterdam means mid-April through mid-October. The peak of the tourist season is July and August, when the weather is at its finest. Weather, however, is never really extreme at any time of year; and if you're one of the growing numbers who favor shoulder- or off-season travel, you'll find the city every bit as attractive during these months. Not only are airlines, hotels, and restaurants cheaper and less crowded during this time (with more relaxed and personalized service), but there are also some very appealing events going on. As an example, the bulb fields near Amsterdam are bursting with color from mid-April to mid-May.

The cultural season is in full swing between September and May in Amsterdam, along with The Hague, Rotterdam, Utrecht, and other nearby towns and cities.

THE WEATHER

In summer, the temperature doesn't often rise above 75°F, making for a pleasant, balmy, urban climate. July and August are the best months for in-line skating in the Vondelpark, soaking up some rays on cafe terraces, eating at an outside restaurant terrace in the evening, and going topless on the beach at Zandvoort. September usually has a few weeks of fine late-summer weather; and there are even sunny spells in winter, when brilliant, crisp weather alternates with clouded skies.

Although the temperature rarely dips below freezing in winter, remember that Amsterdam and much of Holland is below sea level, making fog, mist, and dampness your too-frequent companions. This damp chill often seems to cut through to your very bones, so you'll want to layer yourself in Gore-Tex or something similar in the colder months. There are, however, plenty of bright but cold days in winter, and if the temperature falls far enough, canals, rivers, and lakes freeze to become sparkling highways for skaters through the city and surrounding countryside. Throughout the year, you can also expect some rain. The average annual rainfall is 25 inches. Most of it falls from November through January, though substantial showers can occur year-round.

Some pointers on being prepared for Amsterdam's often unpredictable weather: First, invest in a fold-up umbrella and hope you never have to use it; likewise, carry a raincoat (with a wool liner for winter). Second, pack a sweater or two (even in July) and be prepared to layer your clothing at any time of year. Don't worry: You're allowed to leave some space for T-shirts, skimpy tops, and sneakers.

Amsterdam's Average Monthly Temperature & Days of Rain

	Jan	Feb	Mar	Apr	May	June	July	Aug	Sept	Oct	Nov	Dec
Temp. (°F)	36	36	41	46	54	59	62	62	58	51	44	38
Days of rain	21	17	19	20	19	17	20	20	19	20	22	23

THE BEST OF TIMES

High season is the spring tulip season (early April to mid-May) and the school vacations in July and August. The city is very busy at both times, which means that hotel rooms are hard to find and bargains don't exist at all (but who wants to tiptoe through the tulips in November, or sit on a sidewalk cafe terrace in a snowstorm?). If you're planning to travel at these times, you should book several months in advance. Summer is also the best time for cycling, which is an essential Dutch experience; try a canal bike if you're squeamish about going on the roads.

In winter, room rates are generally cheaper, and cafes and restaurants are less crowded and more genuine in feel. You won't find such a big line to get into the Anne Frank House (though you'll still find a line); you'll be able to stand longer in front of Rembrandt's *The Night Watch* and your favorite van Gogh; and you might get a chance to go skating on the canals. You also get a better view of those canals, because the trees that border them shed their screen of leaves in the winter; and as an added bonus, the lights from all those canal-side windows, whose curtains are never closed, glow with Japanese-lantern charm on the inky surface.

There's no worst of times to visit Amsterdam: It's a year-round stimulation of the brain's pleasure center.

Your Passport to Culture

A sound way to begin your preparations for a trip to Amsterdam is to avail yourself of the **Amsterdam Culture Pass.** This booklet contains around 30 coupons for free and discounted admission to museums such as the Rijksmuseum, Stedelijk Museum, Van Gogh Museum, and for other attractions, excursions, and restaurants. It includes reduced rates for the Museum Boat and the Canal Bus. All this for just Dfl 40 ($18). Total possible savings on the pass are in the region of Dfl 180 ($81).

The coupons are valid only for the person whose signature is on the registration page, and the pass itself is available only from VVV tourist offices. For information and to order the card, contact your local Netherlands Board of Tourism or one of the VVV offices in Amsterdam upon arrival.

HOLIDAYS

A Dutch holiday can add a festive note to your trip, particularly if it involves a parade or special observance somewhere in the country. But expect banks, shops, and most museums to be closed, and public transportation to operate on Sunday schedules for the following holidays: New Year's Day; Good Friday; Easter Sunday and Monday; Ascension Thursday (40 days after Easter); April 30 (Queen's Day—the birthday of the former queen, Juliana, and the anniversary of the coronation of her daughter, Beatrix); Pentecost Sunday (seventh Sunday after Easter) and Monday; Christmas Day; and December 26.

In addition, there are two World War II "Remembrance Days," neither of which is an official holiday, though some establishments close: May 4 honors all those who died in the war; May 5 celebrates the Liberation.

Amsterdam Calendar of Events

One of the biggest and most eagerly awaited winter events in Holland is the **Elfsteden-tocht (Eleven Cities Race),** in which skaters compete over a 125-mile course through the Friesland province north of Amsterdam. The first race was run in 1909, and it has been run only 13 times since. Perhaps the weather and ice conditions will allow the race to be held when you are visiting. If so, it's well worth going out of your way to see—and even to take part in. Contact **Provincial VVV Friesland** (☎ **0900/202-4060**).

The following listing includes events outside Amsterdam, but relatively close by.

January
- **Concert and Theater Season** is in full swing at venues throughout the city, such as the Concertgebouw, Muziektheater, and Stadsschouwburg, but also at lots of smaller places. Contact **VVV Amsterdam** (☎ **0900/400-4040**) or **Amsterdam Uit Buro** (☎ **020/621-1211**). September to May.
- **Rotterdam International Film Festival.** Contact Stichting Film Festival Rotterdam, Postbus 21696, 3001 AR Rotterdam (☎ **010/411-8080;** fax 010/ 413-5132). January 24 to February 2, 2001; similar dates in 2002.

February
- **Carnival.** Amsterdammers' chance to show that they can party just as wildly as their southern compatriots at *their* carnivals in Maastricht and Den Bosch.

An objective observer (one who's still sober) would have to report that the Amsterdammers fail miserably, mainly because the southerners are true experts on the art of going wild. *Note:* The Amsterdam Carnival did not take place in 2000 and there is some uncertainty as to its future. Contact **VVV Amsterdam** (☎ **0900/ 400-4040**). Early February.

- **West Frisian Flora,** Bovenkarspel, North Holland. Bulb and household furnishings trade show, at Veilingweg 1, CNB Halls. Contact **Westfriese Flora** (☎ **0228/511-644**). February 16 to 25, 2001 (a group from the U.S. has been specially invited); similar dates in 2002.

March

- **Windmill Days,** Zaanse Schans. All four working windmills are open to the public at this re-created old village and open-air museum in the Zanstreek, just north of Amsterdam. Contact **VVV Zaandam** (☎ **075/616-2221**). March to October.
- **HISWA,** RAI. This heading might look like some strange hieroglyphic, but it refers to the annual Amsterdam Boat Show at the RAI Congress Center. Holland is big on boats, and here you'll see how big. Contact **RAI** (☎ **020/549-1212**). March 3 to 10, 2001; similar dates in 2002.
- ✪ **Stille Omgang.** This silent procession along Kalverstraat is held by Catholics every year to celebrate the "Miracle of the Host," which occurred in 1345; see "History 101" in appendix A for the full story. The procession begins at the Royal Palace on the Dam and lasts from midnight to 2:30am. Contact the **Gezelschap voor de Stille Omgang** (☎ **020/524-5415**) after 7pm. Sunday closest to March 15.
- ✪ **Opening of Keukenhof Flower Gardens,** Lisse. Spectacular showing of tulips and narcissi, daffodils and hyacinths, bluebells, crocuses, lilies, amaryllis, and many other flowers at this 70-acre garden in the heart of the bulb country. There's said to be around 8 million flowers, but who's counting? This is the greatest flower show on earth. Contact **Keukenhof Gardens** (☎ **0252/465-555**). Late March to May.

April

- **National Museum Weekend.** A weekend during which most museums in Amsterdam, and 400 throughout Holland, offer free and reduced admission and have special exhibitions. Contact **Stichting Museumjaarkaart** (☎ **0900/ 4040-910**). April 14 and 15, 2001; April 13 and 14, 2002.
- **Bloemencorso (Flower Parade).** Floats keyed to a different theme each year parade from Noordwijk to Haarlem. Contact **Corsosecretariat** (☎ **0252/ 438-237**). April 21, 2001; April 20, 2002.
- ✪ **Koninginnedag (Queen's Day).** This nationwide holiday for the House of Orange is vigorously celebrated in Amsterdam, with the city center so jam-packed with people that it's virtually impossible to move. A street market all over the city features masses of stalls, run by everyone from individual kids selling old toys to professional market folk in town to make a killing. Orange ribbons, orange hair, and orange-painted faces are everywhere, as are Dutch flags. Street music and theater combine with probably too much drinking, but Koninginnedag remains a good-natured if boisterous affair. *Tip:* Wear something orange, even if it's only orange suspenders or an orange ribbon in your hair. Contact **VVV Amsterdam** (☎ **0900/400-4040**). Gay and lesbian celebrations center on the city's main gay areas and the Homomonument (see "Other

Monuments & Sights" in chapter 6). There are stage performances, from belly-dancing to drag, stalls publicizing various gay and lesbian organizations, and food and drink. April 30.

May

- **Oosterpark Festival.** A multicultural festival of song and dance held at the Oosterpark in multiracial district Amsterdam Oost (East). Contact **VVV Amsterdam** (☎ **0900/400-4040**). First week of May.

- **Herdenkingsdag (Memorial Day).** Countrywide observance honoring the victims of World War II, principally marked by 2 minutes of silence at 8pm. Be on the street at 8pm. Contact **VVV Amsterdam** (☎ **0900/400-4040**). May 4.

- **Bevrijdingsdag (Liberation Day),** throughout the city. A slightly less frenetic version of Koninginnedag (see April, above), recalling the country's liberation from Nazi occupation at the end of World War II. Canadian troops made it into the city first, so Canadian flags are popular accessories. More street markets, music, and theater. Contact **VVV Amsterdam** (☎ **0900/400-4040**). Gay and lesbian participation includes stage performances, from belly-dancing to drag, stalls publicizing various gay and lesbian organizations, and food and drink. May 5.

- **National Windmill Day,** throughout Holland. Around two-thirds of the country's almost 1,000 windmills spin their sails and are open to the public, including Amsterdam's six. Contact **Vereniging de Hollandse Molen** (☎ **020/623-8703**). Second Saturday in May.

- **National Cycling Day,** throughout Holland. On this day, Dutch people get on their bikes and pedal. So what else is new? Contact **VVV Amsterdam** (☎ **0900/400-4040**) for special events and routes in the city. Second Saturday in May.

- **Drum Rhythm Festival,** Westergasfabriek. Feel the rhythm in your soul at this annual festival that attracts some good acts. Contact **Westergasfabriek** (☎ **020/581-0425**). Mid-May.

- **Floating Amsterdam.** Transforms the lower reaches of the Amstel River into an outdoor theater. Performances are held near the Muziektheater. Contact **VVV Amsterdam** (☎ **0900/400-4040**) or **Amsterdam Uit Buro** (☎ **020/ 621-1211**). Last 2 weeks in May.

- **Vlaggetjesdag (Flag Day),** Scheveningen and IJmuiden. Fishing ports open the herring season with a highly competitive race to bring the first herring back for Queen Beatrix. Dutch flags fly everywhere. Contact **VVV Scheveningen** (☎ **0900/340-3505**) and **VVV IJmuiden** (☎ **0255/515611**). End of May.

- **Open Ateliers,** the Jordaan. Could be subtitled "Artists Working in Garrets," as around 50 Jordaan artists throw open the doors of their studios to an awestruck public. This is a biennial event. Contact **Open Ateliers Jordaan** (☎ **020/ 638-1885**). End of May, 2001.

June

✪ **Holland Festival,** Amsterdam, The Hague, Rotterdam, and Utrecht. Each year, these four cities join forces to present a cultural buffet of music, opera, theater, film, and dance. The schedule includes all the major Dutch companies and visiting companies and soloists from around the world. Although it would seem that a festival taking place in four cities at one time would be impossible to enjoy, Holland is a very compact nation, and the event's organizers skillfully rotate performers among auditoriums in the four cities. Even for tourists, it's possible to see much of the festival's offerings. Don't wait until the last minute to plan for this event, however; it becomes more popular every year. Contact **Holland Festival** (☎ 020/627-6566). Throughout June.

- **Frisian Eleven Cities Cycle Race,** Bolsward, Friesland. A cycling version of Friesland's famous Elfstedentocht Skating Race (see introduction to the "Calendar of Events," above), based on enthusiasm and the idea that roads and bicycles are more reliable than frozen canals and skates. Contact **Provincial VVV Friesland** (☎ 0900/202-4060). Pentecost Monday: June 4, 2001; May 20, 2002.
- **Echo Grachtenloop (Echo Canal Run).** You can either watch or join in as thousands of footloose people run along the city-center canals. The routes are 3, 6, and 11 miles long. Contact **De Echo** (☎ 020/585-9222). Second Sunday in June.
- **Kunst RAI.** An annual arts fair at the RAI Congress Center, in which many Dutch art galleries participate. The theme is the art of a different country each year. Contact the **RAI** (☎ 020/549-1212). June 5 to 10, 2001; similar dates in 2002.
- **Amsterdam Roots Festival.** Various venues. This festival features music and dance from all over the world. Workshops, films, and exhibitions are also offered. Contact **Stichting Melkweg** (☎ 020/624-1777). Early to mid-June.
- **Open Garden Days,** Herengracht, Keizersgracht, and Prinsengracht. If you wonder what the gardens behind the gables of all those fancy canal-side houses look like, this is your chance to find out. A number of the best are open to the public for a few days each June. Contact **Stichting De Amsterdamse Grachtentuin** (☎ 020/422-2379). Mid-June.
- **Vondelpark Open-Air Theater.** Everything goes here: theater, all kinds of music (including full-scale concerts by the famed Concertgebouw Orchestra) and dance, even operetta. Contact **Vondelpark Open-Air Theater** (☎ 020/673-1499). June to end of August.
- **Over Het IJ Festival.** Opposite Centraal Station, on the other side of the IJ channel. Avant-garde theater, music, and dance performed beside the water on an old wharf. Contact **Over Het IJ Festival** (☎ 020/673-1499). End of June to end of July.

July

- **Arts Adventure,** venues throughout the city. An extension of the cultural program through the previously dormant summer months—when most tourists visit the city. It includes more offbeat and informal events across the full range of the arts than would be the case with the main (September to June) cultural program of opera, ballet, and classical music. Contact **VVV Amsterdam** (☎ 0900/400-4040) or **Amsterdam Uit Buro** (☎ 020/621-1211). Throughout July and August.
- **Tourist Market,** Hoorn. Colorful crafts collections are on display in the streets of this pretty harbor town on the IJsselmeer, north of Amsterdam. Contact **VVV Westfriesland** (☎ 0900/403-1055). Every Wednesday from July to mid-August.
- ✪ **North Sea Jazz Festival,** The Hague. One of the world's leading gatherings of top international jazz (and blues) musicians unfolds over 3 concert-packed days at the city's giant Nederlands Congresgebouw. Last-minute tickets are scarce, so book as far ahead as you can. Contact **North Sea Jazz Festival** (☎ 015/214-8900). July 13 to 15, 2001; July 12 to 14, 2002.
- **Skûtsjesilen,** the Frisian Lakes. Sailing races with traditional Frisian sailing ships, called *skûtsjes*. Contact **Provincial VVV Friesland** (☎ 0900/202-4060). Mid-July.

August

- **Gay Pride Festival.** This is a big event in Europe's most gay-friendly city. A crowd of 150,000 people turns out to watch the highlight Boat Parade's display of 100 or so outrageously decorated boats cruising on the canals. In addition, there are street discos and open-air theater performances, a sports program and a film festival. (The entire festival's future is in the balance, and subject to the City Council not revoking its permission on "public order" grounds.) Contact **Gay Business Amsterdam** (☎ and fax **020/620-8807**). Assuming the event goes ahead, dates are August 3 to 5, 2001, Boat Parade August 4; similar dates in 2002.
- **Prinsengracht Concert,** Prinsengracht Canal. Classical music floats up from a boat moored outside the Pulitzer Hotel on an evening in August. Contact **Pulitzer Hotel** (☎ **020/523-5235**). Third week in August.
- ✪ **Holland Festival of Early Music,** Utrecht. Marvelous concerts of music dating from the Middle Ages through the Romantic era. Contact **Organisatie Oude Muziek** (☎ **030/236-2236**). August 24 to September 2, 2001; August 23 to September 1, 2002.
- ✪ **Uitmarkt,** the Dam and other venues. Amsterdam previews the soon-to-open cultural season with this great open market of information on the Dam, and free performances at impromptu outdoor venues and theaters and concert halls. Both professional and amateur groups take part in the shows, which run the gamut of music, opera, dance, theater, and cabaret. Contact **Amsterdam Uitmarkt** (☎ **020/626-2656**). Last weekend in August: August 24 to 26, 2001; August 23 to 25, 2002.
- **International Fireworks Festival.** On the Pier and Boulevard of Scheveningen. Contact **VVV Scheveningen** (☎ **0900/340-3505**). Late August.

September

- **World Port Days.** Events and festivities around Rotterdam's harbor. Contact **VVV Rotterdam** (☎ **0900/403-4065**). Early September.
- **Jordaan Festival.** This loosely organized festival in the trendy Jordaan neighborhood features food, games, fun, and lots of drinking and music in the street and in many cafes in the area. Contact **Jordaan Festival** (☎ **020/624-6908**). Early September.
- ✪ **Bloemencorso,** Aalsmeer to Amsterdam. Every year for nearly half a century, Amsterdam has been the final destination for the Flower Parade that originates in Aalsmeer. The parade features a large number of floats that carry a variety of in-season flowers (so don't expect to see tulips). The parade follows an established route and ends at the Dam. Contact **Stichting Bloemencorso** (☎ **0297/939-393**). First Saturday in September.
- **Open Monumentendag,** all over the country. A chance to see historical buildings and monuments that are usually not open to the public—and to get in free as well. Contact **Vereniging Open Monumentendag** (☎ **020/470-1170**). Second Saturday in September.
- **State Opening of Parliament.** Queen Beatrix rides in a splendid gold coach to the Ridderzaal (Knights' Hall) in The Hague to open the legislative session. Contact **VVV Den Haag** (☎ **0900/3403-5051**). Third Tuesday in September.

October

- **Leidens Ontzet (Relief of Leiden),** Leiden. Procession and festivities commemorating the raising of the 1574 Spanish siege that came close to starving the town into submission. *Haring en witte brood* (herring and white bread) are distributed.

Contact **VVV Leiden** (☎ **0900/222-2333**). October 3 (October 4 when the 3rd is a Sunday).

- **Herfstflora,** Naarden. Splendid display of autumn flowers at this old fortress town in Het Gooi, east of Amsterdam. Contact **VVV Gooi-en Vechtstreek** (☎ **035/694-2836**). Early October.

November

- **Leather Pride** is a growing happening of parties and other events for gays and lesbians from around the world. Contact **Leather Pride Nederland** (☎ and fax **020/422-3737;** www.leatherpride.nl). First weekend of November.
- **International Flower Show.** Largest exhibit of autumn-blooming flowers, in Aalsmeer. Contact KMPT, Afdeling Aalsmeer, Postbus 1454, 1430 BL, Aalsmeer (☎ **0297/344-033;** fax 0297/326-850). Early November.
- **Sinterklaas Arrives.** Holland's equivalent of Santa Claus (Saint Nicholas) launches the Christmas season when he arrives in the city by boat at the Centraal Station pier. Accompanied by black-painted assistants, called Zwarte Piet (Black Peter), who hand out sweets to kids along the way, he goes in stately procession through Amsterdam before being given the keys to the city by the mayor at the Dam. **Contact VVV Amsterdam** (☎ **0900/400-4040**). Third Saturday of November.
- **Crossing Border Festival,** Amsterdam. Literature, pop music, and cinema are combined in this international festival. Contact ☎ **0900/400-4040.** Mid-November.
- **Spiegelkwartier Open House,** Spiegel Quarter. Amsterdam's famous art and antiques quarter throws open its doors to all for 2 days—of course, you won't be locked out at other times either. Late November or early December.

December

- **Sinterklaas,** throughout Holland. Saint Nicholas's Eve is the traditional day in Holland for exchanging Christmas gifts. Join some Dutch friends or a Dutch family if possible. December 5.
- **New Year's Eve,** throughout the center, but mostly at the Dam and Nieuwmarkt. This celebration is wild, and not always so wonderful. Many of Amsterdam's youthful spirits celebrate the New Year with firecrackers, which they cheerfully— you could even say drunkenly—throw at the feet of passersby. This keeps hospital emergency departments busy. December 31.

5 Health & Insurance

STAYING HEALTHY

You will encounter few health problems when traveling in the Netherlands. The tap water is safe to drink, the milk is pasteurized, and health services are good. If a medical emergency arises, your hotel staff can usually put you in touch with a reliable doctor. If not, contact the **Central Medical Service** (☎ **020/592-3434**).

Pack all your vital medicine in your carry-on luggage and bring enough prescribed medications to sustain you during your stay. If you bring copies of your prescriptions, make sure they're written in the generic—not brand-name—form. Your hotel can recommend a doctor if you need one; you also can contact your embassy or consulate.

If you suffer from a chronic illness, talk to your doctor before taking the trip. For such conditions as epilepsy, diabetes, and a heart condition, wear a **Medic Alert Identification Tag.** The tag not only alerts any doctor to your condition but also provides the number of Medic Alert's 24-hour hot line so that a foreign doctor can obtain your medical records. The cost of membership begins at $35. An annual fee of $15 will be charged after the first year's membership. Contact the **Medic Alert Foundation,** 2323 Colorado Ave., Turlock CA 95382-2018 (☎ **800/825-3785;** www. medicalert.org).

Contact the **International Association for Medical Assistance to Travelers (IAMAT)** (☎ **716/754-4833** or 416/652-0137; www.sentex.net~iamat). This organization provides tips on travel and health concerns and lists many local English-speaking doctors.

INSURANCE

Before purchasing any insurance for **trip-cancellation, medical,** and **lost-luggage** coverage, check your homeowner's, automobile, and medical insurance policies and the insurance provided by credit-card companies and auto and travel clubs. You may have adequate off-premises theft coverage, and your credit-card company may even provide flight cancellation coverage if the ticket is charged to the card. If you are prepaying for your vacation or are taking a charter or any other flight that has cancellation penalties, look into cancellation insurance.

Your existing health insurance should cover you if you get sick while on vacation. However, most make you pay the bills up front at the time of care and you get a refund after you've returned and filed all the paper work. In addition to the three classes of insurance referred to above, some companies offer accidental death insurance, emergency evacuation, a 24-hour worldwide emergency hot line, and more.

Note that to submit any claim you must always have thorough documentation, including all receipts, police reports, medical records, and the like.

Members of **Blue Cross/Blue Shield** can now use their cards at select hospitals in most major cities worldwide (☎ **800/810-BLUE;** www.bluecares.com/blue/ bluecards/wwwn for a list of hospitals). **Medicare** covers only U.S. citizens traveling in Mexico and Canada.

If you do require additional insurance, in the United States the following reputable companies can help: **Access America,** 6600 W. Broad St., Richmond, VA 23230 (☎ **800/284-8300**); **Travel Guard International,** 1145 Clark St., Stevens Point, WI 54481 (☎ **800/826-1300**); **Travel Insured International, Inc.,** P.O. Box 280568, East Hartford, CT 06128-0568 (☎ **800/243-3174** in the U.S. or 203/528-7663 outside the U.S., between 7:45am and 7pm EST); **Travelex Insurance Services,** P.O. Box 9408, Garden City, NY11530-9408 (☎ **800/228-9792**). Companies specializing in accident and medical care include: **MEDEX International,** P.O. Box 5375, Timonium, MD 21094-5375 (☎ **888/MEDEX-00** or 410/453-6300; www.medexassist.com); **Travel Assistance International (Worldwide Assistance Services, Inc.),** 1133 15th St. NW, Suite 400, Washington, D.C. 20005 (☎ **800/ 821-2828** or 202/828-5894).

In **Britain,** contact **Columbus Travel Insurance,** 279 High St., Croydon CR0 1QH (☎ **020/7375-0011** in London; www2.columbusdirect.com); students can try **Campus Travel** (☎ **020/7730-3402** in London).

6 Tips for Travelers with Special Needs

FOR TRAVELERS WITH DISABILITIES

The old center of Amsterdam—filled with narrow cobbled streets, steep humpback bridges, zillions of little barrier pillars called *Amsterdammetjes,* and bicycles parked all over the place—can be hard going. But many hotels and restaurants provide easy access for people with disabilities, and some display the international wheelchair symbol in their brochures and advertising. It's always a good idea to call ahead to find out just what the situation is before you book; in particular, bear in mind that many older hotels have no elevator and have steep, narrow stairways. Many, but not all, museums and other sights are wheelchair-accessible, wholly or partly, and some have adapted toilets. Always call ahead to check on accessibility at sights you wish to visit.

The Netherlands Board of Tourism issues a *Holland for the Handicapped* brochure. Schiphol Airport has a service to help travelers with disabilities through the airport. Most Amsterdam trams are inaccessible, or accessible only with difficulty, to wheelchairs; the new trams being introduced on some routes have low central doors that are accessible. The Metro system is fully accessible, but that's not as good as it sounds because few Metro stations are near places where visitors want to go. Taxis are also difficult, but new mini-van taxis are an improvement; or call ahead to book with **Boonstra Taxis** (☎ 020/613-4134), which has wheelchair-accessible cabs.

There's comprehensive assistance for travelers with disabilities throughout the **Netherlands Railways** (☎ 030/235-5555) system, and if you give them a day's notice of your journey by visiting a station or calling ahead they can arrange for assistance along the way.

A World of Options, a book of resources for travelers with disabilities, covers everything from biking trips to scuba outfitters. It costs $35 ($30 for members) and is available from **Mobility International USA,** P.O. Box 10767, Eugene, OR 97440 (☎ 541/343-1284 voice and TDD; fax 503/343-6812; www.miusa.org). Annual membership of Mobility International is $35, which includes their quarterly newsletter, *Over the Rainbow.*

A useful book for travelers with disabilities is *Access to the World: A Travel Guide for the Handicapped,* by Louise Weiss, which can be ordered from Henry Holt & Co. (☎ 800/247-3912). **Twin Peaks Press,** P.O. Box 139, Vancouver, WA 98666 (☎ 360/694-2462), publishes travel-related books for people with disabilities.

The **Moss Rehab Hospital** (☎ 215/456-9600) has been providing friendly and helpful phone advice and referrals to disabled travelers for years through its **Travel Information Service** (☎ 215/456-9603; www.mossresourcenet.org).

You can join the **Society for the Advancement of Travel for the Handicapped (SATH),** 347 Fifth Ave., Suite 610 New York, NY 10016 (☎ 212/447-7284; fax 212/725-8253; www.sath.org), for $45 annually, $30 for seniors and students, to gain access to their vast network of connections in the travel industry. They provide information sheets on travel destinations and referrals to tour operators who specialize in traveling with disabilities. Their quarterly magazine, *Open World for Disability and Mature Travel,* is full of good information and resources. A year's subscription is $13 ($21 outside the U.S.).

An organized tour package can make life on the road much easier. One of the best operators is **Flying Wheels Travel,** 143 West Bridge (P.O. Box 382, Owatonna, MN 55060; ☎ 800/535-6790; www.flyingwheels.com). They offer various escorted tours, with an emphasis on sports, as well as private tours in minivans with lifts. Other reputable specialized tour operators include **Accessible Journeys** (☎ 800/TINGLES or 610/521-0339), for slow walkers and wheelchair travelers; **Guided Tour Inc.** (☎ 215/782-1370); and **Directions Unlimited** (☎ 800/533-5343).

Vision-impaired travelers should contact the **American Foundation for the Blind,** 11 Penn Plaza, Suite 300, New York, NY 10001 (☎ 800/232-5463), for information on traveling with Seeing Eye dogs.

For British travelers, the **Royal Association for Disability and Rehabilitation (RADAR),** Unit 12, City Forum, 250 City Rd., London EC1V 8AF (☎ **020/ 7250-3222**), publishes three holiday "fact packs" for £2 each or £5 for all three. The first one provides general information, including planning and booking a holiday, insurance, and finances; the second outlines transportation available when going abroad and equipment for rent; the third covers specialized accommodations. Another good resource is the **Holiday Care Service,** Imperial Building, 2nd Floor, Victoria Rd., Horley, Surrey RH6 7PZ (☎ **01293/774535;** fax 01293/784647).

FOR GAYS & LESBIANS

The **International Gay & Lesbian Travel Association (IGLTA)** (☎ **800/448-8550** or 954/776-2626; fax 954/776-3303; www.iglta.org), links travelers up with the appropriate gay-friendly service organization or tour specialist. With around 1,200 members, it offers quarterly newsletters, marketing mailings, and a membership directory that's updated quarterly. Membership often includes gay or lesbian businesses, but is open to individuals for $150 yearly, plus a $100 administration fee for new members. It keeps members informed of gay and gay-friendly hoteliers, tour operators, and airline and cruise-line representatives.

Travel agencies for gays and lesbians include **Family Abroad** (☎ 800/999-5500 or 212/459-1800); **Yellowbrick Road** (☎ **800/642-2488**); and, mainly for gay men, **Above and Beyond Tours** (☎ **800/397-2681**).

You may want to pick up a copy of the latest edition of *Frommer's Gay & Lesbian Europe,* which has a fabulous chapter on Amsterdam. Other good guidebooks, both focused on gay men, but including information for lesbians, are the *Spartacus International Gay Guide* and *Gay Travel A to Z.* The gay and lesbian **Ferrari Guides** Web site (www.ferrariguides.com) puts up a good destination guide to Amsterdam, which you can download complete in PDF format.

Out and About, 8 W. 19th St. 401, New York, NY 10011 (☎ **800/929-2268** or 212/645-6922), offers guidebooks and a monthly newsletter packed with good information on the global gay and lesbian scene. A year's subscription to the newsletter costs $49. *Our World,* 1104 N. Nova Rd., Suite 251, Daytona Beach, FL 32117 (☎ **904/441-5367**), is a slick monthly magazine promoting and highlighting travel bargains and opportunities. Annual subscription rates are $35 in the United States, $45 outside the United States.

In Amsterdam, you can get information, or just meet people, by visiting **COC,** Rozenstraat 14 (☎ **020/626-3087;** www.cocamsterdam.nl), the Amsterdam branch of the Dutch lesbian and gay organization. On the premises there is a daytime cafe serving coffee and quiches, a meeting space for special interest groups, weekend discos (mainly men on Friday, women on Saturday), and a special ethnic evening called Strange Fruit on Sundays. The **Gay and Lesbian Switchboard** (☎ **020/623-6565;** www.switchboard.nl), open daily 10am to 10pm, can provide you with all kinds of information and advice.

You shouldn't have much trouble finding information about gay and lesbian bars and clubs because they are well publicized. Also see "Gay & Lesbian Bars" under "The Bar Scene" in chapter 9. The free biweekly listings magazine *Shark,* amusingly subtitled "Underwater Amsterdam," is a great source of cultural information, in particular for the off-beat and alternative scenes, and comes with a centerfold pullout, titled *Queer Fish,* which has excellent lesbian and gay listings. *Gay News Amsterdam* and *Gay & Night,* competing bilingual monthly magazines in both Dutch and English, are available free in gay establishments around the city but lack extensive listings information.

FOR SENIORS

Many major hotel chains offer a **senior citizen's discount,** and you should be sure to ask for the reduction when you make the reservation and carry some kind of identification, such as a passport or driver's license, that shows your date of birth when you check in. Sightseeing attractions and entertainments often offer senior discounts, but many such places only offer these reductions to Dutch citizens, on production of an appropriate ID. Be sure to ask when you buy your ticket.

Members of the **American Association of Retired Persons (AARP),** 601 E St. NW, Washington, DC 20049 (☎ **800//424-3410** or 202/434-2277), get discounts on airfares, hotels, and car rental. AARP's Travel Service puts together packages at moderate rates. The **National Council of Senior Citizens,** 8403 Colesville Rd., Suite 1200, Silver Spring, MD 20910-3314 (☎ **301/578-8800**), offers a newsletter six times a year that's partly devoted to travel tips, and discounts on hotel and car rentals.

Members of **Mature Outlook,** P.O. Box 9390, Des Moines, IA 50306 (☎ **800/336-6330**), receive discounts on hotels (and from Sears) and a bimonthly magazine. Annual membership is $19.95. **Golden Companions,** P.O. Box 5249, Reno, NV 89513 (☎ **702/324-2227**), helps travelers age 45-plus find compatible companions through a personal voice-mail service. Contact them for more information.

The Mature Traveler, a monthly newsletter on senior travel, is a valuable resource. It is available by subscription, $30 a year, from GEM Publishing Group, Box 50400, Reno, NV 89513-0400. Another helpful publication is ***101 Tips for the Mature Traveler,*** available from Grand Circle Travel, 347 Congress St., Suite 3A, Boston, MA 02210 (☎ **800/221-2610** or 617/350-7500; fax 617/346-6700). **Grand Circle Travel** is one of the hundreds of travel agencies specializing in vacations for seniors. Many of these are tour-bus packages. Seniors seeking more independent travel should probably consult a regular travel agent. **SAGA International Holidays,** 222 Berkeley St., Boston, MA 02116 (☎ **800/343-0273**), offers inclusive tours and cruises for those age 50 and over. SAGA also sponsors the more substantial "Road Scholar Tours" (☎ **800/621-2151**), which are fun-loving but with an educational bent.

If you want something more than the average vacation or guided tour, try **Elderhostel** (☎ **877/426-8056;** www.elderhostel.org) or the University of New Hampshire's **Interhostel** (☎ **800/733-9753**), both variations on the same theme of escorted educational tours for senior citizens, led by academic experts, and packed with seminars, lectures, field trips, and sightseeing.

For **British** seniors, **Wasteels,** Victoria Station, London SW1V 1JZ (☎ **020/7834-6744**), provides an over-60s **Rail Europe Senior Card** that offers discounts ranging from 25% to 40% off regular second-class fares. Keep in mind, however, that discounts depend on the time of day and even the type of train. Its price is £5. To qualify, British residents must present a valid British Senior Citizen rail card, which you can get for £16, along with proof of age and British residency, at main railway stations.

In Amsterdam, the **VVV tourist offices** can furnish addresses and telephone numbers for church and social organizations whose activities are slanted toward the upper age brackets. They can also advise you of municipal social agencies for help with specific problems.

FOR FAMILIES

On airlines, you must request a special menu for children at least 24 hours in advance. Bring your own baby food, though; you can ask a flight attendant to warm it to the right temperature.

Arrange ahead of time for such necessities as a crib, bottle warmer, and car seat (in the Netherlands, small children are not allowed to ride in the front seat). For information on baby-sitters, see "Fast Facts: Amsterdam" in chapter 3.

Several books on the market offer tips to help you travel with kids. *Family Travel* (Lanier Publishing International), *How to Take Great Trips with Your Kids* (The Harvard Common Press), and *Adventuring with Children* (Foghorn Press) are reliable and full of good advice that can apply to travel anywhere.

Family Travel Times is published six times a year by **TWYCH (Travel with Your Children;** ☎ **888/822-4388** or 212/477-5524), and includes a weekly call-in service for subscribers. Subscriptions are $40 a year.

Families Welcome!, 92 N. Main, Ashland, OR 97520 (☎ **800/326-0724** or 541/482-6121), a travel company specializing in worry-free vacations for families, offers "City Kids" packages to certain European cities, including Amsterdam.

The University of New Hampshire runs **Familyhostel** (☎ **800/733-9753**), an intergenerational alternative to standard guided tours designed for children age 8 to 15, parents, and grandparents. You live on a European college campus for the 2- or 3-week program, attend lectures and seminars, go on lots of field trips, and do all the sightseeing—all of it guided by a team of experts and academics.

7 Getting There

BY PLANE

FROM THE U.S.   Partner airlines **KLM Royal Dutch Airlines** (☎ 800/374-7747; www.klm.com) and **Northwest Airlines** (☎ 800/447-4747; www.nwa.com), together offer direct flights and easy connections from most U.S. cities to Amsterdam's Schiphol Airport. These include service twice daily from New York; daily from Chicago, Los Angeles, Houston; and two to six times a week from Atlanta, Baltimore, Boston, Detroit, Memphis, Minneapolis/St. Paul, San Francisco, Orlando, and Washington, D.C.

Other airlines fly direct from the U.S. to Amsterdam. **United Airlines** (☎ 800/241-6522; www.ual.com) flies nonstop from Washington Dulles. **Delta Airlines** (☎ 800/241-4141; www.delta-air.com) has daily nonstop service from Atlanta and New York. **Martinair** (☎ 800/627-8462; www.martinairusa.com) has nonstop flights year-round from Miami, Orlando, Tampa, and Denver, and from May to September from Newark, Los Angeles, and Oakland.

FROM CANADA   KLM/Northwest (☎ 800/361-5073; www.klm.com; www.nwa.com) have daily nonstop flights from Toronto, and several flights a week from Calgary, Montréal, Ottawa, Winnipeg, and Vancouver.

Air Canada (☎ 800/555-1212; www.aircanada.ca) flies daily from Toronto to Amsterdam.

FROM BRITAIN   London and many smaller British cities have daily flights by **British Airways** (☎ 0345/222111; www.british-airways.com), **KLM uk** (☎ 08705/074074; www.klmuk.com), and **British Midland** (☎ 0870/6070555; www.britishmidland.co.uk).

FROM IRELAND   Aer Lingus (☎ 01/886-8888; www.aerlingus.ie) flies daily from Dublin.

FROM AUSTRALIA   KLM (☎ 1-800/505747; www.klm.com) flies from Sydney to Amsterdam 3 days a week. **Qantas** (☎ 131313; www.qantas.com.au) flies twice a week.

FROM NEW ZEALAND KLM (☎ **09/309-1782;** www.klm.com) flies from Auckland to Amsterdam.

FROM SOUTH AFRICA KLM (☎ **021/670-2500;** www.klm.com) flies from Johannesburg to Amsterdam.

FLY FOR LESS: TIPS FOR GETTING THE BEST AIRFARES

REGULAR AIRFARES Advance planning and precision timing are the keys to saving money on international airfares; flexibility in scheduling and the ability to stick to the dates you reserve are also a help. The lowest fares in the business these days are called **APEX** (advance-purchase excursion) fares. Requirements vary among airlines, but generally these fares require you to reserve and pick up tickets at least 7 days in advance and to stay abroad a minimum or maximum number of days (or both); there may also be additional charges for cancellations and changes of flights. Fares also vary by season of the year, with the lowest prices offered November through March (except during the Christmas period) and the highest between June and October.

Excursion fares are higher than APEX, but there's no advance-purchase requirement (though most do require a specified minimum stay).

All airlines offer **promotional** fares from time to time. Most have tight restrictions; but no matter when you plan to fly and what airline you choose, it pays to keep a sharp eye out for newspaper, television, and radio advertising in order to take advantage of the considerable savings offered by these fares.

BUCKET SHOPS/CONSOLIDATORS These companies act as clearinghouses for blocks of tickets that airlines discount and consign during normally slow periods of air travel.

Tickets are usually priced 20% to 35% below the full fare. Terms of payment can vary—anything between last-minute and 45 days prior to departure. Tickets can be purchased through regular travel agents, who usually mark up the ticket 8% to 10%, maybe more, thereby greatly reducing your discount. A survey conducted of flyers who use consolidators voiced only one major complaint: Use of such a ticket doesn't qualify you for an advance seat assignment, and you are therefore likely to be assigned a poor seat on the plane at the last minute.

The survey also revealed that most flyers estimated their savings at around $200 per ticket off the regular price. Nearly a third of the passengers reported savings of up to $300 off the regular price. But—and here's the hitch—many people who booked consolidator tickets reported no savings at all, as the airlines will sometimes match the consolidator fare by announcing a promotional fare. The situation is a bit tricky and calls for some careful investigation on your part to determine just how much you're saving.

Bucket shops abound from coast to coast. Look also for their ads in your local newspaper's travel section—they're usually very small and a single column in width. Here are some recommendations:

One of the biggest U.S. consolidators is **Travac,** 989 Sixth Ave., New York, NY 10018 (☎ **800/TRAV-800** or 212/563-3303; www.travac.com). Also try **TFI Tours International,** 34 W. 32nd St., 12th Floor, New York, NY 10001 (☎ **800/ 745-8000**); **Euram Tours,** 1522 K St. NW, 4th Floor, Washington, DC 20005 (☎ **800/848-6789** or 202/789-2255; www.flyeuram.com); and **Travel Avenue,** 10 S. Riverside Plaza, Suite 1404, Chicago, IL 60606 (☎ **800/333-3335** or 312/ 876-6866; www.travelavenue.com).

In addition, **Cheap Tickets** (☎ **800/377-1000**), **1-800/FLY-4-LESS,** and **1-800/ FLY-CHEAP** all specialize in finding the lowest fares out there. You can often get discounted fares on short notice without all the advance-purchase requirements.

Trailfinders (☎ 020/7937-5400 in London) is a consolidator in the United Kingdom that offers access to tickets on major European carriers. There are many other bucket shops around Victoria and Earls Court in London. **CEEFAX,** an information service included on many home and hotel TVs, runs details of package holidays and flights to continental Europe and beyond.

Since dealing with unknown bucket shops can be a little risky, it might be a good idea to call the Better Business Bureau in your area to see if complaints have been filed against the company from which you plan to purchase a fare.

ONLINE BARGAINS   More savvy travelers are finding excellent deals on everything from flights to whole vacation packages by searching the Internet. Although Web sites tend to change as fast as the Internet itself, a good beginning is to engage your favorite search engine, such as Yahoo! or AltaVista, and search for the keyword "travel." Here are some particularly useful sites.

Now incorporating Preview Travel, **Travelocity** (www.travelocity.com, www.previewtravel.com, www.frommers.travelocity.com) is Frommer's online travel planning/booking partner. It offers reservations and tickets for more than 400 airlines, plus reservations and purchase capabilities for more than 45,000 hotels and 50 car-rental companies. An exclusive feature is its Low Fare Search Engine, which automatically searches for the three lowest-priced itineraries based on your criteria. With the Fare Watcher e-mail feature, you can select up to five routes and receive e-mail notices when the fare changes by $25 or more. Travelocity's Destination Guide includes details on some 260 destinations worldwide—supplied by Frommer's.

Moment's Notice (www.moments-notice.com) promotes itself as a travel service, not an agency, providing a bargain-hunter's dream. Updated each morning, many of the deals are snapped up by the end of the day. A drawback is that many of these offerings require you to drop everything and go almost immediately. **Cheap Tickets** (www.cheaptickets.com) has exclusive deals that aren't available through more mainstream channels. At **Priceline** (www.travel.priceline.com), you can "name your price" for domestic and international airline tickets and hotel rooms: You select a route and dates, guarantee with a credit card, and make a bid for what you're willing to pay. If one of the airlines in Priceline's database has a fare lower than your bid, your credit card is automatically charged for a ticket.

At **www.180096hotel.com** you'll be able to make reservations at prestigious hotels all over the world, many accommodations up to 65% off. Booking can be done online, cutting out any travel agent. **Discount Tickets** (www.discount-tickets.com) lists discounts on airfares, accommodations, car rentals, and tours. Several major airlines offer a free e-mail service known as **E-Savers,** via which they'll send you their best bargain airfares on a regular basis. But the fares are cheap, so it's worth taking a look. See the Web addresses given above for each airline. For the latest on airline Web sites, check **www.airlines-online.com** or **www.itn.com**.

In Britain, point your browser at **www.cheapflights.com**.

CHARTER FLIGHTS   In a strict sense, charters book a block of seats (or an entire plane) months in advance and then resell the tickets to consumers. Always ask about restrictions: You may have to purchase a tour package and pay far in advance and pay a stiff penalty (or forfeit the ticket entirely) if you cancel. Charters are sometimes canceled when the plane doesn't fill. In some cases, the charter company will offer you an insurance policy in case you need to cancel for a legitimate reason (such as hospitalization or a death in the family).

There is no way to predict whether a proposed flight to Amsterdam will cost less on a charter or from a bucket shop. You simply have to investigate at the time of your trip.

Council Travel, 205 E. 42nd St., New York, NY 10017 (☎ **800/226-8624** or 212/822-2800; www.ciee.org), arranges charter seats on regularly scheduled aircraft. One of the biggest charter operators is **Travac** (see "Consolidators, above"). For Canadians, good charter deals are offered by **Travel CUTS** (☎ **888/838-CUTS;** www.travelcuts.com), which also has an office in London (☎ **020/7255-1944**).

REBATORS   To confuse the situation even more, rebators also compete in the low-cost air-travel market. These outfits pass part of their commission along to the passenger, though many of them assess a fee for their services. Most rebators offer discounts that range from 10% to 25% (but this could vary from place to place), and charge a $25 handling fee. They are not the same as travel agents, though they sometimes offer similar services, including discounted land arrangements and car rentals.

Rebators include **Travel Avenue,** 10 S. Riverside Plaza, Suite 1404, Chicago, IL 60606-3807 (☎ **800/333-3335** or 312/876-1116); **The Smart Traveler,** 3111 SW 27th Ave., Miami, FL 33133 (☎ **800/448-3338** or 305/448-3338); **Blitz Travel,** 8918 Manchester Rd., St. Louis, MO 63144 (☎ **314/961-2700**); and **Travel Management International (TMI),** 18 Prescott St., Suite 4, Cambridge, MA 02138 (☎ **800/245-3672** or 617/661-8187).

STANDBYS   A favorite of spontaneous travelers with absolutely no scheduled demands on their time, standby fares leave your departure to the whims of fortune and the hopes that a last-minute seat will become available. **Martinair** offers low standby prices on direct flights from its gateways in the United States to Amsterdam.

GOING AS A COURIER   This cost-cutting technique may not be for everyone, but the discounts are excellent. As a courier, you don't actually handle the merchandise you're "transporting" to Europe; you just carry a manifest to present to Customs. Upon arrival, an employee of the courier service will reclaim the company's cargo. You're allowed one piece of carry-on luggage only; your baggage allowance is used by the courier firm to transport its cargo (which, by the way, is perfectly legal—often documents). Another restriction is that you have to fly alone.

Most courier services operate from Los Angeles and New York, but some operate out of other cities, such as Chicago and Miami. Courier services are often listed in the Yellow Pages and in advertisements in travel sections of newspapers. For a start, check **Halbert Express,** 147-05 176th St., Jamaica, NY 11434 (☎ **718/656-8189** from 10am to 3pm daily); or **Now Voyager,** 74 Varick St., Suite 307, New York, NY 10013 (☎ **212/431-1616** from 11:30am to 6pm daily; at other times you get a recorded message announcing last-minute special round-trips).

PACKAGE TOURS   For those travelers who feel more secure if everything is prearranged—hotels, transportation, sightseeing excursions, luggage handling, tips, taxes, and even meals—a package tour is the obvious choice, and it may even help save money.

A good travel agent can tell you about the many excellent bus tours offered in the Benelux region, with all-inclusive rates well below any you could manage on your own. Three leading reliable operators that include the Benelux countries in many of their reasonably priced European tours are: **Globus-Gateway/Cosmos Tours,** 150 S. Roblos Ave., Suite 860, Pasadena, CA 91101 (☎ **800/556-5454** or 818/339-0919); **American Express Travel Service,** P.O. Box 5014, Atlanta, GA 30302 (☎ **800/241-7000**); and **Maupintour,** P.O. Box 807, Lawrence, KS 66046 (☎ **800/255-4266**).

BY TRAIN

Rail service to Amsterdam from other cities in the Netherlands and elsewhere in Europe is frequent and fast. International and Inter City express trains arrive at

Centraal Station from Brussels and Paris, and from several German cities and from more distant locations in eastern Europe, Spain, Austria, Switzerland, and Italy. There's also the Amsterdam/Brussels Inter-City train, and connections can be made in Brussels to the North Express, the Oostende-Vienna Express, the Oostende-Moscow Express, and the Trans-Europe Express. **Nederlandse Spoorwegen** (Netherlands Railways; www.ns.nl) trains arrive in Amsterdam from towns and cities all over Holland. Schedule and fare information on travel in Holland is available by calling ☎ **0900/9292,** and for international trains, call ☎ **900/9296.**

The distinctive burgundy-colored **Thalys** (www.thalys.com) high-speed train, with a top speed of 160 miles per hour (300km per hour), connecting Paris, Brussels, Amsterdam, and (via Brussels) Cologne, has cut travel times from Amsterdam to Paris to 4¼ hours, and to Brussels to 2¼ hours—figures that will be reduced to closer to 3¼ hours and 1¾ hours respectively when the high-speed rail lines in Holland are operational. For Thalys information and reservations in France, call ☎ **08-3635-3536;** in Belgium, ☎ **0800/95-777;** in Germany, ☎ **0221/19419;** and in Holland, ☎ **0900/9296.** Tickets are also available from main train stations and travel agents. One-way weekday first-class (Comfort 1) fares from Paris to Amsterdam in late 2000 were about $120; tourist class (Comfort 2) one-way tickets were about $80; on weekends the respective one-way fares were $75 and $68. Four Thalys trains run between Paris and Amsterdam every day via Brussels.

Britain is connected to the Continent via the Channel Tunnel. On the **Eurostar** (www.eurostar.com) high-speed train (top speed 160 m.p.h.), the travel time between London Waterloo Station and Brussels Midi Station (the closest connecting point for Amsterdam) is 3¼ hours. On weekends the respective one-way fares were £140 ($196) and £100 ($140). Departures from London to Brussels are approximately every 2 hours at peak times. For Eurostar reservations, call ☎ **0345/303030** in Britain, and ☎ **020/423-4444** in Holland.

The **Eurailpass** allows unlimited first-class travel throughout the rail systems of many European countries, including the Netherlands, at a cost of $554 for 15 days, $718 for 21 days, $890 for 1 month, $1,260 for 2 months, and $1,588 for 3 months. The **Eurail Youth Pass** allows unlimited second-class travel to those under 26 years of age at a cost of $388 for 15 days, $499 for 21 days, $623 for 1 month, $882 for 2 months, and $1,089 for 3 months. Other deals are available as well. Both the Eurailpass and the Eurail Youth Pass should be purchased before leaving the United States (they're more expensive if you buy in Europe) and are available through **Rail Europe** (☎ **800/438-7245;** www.raileurope.com), and through travel agents.

BY BUS

Eurolines (www.eurolines.com) coach service operates between London Victoria Bus Station and Amsterdam Amstel Station (via ferry), with four departures daily in the summer. Travel time is just over 12 hours. For reservations, contact Eurolines (☎ **0990/808080** in Britain or 020/560-8787 in Holland). For service to Holland from other major European cities, contact the local Eurolines office. The following are a few of the numbers: **Berlin** (☎ **030/86-0960**); **Brussels** (☎ **02/203-0707**); **Madrid** (☎ **091/528-1105**); **Paris** (☎ **01-49-72-51-51**); **Prague** (☎ **02/2421-3420**); **Rome** (☎ **06 44-23-39-28**); **Vienna** (☎ **01/712-0453**).

BY SHIP

Stena Line (www.stenaline.com) has twice-daily high-speed car-ferry between Harwich in southeast England and Hoek van Holland (Hook of Holland) near Rotterdam; journey time is 3 hours, 40 minutes. In late 2000 a second-class ticket for a foot passenger cost £72 ($100.80); for schedule information and reservations, call ☎ **01233/647047** in Britain or 0174/389-333 in Holland.

If you can afford it, Cunard's ***Queen Elizabeth 2*** makes transatlantic crossings between New York and Southampton, England, from where you can fly, drive, sail and go by train to Amsterdam. The Atlantic crossing takes 5 days. Cunard offers packages that allow you to travel one way by air and one way by ship. For current schedules and fares, contact your travel agent or **Cunard Line,** 555 Fifth Ave., New York, NY 10017 (☎ **800/7-CUNARD** or 212/880-7500; www.cunard.com).

BY CAR

Holland is crisscrossed by a network of major international highways. European expressways E19, E35, E231, and E22 reach Amsterdam from Belgium and Germany. Distances between destinations are relatively short, road conditions are excellent, service stations are plentiful, and highways are plainly signposted.

If you want to drive from Britain to Amsterdam, you can use the fast and efficient **Le Shuttle** auto transporter through the Channel Tunnel from Folkestone to Calais (a 35-minute trip), and drive up from there. Le Shuttle has departures every 15 minutes at peak times, every 30 minutes at times of average demand, and every hour at night. In late 1998, fares ranged from £120 to £190 ($192 to $304) per car, depending on the day, time, and other variables. The cheapest transits are usually midweek between 2 and 5am. For information, call ☎ **0990/353535** for Le Shuttle reservations in Britain, ☎ **03/21-00-61-00** in France, ☎ **020/504-0540** in Holland. Reserving in advance makes sense at the busiest times, but the system is so fast, frequent, and simple that you may prefer to retain travel flexibility by just showing up, buying your ticket, waiting in line for a short while, and then driving aboard.

Driving tip one: The main drawback of driving into Amsterdam lies in the monumental traffic jam you're likely to encounter coming into the city. What's more, to reduce traffic congestion, the authorities have introduced tough measures on parking charges and parking violations. If you must drive into the city, do yourself a favor and park the car in a garage, then walk or use public transportation within the city (see "Getting Around" in chapter 3).

Driving tip two: When passing other cars on a Dutch *snelweg* (expressway), watch out for those all-too-common, brain-free tailgaters who race up behind you, brake hard from 100 miles an hour or more, and then sit right on your trunk trying to force you out of their way, often flashing their lights at you by way of adding drama to the scene. The only thing to do is ignore them as best you can, continue with your own maneuver, and move across when it's safe to do so.

Getting to Know Amsterdam

Amsterdam Center is small enough that its residents think of it as a village. Like a lot of villages, though, it can be confusing until you get the hang of it. It is perfectly possible to think you are headed in one direction along the canal ring only to find out that you are going completely the other way. The concentric rings of major canals are the city's defining characteristic, along with several important squares that act as focal points.

This chapter will explain how the city is laid out, introduce you to its neighborhoods, tell you how to get around, and more.

1 Orientation

ARRIVING

BY PLANE   Amsterdam's **Schiphol Airport,** 18km (11 miles) from the city, and 5m (16 feet) below sea level on the floor of what was once a lake, is the main airport handling international arrivals and departures in the Netherlands. It's easy to figure out; frequent travelers regularly vote Schiphol (pronounced *Skhip*-ol) one of the world's favorite airports, in part because of its massive duty-free shopping center. After you deplane, moving walkways take you to the Arrivals Hall, where you pass through Passport Control, Customs and Baggage Reclaim; facilities such as free luggage carts, currency exchange, baby-rooms, rest rooms, and showers are available. Beyond these, Schiphol Plaza combines railway station access, the Airport Hotel, a shopping mall (which has that most essential Dutch service—a flower shop), bars and restaurants, rest rooms, baggage lockers, airport and tourist information desks, car-rental and hotel reservation desks, check-in for scheduled domestic flights (also available are charter and air-taxi aircraft, including helicopters), and more, all in a single location. Bus, shuttle, and taxi stops are just outside; KLM Road Transport offers coach, minibus and limousine services from its desk in the Schiphol Plaza.

For tourist information and to make hotel reservations, go to the **Holland Tourist Information (HTi)** desk in Schiphol Plaza (☎ **0900/400-4040**); this number, the same as that of the VVV Amsterdam Tourist Office (see "Visitor Information," below), costs Dfl 1 (45¢) per minute and you almost always have to hold. The office is open daily from 7am to 10pm.

Schiphol Plaza has a service to help travelers with disabilities through the airport. For airport and flight information, dial ☎ **0900/0141.**

Schiphol has multistory **parking lots** within walking distance of Schiphol Plaza and a network of short- and long-term parking lots linked by frequent shuttle to the passenger terminal.

Getting to & from the airport   The **KLM Hotel Bus** shuttles between the airport and downtown on two circular routes serving 16 top hotels (Pulitzer, Grand Hotel Krasnapolsky, Holiday Inn Crowne Plaza, Golden Tulip Barbizon Palace, Tulip Inn, Jolly Hotel Carlton, Golden Tulip Amsterdam Center, Park Hotel, Museum Hotel, Cok B.T.S. Class Hotel, Memphis Hotel, Amsterdam Hilton, Le Meridien Apollo, Okura, Holiday Inn Amsterdam, and Novotel), with stops close to many others. The fare is Dfl 17.50 ($7.45) one way; no reservations are needed and buses leave every 20 minutes 7am and 6pm and every 30 minutes 6pm and 9:30pm from in front of Schiphol Plaza. Check at the KLM Hotel Desk for information. If you're not staying at one of the above hotels, the clerks can tell you which shuttle stop is closest to your chosen lodgings.

Trains leave from Schiphol Station, downstairs from Schiphol Plaza, for Amsterdam's Centraal Station and other points. Make sure you get the right train (it's a busy station and if you board the wrong train you could easily find yourself on an express heading for Paris). The VVV Amsterdam Centraal Station tourist offices (and their excellent hotel reservations service), the hotels near Centraal Station and the Dam, those along the canals near the Center, and other hotels along the major tram routes are all served by the Dutch Railways' Schiphol Line (NS Schiphollijn) to Centraal Station (with stops at both the Lelylaan and De Vlugtlaan stations in west Amsterdam on the way). Departures range from six per hour at peak times to one per hour at night. The fare is Dfl 10 ($4.25) one way in first class and Dfl 6.50 ($2.75) one way in second class; the trip takes about 20 minutes.

An alternative route serves other Amsterdam stations: Amsterdam Zuid/WTC (South/World Trade Center) and RAI (beside the city's big RAI congress and exhibitions center). Be sure to check which one is best (including any tram or bus interchange) for your hotel. If you're staying at a hotel near Leidseplein, Rembrandt-plein, in the Museum Quarter, or in Amsterdam South, this route may be a better bet for you. The fare is Dfl 6.50 ($2.75) one way in first class and Dfl 4.25 ($1.80) one way in second class; travel time from the airport is 10 to 12 minutes. After changing at Amsterdam Zuid/WTC, take tram 5 for Leidseplein and the Museum Quarter; from RAI station, take tram 4 for Rembrandtplein.

Among other destinations easily reached by train from Schiphol Station, are The Hague (40 minutes), Rotterdam (45 minutes), and Utrecht (40 minutes).

Taxis are expensive, but they're the preferred choice if your luggage is burdensome or if there are two or more people to share the cost. You find taxi stands at both ends of the sidewalk in front of Schiphol Plaza. Taxis from the airport are all metered. Expect to pay around Dfl 60 ($25.55) to the Center and around Dfl 50 ($21.30) for a trip to hotels in Amsterdam South. Remember, in Holland a service charge—or tip—is already included in the price shown on the meter.

BY TRAIN   Traveling by train in the Netherlands is convenient, with frequent services to most destinations, and modern, clean trains that run on time. Trains arrive at **Centraal Station,** built on an artificial island in the IJ channel. The building itself is an ornate architectural wonder and the focus of much activity. It's at the hub of the city's concentric rings of streets and canals, and is the originating point for most of the city's trams, metro trains, and buses. It houses a VVV Amsterdam tourist office, with another office outside on the station forecourt, and the GWK Bureau de Change, where you can exchange traveler's checks, U.S. dollars, and other currencies (see "Currency Exchange" under "Fast Facts: Amsterdam," later in this chapter); and it's a departure point for canal-boat tours, foot passenger and bicycle ferries across the IJ waterway, taxis, water taxis, and the Museum Boat. There are also usually street musicians performing and a barrel organ or two.

A less welcoming aspect of the station is the pickpocket convention that's in full swing at all times. Messages are broadcast in several languages warning people to be on their guard, but the artful dodgers still seem to do good business. Try to avoid becoming one of their victims by keeping money and valuables under wraps, especially in crowds.

Luggage deposit costs from Dfl 6.50 ($2.75) per day for a large locker to Dfl 4.50 ($1.90) per day for a standard locker. Change is available from machines in the left luggage hall, and staff members are on hand to help if you have problems.

There's comprehensive assistance for travelers with disabilities throughout the Netherlands Railway system.

To get to your hotel by tram, consult one of the **Gemeentevervoerbedrijf (GVB) Amsterdam/Amsterdam Municipal Transport** ticket booths, located in front of the station building, for fare information and schedules. The tram stops are on either side of the main station exit. Or you can head for the taxi stand in front of the station. (Details on transportation within the city can be found under "Getting Around," below.)

BY BUS   International coaches arrive at the bus terminal opposite Amstel Station, where there are easy train, metro, and tram links to the Center.

BY CAR   European expressways E19, E35, E231, and E22 reach Amsterdam from Belgium and Germany.

VISITOR INFORMATION

Few countries have a more organized approach to tourism or are more meticulous in their attention to detailed travel information than Holland. Every province and municipality has its own tourist organization and even small towns and villages have efficient information offices with multilingual attendants on duty. These amazing tourist offices all have the tongue-twisting name **Vereniging voor Vreemdelingenverkeer (Association for Foreigners' Travel),** known simply as the **VVV** (pronounced *vay-vay-vay*). They can book accommodations for you, help with travel arrangements, tell you what's on where, and . . . well, if there's anything they can't do, I have yet to discover it! To find the offices anywhere in the country, look for a blue-and-white roadside sign (often triangular in shape) bearing the letters VVV.

Holland Tourist Information (HTi) has an office in Schiphol Plaza at Schiphol Airport, open 7am to 10pm. Amsterdam's tourist information organization, **VVV Amsterdam** (☎ **0900/400-4040;** fax 020/625-2869; www.visitamsterdam.nl; e-mail: info@amsterdamtourist.nl), has two offices at Centraal Station, one on platform 1, and the other outside the station at Stationsplein 10; and two more at Leidseplein 1 and at the corner of Stadionplein and Van Tuyll van Serooskerkenweg. Handle the telephone number with caution, as it costs a steep Dfl 1 (45¢) a minute, which is tolerable if you get an instant response, but not so good if you have to hold. The correspondence address is Postbus 3901, 1001 AS Amsterdam. VVV Amsterdam will help you with almost any question about the city, and can provide brochures, maps, and so on. There are separate desks for reserving hotel rooms. The offices are open from 9am to 5pm outside the season and on a varying longer schedule as the season proceeds, including Sunday and late evenings. The extended opening hours are somewhat unpredictable, however; the VVV recommends that you call ahead.

Be sure to pick up a copy of ***What's On in Amsterdam*** for 4Dfl ($1.70). This small magazine is full of details about the month's art exhibits, concerts, and theater performances and lists bars, dance clubs, and restaurants. The yellow **Visitors Guide,** free at any tourist office, has a wealth of practical info.

The **Amsterdam Uit Buro (AUB) Ticketshop,** Leidseplein 26 (☎ **020/ 621-1211;** tram: 1, 2, 5, 6, 7, 10, or 20), open Monday to Saturday 10am to 6pm, can give you information regarding cultural events and can book tickets for almost every venue in town. Using their service instead of chasing down tickets on your own can save you precious hours. AUB publishes the free monthly magazine *Uitkrant* (it's in Dutch but it's not difficult to understand the listings information).

CITY LAYOUT

Amsterdammers will tell you it's easy to find your way around their city. However, when each resident offers you a different pet theory of how best to maintain your sense of direction, you begin to sense that the city's layout can be confusing. Some of the natives' theories actually do work. If you try to "think in circles," "follow the canals" (the one I use most), or "watch the way the trams go," you might be able to spend fewer minutes a day consulting a map or trying to figure out where you are and which way to walk to find the Rijksmuseum, a restaurant, or your hotel.

When you step out of Centraal Station's main entrance, you're facing south toward the Center. From here you see the city laid out along five concentric semicircles of canals: Singel, Herengracht, Keizersgracht, Prinsengracht, and Singelgracht. It was along these canals that wealthy 17th-century merchants built their elegant homes, most of which are still standing. The largest and most stately canal houses are along Herengracht. Within these canals are many smaller canals and connecting streets, radiating out from the Center. The area within Singelgracht is the Old City.

Damrak is a busy tourist street leading from Centraal Station to the Dam, location of the former dam on the Amstel River. To the left is the famous Red Light District, where government-licensed prostitutes sit in their windows with red lights glowing, waiting for customers. A block to the right of Damrak is Nieuwendijk (which becomes Kalverstraat when it crosses the Dam), a pedestrians-only shopping street. If you follow Kalverstraat to the end, you'll be at Muntplein beside the old Mint Tower. Cross Singel and continue in the same direction to reach Rembrandtplein, one of the main nightlife areas.

The other main nightlife area is Leidseplein, on the last concentric canal, Singelgracht (not to be confused with Singel, the first concentric canal). Leidseplein is at the end of Leidsestraat, a pedestrians-only shopping street that leads from Singel to Singelgracht and is reached from Kalverstraat by Heiligeweg, another short pedestrians-only shopping street.

The relandscaped green Museumplein, where you find the city's three most famous museums—Rijksmuseum, Van Gogh Museum, and Stedelijk Museum of Modern Art—is a 5-minute walk along Singelgracht from Leidseplein.

One other area worth mentioning is the Jordaan (pronounced Yor-*daan*), a quickly developing old neighborhood now filled with inexpensive restaurants, unusual shops, and small galleries. The Jordaan is between Prinsengracht and Singelgracht in the area bounded by Rozengracht and Brouwersgracht. To reach it, turn right off Damrak at any point between Centraal Station and the Dam. When you cross Prinsengracht, you're in the Jordaan.

STREET MAPS   A map is essential. The maps in this book will help you understand Amsterdam's basic pattern of waterways and the relationships between the major squares or landmarks and the major connecting thoroughfares. Once you get the hang of the necklace pattern of the five major canals and become familiar with the names (or series of names) of each of the five principal roads leading into the Center, all you need to do as you walk along is to keep track of whether you're walking toward or away from the Dam, the heart of the city, or simply circling around it.

The most detailed and helpful maps of Amsterdam are those published by Suurland-Falkplan. Their handy **Amsterdam Tourist Map,** small and easy to unfold, is available from news vendors for Dfl 8 ($3.40). It shows every street and canal; gives tram routes and tram stops; pinpoints churches and many museums; locates address numbers; and identifies one-way streets, bridges, and canals. For more detailed coverage of the entire city and its suburbs, including a street name index, buy Suurland-Falkplan's **Stadsplattegrond Amsterdam** for Dfl 12 ($5.10). The VVV tourist offices have several other maps available, including the small but detailed **VVV Amsterdam** map, which costs Dfl 4 ($1.70).

FINDING AN ADDRESS   Wherever possible in this book, I've made an attempt to locate the addresses given by adding the name of a nearby square, major thoroughfare, adjacent canal, or well-known sight. Street numbers along the canals ascend (as you look at the map) from left to right (west to east); on streets leading away from Centraal Station and out from the Center, they ascend from top to bottom (north to south).

Now, all you need to know is that in Dutch *-straat* means "street," *-gracht* means "canal," *-plein* means "square," and *-laan* means "boulevard," all of which are used as suffixes attached directly to the name of the thoroughfare (for example, Princes' Canal becomes Prinsengracht, one word).

Neighborhoods in Brief

The city of Amsterdam can be divided into six major touristic neighborhoods:

The Center   This area, around the Dam and the Centraal Railway Station, is the oldest part of the city. It includes the major downtown shopping areas and such attractions as the Royal Palace, the Amsterdam Historical Museum, Madame Tussaud's Scenerama, and the canal-boat piers.

The Canal Zone   This semicircular, multistrand "necklace" of waterways (strictly speaking, it's also part of the Center, but it's distinctive enough to be treated separately) was built around the old part of the city during the 17th century. It includes elegant gabled houses, many restaurants, antiques shops, and small hotels, plus such sightseeing attractions as the Anne Frankhuis and the canal-house museums.

The Jordaan   This nest of small streets and canals lies west of the Center, beyond the major canals. Once a working-class neighborhood, it's fast becoming a fashionable residential area, like New York City's SoHo, with a growing number of upscale boutiques and restaurants. Still, its "indigenous" residents are alive and well and show no sign of succumbing to the gentrification going on around them. In its long history, the old Jordaan has seen plenty of trends and fashions come and go, and it will still be there whether the trendy boutiques and restaurants prosper or not.

The Museumplein Area   A gracious residential area surrounds the three major museums of art—Rijksmuseum, Van Gogh Museum, and Stedelijk Museum—and includes Vondelpark, the famous Concertgebouw concert hall, many restaurants and small hotels, and Amsterdam's most elegant shopping streets (P. C. Hooftstraat and Van Baerlestraat).

Amsterdam Neighborhoods

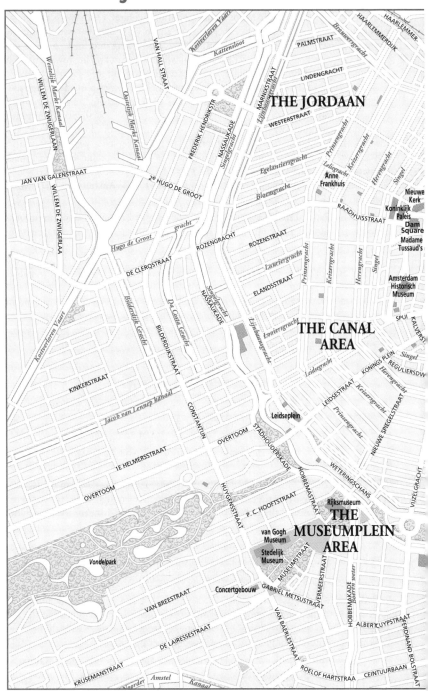

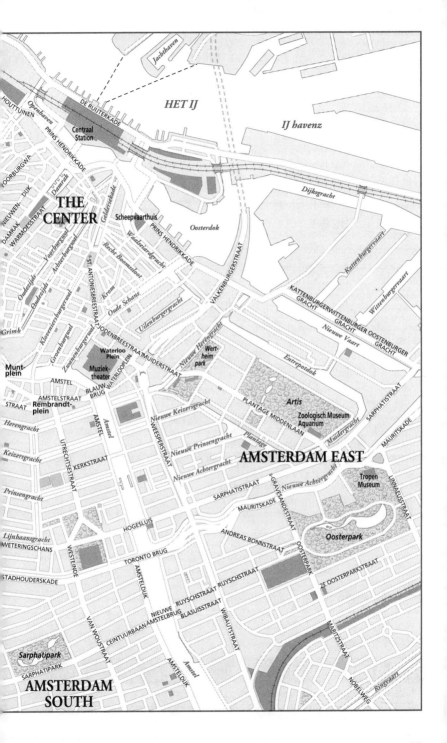

HET IJ

Jachthaven

DE RUIJTERKADE

IJ havenz

HOUTTUINEN

Openhaven

PRINS HENDRIKKADE

Centraal
Station

Damrak

Dijksgracht

VOORBURGWA

NIEUWEN- DIJK

DAMRAK

WARMOESSTRAAT

THE
CENTER

Scheepvaarthuis

PRINS HENDRIKKADE

Oosterdok

VALKENBURGERSTRAAT

Oudezijds Voorburgwal

Oudezijds Achterburgwal

ST. ANTONIESBREESTRAAT

Recht-Boomssloot

Krom

Oude Schans

KATTENBURGERGRACHT

WITTENBURGER
GRACHT

OOSTENBURGER
GRACHT

Kattenburgervaart

Wittenburgervaart

Grimb

Kloveniersburgwal

Geldersekade

Waalseilandgracht

Uilenburgergracht

Zwanenburgwal

Groenburgwal

JODENBREESTRAAT

MUIDERSTRAAT

Nieuwe Herengracht

Wert-
heim
park

Nieuwe Vaart

Entrepotdok

Munt-
plein

Waterloo
Plein

Muziek-
theater

WATERLOOPLEIN

AMSTEL

BLAUW
BRUG

PLANTAGE MIDDENLAAN

Artis

Zoologisch Museum
Aquarium

SARPHATISTRAAT

AMSTELSTRAAT

Rembrandt-
plein

STRAAT

Herengracht

AMSTEL

UTRECHTSESTRAAT

WEESPERSTRAAT

Nieuwe Keizersgracht

Nieuwe Prinsengracht

Nieuwe Achtergracht

Plantage

AMSTERDAM EAST

Muidergracht

MAURITSKADE

Keizersgracht

KERKSTRAAT

Prinsengracht

Nieuwe Achtergracht

Tropen
Museum

LINNAEUSSTRAAT

Lijnbaansgracht

WETERINGSCHANS

WESTEINDE

HOGESLUIS

SARPHATISTRAAT

MAURITSKADE

ANDREAS BONNSTRAAT

's-GRAVESANDESTRAAT

Oosterpark

STADHOUDERSKADE

AMSTELDIJK

TORONTO BRUG

RUYSCHSTRAAT

RUYSCHSTRAAT

OOSTERPARK

2E OOSTERPARKSTRAAT

VAN WOUSTRAAT

CEINTUURBAAN

NIEUWE
AMSTELBRUG

BLASIUSSTRAAT

WIBAUTSTRAAT

Amstel

MAURITSTRAAT

Sarphatipark

SARPHATIPARK

AMSTELDIJK

AMSTERDAM
SOUTH

NOBELWEG

Ringvaart

At Home in the Harbor

Amsterdam's biggest redevelopment project is under way in the Eastern Harbor Area of the IJ channel, which lies east of Centraal Station. Once a major part of Amsterdam Port, this area is now being redeveloped for housing. The city government has touted the project as "a new life on the water." The artificial islands and peninsulas of the harbor complex have been cleared of most of their warehouses and other installations; modern housing and infrastructure are taking their place. A visit here is a good way to see how Amsterdam sees its own future, away from its Golden Age heart.

At present you can reach the redevelopment zone on foot or by bus 28, 32, 59, or 61 to Java Eiland and KNSM Eiland. A *sneltram* (fast tram) line is also planned from Centraal Station and should be in place during the lifetime of this book.

Amsterdam South   The most prestigious modern residential area of Amsterdam is the site of a number of hotels, particularly along the Apollolaan, a wide boulevard that the locals have nicknamed the Gold Coast for its rows of expensive houses.

Amsterdam East   Amsterdam East is another residential area on the far bank of the Amstel River, the location of such sightseeing attractions as the maritime and tropical museums, and also of Artis, the local zoo. It's also the area of Amsterdam where the city's immigrant population is most noticeable.

MAIN ARTERIES & STREETS   There are six major squares in Amsterdam that will be "hubs" of your visit to the city:

The Dam is the heart of the city and the site of the dam across the Amstel River that gave the city its original name, Aemstelledamme. Encircling the square are the Koninklijk Paleis (Royal Palace); the Nieuwe Kerk (New Church); and several department stores, hotels, and restaurants; on the square is the World War II National Monument.

Leidseplein, and the streets around it, is Amsterdam's Times Square, glittering with restaurants, nightclubs, discos, performance centers, and movie theaters.

Rembrandtplein is another entertainment center, bustling with restaurants, cafes, and a casino.

Museumplein and **Waterlooplein** are the cultural hubs, with the Rijksmuseum, Concertgebouw, Van Gogh Museum, and Stedelijk Museum of Modern Art all in and around Museumplein, and the Muziektheater and a superb flea market at Waterlooplein.

Muntplein is essentially a transportation hub, identified by the Munttoren (Mint Tower), from 1620, one of the city's original fortress towers, topped by a distinctive crown ornament. Muntplein affords access to Kalverstraat, one of the city's main shopping arteries.

2 Getting Around

When you look at a map of Amsterdam, you may think the city is too large to explore on foot. This isn't true: It's possible to see almost every important sight on a 4-hour walk. Be sure to wear good walking shoes, as those charming cobbles get under your soles and on your nerves after a time, so leave your thin-soled shoes or boots at home.

Be aware that cars and bikes have the right of way when turning. Don't step in front of one thinking it's going to stop for you. When crossing the street, watch out for trams and bicycles, particularly when you're walking across a dedicated bicycle lane—some cyclists can get unreasonably irritated if you force them to crash into you.

BY PUBLIC TRANSPORTATION

Daytime hours of operation for the public transportation system are 6am to around midnight (trams start at 7:30am on Sunday). A night bus system operates a limited service, with busses usually on an hourly schedule.

FARE INFORMATION   You don't *have* to be a rocket scientist to understand the fare system in Amsterdam, but it sure can't hurt. There are 11 fare zones in greater Amsterdam, though tourists rarely travel beyond the Center zone 5700 (Centrum).

Make sure your ticket is validated for the number of zones you plan to travel through (see below for how to validate). The fare system is based on canceling one strip more than the number of zones you travel through—two strips for one zone, three strips for two zones, and so on. Validated cards can be used for any number of transfers between lines and modes of transportation within 1 hour of the time stamped on them at validation and within the paid-for number of zones (time valid-ity increases up to a maximum $3\frac{1}{2}$ hours as you increase the number of zones validated).

Children age 3 and under travel free; children age 4 to 11 can buy reduced-rate tick-ets for some of the ticket types referred to below.

Several types of tickets are valid on buses, trams, and the metro. An **enkele reis** or **enkeltje (single ticket)** costs Dfl 3 ($1.30) for two strips (one zone) and Dfl 4.50 ($1.90) for three strips (two zones); you buy them from the driver, who stamps them for you. When a three-strip ticket is stamped *vertically,* it becomes an **uurnetkaart** **(1-hour ticket)** and can be used for 1 hour after the time stamped in all Amsterdam fare zones. On some metro trains and on some trams you cannot buy tickets from the driver, but there is an onboard or in-station ticket dispenser; this may sell single tick-ets valid for three zones, for Dfl 6 ($2.55), and four zones, for Dfl 7.50 ($3.20).

You can buy a **Circle-Amsterdam ticket,** valid for the day of purchase and the night following on any tram, bus, and metro train, from any bus or tram driver, con-ductor, or ticket dispenser for Dfl 12 ($5.10). Also available are Circle-Amsterdam tickets valid from 2-day to 9-day with prices from Dfl 16 to Dfl 42.25 ($6.80 to $18); you can purchase these at the GVB/Amsterdam Municipal Transport ticket booths (at Stationsplein in front of Centraal Station). Bear in mind that you need to take a lot of trams for day and multi-day cards to be worthwhile.

If you plan to do a lot of walking and take trams only around the Center, you're probably better off with a **strippenkaart (strip card)** that you can use throughout your stay. You can buy an eight-strip card from drivers and conductors for Dfl 12 ($5.10),

---

Be Careful Where You Step

In such a beautiful city, with high gables in many and varied shapes and forms, there's a temptation to walk along gazing up. But be careful. There's the possibility you may walk straight into a canal, but a graver danger lurks underfoot. Many Am-sterdammers have dogs, and these beasts are often the size of Shetland ponies. Signs on the sidewalk saying HOND IN DE GOOT (DOG IN THE GUTTER) are mostly ignored by both owner and dog. Take your eye off the ground for so much as an instant and you (and your shoes) may live to regret it.

or a 15-strip card for Dfl 12 ($5.10) and a 45-strip card Dfl 35.25 ($15) from railway and metro stations, GVB/Amsterdam Municipal Transport ticket booths, post offices, and many news vendors. The cards must be validated for each trip.

If you are staying in town for a week, a month, or a year, an alternative is to buy a **sterrabonnement (star subscription)** ticket, valid in a certain number of zones, one of which you select as the center zone for the ticket. With one star you can travel only in your chosen center zone; with two stars you can travel in this center zone and one bordering zone in any direction; with three stars you can travel in this center zone and two bordering zones; and so on. An N-star card is valid in all available zones. Prices range from Dfl 18 ($7.65) for a 1-week, one-star ticket, to Dfl 354.50 ($150.85) for a 1-month, N-star ticket; year-tickets cost 10 times the amount of the appropriate month-ticket.

Other complications include special tickets for Circle Tram 20 and night buses (and even more special tickets for some night buses); the option of using the eight-strip card as a day ticket within the city limits (it needs to be stamped *vertically*); multiple-trip tickets valid in between one and seven zones; group tickets for ten or more people; and supplemental tickets; the validity of some tickets on certain local train services.

In short, this is a classic example of a system designed by idiots to be used by geniuses. If you're in doubt about what ticket you need (you won't be alone), ask at the GVB ticket office in front of Centraal Station; the personnel are patient and helpful (and have access to Cray supercomputers to work out your ticket requirement). Once you know what ticket is best for you and have it fixed in your mind, the system is fairly easy to negotiate—trust me.

Validation: Be sure to keep your ticket with you until it's no longer valid and be sure to use the yellow ticket-validating machines in the middle and rear of the tram, or visit the conductor at the rear. To use the machine, just fold your card at the line and punch it in. You don't need to punch in each individual strip—just count down the number of strips you need and punch in the last one; if you need more than one card to cover the required number, stamp the last strip on the old card and the last strip required on a new one. On buses, the driver does this; at metro stations you use machines at platform entrances and on the platforms themselves.

More than one person can use a strip card, so long as the required number of strips is canceled for each passenger.

Most Amsterdam trams either have a conductor or operate on the honor system, but a team of inspectors, in uniform or plain clothes, occasionally hits a tram like gangbusters; in the aftermath of the stampede to reach ticket machines that—ah, too late—have just been turned off, they will ask to see your ticket. The fine for riding without a ticket or not having it properly stamped (you also must have a validated ticket to enter the metro platforms) is Dfl 60 ($25.55), plus Dfl 4.50 ($1.90) for a ticket. Don't think that being foreign and not speaking Dutch, or saying you don't have money on you, or giving Mickey Mouse at 22 Yellow Brick Road as your name and address will help much. The inspectors speak excellent English and they know where Mickey Mouse lives, having accompanied him to the nearest police station often enough.

BY BUS & TRAM   Half the fun of Amsterdam is walking along the canals. The other half is riding the yellow-painted trams that click and clang along every major street. There are 17 ordinary tram routes, 11 of which begin and end at Centraal Station (1, 2, 4, 5, 9, 13, 16, 17, 20, 24, and 25), so you know you can always get back to that central point if you get lost and have to start over again. The other tram routes are 3, 6, 7, 10, 12, and 14. Line 20 is the **Circle Tram,** with trams every 10 minutes at peak times; it gets you close to many of the city's main attractions.

There's a **Tourist Tram,** an old-timer that also does the sights on Sunday and public holidays from Easter to mid-September. It leaves from Prins Hendrikkade in front of Centraal Station; tickets cost Dfl 10 ($4.25) for adults, Dfl 7.50 ($3.20) for seniors and children.

To board a tram, push the *deur open* ("door open") button on the outside of the car beside the door; getting off, you also have to push a *deur open* button. Tram doors in Holland don't open by themselves but do close automatically, and they do it quite quickly, so either step lively or, when getting off, keep one foot on the bottom step to prevent the door from closing until you are off the tram.

An extensive bus network complements the trams. Most bus/tram shelters have maps that show the entire system and all stops have small signs that list the stops yet to be made by the trams or buses that can be boarded at that location (the signs are good for telling you whether you're waiting on the correct side of the street for the direction in which you want to go). If you need it, however, a detailed tram map is available from the VVV or at the offices of GVB/Amsterdam Municipal Transport, Stationsplein. You can also call the transportation information number (☎ **0900/9292**) on Monday to Saturday 7am to 10pm and Sunday 8am to 10pm.

BY METRO   It can't compare to the labyrinthine systems of Paris, London, and New York, but Amsterdam does have its own metro, with four lines—50, 51, 53, and 54—that bring people in from the suburbs. You may want to take them simply as a sightseeing excursion, though to be frank, few of the sights on the lines are worth going out of your way for. On these lines you validate your ticket on the platform before boarding. In 2002, the new Noord/Zuid Metrolijn is due to open, bisecting the city from north to south, from Buikslotermeerplein in Amsterdam Noord, under the IJ to Centraal Station, Rokin, Ceintuurbaan, and Station Zuid/WTC.

BY TRAIN   The train system is not as useful within Amsterdam as the tram, bus, and metro network. In addition to Centraal Station, which is the public transportation hub, there are seven stations in the city: Zuid/WTC (World Trade Center), RAI, and Amstel in the south; Lelylaan, De Vlugtlaan, and Sloterdijk in the west; and Muiderpoort in the east. Because the transportation system is highly integrated, all railway stations are also served by two or more of the other modes. The train comes into its own for longer distances. It's by far the best way to get to Schiphol Airport, Haarlem, Amsterdam's seaside resort Zandvoort, Hoorn on the IJsselmeer shore, and all other points in Holland. The system is Europe's most punctual, with 98% of trains departing and arriving within 4 minutes of the scheduled time.

BY FERRY   **IJ ferries** connect the Center with Amsterdam Noord (North), across the IJ channel. The short crossings are free—making them ideal minicruises for the cash-strapped—and provide a good view of the harbor. Ferries depart from piers behind Centraal Station along De Ruyterkade: the *Buikersloterwegveer* from Landing Stage 7 every 7½ minutes from 6:30am to 9pm, and every 15 minutes thereafter. The *Adelaarswegveer* departs from Landing Stage 8 to a more easterly point on the north shore Monday to Friday from 6:35am to 6:05pm.

BY TAXI

It used to be that you couldn't simply hail a cab from the street in Amsterdam, but nowadays they often stop for you. Otherwise, call **Taxi Centrale** (☎ **020/677-7777**) or find one of the taxi stands sprinkled around the city, generally near the luxury hotels or at major squares such as the Dam, Centraal Station, Spui, Rembrandtplein, Westermarkt, and Leidseplein. Taxis are metered, and fares—which include the tip— begin at Dfl 5.80 ($2.45) when you get in and run up at the rate of Dfl 2.85 ($1.20) per kilometer, or about Dfl 4.60 ($1.95) per mile. Expect to pay Dfl 10 to Dfl 20 ($4.25 to $8.50) for rides within the city.

BY WATER

With all the water Amsterdam has, it makes sense to use it for transportation. Although the options for canal transport are limited (with the exception of cruises and excursions), they do exist, and as an additional benefit they offer a unique and attractive view of the city.

BY WATER BUS   Two services bring you to many of the city's top museums and other attractions. The **Canal Bus** company (☎ **020/623-9886**) has two routes, the Green Line and the Red Line, with a total of six stops that connect important museums, and shopping and entertainment districts: Centraal Station, Westermarkt on both Prinsengracht and Keizersgracht, Leidseplein, Rijksmuseum (with an onward route to the RAI Convention and Exhibition Center when popular events are on there), and Muziektheater. Hours of operation are 10am to 5pm, and there are two buses an hour at peak times. A day pass, valid until noon next day and including a discount on museum admissions, costs Dfl 29.50 ($12.55) for adults, Dfl 17.50 ($7.45) for children age 13 and under. A third route, the Blue Line, is a shuttle service between Centraal Station and the new Metropolis science museum; tickets cost Dfl 7.50 ($3.20).

The **Museumboot (Museum Boat)** (☎ **020/622-2181**)—*boot* is pronounced just like boat—operates a scheduled service every 30 to 45 minutes from Centraal Station to Prinsengracht, Leidseplein, Museumplein, Herengracht, Muziektheater, and the Eastern Dock area. This route brings you to many of the city's top museums and other attractions. A day ticket costs Dfl 27.50 ($11.70) for adults and entitles you to discounts on museum/attraction entry prices. Or you can just buy a ticket at any of the seven stops (see "Organized Tours" in chapter 6 for more details).

BY WATER TAXI   These launches do more or less the same thing as landlubber taxis, except that they do it on the canals and the Amstel River, and in the harbor. They take you where you want to go, or as close to it as they can reach. The advantage of going by boat is that you can move easier on the water than through Amsterdam's streets. As a bonus, you get your very own canal cruise. To order one, call **Watertaxi** (☎ **020/530-1090**), or pick one up at the landing stage outside Centraal Station (to the left of the VVV office). Water taxis hold up to eight people and cost Dfl 115 ($48.95) per 30 minutes, or part thereof, with a further Dfl 50 ($21.30) charge if they have to collect you.

BY MOTORBOAT   SESA (☎ **020/509-5050**) has a mooring on Prinsengracht at Leidsestraat, and another on the Kloveniersburgwal canal at Nieuwmarkt. Their covered salon launches, with mandatory skipper, take up to 12 people, and cost Dfl 350 ($148.95) an hour. They also have self-steer, open sloops, which take up to 10 people, and cost Dfl 100 ($42.55) an hour from June to August, Dfl 80 ($34.05) an hour from September to May; a Dfl 300 ($127.65) deposit is required.

BY WATER BIKE   A water bike is a boat that you peddle with your feet. These vehicles seat two or four and cost Dfl 19.50 ($8.30) for a 1-hour jaunt for two and Dfl 29.50 ($12.55) for four. They can be rented daily from 10am to 11pm in summer (until 7pm at other times) from **Canal Bike** (☎ **020/626-5574**). There are four moorings: Leidseplein; Westerkerk, near the Anne Frankhuis; Stadhouderskade, beside the Rijksmuseum; and at Toronto Bridge on the Keizersgracht, near Leidsestraat. You can rent a water bike at one mooring and leave it at another.

SWIMMING   Believe it or not, some folks (perhaps influenced by too many trips to the "coffeeshop") think this is a good way to get around the canals. It isn't. Swallow so much as one mouthful of that witches' brew and you'll need a session on a hospital stomach pump.

BY BICYCLE & MOPED

Instead of renting a car, follow the Dutch example and ride a bicycle (*fiets*). Sunday, when the city is quiet, is a particularly good day to pedal through the park and to practice riding on cobblestones and dodging trams before venturing forth into the fray of an Amsterdam rush hour. There are some 550,000 bikes in the city, so you'll have plenty of company. Bike-rental rates average Dfl 10 to Dfl 12 ($4.25 to $5.10) per day or Dfl 50 to Dfl 60 ($21.30 to $25.55) per week, with a deposit required.

MacBike rents a range of bicycles, including tandems and six-speed touring bikes. Prices begin at Dfl 12.50 ($5.30) a day and are cheaper the more days you book. A 7-day rental costs Dfl 60 ($25.55). Outlets are located at Mr. Visserplein 2 (☎ 020/620-0985); Marnixstraat 220 (☎ 020/626-6964); and 's-Gravesandestraat 49 (☎ 020/693-2104). **Bike City** at Bloemgracht 70 (☎ 020/626-3721), near the Anne Frankhuis, rents bikes, provides maps and suggested routes both inside and outside the city, and will even store and maintain your own bike. **Damstraat Rent-a-Bike** has a central location near the Dam, at Damstraat 22–24 (☎ 020/625-5029). Rates here and at Bike City are similar to MacBike's. Feminists both male and female might want to give their business to **Zijwind Fietsen,** a women's cooperative, at Ferdinand Bolstraat 168 (☎ 020/673-7026), though it's a bit out from the Center on tram 25.

Warning: Watch out for unpredictable drivers and always lock your bike and its front wheel to something solid and fixed, because theft is common.

If you draw the line at pedaling, maybe a moped, known in these parts as a *bromfiets* or *brommer,* would be more suitable. **Amsterdam First Moped Rental,** Spuistraat 98 (☎ 020/422-0266), rents these noisy but practical little contraptions for Dfl 15 ($6.40) an hour.

BY CAR

To drive in the Netherlands, you need only a valid passport, your driver's license, and if you're bringing your own car, a valid registration and green card proving international insurance.

Don't rent a car to get around Amsterdam. You will regret both the expense and the hassle. The city is a jumble of one-way streets, narrow bridges, and no-parking zones. In addition, it's not uncommon to hear that an automobile, apparently left parked with the hand brake carelessly disengaged, has rolled through a flimsy foot-high railing and into a canal. Spare yourself such anxiety!

If you do choose to park, you need either to feed the meters or to have a parking permit prominently displayed in your car. Sometimes your hotel can sell you this permit, but for short periods it's probably better just to use the meters. The **Dienst Parkeerbeheer (Parking Authority),** responsible for clamping and/or towing away illegally parked cars, is well staffed, efficient, hardworking, and enthusiastic. Its penalties are expensive: Dfl 130 ($55.30) for removing the clamp (also known as the "Texas boot"), and Dfl 300 ($127.65) per day for recovering a towed-away car from a car pound way out in the boonies at Cruquiuskade 25 in the Eastern Dock area (☎ 020/555-9833). If you don't keep your parking meter fed or if you park in an illegal space, you will almost certainly be caught.

Parking meters in the Center cost Dfl 4.75 ($2) per hour Monday to Saturday from 9am to 7pm; Dfl 2.75 ($1.15) per hour Monday to Saturday from 7 to 11pm; and Dfl 2.75 ($1.15) per hour Sunday from noon to 11pm. One- and 3-day street parking permits are available from many hotels for Dfl 30 and Dfl 90 ($12.75 and $38.30), respectively. These permits can be bought from Parking Authority offices at Bakkerstraat 13; Ceintuurbaan 159; Nieuwezijds Kolk parking lot (off Nieuwezijds Voorburgwal); Kinkerstraat 17; and Cruquiuskade 25. Amsterdam intends to further restrict traffic through the Center, so expect even more complications.

To avoid these charges, or private parking lot rates, you can leave your car at the free Park & Ride parking lots at some of the outer metro and railway stations (directions are indicated with blue-and-white P&R signs on the way). Another option is to use the Parkeertaxi (Parking Taxi). Taxis leave every 10 minutes or so from various fixed center-city locations on a regular route covering the main out-of-town parking areas. For further information, contact **Taxi Centrale** (☎ 020/677-7777). Private parking lots are dotted around town and cost from about Dfl 3 to Dfl 6 ($1.30 to $2.55) an hour and Dfl 20 to Dfl 50 ($8.50 to $21.30) a day in summer, depending on the location. The biggest are at Centraal Station, Damrak, under Waterlooplein, adjacent to Leidseplein, and at Marnixstraat.

As if all the parking hassle isn't bad enough, anything left in your car is money on the hoof for every junkie and ne'er-do-well in town. They can withdraw your CD player, cellular phone, and camera faster than you can get cash from an ATM. Cars with foreign license tags are especially tempting, since they are more likely to have something interesting in the trunk.

Outside of the city, driving is another story. You may well want to rent a car for a foray into the Dutch countryside. Rental agencies include **Avis,** Hogehilweg 7 (☎ 020/430-9611); **Budget,** Overtoom 121 (☎ 020/612-6066); **Europcar Interrent,** Overtoom 51–53 (☎ 020/683-2123); and **Hertz,** Overtoom 333 (☎ 020/612-2441). For more information on car and camper rentals, see "Excursions Orientation" at the beginning of chapter 10.

Fast Facts: Amsterdam

Airport   Amsterdam's Schiphol Airport is a 20-minute train ride from Centraal Station (see "Orientation" earlier in this chapter for more details). Some useful airport telephone numbers are: General and flight information ☎ **0900/0141;** Customs ☎ **020/603-7777;** Immigration ☎ **020/603-8111;** tax-free shopping center ☎ **020/601-2497.**

American Express   Offices are at Damrak 66 (☎ **020/504-8777;** tram: 4, 9, 16, 20, 24, or 25) and Van Baerlestraat 39 (☎ **020/673-8550;** tram 2, 3, 5, 12, or 20). Both are open Monday to Friday 9am to 5pm and Saturday 9am to noon. The Damrak office books tours and excursions and offers a full range of services, including currency exchange. The Van Baerlestraat office only books tours and excursions.

Baby-Sitters   Some hotels offer baby-sitting service; ask for details at reception. **Oppascentrale Kriterion** (☎ **020/624/5848**) has vetted baby-sitters over 18. Its prices are Dfl 10 to Dfl 12.50 ($4.25 to $5.30) an hour, plus supplements for administration, Friday and Saturday evening bookings, and for hotels.

Business Hours   Banks are open Monday to Friday 9am to 5pm; some stay open until 7pm on Thursday. Government offices are open Monday to Friday 8:30am to 4pm. Stores are generally open Monday to Friday 9am to 6pm

Saturday until 5pm; some stay open until 9pm on Thursday; some department stores and bigger shops open on Sunday noon to 5pm; most supermarkets are open Monday to Friday 8am to 8pm, Saturday until 6pm. Evening shops open at around 3 to 5pm and stay open until midnight or later.

Car Rentals   See "Getting Around" earlier in this chapter.

Climate   See "When to Go" in chapter 2.

Currency Exchange   The best options for changing money are the VVV tourist offices, a bank, or, if you carry American Express traveler's checks, **American Express** (see above). Other fair options are the 24-hour **Grenswisselkantoor (GWK)** exchanges at Schiphol Airport (☎ **020/653-5121**) and Centraal Station (☎ **020/627-2731**), and at other border checkpoints and main railway stations. The GWK can also provide cash advances for holders of American Express, Diners Club, MasterCard, and Visa credit and charge cards, and handles money transfers via **Western Union** (☎ **0800/0566**) as well. It charges a 4½% commission fee on transactions up to Dfl 5,000 ($2,127.65) and 2½% on transactions above Dfl 5,000. For further information, call GWK's Schiphol or Centraal Station numbers, or the GWK info line (☎ **0800/0566**).

The major Dutch banks with offices in Amsterdam are ABN-AMRO, Centrumbank, Rabobank, VSB, GWK-Grenswisselkantoren, and NMB. Many big U.S. and international banks maintain branches in Amsterdam, including Citibank and Chase Manhattan Overseas. There are clusters of banks around the Dam, the Flower Market, and at Leidseplein. You find centrally located automated-teller machines (ATMs), accessible by cards linked to the Cirrus and Plus networks, Eurocheque cards, and the major credit and charge cards, at **ABN Amro Bank,** Dam 2 and Leidsestraat 1; **Rabobank,** Dam 16 and Van Baerlestraat 100; and **VSB Bank,** Singel 548 (at the Flower Market).

A word of caution: Before you change money or sign over your traveler's checks, be sure to ask not only what exchange rate you get but also what service charge is added. Some exchange services in Amsterdam (not including the ones mentioned above) lure visitors with a generous exchange rate and clobber them with an exorbitant fee. Always know *exactly* how much you are going to get in your hand before agreeing to the transaction.

Dentist   Dentists are listed in the Amsterdam telephone directory; or call the **Central Dental Service** (☎ **020/592-3434**).

Doctor   Doctors are listed in the Amsterdam telephone directory; or call the **Central Medical Service** (☎ **020/592-3434**).

Driving Rules   See "Getting Around" earlier in this chapter.

Drug Laws   Although all narcotic drugs are technically illegal, the authorities in Amsterdam officially tolerate possession of up to 5 grams (0.2 oz.) of cannabis for personal consumption; and you may be in possession of 30 grams (1.2 oz) for your own use. Not all parts of the country are as liberal-minded as Amsterdam when it comes to drug use (and even Amsterdam is not so tolerant that you should just light up anywhere). Peddling drugs to others is a serious offense, as is possession and use of hard drugs. See "Smoking Coffeeshops" in chapter 9.

Drugstores   See "Pharmacies" below.

Electricity   Before you weigh down your luggage with all your favorite appliances, note that the Netherlands runs on 220 volts electricity (North America uses 110 volts). So you need to take with you a small voltage transformer (available in drug and appliance stores and by mail order) that plugs into the round-holed European electrical outlet and converts the Dutch voltage from 220 volts down to 110 volts for any small appliance up to 1,500 watts. Don't try to plug an American appliance directly into a European outlet without a transformer; you may ruin your appliance and possibly even start a fire. Some American appliances (such as some electric shavers) are engineered to operate on either 110 volts or 220 volts, but even with these you usually need to buy a plug adapter for Dutch outlets.

Embassies/Consulates   All embassies are in Den Haag (The Hague), the Dutch governmental city, but many nations have consulates in Amsterdam. The Consulate of the **United States** is at Museumplein 19, Amsterdam (☎ 020/ 575-5309; tram: 3, 5, 12, 16, or 20), open Monday to Friday 8:30am to noon and 1:30 to 3:30pm; the American Embassy is at Lange Voorhout 102, Den Haag (☎ 070/310-9209). The Consulate-General of the **United Kingdom** is at Koningslaan 44, Amsterdam (☎ **020/676-4343;** tram: 2), open Monday to Friday 9am to noon and 2 to 4pm; the British Embassy is at Lange Voorhout 10, Den Haag (☎ **070/310-9209**).

Citizens of other English-speaking countries should contact their embassies in The Hague: **Australia,** Carnegielaan 14, Den Haag (☎ **070/310-8200**); **Canada,** Sophialaan 7, Den Haag (☎ **070/311-1600**); **Ireland,** Dr. Kuyperstraat 9, Den Haag (☎ **070/363-0993**); **New Zealand,** Mauritskade 25, Den Haag (☎ **070/346-9324**); and **South Africa,** Wassenaarseweg 40, Den Haag (☎ **070/392-4501**).

Emergencies   Holland's emergency number to call for the police (*politie*), fire department, and ambulance is ☎ **112.** For routine matters, police headquarters are at Elandsgracht 117 (☎ **020/559-9111**).

Holidays   New Year's Day: January 1; Good Friday; Easter Sunday and Monday; Queen's Day (*Koninginnedag*): April 30; Ascension; Pentecost Sunday and Monday; Christmas Day and Boxing Day: December 25 and 26. Easter, Ascension, and Pentecost are "movable" feast days, so their dates change each year. For 2001, the dates are: Good Friday: April 13; Easter Sunday and Monday: April 15 and 16; Ascension: May 24; Pentecost Sunday and Monday: June 3 and 4. For 2002: Good Friday: March 29; Easter Sunday and Monday: March 31 and April 1; Ascension: May 9; Pentecost Sunday and Monday: May 19 and 20.

Hospitals   These two hospitals have a first-aid department: **Onze Lieve Vrouwe Gasthuis,** Eerste Oosterparkstraat 179 (☎ **020/599-9111;** tram: 3, 6, or 10); and **Academisch Medisch Centrum,** Meibergdreef 9 (☎ **020/ 566-3333;** metro: Holendrecht).

Hotlines   Rape and sexual abuse: **De Eerste Lijn** (☎ **020/612/7576**); drugs: **Drugs Prevention Center** (☎ **020/626-7176**).

Information   See "Visitor Information" earlier in this chapter.

Internet Access   In de Waag, Nieuwmarkt 4 (☎ **020/422-7772**), in the castle in the middle of Nieuwmarkt, is a popular cybercafe and restaurant, with free terminals. **Cyber C@fé,** Nieuwendijk 19 (☎ **020/623-5146**), is an Internet cafe.

Language   Dutch people speak Dutch, of course, but almost everyone speaks at least some English and many locals are fluent. At cinemas, English-language films (mostly American) are usually shown in English with Dutch subtitles.

Laundry/Dry Cleaning   Most Laundromats (*wasserettes*) are open daily 7 or 8am to 9 or 10pm and cost about 12Dfl ($5.10) for 6 kilos (13 pounds) of laundry. **Clean Brothers Launderettes** have several locations throughout Amsterdam, among them Kerkstraat 56 (☎ 020/622-0273), and Westerstraat 26 (☎ 020/627-7376). **Cleancenter,** Ferdinand Bolstraat 7–9 (☎ 020/662-7167), and **Wassalon Java,** Javastraat 23 (☎ 020/668-2483), are two others. For dry cleaning, try **Weerd van Der** at Vaartstraat 64–68 (☎ 020/662-5616), or **Palthé,** Vijzelstraat 59 (☎ 020/623-0337).

Mail   Airmail to the United States and Canada is Dfl 1 (45¢) for a postcard and Dfl 1.60 (70¢) for a letter weighing up to 20 grams (⅔ ounce); cards and letters to other European countries cost Dfl 0.80 (35¢) and Dfl 1 (45¢). Other important post offices are at Sint-Anthoniesbreestraat 16, and Waterlooplein 2. Hotels generally keep a supply of stamps to sell to guests.

Maps   See "City Layout" earlier in this chapter.

Newspapers/Magazines   You find just about every English-language newspaper and magazine you can name (and books, too) at the **American Book Center,** Kalverstraat 185 (☎ 020/625-5537), or **Waterstone's,** Kalverstraat 152 (☎ 020/638-3821). News vendors at Centraal Station have a big choice in international newspapers and magazines.

Pharmacies   In the Netherlands a pharmacy is called an *apotheek.* Try **Dam Apotheek** at Damstraat 2 (☎ 020/624-4331; tram: 4, 9, 14, 16, 20, 24, or 25). All pharmacies have the name of an all-night pharmacy posted on the door. Among convenient *apotheken* in the Center and canal areas are **Dam,** Damstraat 2 (☎ 020/624-4331); **Koek,** Vijzelgracht 19 (☎ 020/623-5949); **Proton,** Utrechtsestraat 86 (☎ 020/624-4333); **Schaeffen en van Tijen,** Vijzelgracht 19 (☎ 020/623-4321); and **Het Witte Kruis,** Rozengracht 57 (☎ 020/623-1051). In the Museum Quarter and Amsterdam South, try **Apollo,** Beethovenstraat 19 (☎ 020/662-8108); **De Lairesse,** De Lairessestraat 42 (☎ 020/662-1022); and **Schaffers,** Ferdinand Bolstraat 11 (☎ 020/662-2240). Go to a drug store (*drogerij*) or supermarket for such items as toothpaste, deodorant, and razor blades.

Police   For police emergencies, dial ☎ 112. For routine matters, police headquarters are at Elandsgracht 117 (☎ 020/559-9111).

Post Office   The main post office is at Singel 250–256 (☎ 020/556-3311; tram: 13, 14, 17, or 20), at the corner of Radhuisstraat. It's open Monday to Friday 9am to 6pm and Saturday 9am to 3pm. To mail a large package, go to the post office at Oosterdokskade 3, a large building to the right as you face Centraal Station.

Radio   The BBC World Service broadcasts on medium-wave, with varying wavelengths and broadcast times. Inquire at your hotel or consult local newspaper listings.

Rest Rooms   Maybe you better sit down for this one. The most important thing to remember about public toilets in Amsterdam—apart from calling them "*toiletten*" (twa-*lett*-en) or "the WC" (*Vay-say*) and not "rest rooms" or "comfort stations"—is not the usual male/female distinction (important though that is) but to **pay the woman** (it generally is a woman) who sits at the entrance. She has a saucer next to her where you put your entrance money. If you don't, she may pursue you into the inner sanctum and interrupt you while you're transacting

A Toilet Tip

If you have a toilet emergency in the Center, the very best address to find relief is the Grand Hotel Krasnapolsky. Just breeze in as if you own the place, swing left past the front desk and along the corridor, past the Winter Garden restaurant, then up a short flight of stairs. Marble washbasins and what look like gold-plated faucets are the least of the wonders therein.

your business. Even if you have paid, in busy places she may have forgotten your face by the time you emerge and will then pursue you out of the toilet and along the street. It's tiresome, but toilets usually costs only a *kwartje* (10¢) or two.

Safety   In Amsterdam, if it isn't bolted to the floor somebody will try to steal it; and even if it is bolted to the floor somebody will try to steal it. Be wary of pickpockets on trams, buses, sightseeing boats, and in train stations (constant public announcements are broadcast at Centraal Station to this effect, and signs on the trams say in a multitude of languages ATTENTION: PICKPOCKETS). Keep an eye on your luggage and personal belongings at Centraal Station and Schiphol Airport—thieves often wait until you are occupied or distracted to make their move. Stay alert. Be aware of your immediate surroundings. Wear a money belt and don't sling your camera or purse over your shoulder. Report any crime committed against you to the police.

Violence is not unknown to Amsterdam, but it's not at all a violent city. It is, however, a drug mecca, and drug-related crime is prevalent, most of it being nonviolent opportunistic thefts such as pickpocketing. People occasionally are held up at knifepoint, and gunpoint even, though such incidents are uncommon. The city may appear safe, but there are some risky areas, especially in and around the Red Light District. Be cautious about walking alone after dark through narrow alleys and along empty stretches of canal side; stick to populated thoroughfares whenever possible. Don't use ATMs at night in quiet areas. It's wise to stay out of Vondelpark at night, but there are cafes on the edge of the park that are busy until closing time.

The rules about not walking alone in poorly lit and unpopulated areas at night apply especially to women. Although you will generally find Amsterdam to be nonthreatening, incidents of harassment do occur, and rape is not unknown. Public transportation is usually busy even late at night, so you generally won't have to worry about being alone in a tram or metro car. Sit close to the driver, where this is possible, if you feel nervous or threatened. Many Amsterdam women like to go by bike at night.

Amsterdam has some weird folks who may lock onto you for one reason or another; if you can't shrug them off, go into a cafe or hotel and either wait until they leave or call a taxi to take you away. Calling the police is also an option, of course.

Note: Listing some of the possible dangers together like this can give a false impression of the threat of crime in Amsterdam. There is no need to be afraid to do the things you want to do. Amsterdammers aren't. Just remember to exercise the usual rules of caution and observation that apply in any big city.

Salons   In addition to beauty salons and barbershops in many major hotels, stylish hairdressers are to be found on P. C. Hooftstraat and on Rokin. **George en Leon,** Leidsegracht 104 (☎ **020/626-3831**), and the **Hair en Beauty**

Center, Rokin 140–142 (☎ **020/623-2381**), are smooth performers. For something a little (or a lot) out of the ordinary, try **Hair Police,** Kerkstraat 113 (☎ **020/420-5841**).

Taxes Citizens from outside the European Union can shop tax-free in Amsterdam. Shops that offer tax-free shopping advertise with a Holland Tax-Free Shopping sign in the window, and they provide you with the form you need to recover value-added tax (VAT) when you leave the European Union. Refunds are available only when you spend more than Dfl 300 ($127.65) in a store. See "The Shopping Scene" in chapter 8 for more details.

Taxis See "Getting Around" earlier in this chapter.

Telephone In the Dutch telephone system, there's a sustained dial tone, and a beep-beep sound for a busy signal. Don't forget that when making local calls in Amsterdam you won't need to use the area codes shown in this book. You may, however, need to use an area code between towns and cities, even if they're only a few kilometers away.

There are two main formats for Dutch telephone numbers: a three-digit area code followed by a seven-digit subscriber number, used for cities and bigger towns; and a four-digit area code followed by a six-digit subscriber number, used for smaller towns and in the countryside.

For a call from Holland to the United States (except Alaska and Hawaii), you pay about Dfl 1.95 (85¢) per minute during business hours, Dfl 1.70 (75¢) on nights and weekends. Calls placed through your hotel switchboard or dialed direct from your room phone are usually more than twice the standard rate. To call the United States or Canada, dial **00** (the international access code) **+ 1** (the country code) + the area code + the number. Other country codes are: Australia, **61;** Great Britain, **44;** Ireland, **353;** New Zealand, **64;** South Africa, **27.**

A 1-minute call within Europe varies according to distance. To a neighboring country like Germany, the call costs Dfl 1.05 (45¢) Monday to Friday between 8am and 8pm and Dfl 0.82 (35¢) during other hours (including the entire weekend); to a more distant country such as Greece it costs Dfl 1.43 (60¢) during peak hours, and Dfl 1.10 (45¢) during off-peak hours.

Almost all public telephones now take a telephone card (*telekaart*) instead of coins; this is a good option for long-distance and international calls. You can buy plastic phone cards at post offices, railway stations, tobacconists, and news vendors for Dfl 10, Dfl 25, and Dfl 50 ($4.25, $10.65, and $21.30).

For a coin-operated Dutch public telephone you need a Dfl 0.25 (10¢) coin, called a *kwartje,* a Dfl 1 (45¢) coin, a Dfl 2.50 ($1.05) coin, or a Dfl 5 ($2.15) coin, which you insert in the appropriate slot. Use smaller coins wherever possible, at least until you are connected, as no change is given from an

Calling Amsterdam

To make an international call from the United States, first dial **011.** The country code for the Netherlands is **31.** The area code for Amsterdam is **020.** If you're phoning an Amsterdam number from the United States or from any other country, don't dial the first **0** of the area code. So from the States, you'd dial **011 + 31 + 20 +** the subscriber number. You don't dial the area code at all if you're phoning an Amsterdam number from within the city. You dial the full area code only if you're phoning an Amsterdam number from elsewhere in Holland.

individual coin. When your call is answered, the coin drops and you can begin to talk. Should there be no answer, hang up and the coin comes back to you. For long calls, and long-distance calls, insert several kwartjes or guilders before you begin; but note that once the call has begun, excess coins will not be returned when you hang up. Phones show a digital reading of your deposit (0.25, 1.00, or whatever); as you talk, the amount shown decreases to let you know when it's time to add more coins. When you're out of money, you're out of conversation; Dutch phones disconnect without a moment's grace. To make additional calls when you still have a coin or coins inserted, do not hang up after each call, but briefly (very briefly) break the connection, and you will get a new dial tone for another call.

For information inside Holland, dial ☎ **0900/8008** (English-speaking operator probable); for international information, dial ☎ **0900/8418** (English-speaking operator assured); for international collect calls, dial ☎ **0900/0410.**

Calling is now easier and less expensive than it used to be, using services like **AT&T Direct.** In Holland you can use any phone to dial the numbers below; you'll be connected immediately and directly to a U.S.-based telephone operator, who then puts your call through (collect, person to person, or with an AT&T Card, station to station) to any number (except 800 numbers) in any of the 48 contiguous states. The AT&T Direct number is ☎ **0800/022-9111.** Similar services are offered by **MCI CallUSA** (☎ **0800/022-9122**); **PhoneUSA** (☎ **0800/022-0224**); **Sprint Express** (☎ **0800/022-9119**); **Canada Direct** (☎ **0800/022-9116**); and **British Telecom** (☎ **0800/022-9944**). Call any of these for rates and reduced time periods.

Television   If your hotel has cable television, you'll be able to watch both BBC 1 and BBC 2, and the local stations, which often show English-language movies with Dutch subtitles. CNN International, CNBC News, BBC World, Sky News, and EuroNews are broadcast in English 24 hours a day.

Time Zone   Holland is on Central European time (CET), which is Greenwich mean time (GMT) plus 1 hour. Amsterdam is normally 6 hours ahead of New York City time and 9 hours ahead of Los Angeles time.

Tipping   The Dutch government requires that all taxes and service charges be included in the published prices of hotels, restaurants, cafes, discos, nightclubs, beauty salons/barbershops and hairdressers, and sightseeing companies. Even taxi fare includes taxes and a standard 15% tip. To be absolutely sure in a restaurant, for example, that tax and service are included, look for the words *inclusief BTW en service* (BTW is the abbreviation for the Dutch words that mean value-added tax), or ask the waiter. The Dutch are so accustomed to having these charges included that many restaurants have stopped spelling it out.

Dutch waitpersons appreciate tips and rely on them to supplement their salary. To tip as the Dutch do, leave any small change up to the next guilder in a cafe or snack bar; in a restaurant, leave up to the next Dfl 5 ($2.15), or Dfl 10 ($4.25) if you think the service was particularly good; for very large tabs, you may want to leave more—or maybe less! An informal survey (I asked a taxi driver) reveals that Americans and British are the best tippers; the worst are the Dutch themselves.

Transit Info   For information regarding tram, bus, metro, and train services dial ☎ **0900/9292** Monday to Saturday from 6am to midnight and Sunday 7am to midnight.

Useful Telephone Numbers   Lost Property: Call ☎ **020/560-5858** for tram, bus, and metro; ☎ **020/557-8544** for trains and stations; and ☎ **020/649-1433** for Schiphol Airport. Don't be optimistic about your chances. There are plenty of honest Amsterdammers, but they're generally out of town when you lose something. **Lost and Stolen Credit Cards: American Express** (☎ **020/504-8000**); **Diners Club** (☎ **0800/0344**); **MasterCard** (☎ **030/283-5555**); **Visa** (☎ **020/660-0611**).

4

Where to Stay

Is your preference old-world charm combined with luxurious quarters? Glitzy modernity with every conceivable amenity? Small, intimate, family-run hotels? A historic canal house that reflects the lifestyle of centuries past? A modern, medium-sized hotel on the fringe of inner-city hustle and bustle? A bare-bones room in a dormitory, which frees up scarce dollars for other purposes? Amsterdam has them all, and more. Some hotels share more than one of these characteristics: A common fusion is that of historic canal house on the outside and glitzy modernity with every conceivable amenity on the inside.

You probably have your own idea of what makes a great hotel. My advice is to let your choice reflect the kind of city Amsterdam is—democratic, adventurous, quirky, and always in search of that enigmatic Dutch quality, *gezelligheid,* which is the ambience that makes a place warm, cozy, friendly, and welcoming. You can find this quality at all prices levels, and especially among the moderately priced hotels owned by local people.

There are around 30,000 hotel and hostel beds available, 40% of which are in four- and five-star hotels. The city has moved in recent years to redress the balance in favor of hotels in the mid- and low-priced categories, but it is inevitably a slow process. If a particular hotel strikes your fancy but is out of your price range, it may pay to inquire if special off-season, weekend, specific weekday, or other packages will bring prices down to what you can afford.

Should your heart be set on, or your financial circumstances dictate, a low-end budget hotel, and you're arriving during almost any period between spring and fall, don't simply brush past the hotel and hostel touts at Centraal Station. Spending a minute to discuss pros and cons with them may save you long hours tramping the cobblestones or waiting in line at a VVV hotel reservation desk. They usually have photographs of the rooms they are offering, but don't commit to taking a place without first eyeballing the bricks-and-mortar reality.

HOTEL ORIENTATION

CHOOSING YOUR HOTEL   For most people, the first consideration in choosing a hotel is money: How much does a particular hotel cost, and is it worth it? The cost of a double room with bathroom averages Dfl 300 ($127.65) per night, but don't despair if you wish to spend less than that. Most Amsterdam hotels, whatever their cost, are still clean and tidily furnished, and in many cases they've been recently renovated or redecorated. Shoddy hotels with unhelpful staff are rare, but they do exist. If circumstance should place you in a hotel different from those recommended below, and you find an unacceptable degree of shabbiness, call around or visit the VVV for a better bet in your price range.

The next consideration is location: How close is a hotel to sights, restaurants, shops, or the transportation to get to them, and what sort of neighborhood is it in? There are neighborhoods that you probably want to avoid; these might include the haunts of drug or sex peddlers (though some of these, like that once notorious shooting gallery, Zeedijk, have been cleaned up, more or less). Amsterdammers accept such phenomena as facts of life, and there are really no "no-go" areas. You'll probably venture into Amsterdam's shady corners in daylight or as an evening lark, but there's no reason to spend your nights in a less-than-desirable area or worry about getting back to your room safely. The hotels described here are all decent hotels in decent neighborhoods.

STANDARD AMENITIES   Until recently, hotel rooms without a private bathroom were quite common in Amsterdam. A major element in the upgrading of low-cost hotels is adding bathrooms, and the city's canal houses and older buildings have posed a major obstacle to efforts to upgrade. One ingenious Dutch solution you may encounter is the "shower/toilet"—a combination shower stall and water closet, fully tiled, that gets the job done but inevitably results in a lot of soggy toilet paper! The term *bathroom,* by the way, is used whether the bathing facilities are a tub, tub/shower combination, shower stall, or one of those silly little shower/toilets.

You can get as much (or as little) out of your hotel-room TV as you might at home. Dutch channels show a number of American programs and air them in English with Dutch subtitles—*Friends* and *The X-Files* are big hits. If you flip the dial and get a German station, you may have the pleasure of watching the stars of *Star Trek: Voyager* speak German. Cable TV is firmly entrenched and many hotels have hookups. That may add BBC, CNN, MTV, Sky, and others to the menu. If you're traveling with the kids, be warned that some Dutch, German, and Luxembourg stations broadcast soft (and some not-so-soft) porn shows late at night.

GAY & LESBIAN HOTELS   Though by law no hotel is allowed to turn away same-sex couples, your reception will probably be more amicable, and tourist advice better tailored, at gay-run accommodations. There are gay hotels aplenty in Amsterdam. Prices and facilities are pretty unexceptional—the knowledge that most guests will be out and about enjoying themselves is the probable reason for hotels not turning up the luxury level.

THE RATES & WHAT THEY INCLUDE   In the following pages, hotels are grouped by price, based on a double room. **Very Expensive:** Dfl 600 ($255.30) and up; **Expensive:** Dfl 400 ($170.20) and up; **Moderate:** Dfl 180 ($76.60) and up; **Inexpensive:** Dfl 180 ($76.60) and under. All rates include applicable taxes and service charges (except in the case of four- and five-star hotels, which add 5% city tax to bills). Room rates increase on average between 5% and 10% each year.

All hotels have been designated according to their high-season rates. Where breakfast is included, this is indicated; if breakfast is not included, expect to pay Dfl 10 to Dfl 30 ($4.25 to $12.75) and up for a continental or full breakfast, depending on the category of your hotel. Single rates are available in many hotels, though not always for a significant reduction over double occupancy. Only those hotels with rooms that all, or nearly all, have private facilities are listed here, even in the inexpensive category, unless there are compelling reasons for including one where this is not the case. Only rates that apply to rooms with bathrooms are used to determine a hotel's price category.

Many Amsterdam hotels, in all price categories, offer significant rate reductions between November 1 and March 31, with the exception of the Christmas and New Year period. The city is as much a delight then as in the tourist-packed summer months. You'll enjoy a calendar full of cultural events, the full blossoming of many traditional Dutch dishes not offered in warm weather, and the fact that streets, cafes, restaurants, and museums are filled more with locals than with visitors.

PARKING   Amsterdam, in particular the old center, has become a free-fire zone for marauding units of the **Dienst Parkeerbeheer (Parking Service Authority).** The locals have learned to keep their heads down and their parking meters loaded at all times. Parking is ruinously expensive, and the Parkeerbeheer will get you for sure if you try to beat the system, so either don't bring the car or stash it on the edge of town and come in by tram.

TIPPING   The standard 16% service charge that's included in hotel rates in Holland eliminates the need to tip under normal circumstances. Tip if you wish for a long stay or extra service, but don't worry about not tipping if that's your style. The Dutch welcome tips but don't expect them (an important distinction if you've ever been hassled by a bellboy who lit every lamp in your room until he heard the rattle of spare change).

RESERVATIONS   This is a popular tourist city, especially during summer months and the tulip season, between early April and mid-May. You are advised always to make your reservation in advance. You can do this directly with any of the hotels below. They will often ask you to confirm by fax or e-mail and/or give your credit-card number. Be sure you provide ample time for them to reply before you leave home. (See "Area Code," under "Fast Facts: Amsterdam" in chapter 3 before dialing; or write to the addresses given below.) You can also make your reservations through a travel agent or through the free hotel-booking service of the Dutch hotel industry: **Netherlands Reservations Center,** P.O. Box 404, 2360 AK Leidschendam (☎ **070/419-5500;** fax 070/419-5519).

Should you arrive in Amsterdam without a reservation, the **VVV Amsterdam Tourist Office** is well organized to help you for a moderate charge of Dfl 5 ($2.15), plus a refundable room deposit of Dfl 5 ($2.15). This is a nice reassurance if you prefer to freelance your itinerary, though at busy periods of the year you have to expect to take potluck. They will always find you something, even at the busiest times, but it may not be what, or where, you want.

IRRITATIONS   **Mosquitoes,** which thrive in the damp conditions on and near the canals and on waterlogged reclaimed land around the city, can be a major nuisance. You can buy various plug-in devices to hold them at bay, but it's better not to let them into your room in the first place.

Amsterdam businesses in general don't much like credit cards—they offend against an ingrained Calvinist prejudice in favor of getting cash on the nail. The result in some Moderate and Inexpensive hotels is a **credit card supplement,** usually 5%.

Also, the lower down the price scale you go, you may find yourself subjected to vexations such as tiny washbasins in which you can just about wash one hand at a time; no soap or shampoo in the bathrooms; a substitute for orange juice at breakfast, even if the juice in question comes out of a carton—talk about being nickel-and-dimed (or dollar-and-pounded) to death.

TRANSPORTATION   Most public transportation connections given are by tram (streetcar) and most, though not all, are from Centraal Station. Never use the Metro system if there is a tram stop within similar distance from your hotel: You won't get such a good view, and the Metro is a less pleasant way to travel. Inevitably, not all

A Canal-House Warning

Elevators are difficult things to engineer into the cramped confines of a 17th-century Amsterdam canal house and cost more than some moderately priced and budget hotels can afford. Many simply don't have them. If lugging your old wooden sea chest up six flights of narrow stairs is liable to void your life insurance policy, better make sure the elevators are in place and working.

Be prepared to climb hard-to-navigate stairways if you want to save money by lodging in a hotel without an elevator. Narrow and steep as ladders, these stairways were designed to conserve space in the narrow houses along the canals. Today they're an anomaly that'll make your stay even more memorable. If you have difficulty climbing stairs, ask for a room on a lower floor.

hotels are right by the tram stop, so you would be better off taking a taxi right from the start if your bags are heavy.

1 Overlooking the Amstel River

VERY EXPENSIVE

✪ Amstel Inter-Continental Amsterdam. Prof. Tulpplein 1 (beside the Torontobrug over the River Amstel), 1018 GX Amsterdam. ☎ **800/327-1177** in the U.S. and Canada, or 020/622-6060. Fax 020/622-5808. www.intercontinenti.com. E-mail: amstel@interconti.com. 79 units. A/C MINIBAR TV TEL. Dfl 925–1,050 ($393.60–$446.80) double; from Dfl 1,250 ($531.90) suite; add 5% city tax. AE, DC, MC, V. Valet parking available. Tram: 6, 7, 10, or 20 to Weesperplein.

The stately Amstel, grande dame of Dutch hotels since its opening in 1867, offers the ultimate in luxury. This is the Rolls Royce of Amsterdam hotels, a place for visiting royalty and superstars hiding from eager fans. Its only possible fault is that it may seem to run a bit *too* smoothly. The hotel sports a mansard roof and wrought-iron window guards, a graceful Grand Hall, and rooms that boast all the elegance of a country manor, complete with antiques and genuine Delft blue porcelain. Each of the large units has a fax machine, personal answering machine, VCR, stereo sound system, and CD player complete with guests' favorite CDs. The Italian marble bathrooms have separate toilets and showers. The staff notes each guest's personal preferences for their next visit.

Dining/Diversions: The French La Rive restaurant has a Michelin star and is one of the hallowed temples of Amsterdam cuisine (see chapter 5 for details). The Amstel Lounge, Amstel Bar & Brasserie, and terraces overlooking the river are more informal.

Amenities: Health club with heated indoor pool, Jacuzzi, sauna, solarium, weight room, Turkish bath, professional masseurs and trainers, beauty specialists, 24-hour room service, dry cleaning and laundry, limousine service, antique motor launch, banquet and conference suites.

✪ Hôtel de l'Europe. Nieuwe Doelenstraat 2–8 (facing Muntplein), 1012 CP Amsterdam. ☎ **0800/223-6800** in the U.S. and Canada, or 020/531-1777. Fax 020/531-1778. www. leurope.nl. E-mail: hotel@leurope.nl. 100 units. A/C MINIBAR TV TEL. Dfl 655–755 ($278.70–$321.27) double; from Dfl 870 ($370.20) and way up suite; add 5% city tax. AE, DC, JCB, MC, V. Valet parking and self-parking Dfl 75 ($31.90). Tram: 4, 9, 14, 16, 20, 24, or 25 to De Munt.

On a stretch of prime riverside real estate in the city center, this elegant, old establishment is one of the Leading Hotels of the World. Its pastel-red and white facade, at the point where the Amstel River flows into the city's canal network, is an iconic element in the classic view of the city. Built in 1896, the de l'Europe has a grand style

Central Amsterdam Accommodations

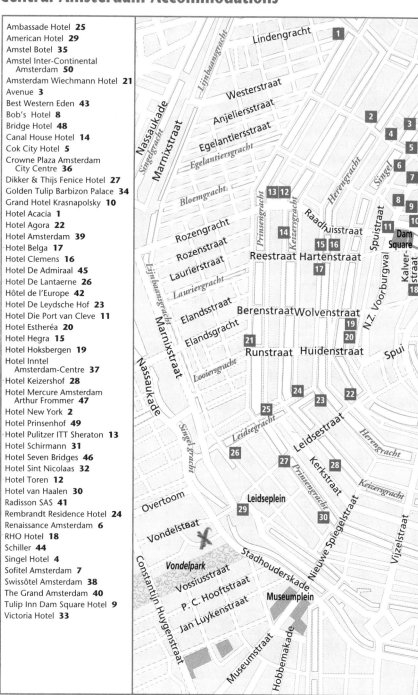

Ambassade Hotel **25**
American Hotel **29**
Amstel Botel **35**
Amstel Inter-Continental Amsterdam **50**
Amsterdam Wiechmann Hotel **21**
Avenue **3**
Best Western Eden **43**
Bob's Hotel **8**
Bridge Hotel **48**
Canal House Hotel **14**
Cok City Hotel **5**
Crowne Plaza Amsterdam City Centre **36**
Dikker & Thijs Fenice Hotel **27**
Golden Tulip Barbizon Palace **34**
Grand Hotel Krasnapolsky **10**
Hotel Acacia **1**
Hotel Agora **22**
Hotel Amsterdam **39**
Hotel Belga **17**
Hotel Clemens **16**
Hotel De Admiraal **45**
Hotel De Lantaerne **26**
Hôtel de l'Europe **42**
Hotel De Leydsche Hof **23**
Hotel Die Port van Cleve **11**
Hotel Estheréa **20**
Hotel Hegra **15**
Hotel Hoksbergen **19**
Hotel Inntel Amsterdam-Centre **37**
Hotel Keizershof **28**
Hotel Mercure Amsterdam Arthur Frommer **47**
Hotel New York **2**
Hotel Prinsenhof **49**
Hotel Pulitzer ITT Sheraton **13**
Hotel Schirmann **31**
Hotel Seven Bridges **46**
Hotel Sint Nicolaas **32**
Hotel Toren **12**
Hotel van Haalen **30**
Radisson SAS **41**
Rembrandt Residence Hotel **24**
Renaissance Amsterdam **6**
RHO Hotel **18**
Schiller **44**
Singel Hotel **4**
Sofitel Amsterdam **7**
Swissôtel Amsterdam **38**
The Grand Amsterdam **40**
Tulip Inn Dam Square Hotel **9**
Victoria Hotel **33**

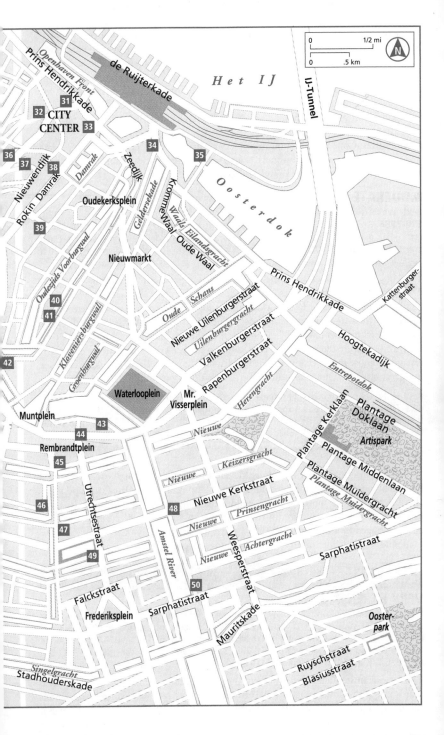

0   1/2 mi
0   .5 km

Openhaven Front

Prins Hendrikkade

de Ruijterkade

Het IJ

IJ-Tunnel

31

32 CITY

CENTER **33**

34

35

O o s t e r d o k

36

37   **38**

Nieuwendijk

Damrak

Zeedijk

Oudekerksplein

Gelderskade

Krommewaal

Waals Eilandsgracht

Oude Waal

Prins Hendrikkade

Kattenburger-straat

Rokin Damrak

39

Oudezijds Voorburgwal

Nieuwmarkt

Oude   Schans

Nieuwe Uilenburgerstraat

Uilenburgergracht

Valkenburgerstraat

Hoogtekadijk

Kloveniersburgwal

40

41

Groenburgwal

Rapenburgerstraat

Entrepotdok

42

Waterlooplein

Mr.
Visserplein

Herengracht

Plantage
Doklaan

Plantage Kerklaan

Muntplein

Nieuwe

Plantage Middenlaan

Artispark

43

44

Rembrandtplein

Keizersgracht

Nieuwe

Plantage Muidergracht

Plantage Muidergracht

45

Nieuwe Kerkstraat

46

Utrechtsestraat

48

Nieuwe

Prinsengracht

47

Nieuwe

Weesperstraat

Achtergracht

Sarphatistraat

49

Amstel River

Nieuwe

Falckstraat

50

Sarphatistraat

Mauritskade

Frederiksplein

Sarphatistraat

Ooster-
park

Singelgracht

Stadhouderskade

Ruyschstraat

Blasiusstraat

and a sense of ease, a smooth combination of aged dignity and modern comforts. Rooms and bathrooms are spacious and bright, furnished with classic good taste. Some rooms have minibalconies overlooking the river and all boast marble bathrooms.

Dining/Diversions: The Excelsior (see chapter 5 for full details), one of the toniest restaurants in town, serves breakfast, lunch, and dinner daily. Le Relais is a less formal setting for light lunches and dinners. Drinks and hors d'oeuvres are served daily in Freddy's Bar and in summer only on La Terrasse, overlooking the Amstel, from 11am to 1am (weather permitting).

Amenities: Concierge, 24-hour room service, dry cleaning and laundry, twice-daily maid service, baby-sitting, business center, secretarial services, heated indoor pool, health club with sauna and massage, gift shop.

MODERATE

Best Western Eden. Amstel 144 (at Rembrandtplein), 1017 AE Amsterdam. ☎ **020/ 530-7888.** Fax 020/623-3267. www.edenhotelgroup.com. E-mail: Res.Eden@edenhotelgroup. com. 410 units. TV TEL. €95.50–€177 ($89.25–$165.40) double. Rates include Dutch buffet breakfast. AE, CB, DC, MC, V. Parking at nearby lot Dfl 45 ($19.15). Tram: 4, 9, or 20 to Rembrandtplein.

The biggest hotel in its class in the center city has a great setting, in several converted 17th-century merchants' houses (and a chocolate factory) beside the Amstel River, just behind Rembrandtplein. Rooms vary quite a lot in size, with some of them on the small side (the 410-room figure includes 70 new ones planned for 2001). Still, they're all well cared for and have bright, modern furnishings. Many have a fine view of the river, and these are the most desirable—and most expensive—ones. All have hair dryers and in-house movie channels. The Garden of Eden brasserie, overlooking the river, is a good place for Dutch specialties and international menu dishes.

Bridge Hotel. Amstel 107–111 (near Theater Carré), 1018 EM Amsterdam. ☎ **020/ 623-7068.** Fax 020/624-1565. www.thebridgehotel.demon.nl. E-mail: postbus@ thebridgehotel.demon.nl. 31 units. TV TEL. Summer Dfl 170–275 ($72.35–$117); winter Dfl 140–275 ($59.55–$117). Children under 4 stay free in parents' room. Rates include continental breakfast. AE, DC, MC, V. Parking Dfl 30 ($12.75). Tram: 6, 7, 10, or 20 to Weesperplein.

The bridge in question is the famous Magere Brug (Skinny Bridge) over the Amstel River. The small and tastefully decorated hotel is also near the Théâtre Carré and probably offers its guests more space per guilder than any other hotel in town. Its pine-furnished rooms seem like studio apartments, with couches, coffee tables, and easy chairs arranged in lounge areas in such a way that there's plenty of room left between them and the beds for you to do your morning exercises.

2 In the Center

VERY EXPENSIVE

The Grand Amsterdam. Oudezijds Voorburgwal 197 (3 blocks east of Spui, then along the canal), 1012 EX Amsterdam. ☎ **800/228-3000** in the U.S. and Canada, or 020/555-3111. Fax 020/555-3222. www.thegrand.nl. E-mail: hotel@thegrand.nl. 182 units. A/C MINIBAR TV TEL. Dfl 820 ($348.95) double; from Dfl 930 ($395.75) and way up suite; add 5% city tax. AE, CB, DC, JCB, MC, V. Parking Dfl 80 ($34.05). Tram: 4, 9, 16, 20, 24, or 25 to Spui.

The Grand Amsterdam is indeed one of the grandest hotels in town. It's in a building that was a 15th-century convent, a 16th-century royal inn, the 17th-century Dutch Admiralty, and the 19th-century Town Hall. To reach the lobby, you walk through a courtyard with a fountain, then through the brass-and-wood revolving door. There are fresh flower arrangements on all the tables in the lobby and lounge area, where tea is served in the afternoon. You also find plenty of art deco style and stained-glass windows. The black-and-white marble floors are covered with Oriental rugs. All this, and only a vigorous stone's throw from the Red Light District.

The individually styled and furnished guest rooms are designed to reflect the different phases of the building's illustrious past and are about the last word in plush (though some rooms put a refreshingly simple slant on this). Most have couches and armchairs; all have a personal safe and a voice-mail answering system for the telephone. The views are good too, onto the 17th-century canals, the hotel garden, or the courtyard. All bathrooms are equipped with hair dryers.

Dining: You can have lunch or dinner at the art deco, brasserie-style Café Roux, where you see an original Karel Appel mural, the *Inquisitive Children.*

Amenities: Indoor pool; health club with Jacuzzi, sauna, Turkish bath, massage, and solarium; concierge; 24-hour room service; twice-daily maid service; dry cleaning and laundry; newspaper delivery; in-room massage; baby-sitting; conference facilities; secretarial services; express checkout; courtesy car.

✪ **Grand Hotel Krasnapolsky.** Dam 9, 1012 JS Amsterdam. ☎ **020/554-9111.** Fax 020/622-8607. www.krasnapolsky.nl. E-mail: book@krasnapolsky.nl. 539 units. A/C MINIBAR TV TEL. Dfl 725 ($308.50) double; Dfl 955–1,495 ($406.40–$636.15) suite; add 5% city tax. Children under 5 stay free in parents' room; children 6–12 are charged half-price. AE, CB, DC, MC, V. Valet parking and self-parking Dfl 40 ($17). KLM Hotel Shuttle service from Schiphol Airport. Tram: 4, 9, 14, 16, 20, 24, or 25 to the Dam.

Living it up at the Hotel Krasnapolsky, one of Amsterdam's landmark hotels, is no great trick. The Krasnapolsky is on the Dam, facing the Royal Palace. It began life as the Wintertuin ("Winter Garden") restaurant, where Victorian ladies and gentlemen sipped wine and nibbled pancakes beneath the hanging plants and lofty skylight ceiling—the Wintertuin still dominates the ground floor. The place was founded in 1866 by a Polish tailor turned entrepreneur. Its original 100 rooms had parquet floors, central heating, and electric lights—the first hotel in Holland to have them.

Over the past century the "Kras" has spread over four buildings on several different levels. The sizes and shapes of the rooms vary, with some tastefully converted into individually decorated apartments. All units have hair dryers and coffeemakers. Recent renovations have added a new wing featuring a Japanese garden and a Dutch roof garden. The hotel's side streets lead into the Red Light District, which may not be the ideal direction to take for a casual evening stroll.

Dining: There are several great dining possibilities here. The Winter Garden is the most elegant place in Amsterdam for lunch. Brasserie Reflet specializes in French cuisine, and there are two fine Japanese restaurants: Edo and Kyo. Certainly the most novel is the Bedouin banquet dinner at the Shibli, from Friday to Sunday; on other evenings the room is open for private parties only.

Amenities: Concierge, 24-hour room service, dry cleaning and laundry, baby-sitting, secretarial services, express checkout, health club, business center, conference rooms, tour desk, beauty salon, boutiques.

EXPENSIVE

✪ **Crowne Plaza Amsterdam City Centre.** Nieuwezijds Voorburgwal 5 (near Centraal Station), 1012 RC Amsterdam. ☎ **020/620-0500.** Fax 020/620-1173. www.crowneplaza. com. E-mail: info&crowneplaza.nl. 270 units. A/C MINIBAR TV TEL. Dfl 435–745 ($185.10–$317) double; add 5% city tax. AE, DC, MC, V. Valet parking and self-parking Dfl 70 ($29.80). Tram: 1, 2, 5, 13, 17, or 20 to Nieuwezijds Voorburgwal.

A red-coated footman greets you at the door when you arrive, and he sets the tone for everything else at this fine hotel. Relaxed luxury is perhaps the best way to describe the Crowne Plaza. Some rooms have the kind of wooden beams that are typical of

ⓘ Family-Friendly Hotels

Crowne Plaza Amsterdam City Centre *(see page 59)* The Crowne Plaza has good and reliable amenities that are comfortable and convenient for traveling families. And it also has an indoor swimming pool.

Estheréa *(see page 71)* Though most of the rooms in this canal-house hotel are rather small, all are tastefully furnished, and a few, ideal for families, are equipped with bunk beds, always a favorite with children.

Sint Nicolaas *(see page 65)* A centrally located hotel run by the warm Mesker family, which welcomes guests into a comfortable and relaxed environment that is child-friendly.

NJHC City Hostel Vondelpark *(see page 68)* An ideal choice for families traveling on a limited budget, offering a good blend of facilities, space, easygoing atmosphere, and security, in addition to a green location in the city's famous Vondelpark.

Amstel Botel *(see page 66)* Although it is more common to find youthful spirits traveling alone or in small groups here, there is no reason why it wouldn't work for families, and there is the added interest for the kids of being on a ship, even if it isn't going anywhere.

canal-side houses in Amsterdam. Each one comes equipped with a hair dryer, trouser press, and coffeemaker, and there are comfortable armchairs and good desks for those of you who want to work. This hotel is ideal for tourists and expense-account travelers alike. An ongoing renovation program ensures that rooms and public spaces are kept up-to-date.

Dining/Diversions: Dorrius is one of Amsterdam's standout, Old Dutch restaurants (see chapter 5 for full details). The Amsterdammer Bar & Patio has the style of a typical local cafe.

Amenities: Indoor pool, health club with Jacuzzi and sauna, concierge, 24-hour room service, dry cleaning, laundry, self-service Laundromat, newspaper delivery, baby-sitting, secretarial services, business center, conference rooms, express checkout, tour desk.

✪ **Golden Tulip Barbizon Palace.** Prins Hendrikkade 59–72 (facing Centraal Station), 1012 AD Amsterdam. ☎ **800/327-1177** in the U.S. and Canada, or 020/556-4564. Fax 020/624-3353. www.goldentulip.com. E-mail: sales@gtbpalace.goldentulip.nl. 268 units. A/C MINIBAR TV TEL. Dfl 425–575 ($180.85–$244.70) double; add 5% city tax. AE, DC, MC, V. Parking Dfl 45 ($19.15). KLM Hotel Shuttle service from Schiphol Airport. Tram: 1, 2, 4, 5, 9, 13, 16, 17, 20, 24, or 25 to Centraal Station.

This sparkling establishment meets every criterion for the ideal Amsterdam hotel. It was built behind the facades of 19 traditional canal houses. Inside, it's fully modern, loaded with amenities, and efficient; it's also centrally located, within walking distance of Centraal Station and the Dam. Many of the rooms feature split-level designs and antique oak beams. A Roman forum may come to mind as you step into the hotel; the lobby is a long promenade of highly polished black-and-white marble floor tiles, with a massive skylight arching above.

Dining: The excellent Restaurant Vermeer has a Michelin star, and the Café Barbizon, serving lighter food, is also pretty good.

Amenities: Health club with Jacuzzi and sauna, business center, conference rooms, secretarial services, car-rental desk, tour desk, beauty salon, boutiques, concierge, 24-hour room service, dry cleaning and laundry, baby-sitting, express checkout.

Hotel Inntel Amsterdam-Centre. Nieuwezijdskolk 19 (off Nieuwezijds Voorburgwal), 1012 PV Amsterdam. ☎ **020/530-1818.** Fax 020/422-1919. www.hotelinntel.com. E-mail: infoamsterdam@hotelinntel.com. 236 units. MINIBAR TV TEL. Dfl 415–575 ($176.60–$244.70) double; add 5% city tax. AE, DC, JCB, MC, V. Nearby parking lot offers guests 25% discount on Dfl 50 ($21.30) day rate. KLM Hotel Shuttle service from Schiphol Airport stops nearby. Tram: 1, 2, 5, 13, 17, or 20 to Nieuwezijds Voorburgwal.

This fine hotel opened in 1996 as part of the redevelopment of Nieuwezijdskolk, a small and relatively quiet side street off the Nieuwezijds Voorburgwal, not far from Centraal Station. The Inntel stands beside the spot where the remains of the 13th-century castle of the Lords of Aemstel (see appendix A for more details) were uncovered by builders and subsequently excavated. The hotel is very modern in its design and facilities. All rooms have coffeemakers, hair dryers, and in-house movies, and only some of the standard rooms do not have air-conditioning. When it opened, the Inntel was considerably less expensive than other upmarket hotels in the area, but instant popularity has allowed it to close the gap rapidly; the American buffet breakfast is no longer included in the room rate.

Dining: The Red, Hot and Blue barbecue steak house aims to make Americans feel at home.

Amenities: Limited-hours room service, laundry, and dry cleaning.

✪ **Radisson SAS.** Rusland 17 (4 blocks east of Spui, then along the canal), 1012 CK Amsterdam. ☎ **800/333-3333** in the U.S. and Canada, or ☎ 020/623-1231. Fax 020/520-8200. www.radisson.com. E-mail: info@amszh.rdsas.com. 243 units. A/C MINIBAR TV TEL. Dfl 480–515 ($204.25–$219.15) double; from Dfl 795 ($338.30) and up suite; add 5% city tax. American buffet breakfast included in business class and suite rates. AE, DC, JCB, MC, V. Valet parking and self-parking Dfl 50 ($21.30). Tram: 4, 9, 16, 24, or 25 to Spui.

You can't get much closer to Old Amsterdam than at this stylish hotel in the higgledy-piggledy heart of the old city. When you walk into the dazzling atrium you face the facade of a vicarage dating from 1650. Because of Amsterdam's strict preservation laws, SAS couldn't knock the building down, so they built around it and incorporated it into the new structure. Two 18th-century merchants' houses and a former paper factory complete the thoroughly renovated ensemble.

The hotel offers four types of rooms. The first is typically Dutch, with oak furnishings and paneling and orange curtains. The other rooms are done in either a Scandinavian, an Asian, or an art deco theme. All offer a standard of comfort and style that has made the SAS a firm favorite in Amsterdam. Each room has a hair dryer. You find a writing desk, and queen-size, king-size, or twin beds in each room.

Dining/Diversions: If you can get past the name, you'll find the LaxenOxen to be an excellent and moodily atmospheric à la carte restaurant. De Palmboom serves breakfast and lunch, while the oak-beamed Pastoriebar, housed in the old vicarage, handles drinks and snacks.

Amenities: Fitness center, solarium, sauna, 24-hour room service and concierge service, dry cleaning and laundry, conference and banquet facilities, express checkout, newspaper delivery, baby-sitting, secretarial services, courtesy car.

Renaissance Amsterdam. Kattengat 1 (between Prins Hendrikkade and Singel), 1012 SZ Amsterdam. ☎ **800/HOTELS1** in the U.S. and Canada, or 020/621-2223. Fax 020/627-5245. www.renaissancehotels.com. E-mail: renaissance.amsterdam@renaissancehotels.com. 405 units. A/C MINIBAR TV TEL. €185–€300 ($172.90–$280.35) double; €231–€346 ($215.90–$323.35) executive room; add 5% city tax. Children under 18 stay free in parents' room. Extra person €46 ($43). Rates for Club-floor rooms include continental breakfast. AE, DC, JCB, MC, V. Parking Dfl 60 ($25.55). Tram: 1, 2, 5, 13, 17, or 20 to Nieuwezijds Voorburgwal.

Van Gogh liked the setting that would one day become the Renaissance well enough to paint part of it. Built around an open central courtyard in an area of old warehouses, the six-story hotel blends with the gabled facades nearby. The influence of antiquity stops at the front door, however: The Renaissance is supermodern, offering big beds, color TVs with in-house movies, electronic security, and message-retrieval systems. Each room has a hair dryer. It's a matter of taste whether you like the hotel's transformation of the adjacent domed Lutheran Koepelkerk, into an "ultramodern conference center." The restored, strikingly beautiful old church, which dates from 1671 and was painted in 1885 by van Gogh, seems more suited to its alternative use as a dining chamber.

Dining/Diversions: The Brasserie Noblesse (see chapter 5 for more details) serves French and international cuisine, in the evenings only. The Koepelcafé serves local dishes all day and the Patio Lounge serves coffee, drinks, and snacks. You can let your hair down at the Boston Club disco.

Amenities: Health club with Jacuzzi and sauna, business center, conference rooms, secretarial services, car-rental desk, tour desk, beauty salon, boutiques, concierge, 24-hour room service, dry cleaning and laundry, newspaper delivery (Club floor only), baby-sitting, express checkout, video rentals.

Swissôtel Amsterdam. Damrak 96 (at the Dam), 1012 LP Amsterdam. ☎ **020/ 522-3000.** Fax 020/522-3223. www.swissotel.com. E-mail: reservations.amsterdam@ swissotel.com. 109 units. A/C MINIBAR TV TEL. Dfl 550–650 ($234.05–$276.60) double; Dfl 700–750 ($297.85–$319.15) suite. Children under 12 stay free in parents' room. Extra person Dfl 100 ($42.55). AE, CB, DC, MC, V. Nearby paid parking lots only. KLM Hotel Shuttle service from Schiphol Airport. Tram: 4, 9, 14, 16, 20, 24, or 25 to the Dam.

If you like to stay at elegant, not-too-big hotels wherever you travel in Europe, you'll be pleased by the Swissôtel Amsterdam. Opened in 1987, this hotel, like so many in Amsterdam, was built anew within the walls of a group of traditional canal-house buildings (Damrak was at one time a canal). The location is superb, just footsteps off the Dam and directly across from De Bijenkorf department store. The service is personal and thoughtful, guest rooms are large and quiet, thanks to double-glazed windows; and hair dryers, coffeemakers, and in-house movie channels are standard. The bathrooms are fully tiled in marble. All guest rooms and the lobby have been renovated in the last few years. You have to go elsewhere to find a health club or a hairdresser, but the Swissôtel offers very good value for money in this prime location.

Dining: Olio takes its inspiration from Mediterranean cuisine.

Amenities: Concierge, 24-hour room service, dry cleaning and laundry, newspaper delivery, in-room massage, baby-sitting, secretarial services, express checkout, gift shop.

Victoria Hotel. Damrak 1–5 (facing Centraal Station), 1012 LG Amsterdam. ☎ **800/ 670 PARK** in the U.S. and Canada, or 020/627-1166. Fax 020/627-4259. www. parkplazaamsterdam.com. E-mail: vicres@parkplazahotels.nl. 305 units. A/C MINIBAR TV TEL. Dfl 430–540 ($183–$229.80) double; Dfl 850–975 ($361.70–$414.90)suite. Extra person Dfl 95 ($40.45). AE, DC, JCB, MC, V. Parking Dfl 42.50 ($18.10) at nearby lot. Tram: 1, 2, 4, 5, 9, 13, 16, 17, 20, 24, or 25 to Centraal Station.

You can survive quite nicely without taking taxis if you stay here, as close as you can be to Centraal Station, where most of the city's trams begin and end their routes, and where you can board a train to other parts of Holland and to Schiphol Airport. To emphasize the point, the hotel offers individual guests free first-class return train travel between Schiphol and Centraal Station. Since 1890, the elegant Victoria has been a turreted landmark at the head of Damrak. It overlooks the canal-boat piers and the stack of bicycles parked outside the station. It can be noisy and tacky out on busy, neon-lit Damrak, but you won't notice that inside. Its original spacious rooms have been recently redecorated and refurnished, and the windows replaced with double-glazed panes. Rooms in the adjacent new block inevitably lack some of the atmosphere of the old. All the rooms have trouser presses and hair dryers, and coffeemakers are available on request. The idea of its owners is to give you a five-star hotel at four-star rates. All this and location, too.

Dining/Diversions: You can enjoy dinner or a quick lunch in the Scandinavian-look Seasons Garden restaurant, or take cocktails at the Tasman Bar and tea at the Brasserie Vic's glassed-in terrace beside Damrak.

Amenities: Heated indoor pool, health club, solarium, business center with secretarial services, concierge, limited-hours room service, dry cleaning and laundry, newspaper delivery, in-room massage, baby-sitting, express checkout, valet parking on request.

MODERATE

Avenue Hotel. Nieuwezijds Voorburgwal 27 (near Centraal Station), 1012 RD Amsterdam. ☎ **020/530-9530.** Fax 020/638-3946. www.emb.hotels.nl. E-mail: info@avenue-hotel.nl. 84 units. TV TEL. Dfl 220–305 ($93.60–$129.80) double. Rates include continental breakfast. AE, DC, MC, V. Parking lot nearby Dfl 55 ($23.40). Tram: 1, 2, 5, 13, 17, or 20 to Nieuwezijds Kolk.

About 2 minutes from Centraal Station, this place has some of the style and many of the amenities of its neighbor, the Crowne Plaza (above), at less than half the price. The rooms aren't huge, but they are bright and have clean furnishings, good-sized bathrooms, some with double sinks, and all with hair dryers. At the time of writing, a major extension and refurbishment was underway, taking the hotel's capacity up from its previous 54 rooms, and renovating existing ones, and a restaurant and cafe should have opened by the time this book is published. There's an elevator, bar, and 24-hour room service.

✪ **Cok City Hotel.** Nieuwezijds Voorburgwal 50 (between Centraal Station and the Dam), 1012 SC Amsterdam. ☎ **800/44-UTELL** in the U.S. and Canada, or 020/422-0011. Fax 020/420-0357. www.cokhotels.nl. E-mail: reserver@cokhotels.nl. 106 units. TV TEL. Dfl 320 ($136.15) double. Extra person Dfl 60 ($25.55). Rates include Dutch buffet breakfast. AE, DC, MC, V. Nearby parking lot offers guests 25% discount on Dfl 50 ($21.30) day rate. Tram: 1, 2, 5, 13, 17, or 20 to Nieuwezijds Voorburgwal.

If you want modern comforts complemented by the personal touch offered by a small, locally owned hotel group, this six-floor hotel located in a converted printing house a 5-minute walk from Centraal Station and the Dam is a good bet. The comfortable, modern rooms are brightly decorated with flair and style, and come equipped with full bathrooms, color TVs, trouser presses, hair dryers, and safes. And you'll be staying in a kind of art gallery, as Cok Hotel Group owners Ger and Jaap Cok are both keen amateur artists, and paintings by the brothers grace the guest rooms and public spaces. Added conveniences include dry cleaning and laundry service; baby-sitting; and food, beverage, and ice dispensers; and rooms equipped for ironing on every floor. Several shops that stay open 24 hours are located on the ground floor. Altogether good value for your money.

✪ **Die Port van Cleve.** Nieuwezijds Voorburgwal 176–180 (behind the Royal Palace), 1012 SJ Amsterdam. ☎ **020/624-4860.** Fax 020/622-0240. www.dieportvancleve.com. E-mail: dieportvancleve.amsterdam@wxs.nl. 120 units. TV TEL. Dfl 425–650 ($180.85–$276.60) double; Dfl 625–850 ($265.95–$361.70) suite; add 5% city tax. Extra person Dfl 100 ($42.55). AE, CB, DC, MC, V. Nearby parking lot Dfl 40 ($17) per day. KLM Hotel Shuttle service from Schiphol Airport. Tram: 1, 2, 5, 13, 17, or 20 to Nieuwezijds Voorburgwal.

Fairly oozing history and charm, this hotel is near the Royal Palace and next to Magna Plaza, a big shopping center in what used to be the city's main Post Office. The hotel

From my favorite spot on the floor I look up at the blue sky and the bare chestnut tree, on whose branches little raindrops glisten like silver, and at the seagulls and other birds as they glide on the wind.

—Anne Frank (February 25, 1944)

itself is one of the city's oldest, and started life in 1864 as the first Heineken brewery. Over the last 100 years it has accommodated many famous guests. The ornamental facade, complete with turrets and alcoves, is original and was fully restored in 1997. Likewise, the interior has been completely renovated, and the rooms, though relatively small, have been furnished comfortably in modern yet cozy style. All have hair dryers and in-house movie channels, and some have stocked minibars. Limited-hours room service, dry cleaning and laundry, and baby-sitting are all provided. You won't eat much more traditionally Dutch than in the Brasserie de Poort, and you can drink in the Bodega de Blauwe Parade watched over by Delft blue tiles.

Hotel Amsterdam. Damrak 93–94 (beside the Dam), 1012 LP Amsterdam. ☎ **020/ 555-0666.** Fax 020/620-4716. www.hotelamsterdam.nl. E-mail: info@hotelamsterdam.nl. 80 units. A/C MINIBAR TV TEL. Dfl 350–420 ($148.95–$178.70) double. Extra person Dfl 70 ($29.80). AE, DC, JCB, MC, V. No parking (nearest lot 800 yards). Tram: 4, 9, 14, 16, 20, 24, or 25 to the Dam.

Only 400 yards from Centraal Station, this hotel, from 1911 and still owned by the same families, possesses an 18th-century facade. Its rooms are supermodern, though, featuring thick carpets, ample wardrobe space, tea- and coffeemaking facilities, and hair dryers. The entire hotel underwent renovation, completed in April 2001. Rooms at the front of the hotel tend to get more light, but are also subjected to more street noise; some have balconies. Room service, in-house movies, and laundry and dry cleaning service are available. The in-house De Roode Leeuw restaurant serves typical Dutch cuisine and daily two-course menus (see chapter 5 for more details). The glassed-in heated terrace overlooking the Dam is a pleasant and relaxing spot for a beer (open daily from 11am to 11:30pm).

Mercure Amsterdam Arthur Frommer. Noorderstraat 46 (off Vijzelgracht), 1017 TV Amsterdam. ☎ **020/622-0328.** Fax 020/620-3208. E-mail: H1032@mercure-hotels.com. 90 units. A/C MINIBAR TV TEL. Dfl 200–295 ($85.10–$125.55) double. AE, DC, MC, V. Limited free parking. Tram: 16, 24, or 25 to Vijzelgracht.

The Mercure (once owned by Arthur Frommer) is tucked away in the canal area off Vijzelgracht. Its entrance opens onto a small courtyard off a side street that runs like an alleyway behind Prinsengracht, with a beautiful canal-side mural painted along the facing wall. It's not easy to find but is well worth finding. A top-to-bottom renovation has transformed the Mercure's rooms, giving them a very stylish decor in soft pastel colors. All rooms have hair dryers and big double or single beds. There's a small, cozy bar. Dry cleaning, laundry, and baby-sitting are available.

Rho Hotel. Nes 5–23 (beside the Dam), 1012 KC Amsterdam. ☎ **020/620-7371.** Fax 020/ 620-7826. 170 units. MINIBAR TV TEL. Dfl 195–235 ($83–$100) double. Rates include continental breakfast. AE, MC, V. Parking Dfl 45 ($19.15). Tram: 4, 9, 14, 16, 20, 24, or 25 to the Dam.

Once you find it, you'll bless this hotel for its easy convenience. Tucked away in a side street just off the National Monument on the Dam, the Rho is housed in a building that once was the offices of a gold company and before that housed a theater dating from 1908 in the space that now holds the reception desk and breakfast area. There are elevators, the rooms are modern and comfortable, having been recently renovated, the price is right, and the location, quiet yet central, is one of the best in town. All rooms have hair dryers and fans, and car rental and tour bookings are available at the reception desk, as are the hotel's own bikes for rent. Who could ask for more?

✪ **Seven Bridges.** Reguliersgracht 31 (at Keizersgracht), 1017 LK Amsterdam. ☎ **020/ 623-1329.** 8 units. TV. Dfl 250–400 ($106.40–$170.20) double. Rates include full breakfast. AE, MC, V. Limited parking available on street. Tram: 16, 24, or 25 to Vijzelstraat.

Owners Pierre Keulers and Gunter Glaner have made the Seven Bridges, which gets its name from its view of seven arched bridges, one of Amsterdam's gems. Each room is individual. There are antique furnishings (art deco, Biedemeyer, Louis XVI, rococo), handmade Italian drapes, hand-painted tiles and wood-tiled floors, and impressionist art posters on the walls. The biggest room, on the first landing, can accommodate up to four and has a huge bathroom with marble floor, double sinks, a fair-sized shower, and a separate area for the lavatory (the sink and shower even have gold-plated taps). The room is enormous, with high ceilings, a big mirror over the fireplace, an Empire onyx table and antique leather armchairs, and an array of potted plants. Attic rooms have sloped ceilings and exposed wood beams, and there are big, bright basement rooms done almost entirely in white.

✪ **Sint Nicolaas.** Spuistraat 1a (corner of Nieuwezijds Voorburgwal), 1012 SP Amsterdam. ☎ **020/626-1384.** Fax 020/623-0979. www.hotelnicolaas.nl. E-mail: info@hotelnicolaas.nl. 24 units. TV TEL. Dfl 200–250 ($85.10–$106.40) double. Rates include continental breakfast. AE, DC, JCB, MC, V. Limited parking available on street. Tram: 1, 2, 5, 13, 17, or 20 to Spui.

Named after Amsterdam's patron saint, this hotel is conveniently near the Centraal Station, in a prominent corner house with a dark facade. It's a typical family hotel with an easygoing atmosphere, and children are welcome. Originally the building was occupied by a factory that manufactured ropes and carpets from sisal imported from the then Dutch colonies. It was converted into a hotel in 1980. The rather basic furnishings are more than compensated for by the ideal location and the Mesker family's friendliness. All rooms have hair dryers.

Tulip Inn Dam Square. Gravenstraat 14–16 (beside the Dam), 1012 NM Amsterdam. ☎ **020/623-3716.** Fax 020/638-1156. 33 units. TV TEL. Dfl 280–320 ($119.15–$136.15) double. Children 12 and under stay free in parents' room. Extra person Dfl 55 ($23.40). Rates include continental breakfast. AE, DC, MC, V. Parking at nearby lot Dfl 50 ($21.30). Tram: 1, 2, 4, 5, 9, 13, 14, 16, 17, 20, 24, or 25 to the Dam.

This hotel is another example of putting an old Amsterdam building to good use housing tourists. This time the old building, behind the Nieuwe Kerk, was a distillery—and a magnificent building it is. Its granite details accentuate the brickwork and massive curve-topped doors with elaborate hinges. Inside, the rooms are all you'll want: modern, bright, comfortable, and attractively priced, and each one has a hair dryer. There is a hotel bar.

INEXPENSIVE

Acacia. Lindengracht 251 (off Prinsengracht), 1015 KH, Amsterdam. ☎ **020/622-1460.** Fax 020/638-0748. www.hotelacacia.nl. E-mail: acacia.nl@wxs.nl. 18 units. TV TEL. Dfl 160 ($68.10) double; Dfl 230 ($97.85) houseboat double. Rates include continental breakfast. MC, V (5% surcharge on credit card payments). Limited parking available on street. Tram: 3 or 10 to Marnixstraat.

Not on one of the major canals, but in the Jordaan, facing a small canal, just a block from the Prinsengracht, the Acacia, shaped like a slice of cake, is run by Hans and

Marlene van Vliet, a friendly young couple that has worked hard to make their hotel welcoming, clean, and well kept. Simple, clean, and comfortable, the rooms have recently been equipped with new beds, writing tables, and chairs. They all have canal views. Breakfast is served in a triangular breakfast room. With windows on two sides, a nice view of the canal, and a breakfast of cold cuts, cheese, a boiled egg, and a choice of coffee or tea, it's a lovely way to start the morning. Two houseboats for guests on nearby Lijnbaansgracht add an authentic local touch.

Amstel Botel. Oosterdokskade 2–4 (beside Centraal Station), 1011 AE Amsterdam. ☎ 020/626-4247. Fax 020/639-1952. 176 units. TV TEL. Dfl 159 ($67.65) double. AE, DC, JCB, MC, V. Limited parking available on quay. Turn left out of Centraal Station, pass the bike rental, and you see it floating in front of you. Tram: 1, 2, 4, 5, 9, 13, 16, 17, 20, 24, or 25 to Centraal Station.

Where better to experience a city on the water than on a boat-hotel? Its cabins are spread out over four decks connected by elevator. Be sure to ask for a room with a view on the water, not on the uninspiring quay. The boat is popular largely because of its location and rates, and for that extra something added by sleeping on a boat. There's a concierge, in-house movie channel, and dry cleaning service. This moored boat-hotel has 352 beds in cabins on four decks, connected by an elevator. The bright, modern rooms are no-nonsense but comfortable, the showers small. To get here, leave the station and turn left, passing the bike rental—the Botel is painted white and directly in front of you. There's no curfew. Hair dryers are available from reception.

Belga. Hartenstraat 8 (between Herengracht and Keizersgracht), 1016 CB Amsterdam. ☎ 020/624-9080. Fax 020/623-6862. 10 units (6 with bathroom). TV TEL. Dfl 150 ($63.85) double with washbasin, Dfl 180 ($76.60) double with bathroom. Rates include continental breakfast. MC, V. Limited parking available on street. Tram: 13, 14, or 17 to Westermarkt.

This basic hotel was apparently designed by Rembrandt's frame-maker and is popular with backpackers who can share the cost of a five-bed room—it's a youth-oriented kind of place staffed by youth-oriented kind of people. You find no frills here, but it's clean and centrally located. New owners have, among other improvements, abandoned the old system of paying for showers via a coin-operated machine.

Bob's Hotel. Nieuwezijds Voorburgwal 92, 1012 SG Amsterdam. ☎ 020/623-0063. Fax 020/675-6446. 150 beds. Dfl 150 ($63.85) double; Dfl 30 ($12.75) per dorm bed. Rates include continental breakfast. No credit cards. Limited parking available on street. Tram: 1, 2, 5, 13, 17, or 20 to Nieuwezijds Kolk.

At this convenient lodging halfway between Centraal Station and the Dam, you are accommodated in doubles or dorms containing anywhere from 4 to 18 bunk beds (four dorms are women-only). Doubles have television. The atmosphere is very international and the clientele is generally young. (Drinking and drug taking are definitely banned, and there's a 3am curfew). During the summer a dinner for Dfl 10 ($4.25) is served. An annex around the corner at Spui 47 has six supermodern apartments with fully equipped kitchenettes accommodating two to four guests; these cost a low Dfl 100 to Dfl 125 ($42.55 to $53.20) per unit.

Clemens. Raadhuisstraat 39 (near to the Westerkerk), 1016 DC Amsterdam. ☎ 020/624-6089. Fax 020/626-9658. www.clemenshotel.nl. E-mail: info@clemenshotel.nl. 8 units (5 with private bathroom). Dfl 120 ($51.05) double. Rates include continental breakfast. AE, DC, MC, V. Limited parking available on street. Tram: 13, 14, 17, or 20 to Westerkerk.

Fully renovated in late 1999, this hotel, a 2-minute walk from the Anne Frankhuis, is spread over four floors in one of those typical steep-staired Dutch buildings, with the reception and breakfast room up one flight of stairs. It's owned and operated by a mother-and-daughter team, Dee and Emely, who keep the fairly spacious rooms in good trim and regularly put in fresh flowers. Rooms 7 and 8 each have a balcony facing the Westerkerk. There's room service from noon to 10pm and each room has an unstocked refrigerator. Particularly good and house-proud guests are in line to win a complimentary fruit basket.

Schirmann. Prins Hendrikkade 23 (facing Centraal Station), 1012 TM Amsterdam. ☎ **020/ 624-1942.** Fax 020/622-7759. 32 units. Dfl 80–280 ($34.05–$119.15) double. Rates include continental breakfast. AE, DC, MC, V. Parking in nearby lot Dfl 38.25 ($16.30). Tram: 1, 2, 4, 5, 9, 13, 16, 17, 20, 24, or 25 to Centraal Station.

A nice, friendly hotel across from Centraal Station—a convenient location but one where budget hotels can often be pretty miserable. Happily, this is not one of those: There's a pool table in the spotlessly maintained lounge, and the rooms are simply but modernly furnished, brightly decorated, and clean and comfortable. During 2001 and 2002, the Schirman will be upgrading to a two-star hotel that offers three-star quality, with an elevator, and telephone and television in each room among other amenities. So, look out for improvements, and more rooms at rates towards the upper end of the range listed above. If you want to stay on Saturday night, you need to book for 2 nights.

3 Around Leidseplein

EXPENSIVE

✪ **American Hotel.** Leidsekade 97 (facing Leidseplein), 1017 PN Amsterdam. ☎ **020/ 624-5322.** Fax 020/625-3236. www.interconti.com. E-mail: american@interconti.com. 188 units. A/C MINIBAR TV TEL. Dfl 550–650 ($234.05–$276.60) double; Dfl 750 ($319.15) suite. AE, CB, DC, JCB, MC, V. Parking at nearby lot Dfl 60 ($25.55). KLM Hotel Shuttle service from Schiphol Airport stops nearby. Tram: 1, 2, 5, 6, 7, 10, or 20 to Leidseplein.

One of the most fascinating buildings on Amsterdam's long list of monuments is this fanciful, castlelike mix of Venetian Gothic and jugendstil, which has been both a prominent landmark and a popular meeting place for Amsterdammers since 1900. While the exterior of the American must always remain an architectural treasure (and curiosity) of turrets, arches, and balconies, in accordance with the regulations of the National Monument Care Office, the interior of the hotel (except that of the café, which is also protected) is modern and chic, though at times a bit gaudy. Rooms are subdued and refined, superbly furnished, and while some have a view of the Singelgracht, others overlook kaleidoscopic Leidseplein. They are always pink and bright, which perhaps appeals to the international rock stars who often stay here. The location, in the thick of the action and near many major attractions, is one of the best in town. Its most recent renovation was in 1998, and all rooms have hair dryers.

Dining/Diversions: The famous Café Américain is one of the most elegant eateries (and bars) in Europe (see chapter 5). There is also the Brasserie and the Nightwatch Bar, which has a closed-in terrace looking out onto Leidseplein.

Amenities: 24-hour room service, concierge, health club with sauna, laundry and dry cleaning, business and secretarial services, gift shop.

Golden Tulip Amsterdam Centre. Stadhouderskade 7 (facing Leidseplein), 1054 ES Amsterdam. ☎ **800/344-1212** in the U.S. and Canada, or 020/685-1351. Fax 020/685-1611. www.goldentuliphotels.nl\gtamsterdamcentre. E-mail: info@gtacentre.goldentulip.nl. 235 units. A/C MINIBAR TV TEL. €240–€280 ($224.30–$261.70) double; €570 ($532.70) suite; add 5% city tax. AE, DC, MC, V. Parking €30 ($28.05) at nearby lot. KLM Hotel Shuttle service from Schiphol Airport. Tram: 1, 2, 5, 6, 7, 10, or 20 to Leidseplein.

The hotel building began life in 1927 as a YMCA to house athletes for the 1928 Amsterdam Olympic Games, and only later became a hotel. Don't worry, the smell of honest sweat has long since vanished. The Amsterdam Centre is gracious, attractive, and imaginatively arranged, with color schemes that reflect those found in the works of the late 19th-century Barbizon school of French landscape painting—restful yet distinctive tones. All rooms have been recently renovated and offer both comfort and efficiency of the kind with which frequent business travelers will be familiar. Each one has a hair dryer.

Dining: Café Ristorante Bice serves Italian food, and the Barbizon Bar Brasserie is open for cocktails in the evening.

Amenities: Concierge, 24-hour room service, health club, laundry and dry-cleaning service, beauty salon.

MODERATE

Best Western AMS Hotel Terdam. Tesselschadestraat 23 (across Stadhouderskade from Leidseplein), 1054 ET Amsterdam. ☎ **0800/0221-455** or 020/612-6876. Fax 020/683-8313. www.hospitality.nl/ams. E-mail: info@ams.nl. 90 units. TV TEL. Dfl 200–300 ($85.10–$127.65) double. Rates include buffet breakfast. AE, DC, JCB, MC, V. Limited parking available on street. Tram: 1 or 6 to Stadhouderskade.

On a quiet street just off Leidseplein and the bustling heart of the city, the AMS Terdam provides spacious rooms with large windows and modern furnishings, all very nicely put together for the price. The last major renovation was in 1996. You find an unusually large array of choices with the Dutch breakfast, and there's a good bar and lounge in art deco style. The hotel offers laundry service and airport shuttle.

INEXPENSIVE

De Lantaerne. Leidsegracht 111 (near Leidseplein), 1017 ND Amsterdam. ☎ **020/623-2221.** Fax 020/623-2683. www.channels.nl/amsterdam.html. E-mail: reservations@lantaerne.com. 24 units (19 with bathroom). TV TEL. Dfl 175 ($74.45) double with bathroom, Dfl 130 ($55.30) double without bathroom. Rates include continental breakfast. AE, MC, V. Limited parking available on street. Tram: 1, 2, 5, 6, 7, 10, or 20 to Leidseplein.

Small and inexpensive, this is perfect for long stays because for a couple of reasons it feels like home. For one, not only are the standard rooms perfectly comfortable but there are four studios that have kitchenettes, color TVs, and minirefrigerators; they're perfect if you're doing Amsterdam on a budget and would like to cook some of your own meals. The other thing that makes this place homey is the breakfast room. It's bright and airy, with an exposed-beam ceiling, large windows, and red-and-white-checked tablecloths. All rooms have hair dryers. If you happen to be sensitive to decibels (and who isn't?), watch out for noisy back rooms: In the back alley is a police station, disco bar, and movie theater. The noise is relentless, especially after 11pm.

De Leydsche Hof. Leidsegracht 14 (off Herengracht), 1016 CR Amsterdam. ☎ **020/623-2148.** 10 units (4 with bathroom). Dfl 110 ($46.80) double. No credit cards. Limited parking available on street. Tram: 1, 2, or 5, to Leidsestraat.

Run by an ex-KLM purser, its greatest advantages are its location and rates, of a level that has almost vanished from Amsterdam. The accommodations are basic but well cared for and clean. The rooms all have a shower; toilets are in the hallway. You cannot get breakfast in the hotel, but there are plenty of cafes in the immediate area.

✪ **NJHC City Hostel Vondelpark.** Zandpad 5 (in Vondelpark), 1054 GA Amsterdam. ☎ **020/589-8996.** Fax 020/589-8955. www.njhc.org/vondelpark. 101 units (475 beds). Dfl 36.25 ($15.45) dorm bed; Dfl 40–48.75 ($17–$20.75) per person in bedroom with

4–8 beds; Dfl 135 ($57.45) double; supplement for nonmembers of IYHF. Rates include continental breakfast. AE, DC, MC, V. No parking. Tram: 1, 2, 5, 6, 7, 10, or 20 to Leidseplein.

"The new generation of city hostel" is how the Dutch youth hostel organization describes this hostel, which opened its doors in 1998, and that's a fair description of a marvelous, great-value lodging just inside Vondelpark. The location, facing Leidseplein, could hardly be better for youthful spirits who want to be near the action. At the hostel's core is a protected monument, a former Girl's Housekeeping School. All rooms are simply but modernly and brightly furnished and all have an en suite bathroom. The four- and six-bed rooms are ideal for families traveling on a limited budget and for groups of friends. Some rooms are adapted for people with disabilities. Although the hostel is open 24 hours a day, security is taken seriously, and all guests have key cards. There are coin-operated Internet stations for those who have to surf, and the Backpacker's Lounge is a pleasant place to meet fellow travelers.

Orfeo. Leidsekruisstraat 14 (near Leidseplein), 1017 RH Amsterdam. ☎ **020/623-1347.** Fax 020/620-2348. 17 units. TV TEL. Dfl 130–215 ($58.50–$96.75) double. Rates include continental breakfast. AE, DC, MC, V. Limited parking available on street. Tram: 1, 2, or 5 to Prinsengracht; 6, 7, 10, or 20 to Leidseplein.

One of the city's longest-standing gay lodgings has for more than 30 years been offering cheap rates for basic, practical facilities and friendly, helpful service. The front desk is in a cozy and sociable lounge and there is a marble-floored breakfast room. Only three guest rooms have a full bathroom, some with charming beamed ceilings; others share shower and/or toilet. One of the perks is a small in-house Finnish sauna, and the largest concentration of city-center restaurants is right on the doorstep.

4 Along the Canal Belt

VERY EXPENSIVE

۞ Hotel Pulitzer Sheraton. Prinsengracht 315–331 (near Westermarkt), 1016 GZ Amsterdam. ☎ **800/325-3535** or 020/523-5235. Fax 020/627-6753. www.sheraton.com. E-mail: res100_amsterdam@sheraton.com. 230 units. MINIBAR TV TEL. Dfl 735–795 ($312.75–$338.30) double; Dfl 1,850 ($787.25)suite; add 5% city tax. Extra person Dfl 100 ($42.55). AE, CB, DC, MC, V. Valet parking and self-parking Dfl 60 ($25.55). KLM Hotel Shuttle service from Schiphol Airport. Tram: 13, 14, 17, or 20 to Westermarkt.

The recently renovated Pulitzer has spread through 25 old canal houses, giving it frontage on the historic Prinsengracht and Keizersgracht canals. The houses date from the 17th and 18th centuries and adjoin one another, side by side and garden to garden. You walk between two houses to enter the lobby, or climb the steps of a former merchant's house to enter the ever-crowded and cheerful bar. With the exception of bare beams or brick walls here and there, history stops at the Pulitzer's many thresholds. Rooms are spacious and modern, with wickerwork furnishings. All have hair dryers. The rooms with the best views look out over either the canals or the hotel garden.

The Pulitzer is big on culture, with its own art gallery, and every August the hotel sponsors a popular classical music concert performed by musicians on barges in the canal. As icing on the cake, the Pulitzer owns a restored saloon cruiser dating from 1909, which awaits your pleasure at the hotel's own jetty.

Dining/Diversions: In the French De Goudsbloem (Marigold) restaurant, open 6 to 11pm, you have one of Amsterdam's toniest dining experiences. Café Pulitzer has a canal-side entrance and serves lunch and snacks. The Pulitzer Bar is for a quiet drink.

Amenities: Concierge, 24-hour room service, laundry and dry cleaning, newspaper delivery, in-room massage, baby-sitting, secretarial services, valet parking, conference rooms, tour desk.

EXPENSIVE

✪ **Dikker & Thijs Fenice.** Prinsengracht 444 (at Leidsestraat), 1017 KE Amsterdam. ☎ **020/626-1212.** Fax 020/625-8986. www.dtfh.nl. E-mail: info@dtfh.nl. 42 units. MINI-BAR TV TEL. Dfl 325–750 ($138.30–$230.75) double. Children 12 and under stay free in parents' room. Rates include continental breakfast. AE, DC, JCB, MC, V. Parking at nearby lot. Dfl 50 ($21.30). Tram: 1, 2, or 5, to Prinsengracht.

On the Prinsengracht, at the intersection of the lively Leidsestraat, is this small and homey hotel whose smart but cozy character is indicated by the new marble-rich lobby. The stylish facade has hosted Dikker & Thijs here since 1921. Upstairs, the spacious and tastefully styled rooms are clustered in groups of two or four around small lobbies, which makes the Dikker & Thijs feel more like an apartment building than a hotel. Welcoming touches are flowers in the rooms, a subtle but elegantly modern art deco decor, and double-glazed windows to eliminate the noise rising up from Leidsestraat at all hours of the day and night. All rooms were renovated during 1997 and 1998, and have hair dryers and in-house movies. Those at the front have a super view of the classy Prinsengracht.

Dining/Diversions: The Prinsenkelder restaurant and bar serves good French and Italian dinners, and the adjacent cellar bar is worth a visit.

Amenities: Concierge, room service, dry cleaning and laundry, in-room massage, baby-sitting, secretarial services, bicycle rental, tour desk.

MODERATE

Agora. Singel 462 (at Koningsplein), 1017 AW Amsterdam. ☎ **020/627-2200.** Fax 020/627-2202. www.hotelagora.nl. E-mail: info@hotelagora.nl. 16 units (13 with bathroom). TV TEL. Dfl 235–260 ($100–$110.65) double with bathroom, Dfl 165 ($70.20) double without bathroom. Extra person Dfl 40 ($17). Rates include buffet breakfast. AE, DC, MC, V. Parking Dfl 45 ($19.15). Tram: 1, 2, or 5 to Koningsplein.

Old-fashioned friendliness is the keynote at this efficiently run and well-maintained lodging, a block from the Flower Market. Owners Yvo Muthert and Els Bruijnse like to keep things friendly and personal. Although the hotel occupies a canal house built in 1735, it has been fully restored in an eclectic style. Furniture from the 1930s and 1940s mixes with fine mahogany antiques. Bouquets greet you as you enter, and a distinctive color scheme creates an effect of peacefulness and drama at the same time. They have installed an abundance of overstuffed furniture; nearly every room has a puffy armchair you can sink into after a wearying day of sightseeing. All rooms have hair dryers. Upgrading of the bathrooms is proceeding apace and all beds have been recently renewed. Rooms with a canal view cost the most, but the extra few guilders are worth it, though the hustle and bustle out on the street can make them somewhat noisy by day; the large family room has three windows overlooking the Singel. Those rooms that don't have a canal view look out on a pretty garden at the back.

Ambassade. Herengracht 335–353 (near Spui), 1016 AZ Amsterdam. ☎ **020/555-0222.** Fax 020/555-0277. www.ambassade-hotel.nl. E-mail: info@ambassade-hotel.nl. 52 units. TV TEL. Dfl 350–380 ($148.95–$161.70) double; Dfl 425–620 ($180.85–$263.85) suite. Extra person Dfl 60 ($25.55). AE, DC, MC, V. Limited parking available on street; parking in nearby lot Dfl 40 ($17). Tram: 1, 2, or 5 to Spui.

Perhaps more than any other hotel in Amsterdam, this one, in 10 old canal houses on the Herengracht and Singel canals, re-creates the feeling of living in an elegant canal house. The rooms are individually styled and their size and shape vary according to the character of the individual houses. All have hair dryers, and the hotel offers such services as concierge, 24-hour room service, dry cleaning and laundry, baby-sitting, secretarial services, newspaper delivery, video rentals, and bicycle rental. Each year one of the houses is completely renovated. Everyone who stays at the Ambassade enjoys the view each morning with breakfast in the bilevel, chandeliered breakfast room or each evening in the adjoining parlor, with its Persian rugs and stately grandfather clock ticking away. To get to some guest rooms, you cope with a typically Dutch steep and skinny staircase, though other rooms are accessible by elevator. For the nimble-footed who can handle the stairs, the rewards are a spacious room with large multipane windows overlooking the canal.

✪ Amsterdam Wiechmann. Prinsengracht 328–330 (at Looiersgracht), 1016 HX Amsterdam. ☎ **020/626-3321.** Fax 020/626-8962. 40 units. TV TEL. Dfl 195–250 ($83–$106.40) double. Rates include continental breakfast. MC, V. Limited parking available on street. Tram: 1, 2, or 5 to Prinsengracht.

It takes only a moment to feel at home in the antique-adorned Amsterdam Wiechmann. Owned by American T. Boddy and his Dutch wife, Nicky, for a number of years, the Wiechmann is a classic, comfortable, casual sort of place, in spite of the suit of armor you encounter just inside the front door. Besides, the location is one of the best you find in this or any price range: 5 minutes in one direction is the Kalverstraat shopping street; 5 minutes in the other, Leidseplein. Most of the rooms are standard, with good-sized twin beds or double beds, and some have big bay windows. Furnishings are elegant, and Oriental rugs grace many of the floors in the public spaces. The higher-priced doubles have antique furnishings, and many have a view of the Prinsengracht. The breakfast room has hardwood floors, lots of greenery, and white linen cloths on the tables. There is a lounge and bar.

Canal House. Keizersgracht 148 (near Leliegracht), 1015 CX Amsterdam. ☎ **020/622-5182.** Fax 020/624-1317. www.canalhouse.nl. E-mail: info@canalhouse.nl. 26 units. TEL. Dfl 225–265 ($95.75– $112.75) double. Rates include continental breakfast. AE, DC, MC, V. Limited parking available on street. Tram: 13, 14, 17, or 20 to Westermarkt.

A contemporary approach to reestablishing the elegant canal-house atmosphere has been taken by the American owner of the Canal House Hotel. This small hotel below Raadhuisstraat is in three adjoining houses that date from 1630; they were gutted and rebuilt to provide private bathrooms and filled with antiques, quilts, and Chinese rugs. Fortunately, it's blessed with an elevator (though one that does not stop at every floor, so you may still have to walk a short distance up or down stairs), along with a (steep) staircase that still has its beautifully carved old balustrade, and overlooking the back garden, which is illuminated at night, a magnificent breakfast room that seems to have been untouched since the 17th century. Plus, on the parlor floor the owner has created a cozy Victorian-era saloon. It is, in short, a home away from home. All rooms have hair dryers.

✪ Estheréa. Singel 303–309 (near Spui), 1012 WJ Amsterdam. ☎ **020/624-5146.** Fax 020/623-9001. E-mail: estherea@xs4all.nl. 75 units. MINIBAR TV TEL. Dfl 290–495 ($123.40–$210.65) double; add 5% city tax. One child 12 or under stays free in parents' room. Extra person Dfl 50 ($21.30). AE, DC, JCB, MC, V. Parking nearby Dfl 40 ($17) per day. Tram: 1, 2, or 5, to Spui.

The Estheréa has been owned by the same family since its beginnings and is built within the walls of neighboring 17th-century canal houses. The family touch shows in careful attention to detail and a breezy but professional approach. It offers the blessed advantage of an elevator, a rarity in these old Amsterdam homes. In the 1930s the owners spent a lot of money on wood paneling and other structural additions; more recent owners have had the good sense to leave all of it in place. While it will look dated to some, the wood bedsteads and dresser-desks in fact lend warmth to the recently renovated and upgraded rooms. The room sizes vary considerably according to their location in the canal houses, and a few are quite small, though not seriously so. Most of the rooms will accommodate two, but some rooms have more beds, which make them ideal for families. All rooms have hair dryers. The excellent small Greek restaurant Traîterie Grekas, next door (see chapter 5 for full details), provides room-service meals, and the Estheréa offers a concierge, limited-hours room service, dry cleaning and laundry, in-room massage, baby-sitting, secretarial services, bicycle rental, tour desk, and free coffee in the lobby.

New York. Herengracht 13 (near Centraal Station), 1015 BA Amsterdam. ☎ **020/624-3066.** Fax 020/620-3230. 18 units. TV TEL. Dfl 220–270 ($93.60–$114.90) double. Rates include continental breakfast. AE, DC, MC, V. Limited private parking Dfl 35 ($14.90). Tram: 1, 2, 5, 13, 17, or 20 to Martelaarsgracht.

Three 17th-century buildings on one of the city's most picturesque canals have been joined to create this gay-run hotel, which has considerable charm and overlooks the famous Milkmaid's Bridge. It's only a short walk to the Nieuwezijdskolk and War-moesstraat bars, and Centraal Station train and tram connections are close at hand. Guest rooms range in size from spacious to quaintly cramped and are furnished in a clean modern style. Additional facilities and services include a cocktail lounge and same-day laundry service. Note that this four-floor hotel has no elevator and a warren of narrow stairs and walkways to navigate.

Rembrandt Residence. Herengracht 255 (at Hartenstraat), 1016 BJ Amsterdam. ☎ **020/ 623-6638.** Fax 020/625-0630. www.bookings.nl/hotels/rembrandt. E-mail: rembrandt. residence.hotel@tip.nl. 111 units. TV TEL. Dfl 360–395 ($153.20–$168.10) double; Dfl 440 ($187.25) executive room. Children 14 and under stay free in parents' room. Extra person Dfl 75 ($31.90). AE, DC, MC, V. Limited parking available on street. Tram: 1, 2, 5, 13, 14, 17, or 20 to the Dam.

Following the example of the Hotel Pulitzer, the Rembrandt Residence was built anew within old walls. In this case the structures are a wide 18th-century building on a canal above Raadhuistraat and four small 16th-century houses directly behind it on the Sin-gel canal. The look of the place is best described as basic, but rooms tend to be large (in all sizes and shapes) and fully equipped (down to the trouser press); some still have their old fireplaces (not working) with elegant wood or marble mantels. And as you walk around, occasionally you see an old beam or pass through a former foyer on the way to your room.

Singel Hotel. Singel 13 (near Centraal Station), 1012 VC Amsterdam. ☎ **020/626-3108.** Fax 020/620-3777. 30 units. TV TEL. Dfl 235–275 ($100–$117) double. Extra person Dfl 55 ($23.40). Rates include Dutch buffet breakfast. AE, DC, MC, V. Limited parking available on street. Tram: 1, 2, 4, 5, 9, 13, 16, 17, 20, 24, or 25 to Centraal Station.

Style marries tradition in the elegant little Singel, near the head of the Brouwersgracht in one of the most pleasant and central locations in Amsterdam. Three renovated canal houses have been united in harmony to create this hotel. The decor is bright and wel-coming. The modernly furnished rooms are spacious for a small hotel. Some of the rooms have an attractive view of the Singel canal; all have hair dryers. An elevator ser-vices the building's four floors.

Toren. Keizersgracht 164 (near Leliegracht), 1015 CZ Amsterdam. ☎ **020/622-6352.** Fax 020/626-9705. www.toren.nl. E-mail: hotel.toren@tip.nl. 43 units. TV TEL. Dfl 220–275 ($93.60–$117) double; Dfl 420 ($178.70) suite. Rates include continental breakfast. AE, DC, MC, V. Parking in nearby lot Dfl 30 ($12.75). Tram: 13, 14, 17, or 20 to Westermarkt.

The Toren is a sprawling enterprise that encompasses two buildings, separated by neighboring houses. With so many rooms, it's a better bet than most canal-house hotels during the tourist seasons in Amsterdam. Clean, attractive, and well maintained, the

Toren promises private facilities with every room, though in a few cases that means a private bathroom located off the public hall (with your own private key, however). There's a bridal suite here, complete with a blue canopy and a Jacuzzi. There's also a little private guesthouse off the garden that's done up in Laura Ashley prints. Each room has a hair dryer. All this and a canal-side location, too.

INEXPENSIVE

De Admiraal. Herengracht 563 (at Thorbeckeplein), 1071 CD Amsterdam. ☎ **020/ 626-2150.** Fax 020/623-4625. 9 units. TV TEL. Dfl 125–180 ($53.20–$76.60) double. MC, V (5% supplement). Limited parking available on street. Tram: 4, 9, 14, or 20 to Rembrandtplein.

De Admiraal is located in a building dating from 1666, part of which was originally a warehouse for spices from the East Indies unloaded on the canal quay outside, and that appeared more than 3 centuries later in the movie *Puppet on a Chain*. It still retains a nautical and exotic feel, with a bar/breakfast room that looks like an old-time sailing-ship's officer's quarters. The rooms are at all angles and places and are reached by a narrow staircase. They are simple but clean and comfortably furnished and have a fine view of the canal or adjacent Thorbeckeplein (there are some strip clubs on this otherwise pleasant little square, but it cannot be called sleazy). Room 6 is the hotel's star, with two double beds and a view on Herengracht, Reguliersgracht, and Thorbeckeplein.

Hegra. Herengracht 269 (near Hartenstraat), 1016 BJ Amsterdam. ☎ **020/623-7877.** Fax 020/623-8159. 11 units (6 with bathroom). Dfl 175 ($74.45) double with bathroom, Dfl 120 ($51.05) double without bathroom. Extra person Dfl 60 ($25.55). Rates include continental breakfast. AE, DC, MC, V. Limited parking available on street. Tram: 1, 2, 5, 13, 14, 17, or 20 to the Dam.

Housed in a 17th-century building and a 5-minute walk from the Dam, this cozy little hotel has been under the same management for two generations. Robert, the owner, is extremely helpful and friendly. The rooms are small but tastefully furnished and have beamed ceilings. Note that there is no elevator, so you have to climb four stories if you get a room on the top floor. Hair dryers are available.

Hoksbergen. Singel 301 (near Spui), 1012 WA Amsterdam. ☎ **020/626-6043.** Fax 020/638-3479. www.hotelhoksbergen.com. E-mail: hotelhoksbergen@wxs.nl. 14 units. TV TEL. Dfl 160–190 ($68.10–$80.85) double. Children 4 and under stay free in parents' room. Extra person Dfl 25 ($10.65). Rates include continental breakfast. AE, DC, JCB, MC, V. Limited parking available on street with permit from hotel Dfl 39.25 ($16.70); at nearby lot Dfl 50 ($21.30). Tram: 1, 2, or 5 to Spui.

At a tranquil point on the historic Singel canal, this inexpensive hotel in a 300-year-old canal house is not flashy or elegant, but it's bright and fresh and recently renovated, which makes it appealing to budget-conscious travelers who don't want to swap creature comforts for guilders. Its central location makes it easy to get to all the surrounding sights and attractions. All rooms have fans, and hair dryers are available at the reception desk. Rooms at the front have a canal view.

Keizershof. Keizersgracht 618 (at Nieuwe Spiegelstraat), 1017 ER Amsterdam. ☎ **020/ 622-2855.** Fax 020/624-8412. www.vdwp.nl/keizershof. E-mail: keizershof@vdwp.nl. 6 units (3 with bathroom). Dfl 180 ($76.60) double with bathroom, Dfl 140 ($59.55) double without bathroom. Rates include buffet breakfast. MC, V. Limited parking available on street. Tram: 16, 24, or 25 to Keizersgracht.

Owned by the genial De Vries family, this hotel in a four-story canal-house from 1672 has six rooms named after movie stars—though a greater claim to fame is that members of the Dutch royal family were regular visitors in its prehotel days. Several other touches make a stay here memorable. From the street-level entrance a wooden spiral staircase built from a ship's mast leads to the beamed rooms. Note that there's no elevator. There is, however, a television and a grand piano in the cozy lounge. All rooms have hair dryers. In good weather, breakfast, which includes excellent omelettes and pancakes, is served in the flower-bedecked courtyard. Because the hotel is has so few rooms, you need to book ahead; the earlier the better.

Prinsenhof. Prinsengracht 810 (at Utrechtsestraat), 1017 JL Amsterdam. ☎ **020/623-1772.** Fax 020/638-3368. www.hotelprinsenhof.com. E-mail: info@hotelprinsenhof.com. 10 units (3 with bathroom). TEL. Dfl 165 ($70.20) double with bathroom, Dfl 125 ($53.20) double without bathroom. Rates include continental breakfast. AE, MC, V. Limited parking available on street; two nearby parking lots Dfl 45 ($19.15). Tram: 4 to Prinsengracht.

A modernized canal house near the Amstel River, this hotel offers rooms with beamed ceilings and basic yet reasonably comfortable beds. The place has been recently refurbished, and new showers and carpets installed. Front rooms look out onto the Prinsengracht, where colorful houseboats are moored. Breakfast is served in an attractive blue-and-white decorated dining room. The owners, Rik and André van Houten, take pride in their hotel and will make you feel welcome. There's no elevator, but a pulley hauls your luggage up and down the stairs. Hair dryers are available from reception.

Van Haalen. Prinsengracht 520 (between Nieuwe Spiegelstraat and Leidsestraat), 1017 KJ Amsterdam. ☎ **020/626-4334.** 20 units (10 with bathroom). TV TEL. Dfl 195 ($83) double with bathroom, Dfl 125 ($53.20) double without bathroom. Rates include continental breakfast. No credit cards. Free parking. Tram: 1, 2, or 5 to Prinsengracht.

If you're looking for a canal hotel decorated with the dark woods and bric-a-brac you associate with Old Holland, you'll like the Hotel van Haalen. You'll also like the friendly owners, who've done a lot of work around the place, including building the platform beds. Location is another advantage: The Van Haalen is near a bustling shopping street and the premier main antiques district.

5 Around Rembrandtplein

EXPENSIVE

✪ **Hotel Schiller.** Rembrandtplein 26–36, 1017 CV Amsterdam. ☎ **020/554-0700.** Fax 020/624-0098. www.goldentuliphotels.nl/gtschiller. E-mail: sales@gtschiller.goldentulip.nl. 92 units. MINIBAR TV TEL. Dfl 385–495 ($163.85–$210.65) double; from Dfl 525 ($223.40) suite. AE, DC, MC, V. Parking in nearby lot Dfl 45 ($19.15). Tram: 4, 9, 14, or 20 to Rembrandtplein.

A historic Amsterdam gem, now fully restored, this hotel boasts a blend of jugendstil and art deco in its public spaces that is reflected in tasteful decor and furnishings in the rooms. Its sculpted facade, wrought-iron balconies, and stained-glass windows stand out on the often brash Rembrandtplein. Café Schiller, next door to the hotel, is one of the trendiest watering holes in town. The hotel takes its name from the painter Frits Schiller, who built it in 1912. His outpourings of artistic expression, in the form of 600 portraits, landscapes, and still lifes, are displayed in the halls, rooms, stairwells, and public areas; and their presence fills this hotel with a unique sense of vitality, creativity, and personality. All rooms have a coffeemaker and a hair dryer. Perhaps the happiest outcome of the revitalization of the Schiller is the new life it brings to the hotel's gracious oak-paneled dining room and to the Café Schiller, one of Amsterdam's few permanent, and perfectly situated, sidewalk cafes.

Dining/Diversions: Experience classic French and Dutch cuisine and the hotel's own beer, Frisse Frits, in the jugendstil Brasserie Schiller (see chapter 5 for more details), or join the in crowd next door for a drink amid the art deco splendor of the Café Schiller.

Amenities: 24-hour room service, laundry and dry cleaning, baby-sitting, health club, conference rooms.

6 Around Museumplein & Vondelpark

MODERATE

Atlas. Van Eeghenstraat 64 (near Vondelpark), 1071 GK Amsterdam. ☎ **020/676-6336.** Fax 020/671-7633. 23 units. TV TEL. Dfl 220 ($93.60) double. Extra person Dfl 45 ($19.15). Rates include continental breakfast. AE, DC, JCB, MC, V. Limited parking available on street. Tram: 2, 3, 5, 12, or 20 to Van Baerlestraat.

Off Van Baerlestraat, the Atlas is a converted house with a convenient location for shoppers, concertgoers, and museum lovers. The staff backs up the homey feel with attentive service. The guest rooms are small but tidy, decorated attractively in gray with blue comforters on the beds and a welcoming basket of fruit on the desk. Leather chairs fill the front lounge, which has a grandfather clock ticking in the corner. There is also a small bar/restaurant providing 24-hour room service. Laundry and dry-cleaning service is available during the week. A hair dryer is available at the reception desk.

Cok Superior Tourist Class Hotel. Koninginneweg 34–36 (at Valeriusplein), 1075 CZ Amsterdam. ☎ **800/44 UTELL** in the U.S. and Canada, or 020/664-6111. Fax 020/664-5304. www.cokhotels.nl. E-mail: reserver@cokhotels.nl. 110 units. TV TEL. Dfl 275–310 ($117–$131.90) double. Rates include full breakfast. AE, DC, JCB, MC, V. Parking day permit Dfl 18.50 ($7.85). Tram: 2 to Koninginneweg.

State-of-the-art rooms and the design and the kind of artistic flair imparted by the Cok brothers Ger and Jaap in all of their small Amsterdam chain make this place a good bet for travelers who want that extra something in their hotel. Each room has a hair dryer, trouser press, and coffeemaking facilities; some have balconies. Club class rooms have a minibar. For an added touch of luxury, book one of the five suites that have a Jacuzzi. Koninginneweg is within easy walking distance of Vondelpark.

De Filosoof. Anna van den Vondelstraat 6 (at Vondelpark), 1054 GZ Amsterdam. ☎ **020/683-3013.** Fax 020/685-3750. www.xs4all.nl/~filosoof. E-mail: filosoof@xs4all.nl. 28 units. TV TEL. 215Dfl–245Dfl ($91.50–$104.25) double. Rates include buffet breakfast. AE, MC, V. Limited parking available on street. Tram: 1 or 6 to 1e Constantijn Huygensstraat; 3 or 12 to Overtoom.

On a quiet street facing Vondelpark, this hotel might be the very place if you fancy yourself as something of a philosopher king or queen. One of the owners, a philosophy professor, has chosen posters, painted ceilings, framed quotes, and unusual objects to represent philosophical and cultural themes. each room is dedicated to a mental maestro—Goethe, Wittgenstein, Nietzsche, Marx, and Einstein are among those who get a look-in—or are based on motifs like Eros, the Renaissance, astrology, and women. Rooms in an annex across the street are larger; some open onto a private terrace. In 2000, all-round improvements in services and facilities raised the hotel's local rating from two stars to three.

Jan Luyken. Jan Luykenstraat 54–58 (near Rijksmuseum), 1071 CS Amsterdam. ☎ **020/573-0730.** Fax 020/676-3841. www.janluyken.nl. E-mail: info@janluyken.nl. 63 units. MINIBAR TV TEL. Dfl 370–540 ($157.45–$229.80) double. Children 4–12 are charged half-price; children under 4 stay free in parents' room. Extra person Dfl 85 ($36.15). Rates include Dutch buffet breakfast. AE, DC, V. Limited parking available on street. Tram: 2, 3, 5, 12, or 20 to Van Baerlestraat.

One block from the Vincent van Gogh Museum and from the elegant P. C. Hooftstraat shopping street, the Jan Luyken is best described as a small hotel with many of

Museumplein Area & Amsterdam South Accommodations

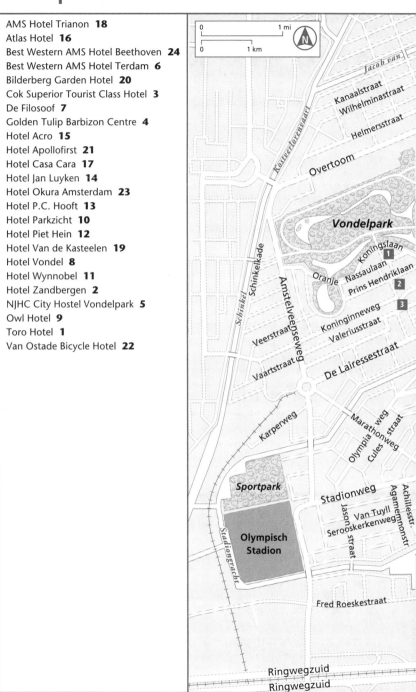

the amenities and facilities of a big hotel. Everything here is done with perfect attention to detail. The Jan Luyken maintains a balance between its sophisticated lineup of facilities (double sinks and bidets, elevator, lobby bar with fireplace, and meeting rooms for business) and an intimate and personalized approach that's appropriate to this 19th-century residential neighborhood. That residential feel extends to the rooms, which look much more like a well-designed home than a standard hotel room. The owners are proud of the atmosphere they've created, and are constantly improving the look of the hotel.

Toro. Koningslaan 64 (off Oranje Nassaulaan), 1075 AG Amsterdam. ☎ **020/673-7223.** Fax 020/675-0031. 22 units. MINIBAR TV TEL. Dfl 250 ($106.40) double. Rates include buffet breakfast. AE, DC, MC, V. Parking Dfl 16.50 ($7), except Sun. Tram: 2 to Valeriusplein.

On the fringes of Vondelpark in a quiet residential district, this beautiful hotel in a completely renovated mansion dating from 1900 is one of Amsterdam's top moderately priced choices. Both on the inside and the outside, it is as near as you can get in Amsterdam to staying in a country villa. The house is furnished and decorated with taste, combining Louis XIV and Liberty styles and featuring stained-glass windows and Murano chandeliers. The guest rooms are worthy of being featured in *Better Homes & Gardens*. The house also affords guests a private garden and terrace, and there is a dry cleaning and laundry service. All rooms have hair dryers. It's about a 10-minute walk through Vondelpark to Leidseplein.

Vondel. Vondelstraat 28–30, 1054 GE Amsterdam. ☎ **020/612-0120.** Fax 020/685-4321. E-mail: bhsnl@xs4all.nl. 74 units. MINIBAR TV TEL. Dfl 340–410 ($144.70–$174.45) double; Dfl 550 ($234.05) suite. Rates include continental breakfast. AE, DC, MC, V. Limited parking available on street. Tram: 1 or 6 to 1e Constantijn Huygensstraat; 3 or 12 to Overtoom.

Named after the famous 17th-century Dutch poet Joost Van den Vondel, this five-floor hotel opened in late 1993 and has since become one of the leading three-star hotels in Amsterdam. Each room is named after one of Vondel's poems, like Lucifer or Solomon. Three of the rooms (all with soundproof windows) are on the first floor and are ideal for travelers with disabilities. The furniture is solid, the rooms are spacious, with hair dryers in each, and the service is good. This is a comfortable place, conveniently located in a quiet and popular area close to the museum area and Leidseplein.

Wynnobel. Vossiusstraat 9 (off Stadhouderskade), 1071 AB Amsterdam. ☎ **020/662-2298.** 11 units (none with bathroom). Dfl 180–200 ($76.60–$85.10) double. Rates include continental breakfast. No credit cards. Limited parking available on street. Tram: 2, 5, or 20 to Hobbemastraat.

Just around the corner from the boutiques on P. C. Hooftstraat and only a few minutes' walk from the Rijksmuseum, the hotel overlooks a corner of Vondelpark and is managed by Pierre Wynnobel and his wife, Joan, who always make sure the hotel is clean and their guests are happy. One way they achieve this is by serving you breakfast in bed, if you want it. The large rooms are furnished with old-fashioned or antique pieces. A steep but striking central stairway leads to the hotel's four floors.

Zandbergen. Willemsparkweg 205 (at Vondelpark), 1071 HB Amsterdam. ☎ **020/ 676-9321.** Fax 020/676-1860. www.hotel-zandbergen.com. E-mail: info@hotel-zandbergen. com. 21 units. MINIBAR TV TEL. Dfl 245–295 ($104.25–$125.55) double. Rates include continental breakfast. AE, DC, MC, V. Limited parking available on street. Tram: 2 to Cornelis Schuytstraat.

Beside Vondelpark, this place nearly outdoes the Amstel in its use of shiny brass handrails and door handles. Rebuilt in 1979, the Zandbergen has been efficiently divided into a variety of room types and sizes by the use of simple but attractive brick wall dividers between rooms. Wall-to-wall carpets and a color scheme based on bright tones of sand and blue-gray make the rooms seem more spacious and inviting, and all are outfitted with some flair and have good comfortable beds. You have a hair dryer and coffeemaker in each room. There's also a great family-size room with a garden patio for between two and four guests. Recent improvements include new bathrooms and air-conditioning in the reception and breakfast area.

INEXPENSIVE

✪ **Acro.** Jan Luykenstraat 44 (near Rijksmuseum), 1071 CR Amsterdam. ☎ **020/662-5538.** Fax 020/675-0811. 57 units. TV TEL. Dfl 165–205 ($70.20–$87.25) double. Rates include continental breakfast. AE, DC, MC, V. Parking Dfl 25 ($10.65). Tram: 2, 3, 5, 12, or 20 to Van Baerlestraat.

The Acro, in a townhouse on a fairly quiet street near Vondelpark and close to the main museums, tends to appeal especially to young travelers. The hotel is modern on the inside, with crisp-and-clean bedspreads and furniture and walls all colored light blue-gray. Most rooms have twin beds—some have three and some four—and all have hair dryers. You find more ambience in the hotel bar than in many street cafes. The Acro is definitely value for your money.

AMS Hotel Trianon. J.W. Brouwersstraat 3–7 (beside the Concertgebouw), 1071 LH Amsterdam. ☎ **020/673-2073.** Fax 020/673-8868. www.hospitality.nl/ams. E-mail: info@ams.nl. 52 units. TV TEL. Dfl 160–220 ($68.10–$93.60) double. Extra person Dfl 50 ($21.30). Rates include continental breakfast. AE, DC, JCB, MC, V. Limited parking available on street. Tram: 3, 5, 12, or 20 to Museumplein; 16 to Concertgebouwplein.

A top-to-bottom renovation, redecoration, and redirection took this hotel from serviceable to sophisticated in one big leap, giving it an excellent quality/price ratio. Located directly behind the Concertgebouw concert hall, it's also home to an Italian restaurant. The hotel was last renovated in 1998. All rooms have hair dryers, and there is a laundry service, baby-sitting service, and airport shuttle. Should the Trianon be fully booked, the AMS Hotel Holland is in the same class and close by, at P. C. Hooftstraat 162 (bookable through the Trianon).

Casa Cara. Emmastraat 24 (at Koninginneweg), 1075 HV Amsterdam. ☎ **020/662-3135.** Fax 020/679-9741. www.com-all.nl/hotels/casa-cara/. 9 units (6 with bathroom). TV TEL. Dfl 100–120 ($42.55–$51.05) double without bathroom, Dfl 130–155 ($55.30–$65.95) double with bathroom. Summer rates include continental breakfast. AE, CB, DC, DISC, MC, V. Limited parking available on street. Tram: 2 or 16 to Emmastraat.

Near Vondelpark, this family-owned hotel is a simple but well-crafted conversion of a residential home, in a neighborhood with deep front lawns. It offers three large rooms on each floor with private bathroom, and a trio of rooms without bathroom that, as a result, have the hall facilities almost to themselves; two rooms have balconies.

✪ **Owl.** Roemer Visscherstraat 1 (off 1e Constantijn Huygensstraat), 1054 EV Amsterdam. ☎ **020/618-9484.** Fax 020/618-9441. E-mail: manager@owl-hotel.demon.nl. 34 units. TV TEL. Dfl 170–260 ($72.35–$110.65) double. Rates include continental breakfast. AE, DC, JCB, MC, V. Limited parking available on street, and at nearby parking lot Dfl 25 ($10.65). Tram: 1 or 6 to Constantijn Huygensstraat; 3 or 12 to Overtoom.

If small but chic and reasonably priced seems to describe the sort of hotel you prefer, you'll be pleased to learn about the Owl, located in the pleasant residential area around Vondelpark, behind the Marriott. One of Amsterdam's best buys, the Owl Hotel has been owned by the same family since 1972 and is bright, tidy, and well kept. Rooms are not very big but are not cramped, and the bathrooms, all of which were renovated in 1997, are tiled floor to ceiling. There's also a pleasant lounge/bar overlooking a small garden. The Owl offers a concierge, limited-hours room service, dry cleaning and laundry, baby-sitting, and secretarial services. All rooms have hair dryers.

P. C. Hooft. P. C. Hooftstraat 63 (near van Gogh Museum), 1071 BN Amsterdam. ☎ **020/ 662-7107.** Fax 020/675-8961. 15 units (3 with bathroom). Dfl 150 ($63.85) double with bathroom, Dfl 125 ($53.20) double without bathroom. Extra person Dfl 35 ($14.90). AE, MC, V. Parking in nearby lot Dfl 25 ($10.65). Tram: 2, 3, 5, 12, or 20 to Van Baerlestraat.

One of the spiffiest little budget lodgings in town, the P. C. Hooft seems to have picked up a sense of style from the smart shops on the street without picking up their tendency toward upscale pricing. Rooms are bright and tidy, and the building also houses a coffee shop, which is a handy spot to stop for a quick bite before you hit the sights or the shops.

Parkzicht. Roemer Visscherstraat 33 (off 1e Constantijn Huygensstraat), 1054 EW Amsterdam. ☎ **020/618-1954.** Fax 020/618-0897. 14 units (10 with bathroom). TV TEL. Dfl 160–180 ($68.10–$76.60) double with bathroom. Rates include continental breakfast. AE, MC, V. Limited parking available on street. Tram: 1 or 6 to Constantijn Huygensstraat; 3 or 12 to Overtoom.

A characterful place owned and managed by the same man, Mr. Cornelissen, since 1970, this hotel features large rooms with brass beds, old Dutch wooden furniture, fireplaces in some units, and bathrooms as large as the bedrooms. Many of the guests who stay here are English-speaking—Americans, British, Australians, New Zealanders. Try to book one of the large apartment-like doubles on the second floor (no. 5 or 6), overlooking Vondelpark.

Piet Hein. Vossiusstraat 52–53 (off Van Baerlestraat), 1071 AK Amsterdam. ☎ **020/ 662-7205.** Fax 020/662-1526. www.hotelpiethein.com. E-mail: info@hotelpiethein.nl. 36 units. TV TEL. Dfl 135–275 ($57.45–$117) double. Rates include continental breakfast. AE, DC, JCB, MC, V. Limited parking available on street. Tram: 2, 3, 5, 12, or 20 to Van Baerlestraat.

Facing Vondelpark, and close to the city's most important museums, this appealing, well-kept hotel is in a villa named after a 17th-century Dutch admiral who captured a Spanish silver shipment. Its spacious rooms are well-furnished and the staff is charming and professional. Half the rooms overlook the park, two second-floor double rooms have semicircular balconies, and the honeymoon suite has a water bed. The lower-priced rooms are in an annex behind the main hotel. Hair dryers are available on request, and the hotel provides concierge, room service for drinks, dry cleaning and laundry, baby-sitting, and in-house movies.

Van de Kasteelen. Frans van Mierisstraat 34 (off Van Baerlestraat), 1071 RT Amsterdam. ☎ **020/679-8995.** Fax 020/670-6604. E-mail: hotel@kastele.A2000.nl. 15 units (6 with bathroom). Dfl 140–180 ($59.55–$76.60) double without bathroom, Dfl 195–230 ($83–$97.85) double with bathroom. AE, DC, MC, V. Limited parking available on street. Tram: 3, 5, 12, 16, or 20, to Concertgebouwplein; 24 to Roelof Hartplein.

On a relatively quiet side street off Van Baerlestraat, not far from the Concertgebouw, this hotel is run by a young Dutch-Indonesian couple who give a gracious welcome to their guests, including a complimentary welcome drink. The rooms are Spartan but clean; some have balconies. A simple breakfast is served in the lounge, where there is also a television that guests may watch in the evening. A hair dryer is available at the reception desk.

7 In Amsterdam South

EXPENSIVE

✪ **Bilderberg Garden Hotel.** Dijsselhofplantsoen 7 (off Apollolaan), 1077 BJ Amsterdam. ☎ **0800/777-96735** in the U.S. and Canada, or 020/664-2121. Fax 020/679-9356. www.bilderberg.nl. E-mail: garden@bilderberg.nl. 124 units. A/C MINIBAR TV TEL.

Dfl 295–675 ($125.55–$287.25) double; Dfl 75 ($31.90) supplement for executive rooms; add 5% city tax. Extra person Dfl 50 ($21.30). AE, DC, JCB, MC, V. Limited parking available on street. KLM Hotel Shuttle service from Schiphol Airport. Tram: 5 or 24 to Apollolaan.

This is the smallest and most personal five-star hotel in town. Because of its excellent Mangerie de Kersentuin restaurant (see below), the Garden considers itself a "culinary hotel," an idea that extends to the rooms, whose color schemes are salad-green, salmon-pink, *parfait d'amour* lilac, and grape-blue—and you can choose whichever suits you best. The rooms themselves are furnished and equipped to the highest standards and with refined taste; only executive rooms have coffeemakers. Bathrooms are in marble, and are equipped with Jacuzzi tubs and hair dryers. The Garden's spectacular lobby has a wall-to-wall fireplace with a copper-sheathed chimney.

Dining: The Mangerie de Kersentuin (Cherry Orchard) restaurant, a member of Les Etappes du Bon Goût, has an international reputation (see chapter 5 for full details) and moderate prices. The Kersepit (Cherry Pit) is a cozy bar with an open fireplace.

Amenities: Conference room, 24-hour room service, dry cleaning and laundry, newspaper delivery, baby-sitting, secretarial services, health club across the street, car-rental and tour desk.

Okura Hotel Amsterdam. Ferdinand Bolstraat 333 (at the Amstel Canal), 1072 LH Amsterdam. ☎ **020/678-7111.** Fax 020/671-2344. www.okura.nl. E-mail: sales@okura.nl. 370 units. A/C MINIBAR TV TEL. Dfl 525–825 ($223.40–$351.05) double (includes executive rooms); from Dfl 1,490 ($634.05) and way up suite; add 5% city tax. AE, DC, JCB, MC, V. Free parking. Tram: 25 to Ferdinand Bolstraat.

The 23-story Japanese-owned hotel doesn't have much in the way of traditional Dutch looks, but on the inside it provides an unrivaled standard of excellence and style. Guest rooms offer Western-style twin beds, an easy-on-the-eyes decor, well-appointed bathrooms, and sweeping views over the city from large windows.

A complete room renovation program was finished at the end of 1998, bringing all rooms up to a new standard of comfort. All rooms have a fax machine, telephones with voice mail, trouser press, and hair dryer. Perhaps the greatest charm of the Okura is its blending of Japanese and Western style.

Dining/Diversions: On the top floor you'll find the classical French Ciel Bleu restaurant and bar, a culinary highlight whose big picture windows give a panoramic view of the city. Two Japanese restaurants, the traditional Yamazato, which has a sushi bar and seven private rooms, one of which is a tatami room, and the Sazanka Teppanyaki, are both top-notch. The Camelia Brasserie offers an international menu and La Serre Bar is an airy place for an informal drink or snack.

Amenities: Indoor swimming pool; health club with Jacuzzi, sauna, Turkish cold bath, and massage, traditional Japanese sauna and massage; concierge; 24-hour room service; shopping arcade; airport shuttle; car hire; secretarial services; same-day laundry and dry cleaning; hairdresser and beauty salon.

MODERATE

Apollofirst. Apollolaan 123 (off Minervalaan), 1077 AP Amsterdam. ☎ **020/673-0333.** Fax 020/675-0348. E-mail: apolfi@xs4all.nl. 40 units. TV TEL. Dfl 295–325 ($125.55–$138.30) double; Dfl 525 ($223.40) suite. Rates include continental breakfast. AE, DC, MC, V. Limited parking available on street. Tram: 5 or 24 to Apollolaan.

The small and very elegant Apollofirst, a family owned hotel set amid the Amsterdam school architecture of Apollolaan, advertises itself as the "best quarters in town in the town's best quarter." Their claim may be debatable, but the Venman family's justifiable pride in their establishment is not. All the accommodations of this intimate hotel are quiet, spacious, and grandly furnished. Bathrooms are fully tiled, and rooms at the back of the hotel overlook the well-kept gardens of the hotel and its neighbors, and the summer terrace where guests can have a snack or a cocktail. Room service and a laundry and dry-cleaning service are available. The hotel's elegant Restaurant Chambertin is a French fin de siècle affair.

Best Western AMS Hotel Beethoven. Beethovenstraat 43 (near Apollolaan), 1077 HN Amsterdam. ☎ **0800/0221-455** or 020/664-4816. Fax 020/662-1240. www.hospitality.nl/ams. E-mail: ams@hospitality.nl. 52 units. MINIBAR TV TEL. Dfl 240–340 ($102.10–$144.70) double. Extra person Dfl 70 ($29.80). AE, DC, JCB, MC, V. Limited parking available on street. Tram: 5 or 24 to Apollolaan.

If you like to stay in a neighborhood atmosphere wherever you travel, make note of the AMS Hotel Beethoven. It's located in the heart of one of Amsterdam's most desirable areas, on one of its most beautiful shopping streets. The Beethoven was treated to a top-to-bottom redecoration in 1997. Plus, to the delight of local people and hotel guests, the Beethoven also gained an attractive restaurant, Brasserie Beethoven, that has a year-round sidewalk cafe (which closes at 7:30pm). All rooms have hair dryers, and there is a laundry service, baby-sitting service, and airport shuttle.

INEXPENSIVE

Van Ostade Bicycle Hotel. Van Ostadestraat 123 (off Ferdinand Bolstraat), Amsterdam 1072 SV. ☎ **020/679-3452.** Fax 020/671-5213. www.etrade.nl/bicyclehotel. E-mail bicyclehotel@ capitolonline.nl. 16 units, 8 with bathroom. TV. Dfl 100–120 ($42.55–$51.05) double without bathroom, Dfl 125–160 ($53.20–$68.10) double with bathroom. Rates include continental breakfast. No credit cards. Tram: 25 to Ceintuurbaan; 3, 12, 20, or 24 to Ferdinand Bolstraat.

The young owners of this establishment have hit on an interesting idea: They cater to visitors who wish to explore Amsterdam on bikes and they are helpful in planning biking routes through and around the city. You can rent bikes for only Dfl 7.50 ($3.20) daily, no deposit, and stable your trusty steed indoors. The recently renovated rooms have new carpets and plain but comfortable modern furnishings; some have kitchenettes and small balconies, and there are large rooms for families. The hotel is a few blocks from the popular Albert Cuyp street market, in the somewhat raggedy De Pijp neighborhood. An old bike hangs on the hotel's facade, and there are always bikes parked in front.

8 Near the Airport

VERY EXPENSIVE

Sheraton Amsterdam Airport. Schiphol Boulevard 101, 1118 BG Schiphol Airport. ☎ **800/325-3535** in the U.S. and Canada, or 020/316-4300. Fax 020/316-4399. www.sheraton.com/amsterdam. 408 units. A/C MINIBAR TV TEL. Dfl 690–870 ($293.60– $370.20) double; Dfl 1,450–1,800 ($617–$765.95) suite; add 5% city tax. Rates include breakfast for executive rooms and suites. AE, DC, MC, V. Parking Dfl 56 ($23.85); 25% reduction if paid at hotel reception.

You could only be more convenient to the airport by lodging on the runway. There's all the comfort you would expect of a top-flight Sheraton, including soundproofed rooms with big, comfortable beds, marble bathrooms with separate shower and hair dryer, and a well-equipped fitness center with swimming pool. Room style ranges from modern and functional to unashamed luxury in the suites.

  Dining/Diversions: The Voyager restaurant has an international, à la carte menu. The Dutch Runway Café serve drinks and delicatessen snacks. The Boomerang Bar and the Cascade Bar.

Amenities: Concierge, 24-hour room service, laundry and dry cleaning, newspaper delivery, secretarial services, express checkout, indoor heated swimming pool, health club, sauna, business center, conference rooms.

EXPENSIVE

Dorint Schiphol Amsterdam. Sloterweg 299, 1171 VB Badhoevedorp. ☎ **020/658-8111.** Fax 020/658-8100. E-mail: sales@dha.dorint.nl. 216 units. A/C MINIBAR TV TEL. Dfl 380–440 ($161.70–$187.25) double; add 5% city tax. AE, DC, MC, V. Free parking.

Though comparisons are invidious, you get many of the same amenities here for less than you'd pay at the Sheraton, and even if you do have to travel a few miles to get there, you do so by hotel shuttle. That said, the Dorint is no fount of Dutch tradition. Blocky and modern is the kindest thing I can say about the exterior, which is what you'd expect of a hotel in this business-park zone. The inside story is better, with rooms that bring a touch of style to their mission of lodging itinerant businesspeople. All have hair dryers.

Dining/Diversions: The Winter Garden restaurant has an international, à la carte menu. The English-style Pub lounge-bar is a relaxed place for a drink.

Amenities: Concierge, 24-hour room service, laundry and dry cleaning, newspaper delivery, secretarial services, express checkout, indoor heated swimming pool, indoor and outdoor tennis courts, health club, sauna, business center, conference rooms.

5 Where to Dine

If cities get the cuisine they deserve, this one's ought to be liberal, multiethnic, and adventurous. Guess what—it is. As a port and trading city with a true melting-pot character, Amsterdam has absorbed culinary influences from far, wide, and yonder, and rustled them all up to its own satisfaction. More than 50 different national cuisines are served at its restaurants. Better yet, many of these eateries satisfy the sturdy Dutch insistence on getting maximum value out of each guilder spent.

From elegant 17th-century dining rooms to cozy canal-side bistros, to exuberant taverns with equally exuberant Greek attendants to exotic Indonesian rooms attended by turbaned waiters, to the *bruine kroegjes* (brown cafes) with their smoke-stained walls and friendly table conversations, the eateries of Amsterdam confront the tourist with the exquisite agony of being able to choose only one or two from their vast numbers each day. Dutch cooking, of course, is part of all this, but you won't be stuck with *biefstuk* (beefsteak) and *kip* (chicken) every night, unless you want to be. Dutch practicality has also produced a wide selection of restaurants in all price ranges.

A relatively recent and popular trend is the emerging **grand cafe** scene. These are cafes in the, well, grand tradition of Paris, Vienna, and Rome, with lots of style, ambience, and balconies or terraces—see-and-be-seen kind of places. Grand cafes are distinguished by their emphasis on food and drink, architecture, production values, and style. The grand cafes listed below are truly grand, but there are others that use the name even though they may not be particularly impressive. The definition is an elusive one, merging into restaurants with terraces at one end and more-or-less ordinary cafes at the other.

There are a few distinctively **Dutch foods** whose availability is seasonal. Among them: asparagus, beautifully white and tender, in May; "new" herring, fresh from the North Sea and eaten raw, in May or early June (great excitement surrounds the first catch of the season, part of which goes to the queen and the rest to restaurateurs amid spirited competition); and Zeeland oysters and mussels (*Zeeuwsoesters* and *Zeeuwsmosselen*), from September to March.

RESTAURANT ORIENTATION

Dutch menus list appetizers, not main courses, under the title "entree." Restaurants are required to include in their prices a 15% service charge plus value-added tax (BTW) and any local taxes.

HOURS   Most restaurants are open noon to 2:30pm for lunch, and 6 or 7 to 10 or 11pm for dinner. In general, with the exception of late-night restaurants, kitchens in Amsterdam take their last dinner orders between 10 and 11pm. Even if a restaurant is open until 11pm or midnight, you won't get served unless you arrive well before then—how much before varies with the restaurant, and maybe with the mood of the staff, but it should be at least half an hour in moderate and budget places, and at least an hour further upmarket. The trend in recent years has been for restaurants to stay open later. (It used to be common for kitchens to close at 9pm.)

TIPPING   Since a 15% service charge is automatically included in the prices shown on the menus, you needn't leave a tip beyond the amount shown on the tab—but if you want to do as the Dutch do, round up to the next guilder or two, or in the case of a large check, up to the next 5 or 10 guilders.

RESERVATIONS   On the weekends, unless you eat especially early or late, reservations are generally recommended at top restaurants and at those on the high end of the moderate price range. A call ahead to check is a good idea at any time in Amsterdam, where restaurants are often small and may be crowded with neighborhood devotees. Note that restaurants with outside terraces are always in big demand on pleasant summer evenings; make a reservation, if the restaurant will let you—if not, get there early or forget it.

WINE WITH DINNER   Estate-bottled imported wines are expensive in Holland, and even a bottle of modest French wine can add at least Dfl 25 to Dfl 30 ($10.65 to $12.75) to a dinner tab. House wine, on the other hand—which may be a carefully selected French estate-bottled wine—will be a more economical choice in restaurants at any price level. Wine by the glass costs anywhere from Dfl 5 to Dfl 8 ($2.15 to $3.40).

LUNCH & SNACK COSTS   Unless you want it to be, lunch doesn't have to be an elaborate affair (save that for the evening). Typical Dutch lunches are light, quick, and cheap (see "Dutch Cuisine," below). A quick midday meal can cost Dfl 12 to Dfl 25 ($5.10 to $10.65). An afternoon pit stop for cake and cappuccino or pastry and tea will set you back around Dfl 6 to Dfl 12 ($2.55 to $5.10).

BUDGET DINING   Eating cheaply in Amsterdam is not an impossible dream. And, I'm happy to report, in some cases you can even eat cheaply in style, with candles on the table, flowers in the window, and music in the air. The practical Dutch don't like to spend unnecessary guilders, so almost every neighborhood has its modestly priced restaurant and new budget places are popping up all over town like spring tulips. In this category you should look out particularly for *eetcafés,* which are essentially brown cafes with a hardworking kitchen attached. The food in these places is generally unpretentious, mainstream Dutch (though some are more adventurous), and the price for their *dagschotels* (plates of the day), which come with meat, vegetable, and salad all on one large plate, is usually in the Dfl 12 to Dfl 20 ($5.10 to $8.50) range. Another way to combat escalating dinner tabs is to take advantage of the tourist menu that many restaurants offer.

1 Dutch Cuisine

Dutch national dishes tend to be of the ungarnished, hearty, wholesome variety—solid, stick-to-your-ribs stuff. A perfect example is *erwtensoep,* a thick pea soup cooked with ham or sausage that provides inner warmth against cold Dutch winters and is filling enough to be a meal by itself. Similarly, *hutspot,* a potato-based "hotchpotch," or stew, is no-nonsense nourishment that becomes even more so with the addition of *klapstuk* (lean beef). Hutspot also has an interesting intangible ingredient—a story behind its name that's based on historical fact (see "History 101" in appendix A).

Seafood, as you might imagine in this traditionally seafaring country, is always fresh and simply—but very well—prepared. Fried sole, oysters from Zeeland, mussels, and herring (fresh in May, pickled other months) are most common. In fact, if you happen to be in Holland for the beginning of the herring season, it's an absolute obligation—at least once—to interrupt your sidewalk strolls for a "green" herring from a pushcart; prices run the gamut from dirt cheap to astronomical. Look for signs saying HOLLANDSE NIEUWE, or MAATJE HARING. The Dutch are also uncommonly fond of eel.

Far-ranging Dutch explorers and traders brought back recipes and exotic spices, and the popular Indonesian rijsttafel (rice table), a feast of 15 to 30 small portions of different dishes eaten with plain rice, has been a national favorite ever since it arrived in the 17th century. If you've never experienced this minifeast, it should definitely be on your "must eat" list for Holland. Should you part company with the Dutch and their love of Indonesian food, you'll find the cuisines of China, France, Greece, India, Italy, Japan, Spain, Turkey, Yugoslavia, and several other nationalities well represented.

At the top of the restaurant scale are those posh dining rooms affiliated with the prestigious **Alliance Gastronomique Néerlandaise** or the **Relais du Centre.** They're likely to be elegant and sophisticated or atmospherically old world and quaint. They will certainly be expensive. Then there are the numerous moderately priced restaurants and little brown cafes. Dutch families gravitate to the restaurants, while the brown cafes are cozy social centers with simple but tasty food, often served outside on sidewalk tables. Sidewalk vendors, with fresh herring and the ubiquitous *broodjes* (sandwiches) or other light specialties, are as popular as the brown cafes.

MEALS

The first step in getting to know Dutch gastronomy is to forget that in American restaurants the word *entree* means a main course; in Holland, an entree is an appetizer, and main courses, also known as *hoofdgerechten,* are listed separately as *vis* (fish) or *vlees* (meat), and in some restaurants, as *dagschotel* (dish of the day). The other courses you will see on Dutch menus are *soepen* (soups), *warme* or *koude voorgerechten* (warm or cold appetizers), *groenten* (vegetables), *sla* (salad), *vruchten* (fruits), *nagerechten* (desserts), *dranken* (beverages), and *wijn* (wine).

The next step is to understand that Dutch is a language of compound words, and just as Leiden Street becomes Leidsestraat—one word for two ideas—you'll notice on menus that beef steak becomes *biefstuk,* pork chop becomes *varkenscotelette,* and so on.

Similarly, you'll find listings for *gehakte biefstuk* (chopped beef) or *gebakken worst* (fried sausage). The clue is to look for the following key words and word endings as you scan a menu for basic information on the cuts of meat available and the modes of preparation of the dishes from which you are choosing:

- For cuts of meat: *-stuk* (steak or, literally, piece), *-scotelet* or *-scotelette* (chop), *-kotelet* or *-kotelette* (cutlet).
- For modes of preparation: *gekookt* or *gekookte* (boiled), *gebakken* (fried), *gebraden* (roasted), *geroosteerd* (broiled), *gerookte* (smoked).
- For meat cooked to your taste: *niet doorgebakken* (rare), *half doorgebakken* (medium), *goed doorgebakken* (well done).

MENU CHOICES

BREAKFAST   The Dutch don't eat bacon and eggs or drink orange juice, but they eat nearly as much as Americans do in the morning. Dutch hotel restaurants serve the same kind of breakfast the Dutch make for themselves at home, with the cost

What'll You Have with Your Kip?

If you're unfamiliar with terms used on menus, see "Dutch Menu Savvy" in appendix B.

sometimes incorporated in your room rate. Bring a good appetite to the table, however, because a typical Dutch morning begins with a selection of breads—whole meal, nutty, or rye—fresh from the *warme bakker,* rusks (crunchy toasted rounds, like Zwieback), and *ontbijtkoek* (spicy gingerbread cake); a platter of cheese and sliced meats (ham, roast beef, salami); butter, jam, *hagelslag* (chocolate sprinkles), and *muisjes* (sugar-and-aniseed sprinkles), which are a favorite with Dutch children, and *apelstroop* (apple, or pear, syrup); coffee (thicker and stronger than American coffee, and often served with *koffiemelk,* gunk similar to condensed milk, which does to coffee what Hitler's bombers did to Rotterdam) or tea. Some hotels include a boiled egg, yogurt, a glass of fruit juice, or all three.

This at any rate is the ideal spread, but in cheaper hotels you may find a few sorry-looking, curled-up-at-the-edges slices of cheese, assorted cold meats of indeterminate provenance, and eggs boiled hard enough to sink an enemy submarine.

LUNCH & SNACK SPECIALTIES   Below are a number of dishes you may notice on lunch menus or may want to look for as typically Dutch choices for your midday meal:

Bami/Nasi Goreng & Nasi Rames   Miniature versions of an Indonesian rijsttafel (see below) that are served in a bowl on a bed of either noodles or rice, with spiced meat and possibly a fried egg or stick of satay (a grilled kabob) on top.

Bitterballen   Fried potato balls, or croquettes, that are generally quite spicy.

Broodjes   Small sandwiches on round buttered rolls, made with ham, cheese, roast beef, salami, or other fillings. They're often ordered in pairs and eaten standing up or perched at a narrow counter in a *broodjeswinkel,* or sandwich shop.

Croquetten   Fried croquettes of meat, prawns, or cheese that may be quite gooey inside but are at their best when served piping hot with a blob of mustard for dunking.

Erwtensoep   Pea soup, thick and creamy and chock-full of chunks of ham, carrots, and potatoes—a meal by itself. (This is what the Dutch call a winter dish, so you may have trouble finding it on menus in summer.)

Nieuwe Haring   New herring, the fresh-caught fish that is eaten whole (or chopped if you're squeamish) with minced onion at stands all over town during summer; during the rest of the year it's eaten pickled as *maatjes.*

Pannekoeken & Poffertjes   Dutch pancakes that are the equivalent of French crepes, served flat on a dinner plate and topped with plain sugar, confectioners' sugar, jam, syrup, hot apples, or—typically Dutch—hot ginger sauce. Less common are pannekoeken with meat. Poffertjes are small "puffs" of a fried pancake mixture coated with confectioners' sugar and filled with syrup or liqueur.

Saucijzenbrood   A Dutch hot dog, except in this case the bun is flaky pastry and the hot dog is a spicy Dutch wurst, or sausage.

Tostis   Grilled ham-and-cheese sandwiches.

Uitsmijter   An open-faced sandwich consisting of a slice of bread (or two), buttered and topped with cold slices of ham or roast beef and one or two fried eggs. (The name, incidentally, is the same as for "bouncer," the burly doorman at discos and clubs.)

Vlammetjes (little flames)   These belong to the same general family of *borrelhapjes* (drinking snacks) as bitterballen, but are more like diminutive spring rolls which, like Napoléon, make up in fiery aggression for what they lack in size.

DINNER SPECIALTIES   With the exception of one excellent taste treat—an Indonesian rijsttafel (see below)—the Dutch may seem to many tourists to be less inventive in the area of dinner specialties than they are for lunch and snacks. This is partly due to the fact that many traditional, typically Dutch dishes closely resemble dishes popular in the United States and elsewhere in Europe, but mostly it's due to modern Holland's ongoing and ever-growing (and finally, pretty tiresome) love affair with French cuisine. Here, however, are a few typically Dutch menu choices you may encounter, particularly in winter, when the stick-to-the-ribs nature of real Dutch cooking can be best appreciated:

Asperges   Asparagus, the thick, white cultivated variety that grows during a 7-week season beginning with Queen's Day on April 30 and continuing until late June. Most of it comes from Limburg, so it is marketed as "the white gold of Limburg"—but most folks just call it asparagus.

Capucijners Met Spek   Marrow beans with bacon.

Gember Met Slagroom   The typically Dutch sweet-and-sour dessert of tangy slices of fresh ginger, topped with whipped cream.

Gerookte Paling   Smoked eel, a typically Dutch appetizer, most of which come from the IJsselmeer, though many eels are now imported.

Hazepeper   Jugged hare.

Hutspot   A stew made of ribs of beef, carrots, onions, and potatoes, often mashed together. This is a dish with historic significance, particularly for the people of Leiden: It's the Dutch version of the stew found in the boiling pots left behind after the Spaniards were routed from their city at the end of the long siege during the Eighty Years' War.

Krabbetjes   Dutch spareribs, usually beef ribs rather than pork.

Mosselen   Mussels, raised in the clean waters of the Oosterschelde (Eastern Scheldt) estuary in Zeeland. The mussel season begins with great fanfare in mid-August, and the first of the crop are eagerly awaited; it runs until April. The mussels are often eaten steamed in a little white wine–and–vegetable stock.

Rolpens   A combination of minced beef, fried apples, and red cabbage.

Stampot   Cabbage with smoked sausage.

Zuurkool Met Spek en Wurst   Sauerkraut with bacon and sausage.

A SPECIAL FEAST   The Indonesian feast **rijsttafel** is Holland's favorite meal and has been ever since the Dutch East India Company captains introduced it to the wealthy burghers of Amsterdam in the 17th century. The rijsttafel (literally "rice table") originated with Dutch plantation overseers in Indonesia, who liked to sample selectively from Indonesian cuisine. It became a kind of tradition, one upheld by Indonesian immigrants to Holland who opened restaurants and, knowing the Dutch fondness for rijsttafel, made it a standard menu item. Rijsttafels are only a small part of the menu in an Indonesian restaurant, and there is a trend among the Dutch to look down on them as being just for tourists; the Dutch generally have a good understanding of Indonesian cuisine and prefer to order an individual dish rather than the mixed hash of flavors of a rijsttafel. However, rijsttafels remain popular, and many Chinese, Japanese, Vietnamese, and Thai restaurants in Holland have copied the idea.

The Search for Gezelligheid

When in Amsterdam, do as the Dutch do: Look for someplace *gezellig,* and treasure it if you find it.

So what is *gezellig,* or *gezelligheid* (the state of being *gezellig*)?

Ah . . . it's a simple idea, yet one that underlines everyday life; one of those imprecise, enigmatic, and finally untranslatable-in-a-single-word concepts for a mood and an attitude that you'll recognize right away when you find it, and then you'll say with quiet satisfaction, "Ah, this place looks *gezellig.*"

So what *is* it then?

The special *something* that makes a place comfortable, congenial, cozy, familiar, friendly, intimate, memorable, tolerant, warm, and welcoming. Dutch, in fact. You find it in abundance in brown cafes; in a candle-lit restaurant where the atmosphere is unforced and there's a view of a softly illuminated canal; in a Dutch home where you are made to feel one of the family; even on a packed-to-the-gills tram where everyone is in good humor and sees the funny side of the situation.

The great thing about gezelligheid is that it's free. Box some up and take it home with you.

Rijsttafel is an acquired taste, and unless you already have a stomach for both Chinese and Indian cooking, you may not like much of what you eat. But to be in Holland and not at least try a rijsttafel is as much a pity as it would be to miss seeing Rembrandt's *The Night Watch* while you had the chance. Besides, with more than 20 different dishes on the table, you're bound to find a few you enjoy.

The basic concept of a rijsttafel is to eat a bit of this and a bit of that, blending the flavors and textures. A simple, unadorned bed of rice is the base and the mediator between spicy meats and bland vegetables or fruits, between sweet-and-sour tastes, soft-and-crunchy textures. Although a rijsttafel for one is possible, this feast is better shared by two or by a table full of people. In the case of a solitary diner or a couple, a 17-dish rijsttafel will be enough food; with four or more, order a 24- or 30-dish rijsttafel and you can experience the total taste treat.

Before you begin to imagine 30 dinner-sized plates of food, it's important to mention that the dishes used to serve an Indonesian meal are small and the portions served are gauged by the number of people expected to share them. Remember, the idea is to have tastes of many things rather than a full meal of any single item. Also, there are no separate courses in an Indonesian rijsttafel. Once your table has been set with a row of low, Sterno-powered plate warmers, all 17 or 24 or 30 dishes arrive all at one time, like a culinary avalanche, the sweets along with the sours and the spicy, so you're left to plot your own course through the extravaganza. (Beware, however, of one very appealing dish of sauce with small chunks of what looks to be bright-red onion—that is *sambal badjak,* or simply *sambal,* and it's hotter than hot.)

Among the customary dishes and ingredients of a rijsttafel are *loempia* (classic Chinese-style egg rolls); *satay,* or *sateh* (small kabobs of pork, grilled and served with a spicy peanut sauce); *perkedel* (meatballs); *gado-gado* (vegetables in peanut sauce); *daging smoor* (beef in soy sauce); *babi ketjap* (pork in soy sauce); *kroepoek* (crunchy, puffy shrimp toast); *serundeng* (fried coconut); *roedjak manis* (fruit in sweet sauce); and *pisang goreng* (fried banana).

DESSERT   Desserts at any meal lean toward fruit with lots of fresh cream, ice cream, or *appelgebak,* a lovely and light apple pastry.

DRINK

Wines from all over the world are readily available. The Dutch are most famous for their gin, or *jenever,* and their beer. The former is a fiery, colorless liquid served ice cold to be drunk "neat"—it's not a mixer. You can get flavored jenever—from berry to lemon—and just as with cheese, you can get *oude* or *jonge* (old or young) jenever, and every bar has a wide selection of most or all of the above on its shelves. Jonge is less sweet and creamy than the oude variety, but both are known for their delayed-action effectiveness.

As for **beer,** you can get the regular Heineken, Grolsch, or Amstel—called *pils* in Amsterdam, or you can try something different as you make the rounds of the brown cafes (the world-renowned Dutch beer halls). I happen to like the *witte* (white) beer, which is sweeter than pils. Or, on the opposite end of the spectrum, you can have a Belgian dark beer, like De Koninck or Duvel, or a white beer like Hoegaarden. (Belgian beers are very popular in Holland and are, in general, better made, more "artisanal," than the native brews.)

There are also very good Dutch liqueurs, such as Curaçao and Triple Sec.

2 Restaurants by Cuisine

AMERICAN
Brasserie Noblesse (p. 96)
L'Entrecôte (p. 116)

ASIAN
Dynasty (p. 97)
Manchurian (p. 110)

BISTRO
Bistro La Forge (p. 109)

CARIBBEAN
Rum Runners (p. 106)

CHINESE
Dynasty (p. 97)
Nam Kee (p. 103)
Treasure (p. 102)

CONTINENTAL
Bodega Keyzer (p. 113)
Café Américain (p. 107)
Café-Restaurant Amsterdam (p. 97)
Café-Restaurant Blincker (p. 103)
Café van Puffelen (p. 104)
De Balie (p. 109)
De Belhamel (p. 105)
Excelsior (p. 92)
In de Waag (p. 99)
Kort (p. 105)

Sluizer (p. 101)
Spanjer & Van Twist (p. 112)

DUTCH
1e Klas (p. 102)
Brasserie Schiller (p. 110)
Café van Puffelen (p. 104)
De Blauwe Hollander (p. 109)
De Boemerang (p. 109)
De Knijp (p. 116)
De Magere Brug (p. 93)
De Nissen (p. 98)
De Poort (p. 99)
De Prins (p. 106)
De Silveren Spiegel (p. 96)
Dorrius (p. 97)
Enfant Terrible (p. 107)
Haesje Claes (p. 99)
Het Stuivertje (p. 112)
Keuken van 1870 (p. 103)
Restaurant d'Vijff Vlieghen (p. 96)
't Swarte Schaep (p. 108)

FILIPINO
At Mango Bay (p. 112)

FRENCH
Brasserie Schiller (p. 110)
Bordewijk (p. 111)

Christophe's (p. 96)
Cyrano (p. 112)
De Goudsbloem (p. 103)
De Kelderhof (p. 105)
De Knijp (p. 116)
De Prins (p. 106)
De Silveren Spiegel (p. 96)
Gare de l'Est (p. 99)
Het Stuivertje (p. 112)
La Rive (p. 92)
L'Entrecôte (p. 116)

FUSION
De Luwte (p. 98)

GRAND CAFE
Café de Jaren (p. 93)
Café Dulac (p. 102)
Café Luxembourg (p. 102)
Café-Restaurant Wildschut (p. 116)
De Balie (p. 109)
Grand Café l'Opéra (p. 110)
Het Land van Walem (p. 105)
Ovidius (p. 100)
Royal Café de Kroon (p. 111)

GREEK
Aphrodite (p. 109)
Traîterie Grekas (p. 106)

INDIAN
Akbar (p. 108)
Memories of India (p. 111)

INDONESIAN
Kantjil en de Tijger (p. 100)
Purnama (p. 101)
Sama Sebo (p. 117)
Sarang Mas (p. 101)
Speciaal (p. 113)
Tempo Doeloe (p. 102)

INTERNATIONAL
Brasserie Noblesse (p. 96)
Breitner (p. 92)
Les Quatre Canetons (p. 104)
Mangerie de Kersentuin (p. 117)

ISRAELI
Falafel Koning (p. 111)

ITALIAN
Casa di David (p. 104)
Hostaria (p. 112)
Ristorante Mirafiori (p. 116)
Toscanini (p. 113)

JAPANESE
Osaka (p. 93)
Umeno (p. 118)

JAVANESE
Kantjil en de Tijger (p. 100)

LEBANESE
Artist (p. 118)

LIGHT FARE
Lunchcafé Singel 404 (p. 106)

MEDITERRANEAN
Gare de l'Est (p. 99)
Vertigo (p. 117)

MEXICAN
Alfonso's (p. 108)
Rose's Cantina (p. 101)

NEPALESE/TIBETAN
Sherpa (p. 110)

PANCAKES
Pancake Bakery (p. 106)

SEAFOOD
De Oesterbar (p. 108)
Le Pêcheur (p. 100)
Lucius (p. 97)
Sluizer (p. 101)

SPANISH
Tapas Café Duende (p. 113)

THAI
Rakang Thai (p. 112)

TIBETAN
Sherpa (p. 110)

VEGETARIAN
Bolhoed (p. 104)
Oibibio (p. 100)

3 Overlooking the Amstel

VERY EXPENSIVE

✪ Excelsior. In the Hôtel de l'Europe, Nieuwe Doelenstraat 2–8 (facing Muntplein, near the Muziektheater). ☎ **020/531-1777.** Main courses Dfl 48.50–78.50 ($20.65–$33.40); fixed-price menus Dfl 95–165 ($40.45–$70.20). AE, DC, JCB, MC, V. Daily 7–11am, 12:30–2:30pm (except Sat), 7–10:30pm. Tram: 4, 9, 14, 16, 20, 24, or 25 to the Munt. CONTINENTAL.

One of the city's most famous restaurants derives its reputation from its cuisine and service. Crystal chandeliers, elaborate moldings, crisp linens, fresh bouquets of flowers, and picture windows overlooking the Amstel River help to give this lovely place a baronial atmosphere. Formal attire (jackets for men) is required. If your budget cannot compete with that of the royalty or showbiz stars who often dine here, try the Excelsior's three-course menu du théâtre, which makes fine dining more affordable. It includes such choices as smoked eel with dill (a Dutch specialty) or marinated sweetbreads of lamb with salad for starters, fillet of halibut with caper sauce or fillet of veal with leek sauce as main courses, and desserts such as orange pie with frozen yogurt or raspberry bavaroise with mango sauce. A meal here is a lovely way to start an evening at the ballet or the opera, especially as there is live piano music every evening to get you into the swing.

✪ La Rive. In the Amstel Intercontinental Hotel, Professor Tulpplein 1 (off Weesperstraat). ☎ **020/622-6060.** Main courses Dfl 50–130 ($21.30–$55.30); fixed-price menus Dfl 135–195 ($57.45–$83). AE, DC, MC, V. Mon–Fri noon–2pm; Mon–Sat 6:30–10:30pm. Tram: 6, 7, 10, or 20 to Sarphatistraat. FRENCH.

La Rive, which sports a pair of prestigious Michelin stars, overlooks the river, and in summer it opens onto a grassy terrace along the embankment. The atmosphere here suggests a small private library called into service for a dinner party. The walls are paneled in cherry and punctuated with tall cabinets filled with books and brass objects. Along one wall is a row of particularly romantic private booths that overlook the other tables and provide a view through the tall French windows to the water. The service and wine cellar here are in the finest modern French traditions. Specialties include grilled baby abalone with citrus-pickled onion puree and garlic juice, and grill-roasted rack of lamb with dates and Zaanse mustard.

MODERATE

✪ Breitner. Amstel 212 (beside the Blauwe Brug). ☎ **020/627-7879.** Reservations recommended at theater time. Main courses Dfl 21.50–49.50 ($9.15–$21.05); fixed-price lunch Dfl 59.50 ($25.30), fixed-price dinner Dfl 72.50–87.50 ($30.85–$37.25). AE, DC, MC, V. Tues–Fri noon–2:30pm and 6–10:30pm, Sat 6–10:30pm. Tram: 4 to Keizersgracht; 9, 14, or 20 to Waterlooplein. INTERNATIONAL.

An Amsterdam Dinner Cruise

A delightful way to combine sightseeing and leisurely dining is the ✪ **Amsterdam Dinner Cruise,** offered by Holland International (☎ **020/622-7788**). During this 3-hour canal cruise (with a multilingual guide) you get to enjoy a four-course dinner that includes a cocktail and wine with dinner, coffee with bonbons, and a glass of cognac or a liqueur to finish. The cost is Dfl 160 ($68.10) per person and includes transportation from all major hotel areas. The cruise operates April to November, nightly at 8pm; December to March, on Tuesday and Friday at 7pm. Reservations are required.

A fast, last-minute dash from here should get you to the Muziektheater or Theater Carré just in time for the evening curtain rise, but that would involve dining in unseemly haste (the expression "wolfing down" comes to mind), and undervalues the performance of the kitchen. The plush red carpet, chandelier and a wine cupboard standing against one wall suggest timelessness, yet cool, modern decor and paintings tell a different story. Named after Amsterdam's impressionist painter George Hendrik Breitner, this restaurant has found a way to fuse a classic French foundation with the cosmopolitan spirit of by this world city. The smoked rib-eye starter with Szechuan pepper, and turbot stew with Indonesian vegetables are just two examples. Light floods in from big riverside and canal-side windows.

Café de Jaren. Nieuwe Doelenstraat 20–22 (near Muntplein). ☎ **020/625-5771.** Main courses Dfl 16–30 ($6.80–$12.75); fixed-price menus Dfl 20–28 ($8.50–$11.90). No credit cards. Sun–Thurs 10am–1am, Fri–Sat 10am–2am. Tram: 4, 9, 14, 16, 20, 24, or 25 to the Munt. GRAND CAFE.

One of the city's biggest cafes, de Jaren has 300 seats inside and can seat more out on a terrace beside the Amstel River, a marvelous place in the sun that is much in demand in good weather. Many students from the nearby university who are tired of cafeteria food eat lunch here, and it's popular with the media crowd. You can enjoy everything from a cup of coffee and a glass of *jenever* (gin) to spaghetti bolognese and rib-eye steak. The building, which originally served as a bank, is spacious and has unusually high ceilings.

De Magere Brug. Amstel 81 (near Theater Carré). ☎ **020/622-6502.** Reservations recommended at theater time. Main courses Dfl 20–30 ($8.50–$12.75). AE, DC, V. Tues–Thurs noon–1am, Fri–Sat 5pm–2am. Tram: 9, 14, or 20 to Waterlooplein. DUTCH.

This plain, down-home, cafe-restaurant, which looks out on the Magere Brug, the famous "Skinny Bridge" across the Amstel, is a good choice if you're planning to have dinner before taking in a concert, ballet, or show at the nearby Muziektheater or Theater Carrére. Owner Christiaan Dijkstra, who also handles catering at the Carré, likes to keep things simple and friendly—a refreshing change from the snooty style affected by many Amstelside establishments. In addition to locals, it attracts visiting stars from the performance venues, who seem attracted by a change of pace. Rod Stewart is just one who has signed the visitors' book—"Nice ham 'n' eggs," he wrote. The food reaches higher than Rod's favorite, however. Smoked halibut, eel and salmon steaks find a place on the menu, along with simpler fare.

4 In the Center

VERY EXPENSIVE

Osaka. 12th Floor, Het Havengebouw, De Ruijterkade 7 (beside the harbor, west of Centraal Station). ☎ **020/638-9833.** Fixed-price menus Dfl 67.50–165 ($28.70–$70.20). AE, DC, MC, V. Mon–Fri noon–midnight, Sat–Sun 6pm–midnight. Tram: 1, 2, 4, 5, 9, 13, 16, 17, 20, 24, or 25. JAPANESE.

The name of Japan's main port city is an appropriate one for a Japanese restaurant on the twelfth floor of the 13-story Havengebouw, overlooking Amsterdam harbor. Amsterdam doesn't have many tall buildings, so this place offers a grand view for dinner. Only the section where traditional Japanese food is served has the water view, however; those who go for teppanyaki get to look out over the Centraal Station and its rail-line network. But no matter where you sit, the food is worth it. This is one of the Japanese restaurants that have borrowed the Indonesian rijsttafel concept—a little bit of this and a little bit of that—and applied it to Japanese cuisine. Otherwise, the menu is standard Japanese, with sushi in an extensive seafood menu, and with chefs

Central Amsterdam Dining

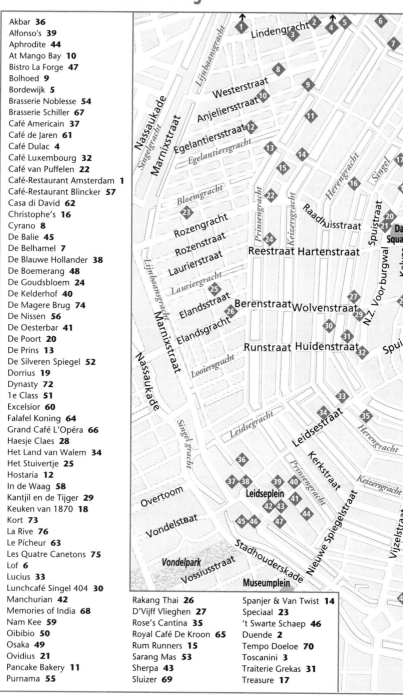

Openhaven Front
Prins Hendrikkade
50
de Ruijterkade
51
CITY CENTER
Het IJ
IJ-Tunnel

0   1/2 mi
0   .5 km
N

52 53
54
55
Nieuwendijk
Damrak
Damrak
Rokin
Zeedijk
Oudekerksplein
Geldersekade
Kromme Waal
Wads Eilandsgracht
Oude Waal
Oosterdok
Kattenburger-straat

56
57
Oudezijds Voorburgwal
58 59
Nieuwmarkt
60

Prins Hendrikkade
Hoogtekadijk

Oudezijds Voorburgwal
Kloveniersburgwal
Groenburgwal
61
Oude Schans
Nieuwe Uilenburgerstraat
Uilenburgergracht
Valkenburgerstraat
Rapenburgerstraat
Herengracht
Entrepotdok
Plantage Doklaan
Plantage Kerklaan
Artispark

Muntplein
62
63
64 65 66
Rembrandtplein
67
68
Waterlooplein
Mr. Visserplein
Nieuwe
Keizersgracht
Nieuwe Kerkstraat
Plantage Middenlaan

69
70
71
Nieuwe
Prinsengracht
Plantage Muidergracht
Plantage Muidergracht

72
73
Utrechtsestraat
74
Nieuwe
Achtergracht
Weesperstraat
Sarphatistraat

75
Amstel River
76

Falckstraat
Frederiksplein
Sarphatistraat
Mauritskade
Ooster-park

Singelgracht
Stadhouderskade
Ruyschstraat
Blasiusstraat

who are fast on the draw with knives and salt and pepper shakers in the teppanyaki grill section. Note that à la carte prices on the traditional menu can take you way above the top menu price listed here, depending on what choices you make.

EXPENSIVE

Brasserie Noblesse. In the Amsterdam Renaissance Hotel, Kattengat 1 (off Singel). ☎ **020/ 551-2044.** Main courses Dfl 38.50–59.50 ($16.40–$25.30). AE, DC, MC, V. Daily 6–10pm. Tram: 1, 2, 5, 13, 17, or 20 to Martelaarsgracht. AMERICAN.

This fine American-style restaurant offers a short but satisfying menu. The surf and turf (tender fillet steak with a broiled langoustine tail) "comes from Michel's at the Colony Surf, Honolulu," says the menu—it tastes so fresh that it must be shipped over by Lockheed SR-71 Blackbird. The ahi tuna steak (grilled tuna steak flavored with oyster sauce and Polynesian-style vegetables) "is a 50-year-old success story from Ernie's Restaurant in San Francisco"—no way that tuna steak's 50 years old. You might well laugh at the menu—I sure did—but I don't think you'll laugh at the food.

Christophe's. Leliegracht 46 (between Prinsengracht and Keizersgracht). ☎ **020/625-0807.** Main courses Dfl 55–65 ($23.40–$27.65); fixed-price menus Dfl 85–105 ($36.15–$44.70). AE, DC, MC, V. Tues–Sat 6:30–10:30pm. Tram: 13, 14, 17, or 20 to Westermarkt. MODERN FRENCH.

The star of this show is owner and chef Jean Christophe, who combines influences from his youth in Algeria and southwest France with his experience at top restaurants in New York, Baltimore, and Massachusetts to create an updated version of classic French cuisine. Christophe serves sensuous, sophisticated food in an elegant setting featuring dark cherry-wood paneling, thick carpets, rice-paper lamp shades, stately cacti by the windows, and floral paintings by contemporary Dutch artist Martin van Vreden. The food is similarly refined, using traditional Mediterranean ingredients— figs, truffles, olives, and saffron—in exciting new ways. Try the roasted milk-fed Pyreneean lamb, or roasted turbot in a light curry sauce, and finish with a light tart of prunes in Armagnac.

۞ D'Vijff Vlieghen. Spuistraat 294–302 (entrances on Singel and Spuistraat). ☎ **020/ 624-8369.** Main courses Dfl 48–60 ($20.45–$25.55); seasonal menu Dfl 75–97.50 ($31.90–$41.50). AE, CB, DC, DISC, MC, V. Daily 5:30pm–midnight. Tram: 1, 2, or 5 to Spui. DUTCH.

You know those jokes that begin, "Waiter, there's a fly in my soup . . ."? Well, how about five flies? D'Vijff Vlieghen (Five Flies), among the most famous restaurants in town, occupies five canal houses (hence the name). The decor is Old Dutch, though each of the seven separate dining rooms has a different character. There's the Glass Room, which has a collection of Golden Age handmade glass, and the Rembrandt Room, which sports four original etchings by the artist, to name just two. The chef is out to convey the culinary excellence inherent in many traditional Dutch recipes, but in an updated, "New Dutch" form. You can enjoy quite a mouthful by choosing the *geroosterde tamme eend op een bedje van appeltjes en tuinboontjes overgroten met een vinaigrette van rode en groene pepers* (roasted tame duck on a layer of apples and broad beans drizzled with a vinaigrette of red and green peppers). Or select from an extensive range of fish and vegetarian options.

۞ De Silveren Spiegel. Kattengat 4–6 (off Singel). ☎ **020/624-6589.** Main courses Dfl 47.50–55 ($20.20–$23.40); fixed-price menus Dfl 75–85 ($31.90–$36.15). AE, MC, V. Daily 6–11pm (open for lunch by reservation). Tram: 1, 2, 5, 13, 17, or 20 to Martelaarsgracht. DUTCH/FRENCH.

The owner of this traditional old restaurant, one of the best known in Amsterdam, has introduced a fresh approach. The two houses that form the premises were built in

1614 for a wealthy soap-maker, Laurens Jansz Spieghel. It's typically Old Dutch inside, with the bar downstairs and more dining rooms where the bedrooms used to be. The whole place emanates a traditionally Dutch tidiness that's very welcoming. There's a garden in back. The menu has been updated and now offers new, finely prepared seafood and meat dishes, such as baked sole fillets with wild spinach, and trilogy of lamb with ratatouille—but just as in the old days, the lamb is still Holland's finest, from Texel, and traditional Zaanse mustard is never far away.

Dorrius. In the Crowne Plaza Hotel, Nieuwezijds Voorburgwal 5 (near Centraal Station). ☎ **020/620-0500.** Main courses Dfl 34.50–55 ($14.70–$23.40); fixed-price menus Dfl 55–90 ($23.40–$28.30). AE, DC, MC, V. Daily 6–11pm. Tram: 1, 2, 5, 13, 17, or 20 to Martelaarsgracht. CLASSIC DUTCH.

Housed in adjoining canal houses from 1890, this is one of Amsterdam's most elegant dining rooms. Its traditional atmosphere, which particularly suits quiet business discussions, is enhanced by beamed ceilings and a black-and-white marble floor. Among the specialties are fried pike perch with raspberry sauce, and fillet steak with duck liver and truffle sauce. Or you can choose from the Dorrius Classics—a list of old-fashioned Dutch dishes, including such delicacies as Zeeland oysters, home-style marrowfat peas, and braised beef with red cabbage. Although the wine list changes seasonally, you may be lucky enough to find on it some of the small production of white wines from the Slavante and Apostelhoeve wineries in the south of Holland, near Maastricht.

Dynasty. Reguliersdwarsstraat 30 (behind the Flower Market, between the Singel and Herengracht canals). ☎ **020/626-8400.** Main courses Dfl 36–67.50 ($15.30–$28.70); fixed-price menus Dfl 72–98 ($30.65–$41.70). AE, DC, MC, V. Wed–Mon 5:30–11pm. Tram: 1, 2, or 5 to Konings-plein. CHINESE/ASIAN.

For summer dining in a formal Louis XV–style canal-house garden or winter dining in a cozy cavern of exotic colors and upturned Chinese umbrellas, try Dynasty. It offers a selection of imaginative Chinese and Asian specialties, including Thai, Malay, and Filipino favorites. Among the intriguing possibilities is Promise of Spring, an appetizer of crisp pancakes filled with bamboo shoots and minced meat. Or perhaps you'll think it's more fun to get together a group of six like-minded diners to share the magnificent 10-course Festive Meal, an extravaganza of flavors—among its delights are lobster, coquillage, duck, lamb, pigeon, and Szechuan beef.

Lucius. Spuistraat 247 (near Spui). ☎ **020/624-1831.** Main courses Dfl 37.50–75 ($15.95–$31.90); fixed-price menus Dfl 52.50–65 ($22.35–$27.65). AE, DC, MC, V. Daily 5pm–midnight. Tram: 1, 2, or 5 to Spui. SEAFOOD.

Lucius, which means "pike" in Latin, has earned a reputation for fine seafood at fairly reasonable prices. Oysters and lobsters imported from Norway and Canada are the specialties. The three-course menu is also very popular. Among the half dozen or so choices featured on the chalkboard menu, you might find fish soup to start, followed by grilled plaice, Dover sole, bass, or John Dory. The spectacular seafood plate includes 6 oysters, 10 mussels, clams, shrimp, and half a lobster. The long, narrow dining room is cooled by ceiling fans and features an aquarium. In summer, chairs are placed out on the sidewalk.

MODERATE

✪ **Café-Restaurant Amsterdam.** Watertorenplein 6 (off Haarlemmerweg). ☎ **020/682-2666.** Reservations recommended on weekends. Main courses Dfl 17.50–40 ($7.45–$17). AE, DC, MC, V. Daily 11:30am–1am. Tram: 10 to Van Halstraat. CONTINENTAL.

Think of it as *Amsterdam: the Restaurant,* because it's quite a performance. Café-Restaurant Amsterdam is based in a century-old water-pumping station, complete

A Culinary Critic

Most Americans are more familiar with Jean-Claude van Damme than with the Dutch food critic Johannes van Dam, but though the latter isn't a martial arts movie star, his restaurant reviews in the Dutch daily *Het Parool* still pack quite a wallop. In recent years van Dam has emerged as the most influential voice on Amsterdam's dining scene, ensuring the popularity of restaurants he praises and dooming to obscurity those he disdains. His 10-point rating system is applauded by some Amsterdam restaurateurs for its honesty and decried by others for its harshness. The popular and elegant Dorrius Restaurant (see p. 97) garnered a measly 5.5, while the highest mark van Dam has awarded to date, a 9.5, went to Bordewijk, a popular French restaurant in the Jordaan (see p. 111), though there are many more refined and aristocratic places in town. Despite the controversies around his grades, Van Dam's readers and Amsterdam chefs seem to agree that his qualifications as a culinary expert are first-rate and that his intentions are sincere. What he wants is to reward fine restaurants, and to force mediocre ones to improve (or, perhaps, to give up and close down).

Van Dam's reviews are plastered in the windows of Amsterdam restaurants, and many also appear in the English-language *Now in Amsterdam,* which is widely available at city newsstands. See if your tastes are as selective as those of Amsterdam's most discriminating food critic.

with diesel-powered engine. It has taken this monument of Victorian industrial good taste and made of it a model of contemporary good eats. You dine amidst a buzz of conviviality in the big, brightly lit, former pumping hall, which had been so carefully tended by the water workers that some of its elegant decoration didn't even need repainting. Service is friendly and the food is good and moderately priced. The fried sweetbreads are popular. If you're feeling flush, spring for a double starter of half lobster with six Zeeland oysters. The Amsterdam is a little bit off the Center, but easily worth the tram ride.

De Luwte. Leliegracht 26–28 (between Keizersgracht and Herengracht). ☎ **020/625-8548.** Main courses Dfl 27.50–32.50 ($11.70–$13.85). No credit cards. Daily 6–11pm. Tram: 13, 14, 17, or 20 to Westermarkt. FUSION.

Graceful is the term that seems best to sum up this fine restaurant, though that quality never descends into stiffness. It gets its grace from Florentine wall murals, floor-to-ceiling art deco lamps, drapes, hangings, ceiling mirrors painted with flowers and vines, a candle on each table, and not least from an elegant canal-side location. And it avoids being starchy by a characteristic Amsterdam exuberance and buzz. In either of the twin rooms, try for one of the window tables that look out on the canal. The menu ranges across the globe for inspiration. Look out for items such as the vegetarian coconut curry crepes filled with spinach, lentils, and nuts; and stir-fried guinea fowl with nuts and bok choy.

De Nissen. Rokin 95 (between the Dam and Muntplein). ☎ **020/624-2825.** Main courses Dfl 27.50–42.50 ($11.70–$18.10); fixed-price menus Dfl 29.50–57.50 ($12.55–$24.45). AE, DC, MC, V. Mon–Sat noon–9:30pm. Tram: 4, 9, 16, 20, 24, or 25 to Rokin. DUTCH.

This Old Dutch–style spot has nooks and crannies that give it the atmosphere of an old wine cellar. The menu is typically Dutch and reasonably priced, and the mood is casual. Fresh fish here is a must. Try lobster bisque to start, fried fillets of flounder as a main dish, and hot apple pie with cinnamon ice cream for dessert. At lunch, De Nissen is popular with people who work nearby, so you may have to wait for a table.

✪ **De Poort.** In the Hotel Die Port van Cleve, Nieuwezijds Voorburgwal 176–180 (behind the Dam). ☎ **020/624-0047.** Main courses Dfl 28–42.50 ($11.90–$18.10); fixed-price menu Dfl 39.50 ($16.80). AE, DC, JCB, MC, V. Daily 7am–10:30pm. Tram: 1, 2, 5, 13, 14, 17, or 20 to the Dam. DUTCH.

This restaurant, in a former beer hall, has been offering its steaks and typically Dutch dishes for more than 100 years. Its beamed and tiled Dutch-tavern dining room has recently been fully restored along with its parent hotel. De Poort still maintains a tradition that has become legendary among its patrons: Each of its steaks is numbered, and if the number on yours is a round thousand, you're the winner of a free bottle of wine. They're almost up to steak 6 million! The restaurant is also famous for its Dutch pea soup.

Gare de l'Est. Cruquiusweg 9 (at the East Harbor). ☎ **020/463-0620.** Reservations recommended on weekends. Fixed-price menu Dfl 52 ($22.10). No credit cards. Daily 6–11pm. Tram: 7 or 10 to Zeeburgerdijk; bus: 39 or 59 to Cruquiusweg. FRENCH/MEDITERRANEAN.

This detached, distinctive house, with a recently added conservatory extension and a large sidewalk terrace, was originally built as a coffeehouse for workers at the docks. Many a poor slob, er, visitor, victim of the merciless parking authority, has had to make his or her way out here from the city center to pick up a towed-away car from the nearby pound. This is an altogether better reason for the trip to part of town that is by no means fashionable. As the restaurant's name indicates, the cuisine is French, traditional, though with Mediterranean touches. Service is both relaxed and knowledgeable, and as the fixed-price menu is excellent value for money any surprises appear on your plate rather than on the check. The strict five-course formula (starter, salad, main course of meat or fish, cheese, and dessert) leaves no room for choice—except for the main course—but plenty for market-fresh ingredients and culinary creativity. How does this sound: pulpo estofado with risotto nero (ink-fish stew with black rice) as a starter, and roast lamb with gazpacho and farfalle as a main course?

Haesje Claes. Spuistraat 273–275 (at Spui). ☎ **020/624-9998.** Main courses Dfl 24.50–34.50 ($10.45–$14.70). AE, DC, MC, V. Daily noon–midnight. Tram: 1, 2, or 5 to Spui. DUTCH.

If you're yearning for a cozy Old Dutch environment and hearty Dutch food at moderate prices, try this inviting place. Lots of nooks and crannies decorated with Delftware and wooden barrels, brocaded benches and traditional Dutch hanging lamps with fringed covers give an intimate, comfortable feel to the setting. The menu covers a lot of ground, from canapés to caviar, but you have the most luck with Dutch stalwarts ranging from omelettes to tournedos, and taking in *hutspot* (stew), *stampot* (mashed potatoes and cabbage), and various fish stews, including those with IJsselmeer *paling* (eel), along the way.

In de Waag. Nieuwmarkt 4. ☎ **020/422-7772.** Main courses Dfl 28.50–38 ($12.15–$16.15). AE, DC, MC, V. Daily 10am–1am. Metro: Nieuwmarkt. CONTINENTAL.

This cafe-restaurant is called In de Waag because it's in the Waag (see, you *can* speak Dutch). And what is the Waag? In medieval times it was the St. Antoniespoort Gate in the city walls; by the Golden Age, it had become a weigh house: De Waag. Dissections were once carried out on the top floor. Nowadays, this castlelike structure holds one of Amsterdam's newest and most stylish cafe-restaurants. It's an indelibly romantic place, ablaze with candlelight in the evening. You can mix easily with other diners at the long banquet-style tables. The breast of Barbary duck with sesame-cracker and sherry dressing is pretty good, as is the vegetarian Kashmir bread with braised vegetables and coriander-yogurt sauce.

⭐ **Kantjil en de Tijger.** Spuistraat 291 (beside Spui). ☎ **020/620-0994.** Reservations recommended on weekends. Main courses Dfl 22.50–30.50 ($9.55–$13); rijsttafels Dfl 77.50–97.50 ($33–$41.50) for two. AE, DC, MC, V. Daily 4:30–11pm. Tram: 1, 2, or 5 to Spui. JAVANESE/INDONESIAN.

Unlike many Indonesian restaurants that wear their ethnic origins on their sleeves, the Antelope and the Tiger is chic, modern, and cool. Moreover, it attracts customers who like their Indonesian food not only chic, modern, and cool, but good as well. The two best-sellers in this very popular restaurant are *nasi goreng Kantjil* (fried rice with pork kabobs, stewed beef, pickled cucumbers, and mixed vegetables) and the 20-item rijsttafel for two. Other choices include stewed chicken in soja sauce, tofu omelette, shrimp with coconut dressing, Indonesian pumpkin, and mixed steamed vegetables with peanut-butter sauce. Finish off your meal with the multilayered cinnamon cake or (try this at least once) the coffee with ginger liqueur and whipped cream.

Le Pêcheur. Reguliersdwarsstraat 32 (behind the Flower Market). ☎ **020/624-3121.** Main courses Dfl 35–45 ($14.90–$19.15); fixed-price menu Dfl 65 ($27.65). AE, MC, V. Mon–Fri noon–midnight, Sat 5pm–midnight. Tram: 1, 2, or 5 to Koningsplein. SEAFOOD.

Popular and appealing, Le Pêcheur has a marble floor, a muraled ceiling, and a garden for summer dining. Fish is the preoccupation here. In season, come for the coquilles St-Jacques (scallops) and the mussels and oysters from the southern province of Zeeland. You could also try poached brill with onion sauce, fried wolf-fish with light mustard sauce, or sashimi. Tournedos of beef cooked to your liking are available for nonseafood-lovers.

Lof. Haarlemmerstraat 62 (near Centraal Station). ☎ **020/620-2997.** Reservations required. Main courses Dfl 19.50–37.50 ($8.30–$15.95), fixed-price menus Dfl 52.50–75 ($22.35–$31.90). No credit cards. Tues–Sun 6–11pm. Tram: 1, 2, 4, 5, 9, 13, 16, 17, 20, 24, or 25 to Centraal Station. EUROPEAN.

It's tough to pin down this fashionable, vaguely French/Italian eatery. For one thing, there's no menu. Its youthful chefs describe their creations as *cuisine spontane*—they go to the markets, spontaneously pick out whatever's fresh and takes their fancy, and equally spontaneously figure out what to do with it back at base. The results are invariably splendid. Oysters are a regular feature among three or four starters; then, choose from three main courses: meat, fish, and vegetarian; and finish with a *torte*. You dine on one of two levels, at plain tables in a cozy setting with bare brick walls, and a view of proceedings in the open kitchen.

Oibibio. Prins Hendrikkade 20–21 (facing Centraal Station). ☎ **020/553-9328.** Main courses Dfl 27.50–34.50 ($11.70–$14.70). AE, DC, V. Mon noon–6:30pm, Tues–Sun 10am–6:30pm. Tram: 1, 2, 4, 5, 9, 13, 16, 17, 20, 24, or 25. VEGETARIAN.

Oibibio is one of the more interesting of the new breed of Amsterdam eateries. You're looking at vegetarian with added value here. The "New Age" complex boasts a grand cafe, tea garden, department store, healing center, sauna, and concert space. The complex's culinary end, the restaurant, is a stylish affair with a bar, wooden tables, a terracotta floor, and a glass roof. The decor and the ethereal music wafting through the place give the restaurant a light, airy feeling that transmits itself to the food. Wash the wide range of inventive vegetarian dishes down with biodynamic beet juice.

Ovidius. Spuistraat 137 (at Magna Plaza shopping center). ☎ **020/620-8977.** Main courses Dfl 15.50–27.50 ($6.60–$11.70). AE, DC, MC, V. Tues–Sat 9am–9pm (Thurs until 11pm), Sun–Mon 10am–9pm. Tram: 1, 2, 5, 13, 14, 17, or 20 to the Dam. GRAND CAFE.

Though it's not the grandest of the grand cafes, the Ovidius is still a stylish brasserie with lots of polished wood and brass, and tables arranged on three levels. It makes for a good timeout from shopping at the Magna Plaza. A sign at its entrance reads, VENI, VIDI, VERBAZI, which roughly translates as "I came, I saw, I was astonished" (*verbazi* is derived from the Dutch *verbazen*, to be surprised). I can't promise astonishment, but atmosphere and style are certainly here, along with healthful, snacky food, such as salads, roast chicken and avocado, and the Indonesian specialties saté (roast meat) and vlammetjes (deadly hot "little flames," like small and spicy spring rolls).

Purnama. Nieuwendijk 33 (near Centraal Station). ☎ **020/620-5325.** Main courses Dfl 18.50–26.50 ($7.85–$11.30); rijsttafels Dfl 29.50–49.50 ($12.55–$21.05). AE, DC, MC, V. Daily noon–10pm. INDONESIAN.

This small restaurant is always crowded with locals enjoying the high-quality food. Among the favorite dishes are the 11-item minirijsttafel and the 15-item special rijsttafel. Both combine foods with sweet-and-sour tastes and other contrasting flavors. If a rijsttafel is too much for you, try the nasi or bami goreng or choose one of the 8 meat and 10 fish dishes. For starters, try the sot ayam, a spicy soup.

✪ **Rose's Cantina.** Reguliersdwarsstraat 38–40 (1 block behind the Flower Market). ☎ **020/625-9797.** Main courses Dfl 19.50–42.50 ($8.30–$18.10). AE, DC, MC, V. Daily 5–11pm. Tram: 1, 2, or 5 to Koningsplein. TEX-MEX.

Rose's attracts English-speaking guests with typical American favorites like hamburgers and meatballs, though the decor and most of the cuisine are Mexican inspired. A meal starting with tortilla chips and salsa, followed by a plato mixto or fried galinhas (roast chicken with fries and red peppers), and accompanied by a Mexican beer will cost you less than Dfl 50 ($21.30). The tables are oak, the service is decent (though a bit slow), and the atmosphere is Latin American and buzzing with good cheer. Just be careful of long waiting times—the basic rate of continental drift is a good comparison—during which you sit at the bar downing one after another of Rose's deadly margaritas.

Sarang Mas. Damrak 44 (near Centraal Station). ☎ **020/622-2105.** Main courses Dfl 25–40 ($10.65–$17); rijsttafels Dfl 52.75–65.75 ($22.45–$28). AE, DC, MC, V. Daily 11:30am–11pm. Tram: 1, 2, 4, 5, 9, 13, 16, 17, 20, 24, or 25, or 4, 9, 16, 20, 24, or 25 to the Dam. INDONESIAN.

This intimate Indonesian restaurant is near the canal-boat piers, so you get a nice view while you dine on traditional Indonesian dishes, including a decent selection of rijsttafels. The pink, white, and green color scheme is a refreshing and contemporary alternative to the usual basic decor found in Indonesian restaurants. The big drawback is location: Damrak is central enough but is also the center of "tacky" Amsterdam; Sarang Mas is surrounded by sex boutiques, souvenir shops, fast-food joints, and video-game parlors. Still, the ruckus ends at the restaurant door, and Sarang Mas hasn't let its standards slip by being in a tourist ghetto.

Sluizer. Utrechtsestraat 41–43 and 45 (between Herengracht and Keizersgracht). ☎ **020/622-6376** (Continental) or 020/626-3557 (seafood). Main courses Dfl 22.75–59.75 ($9.70–$25.45); optional menu Dfl 27.50 ($11.70). AE, DC, MC, V. Mon–Fri noon–2:30pm and 5pm–1am, Sat–Sun 5pm–1am. Tram: 4 to Utrechtsestraat. CONTINENTAL/SEAFOOD.

Two notable restaurants (sadly, not for the price of one), stand side by side in convivial harmony. No. 45 is an old-fashioned brasserie with an eclectic menu that has a slightly French bias, in such items as *entrecôte Dijon* (steak with mustard sauce) and *poulet à la Provençal* (chicken with olives, sage, rosemary, and tomato). Next door, at nos. 41–43, the vaguely art deco *Visrestaurant* (Fish restaurant) has at least 10 specials daily, ranging from simple cod or eel to *coquille St-Jacques* (scallops), crab casserole, Dover sole, halibut, and octopus. Meat dishes, such as beef stroganoff and chicken supreme, also appear on the menu.

Tempo Doeloe. Utrechtsestraat 75 (between Herengracht and Keizersgracht). ☎ **020/ 625-6718.** Main courses Dfl 25.50–62.50 ($10.85–$26.60); rijsttafel Dfl 49.50 ($21.05) and Dfl 59.50 ($25.30). AE, DC, MC, V. Daily 6–11:30pm. Tram: 4 to Utrechtsestraat. INDONESIAN.

For authentic Indonesian cuisine this place is hard to beat, though its local reputation goes up and down with the tide. The attractive decor and fine china are unexpected pluses. You eat in an ambience that's Indonesian, of course, but not to the extent of being kitsch. Try the rijsttafel, the *nasi koening*, or any of the vegetarian dishes. Finish with the *spekkoek*, a layered spice cake. One caution: When something on the menu is described as *pedis*, meaning hot, that's *exactly* what it is—a fire-extinguisher would be a useful accessory for these dishes.

Treasure. Nieuwezijds Voorburgwal 115–117 (near the Dam). ☎ **020/623-4061.** Main courses Dfl 18–27 ($7.65–$11.50); fixed-price menus Dfl 27.50–75 ($11.70–$31.90). AE, JCB, MC, V. Daily noon–11pm. Tram: 1, 2, 5, 13, 14, 17, or 20 to the Dam. CHINESE.

In a city with a passion for Indonesian food, it can be difficult to find traditional Chinese cuisine, let alone good traditional Chinese cuisine. Don't despair—make a beeline for Treasure, a legend in its own lunchtime (and dinnertime), rated among the best restaurants in Amsterdam by *Avant Garde.* It offers a wide array of classic Chinese choices in a classic Chinese setting, with lots of lanterns, watercolor paintings, and Chinese scripts. You can eat dishes from any of the four main styles of Chinese cooking—Beijing, Shanghai, Cantonese, and Szechuan. Look for specialties such as Beijing duck, Szechuan-style prawns (very spicy), and steamed dumplings.

INEXPENSIVE

✪ **1e Klas.** Platform 1, Centraal Station. ☎ **020/627-3306.** Main courses Dfl 15–20 ($6.40–$8.50); dish of the day Dfl 19.50 ($8.30). No credit cards. Mon–Sat 7am–10pm, Sun 8am–10pm. DUTCH.

For a little bit of art deco elegance with your budget meal, try this self-service Centraal Station restaurant, in a lofty wood-paneled chamber with chandeliers. The place used to be the first-class waiting room. Each month there's a different special plate offered here at a rock-bottom price, and it's not the usual boring blue-plate fare. Trout, jugged hare, and coq au vin have all been the special in the recent past, always with salad, vegetable, and other appropriate accompaniments.

Café Dulac. Haarlemmerstraat 118 (parallel to Brouwersgracht). ☎ **020/624-4265.** Main courses Dfl 19.50–32.50 ($8.30–$13.85). No credit cards. Mon–Fri 4pm–1am, Sat 2pm–2am, Sun 2pm–1am. Bus: 18 or 22 to Haarlemmer Houttuinen. GRAND CAFE.

This establishment used to be a bank, though it's a sure bet that none of its former staff or customers would recognize it now. The decor in the gloomily lit main room is bizarre: angels and devils on the ceilings, and skyscraper models sticking out at right angles above the bar. Still, the Dulac is one of the most popular grand cafes. There's a nice little garden terrace at the back, what's said to be the biggest pool table in Amsterdam, and a DJ on Friday and Saturday, when the lack of a true dance floor can't prevent many patrons from dancing. Friendly, youth-oriented service complements Mediterranean food specialties. Try the Portuguese mussels.

✪ **Café Luxembourg.** Spuistraat 24 (beside Spui). ☎ **020/620-6264.** Snacks Dfl 9.50–19.50 ($4.05–$8.30). MC, V. Mon–Thurs 9am–1am, Fri–Sat 9am–2am. Tram: 1, 2, or 5 to Spui. GRAND CAFE.

"One of the world's great cafes," wrote *The New York Times* about this stylish place. Unlike other cafes in Amsterdam, which often draw a distinctive clientele, Café

Luxembourg attracts all kinds of people because it offers amazingly large portions of food at reasonable prices. Soups, sandwiches, and such dishes as meat loaf are available. A special attraction is that some of the dishes are specialties from other well-known Amsterdam restaurants—for example, the dim sum comes from the China Treasure and the chicken salad from Café Wildschut. You're encouraged to linger in this relaxing place and read one of the many international newspapers. In summer there's sidewalk dining.

Café-Restaurant Blincker. St. Barberenstraat 7 (off Rokin). ☎ **020/627-1938.** Main courses Dfl 10–30 ($4.25–$12.75). AE, DC, MC, V. Mon–Sat 4pm–1am. Tram: 4, 9, 16, 20, 24, or 25 to Rokin. CONTINENTAL.

To find Café Blincker, turn into Ness from the Dam (which runs parallel to Rokin), then turn left after the Frascati Theater. This intimate restaurant in the Frascati Theater building attracts actors, journalists, artists, and other assorted bohemians. At night the place is jammed with people around the bar. The simple but tasty fare includes lamb chops with garlic, pancakes with cheese and mushrooms, homemade pasta, and cheese fondue.

Keuken van 1870. Spuistraat 4 (at Martelaarsgracht). ☎ **020/624-8965.** Main courses Dfl 11.50–17.50 ($4.90–$7.45). AE, DC, MC, V. Mon–Fri 12:30–8pm, Sat–Sun 4–9pm. Tram: 1, 2, 5, 13, 17, or 20 to Martelaarsgracht. DUTCH.

Keuken van 1870 is one of the cheapest (and plainest) places to eat in Amsterdam. Built in 1870 as a public soup kitchen, it's still a nonprofit concern. There's absolutely no attempt at decor here; meals are served cafeteria style; tables are bare; and dishes are plain—but the food is good. Pork chops, fish, and chicken—all accompanied by vegetables and potatoes—are some of the unremarkable but reliable main courses available on the menu. This place is typical Dutch, popular with Amsterdammers, and good for travelers on a tight budget.

Nam Kee. Zeedijk 111–113 at Nieuwmarkt. ☎ **020/624-3470.** Main courses Dfl 12–31.50 ($5.10–$13.40). AE, DC, MC, V. Daily 11:30am–midnight. Metro: Nieuwmarkt. CHINESE.

The area around Zeedijk and Nieuwmarkt, which a few years back was a shooting gallery for heroin addicts, has been cleaned up and is moving upmarket. The city's growing Chinatown is here, along with some good, genuine Chinese restaurants. Nam Kee has a long interior with few obvious graces and no plastic Ming Dynasty knick-knacks. Its food is excellent and its menu boasts 140 items. The steamed duck with plum sauce is to die for. Judging by the number of Chinese customers clicking chopsticks around, Nam Kee does okay when it comes to ethnic credibility.

5 Along the Canal Belt

EXPENSIVE

De Goudsbloem. In the Hotel Pulitzer, Reestraat 8 (on the corner of Prinsengracht). ☎ **020/523-5283.** Reservations recommended on weekends. Main courses Dfl 39.50–45 ($16.80–$19.15); fixed-price menus Dfl 59.50–95 ($25.30–$40.45). AE, DC, MC, V. Daily 6pm–midnight. Tram: 13, 14, 17, or 20 to Westermarkt. FRENCH.

The Goudsbloem is noted for its contemporary decor, its wildly colored service plates, its intimacy—so rare in hotel dining rooms—and its kitchen staff, supervised by the Pulitzer's executive chef. Try the fried North Holland blue chicken with a sauce of white grapes, or the smoked salmon in goose gravy, with capers, vinaigrette, scallions, and quail eggs. You can even visit the extensive wine cellar—one of only four worldwide to win *Wine Spectator* magazine's Grand Award in 1997—by appointment only, Monday to Friday 6 to 6:30pm.

Les Quatre Canetons. Prinsengracht 1111 (near the Amstel River). ☎ **020/624-6307.** Main courses Dfl 49–55 ($20.85–$)23.40; menu surprise Dfl 65–105 ($27.65–$44.70); wine arrangement Dfl 35–55 ($14.90–$23.40). AE, CB, DC, DISC, MC, V. Mon–Fri noon–2:30pm and 6–11pm, Sat 6–11pm. Tram: 4 to Utrechtsestraat. INTERNATIONAL.

This is a longstanding favorite among Amsterdammers. The "Four Ducklings," in what used to be the garden of a 17th-century canal house, is one of Amsterdam's most stylish restaurants. The interior evokes the atmosphere of a garden behind the gables, bright and airy, with delicate countryside images on the walls. Yet the emphasis is more on food than fuss. Owners Ailko Faber and Jacques Roosenbred, who have been here since 1979, are credited, along with others, for elevating Amsterdam to the rank of European culinary capital. Seasonal specialties and imaginative choices, such as duck breasts with prunes, make this a delightful place to dine. The menu changes frequently and the *menu surprise* changes every day (otherwise it wouldn't be a surprise). In summer, the restaurant deploys a sidewalk terrace.

MODERATE

✪ **Bolhoed.** Prinsengracht 60–62 (near Noordermarkt). ☎ **020/626-1803.** Main courses Dfl 22.50–27.50 ($9.55–$11.70). No credit cards. Sun–Fri noon–11pm, Sat 11am–11pm. Tram: 13, 14, 17, or 20 to Westermarkt. VEGETARIAN.

Forget the corn-sheaf 'n' brown-rice image affected by so many vegetarian restaurants, that worthy but dull message: "This stuff is good for you." Instead, garnish your healthful habits with a dash of zest. Latin style, world music, a changing program of ethnic exhibitions, evening candlelight, and a fine view of the canal from each of its two cheerful rooms distinguish a restaurant for which *vegetarian* is a tad too wholesome-sounding. Service is delivered with equal amounts of gusto and attention. Try such veggie delights as *ragoût croissant* (pastry filled with leeks, tofu, seaweed, and curry sauce), and *zarzuela*. If you want to go whole hog, so to speak, and eat vegan, most of Bolhoed's dishes can be so prepared on request, and in any case most are made with organically grown produce.

Café van Puffelen. Prinsengracht 377 (facing Lauriergracht). ☎ **020/624-6270.** Main courses Dfl 12.50–40 ($5.30–$17); dish of the day Dfl 27.50–35 ($11.70–$14.90). AE, DC, MC, V (for amounts over Dfl 50 [$21.30] only). Mon–Thurs 3pm–1am, Fri 3pm–2am, Sat noon–2am, Sun noon–1am. Tram: 13, 14, 17, or 20 to Westermarkt. DUTCH/CONTINENTAL.

A big cafe-restaurant near the Westerkerk. Among the menu dishes that show flair, creativity, and a seemingly inexhaustible supply of ingredients, you can try fried butterfish with a tarragon, coriander, and pesto cream sauce served on bacon and tomato spaghetti; and the main course Salad van Puffelen, served with tandoori chicken, smoked turkey, smoked salmon, roast veal and Cajun shrimps. Other choices include vegetable platters and mozzarella with tomato. Save room for the delicious handmade chocolates that are house specialties.

Casa di David. Singel 426 (at the Flower Market). ☎ **020/624-5093.** Main courses Dfl 20–40 ($8.50–$17). AE, DC, MC, V. Daily 5pm–midnight. Tram: 1, 2, 5, or 20 to Spui. ITALIAN.

A friend recommended Casa di David as the best Italian restaurant in Amsterdam, and she's probably right. The ambience is very romantic and typically Italian—dark paneling, red-and-white-checked tablecloths, and wine casks—but mingled with the flavor of an old wood-beamed Amsterdam canal house. There's a view of both the Singel and Herengracht canals from the restaurant's two floors. Casa di David is most famous for its freshly made in-house pasta and its pizzas for one.

✪ **De Belhamel.** Brouwersgracht 60 (at Herengracht). ☎ **020/622-1095.** Main courses Dfl 28.50–39.50 ($12.15–$16.80); specials Dfl 32.50 ($13.80). AE, MC, V. Daily 6pm–midnight. Tram: 1, 2, 5, 13, 17, or 20 to Martelaarsgracht. CONTINENTAL.

Soft classical music complements a graceful art nouveau setting at this two-level restaurant overlooking the photogenic junction of the Herengracht and Brouwersgracht canals. The tables fill up quickly most evenings, so make reservations or go early. The menu changes seasonally, but if you're like me you'll hope that something like, or as good as, this will be on the list: puffed pastries layered with salmon, shellfish, crayfish tails, and chervil beurre-blanc to start; and beef tenderloin in Madeira sauce with zucchini rösti and puffed garlic for a main course. You can also get vegetarian dishes. Try for a window table and take in the superb canal views. Although generally excellent, De Belhamel does have two minor flaws: The wait staff is occasionally a bit too laid-back, and when the place is full, as it often is, the noise level can approach that of a boiler factory; this is a matter of acoustics, not rowdiness.

De Kelderhof. Prinsengracht 494 (near Leidsestraat). ☎ **020/622-0682.** Main courses Dfl 30–47.50 ($12.75–$20.20). AE, DC, MC, V. Daily 5:30–11pm. Tram: 1, 2, or 5, to Leidsestraat. MODERN MEDITERRANEAN/CLASSIC FRENCH.

Rattan chairs, wooden tables, lots of plants, and a cobbled floor give this cellar restaurant a French Mediterranean–village atmosphere, and the French wine list adds to the feeling. The menu, though not extensive, has a good mix of soups, seafood, and grilled meat dishes, all prepared Mediterranean style. The fresh seasonal fish is close to the "heaven on earth" they claim for it, and the Caesar salad is pretty mean, too. Live music plays Wednesday to Sunday. This restaurant is a double bill: Round the corner, at Lange Leidsedwarsstraat 53–59, is Brasserie De Kelderhof (☎ **020/638-0519**), a fine fish restaurant in the style of a Portuguese *cantine.*

Het Land van Walem. Keizersgracht 449 (beside Leidsestraat). ☎ **020/625-3544.** Main courses Dfl 22.50–39.50 ($9.55–$16.80). AE, DC, MC, V. Sun–Thurs 9am–1am, Fri–Sat 9am–2am. Tram: 1, 2, or 5 to Leidsestraat. GRAND CAFE.

Het Land van Walem may have lost a few of its accumulated brownie points since a few years ago when it was one of the hottest addresses in town, but that only means it's easier to get a seat on one of its two terraces: one outside beside the canal and the other at the back in a garden patio. The space between them isn't bad either; it was designed by the noted Dutch architect Rietveld, with small tables in front of and beside the long bar, where daily newspapers are provided. This cafe-restaurant's standards have not slipped at all, so don't worry about being seen in yesterday's in-place. Menu items include pasta specialties, and also steak, chicken, and salads.

✪ **Kort.** Amstelveld 12 (at Prinsengracht). ☎ **020/626-1199.** Reservations required for outside terrace. Main courses Dfl 35–45 ($14.90–$19.15). AE, CB, DC, MC, V. Summer, daily 11:30am–midnight; winter, Wed–Mon 11:30am–midnight. Tram: 4 to Utrechtsestraat. CONTINENTAL.

Few restaurants in the city take reservations for eating outdoors on a warm summer evening, when most sidewalk terraces fill up in the blink of an eye. Kort does. Its tree-shaded terrace on a wide, open square beside the Prinsengracht is just far enough from the canal-side street to be little affected by traffic noise. Service is friendly and the food is both adventurous and consistently excellent. I would rave about my ricotta, Parmesan, forest mushrooms, and wild-spinach tart, but as the menu changes seasonally it likely won't be available when you visit. Don't worry, I'm sure there'll be another mouthwatering vegetarian choice, along with fish, steak and poultry menu dishes. Inside the main restaurant, you dine amid the ambience of a restored and converted 17th-century timber church, the Amstelkerk.

Rum Runners. Prinsengracht 277 (beside Anne Frankhuis). ☎ **020/627-4079.** Main courses Dfl 21.50–34.50 ($9.15–$14.70); fixed-price menus Dfl 35–45 ($14.90–$19.15). AE, DC, MC, V. Mon–Thurs 2pm–1am, Fri–Sun 2pm–2am. Tram: 13, 14, 17, or 20 to Wester-markt. CARIBBEAN.

In the former coach house of the Westerkerk (yes, the church) is Rum Runners, a two-level, laid-back, tropical kind of place where the atmosphere and cuisine are inspired by the Caribbean. Two gigantic bamboo birdcages greet you as you enter. You sit beneath gently circling ceiling fans and among towering potted palms that stretch to the lofty rafters. At night the reggae beat of the music often lasts until the wee hours. Try asopao, a Caribbean rice dish, or a Caribbean barbecue. You can also just drink cocktails to your heart's content and fill up on some of the best guacamole in town.

INEXPENSIVE

✪ **De Prins.** Prinsengracht 124 (at Leliegracht). ☎ **020/624-9382.** Main courses Dfl 12–25 ($5.10–$10.65); dish of the day Dfl 19.50 ($8.30); specials Dfl 23.50–27.50 ($10–$11.70). AE, MC, V. Daily 10am–midnight. Tram: 13, 14, 17, or 20 to Westermarkt. DUTCH/FRENCH.

This companionable restaurant, housed in a 17th-century canal house, has a smoke-stained, brown-cafe style and food that could easily grace a much more expensive place. De Prins offers an unbeatable price-to-quality ratio for typically Dutch/French menu items, and long may it continue to do so. The youthful clientele is loyal and enthusiastic, so the relatively few tables fill up quickly. This is a quiet neighborhood place—nothing fancy or trendy, but quite appealing in a human way. There's a bar on a slightly lower level than the restaurant. From March to September De Prins spreads a terrace out onto the canal-side.

Lunchcafé Singel 404. Singel 404 (near Spui). ☎ **020/428-0154.** No credit cards. Snacks Dfl 4–13.50 ($1.70–$5.75). Daily 10am–8pm. Tram: 1, 2, or 5 to Spui. LIGHT FARE.

If you find yourself growing weary of eating at local grand cafes, where they charge you an arm for ambience and a leg for lunch, Singel 404 makes an acceptable alter-native. It has the blessing of simplicity and the advantage of low cost. You won't have to pretend that you're cool, or smart, or hip; you can just eat. Service is friendly and the salads and sandwiches are very good.

Pancake Bakery. Prinsengracht 191 (near Westermarkt, a block from the Anne Frankhuis). ☎ **020/625-1333.** Reservations required for large groups. Pancakes Dfl 8–20 ($3.40–$8.50). AE, MC, V. Daily noon–9:30pm. Tram: 13, 14, 17, or 20 to Westermarkt. PANCAKES.

This two-story canal-house restaurant serves almost nothing but pancakes—an appro-priate choice for any meal. The satisfyingly large pancakes come adorned with all sorts of toppings, both sweet and spicy, including Cajun chicken (on the spicy end of the taste spectrum), ice cream and liqueur (on the sweet end), and curried turkey with pineapple and raisins (for a little bit of both). The decor is simple, with winding stair-cases and exposed beams contributing to the pleasant ambience, and the windows pro-vide a pretty view over the Prinsengracht. In the summertime you can dine outside at long wooden tables, but beware: All the syrup, honey, and sugar being passed around tends to attract bees and hornets. Nonetheless, the Pancake Bakery remains a firm local favorite, especially among children.

✪ **Traîterie Grekas.** Singel 311 (near Spui). ☎ **020/620-3590.** Main courses Dfl 15–21 ($6.40–$8.95). No credit cards. Tues–Fri and Sun 4–9:30pm, Sat 1–9:30pm. Tram: 1, 2, or 5 to Spui. GREEK.

With a maximum of seven tables and room for only 14 diners, Grekas would be more of a frustration than anything else, except that its main business is its takeout service.

🚸 Family-Friendly Restaurants

New York Pizza *(see page 120)*   When your kids are longing for that all-American Italian food, head to New York Pizza, Damrak 59 (☎ **020/639-0494**), Amsterdam's answer to Pizza Hut. You can order three different kinds of pizza—traditional, deep pan, or whole meal.

Pancake Bakery *(see page 106)*   I have yet to meet a kid who doesn't love pancakes, and this restaurant at Prinsengracht 191 (☎ **020/625-1333**) is *the* best pancake source in town. Pancakes come with various inventive toppings (sweet and savory). Suitably colorful ornaments such as umbrellas and clowns accompany child-oriented meals and desserts. Toys, children's chairs, and special menus complete the picture. There are also pancakes big enough to satisfy the most adult of tastes.

De Orient   Kids will have fun sampling the different Indonesian foods of the rijsttafels (comprising 12, 19, or 25 dishes) at De Orient, Van Baerlestraat 21 (☎ **020/673-4958**). There are a couple of dishes made especially for children who don't like spicy food.

De Rozenboom   The tiny De Rozenboom, Rozenboomsteeg 6 (☎ **020/ 622-5024**), in an alley leading to the Begijnhof, serves hearty Dutch meals and has a special children's menu. Eating here is like having dinner in a doll's house.

Enfant Terrible   This cafe at De Genestetstraat 1 (☎ **020/612-2032**) is in a quiet residential area, not far from Leidseplein. In front is a large play room. You can take a break and have a coffee on your own, or have lunch or dinner together with the children. There's even a playpen for the very young. The cafe also offers a baby-sitting service (maximum 3 hours).

✪ KinderKookKafé   Children are the chefs and waiters at this small restaurant at Oudezijds Achterburgwal 193 (☎ **020/625-3527**). With the help of some adults, they prepare dinner on Saturday and bake cookies and pies for high tea on Sunday. If your kids want to, they can join the kitchen brigade; or you can all just relax and enjoy the meal. Kids must be at least 8 years old to help with the Saturday dinner, and 5 for the Sunday bake.

If you're staying at one of the hotels in this neighborhood (particularly next door at the Estheréa, to which Grekas provides room service), this place can even become your local diner. The food is fresh and authentic, and you can choose your meal like you would in Mykonos, by pointing to the dishes you want. If there are no free tables, you can always take your choices back to your room, or eat alfresco on the canal side. Menu items are standard Greek but with a freshness and taste that are hard to beat. The moussaka and pasticcio are heavenly; the roast lamb with wine, herbs, olive oil, and bouillon is excellent; the calamari in the calamari salad seems to have come straight out of Homer's wine-dark sea; and there's a good Greek wine list, too. Take-out dishes cost a few guilders less.

6 Around Leidseplein

EXPENSIVE

✪ Café Américain.   In the American Hotel, Leidsekade 97 (at Leidseplein). ☎ **020/ 624-5322.** Main courses Dfl 35–52 ($14.90–$22.15). AE, DC, MC, V. Daily 10:30am–midnight. Tram: 1, 2, 5, 6, 7, 10, or 20 to Leidseplein. CONTINENTAL.

The Knives Are Out

In the 1960s, satirist Gerrit Komrij described the Café Américain's famously brusque waiters as "unemployed knife-throwers."

The lofty dining room here is a national monument of Dutch jugendstil. Since its opening in 1900 the place has been a hangout for Dutch and international artists, writers, dancers, and actors. Seductress/spy Mata Hari held her wedding reception here in her preespionage days. Leaded windows, newspaper-littered reading tables, bargello-patterned velvet upholstery, frosted-glass chandeliers from the 1920s, and tall carved columns are all part of the dusky sit-and-chat atmosphere. Seafood specialties include monkfish, perch, salmon, and king prawns; meat dishes include rack of Irish lamb and rosé breast of duck with creamed potatoes. Jazz lovers can stock up on good music and good food at the Sunday jazz brunch.

De Oesterbar. Leidseplein 10. ☎ **020/623-2988.** Main courses Dfl 39.50–90 ($16.80–$38.30). AE, DC, MC, V. Daily noon–1am. Tram: 1, 2, 5, 6, 7, 10, or 20 to Leidseplein. SEAFOOD.

De Oesterbar, which is more than 50 years old, is the best-known and most popular fish restaurant in Amsterdam. Its seafood is delivered fresh twice daily. The decor is a delight: all white tiles with fish tanks bubbling at your elbows on the street level, and Victorian brocades and etched glass in the more formal dining room upstairs. The menu is a directory of Dutch seafood dishes, but it also includes a few meat selections. Choices include sole Danoise with the tiny Dutch shrimp; sole Véronique with muscadet grapes; stewed eel in wine sauce; and the assorted fish plate of turbot, halibut, and fresh salmon.

't Swarte Schaep. Korte Leidsedwarsstraat 24 (at Leidseplein). ☎ **020/622-3021.** Main courses Dfl 45–55 ($19.15–$23.40); fixed-price menu Dfl 77.50 ($33). AE, DC, JCB, MC, V. Daily noon–11pm. Tram: 1, 2, 5, 6, 7, 10, or 20 to Leidseplein. DUTCH.

't Swarte Schaep is much better known by its English name, "The Black Sheep." It's in a house that dates from 1687 and still seems like an old Dutch home. You climb a steep flight of tiled steps to reach the second-floor dining room, where the oak beams and ceiling panels are dark with age. This cozy, almost crowded, place is made both fragrant and inviting by the fresh flowers that stand on every table and spill from the polished brass buckets hanging from the ceiling beams. The Black Sheep is well known for its wine list and its crêpes suzette. Menu choices might include sole meunière with asparagus or grilled salmon with fresh thyme.

MODERATE

Akbar. Korte Leidsedwarsstraat 15 (off Leidseplein). ☎ **020/624-2211.** Main courses Dfl 22–40 ($9.35–$17). Special Indian dinners Dfl 35–47.50 ($15.30–$20.20). AE, DC, MC, V. Daily 5pm–midnight. Tram: 1, 2, 5, 6, 7, 10, or 20 to Leidseplein. INDIAN.

This is the best Indian restaurant in the Leidseplein area. Akbar has shifted sideways a few doors from its previous location, but is still on the same side street off the square. It's a consistently good performer across the range of Indian cuisine—tandoori, curry, vegetarian, and seafood—without being exactly outstanding in any category. The set meals are a good value, and service is friendly and prompt. There's also a takeout service.

Alfonso's. Korte Leidsedwarsstraat 69 (off Leidseplein). ☎ **020/627-0580.** Main courses Dfl 21–33 ($8.95–$14.05); fixed-price menus Dfl 30–55 ($12.75–$23.40). AE, DC, MC, V. Daily 5–11:30pm. Tram: 1, 2, 5, 6, 7, 10, or 20 to Leidseplein. MEXICAN.

If you suddenly get a craving for Mexican food while you're in Amsterdam, you won't have to go far to find Alfonso's. The large dining room is decorated in Mexican style, with sombreros, clay pottery, and cacti. Alfonso's offers enchiladas con queso, burritos, tacos, and other traditional favorites. You can order margaritas by the pitcher.

Aphrodite. Lange Leidsedwarsstraat 91 (off Leidseplein). ☎ **020/622-7382.** Main courses Dfl 15–25 ($6.40–$10.65). No credit cards. Daily 5pm–midnight. Tram: 1, 2, 5, 6, 7, 10, or 20 to Leidseplein. GREEK.

In an area awash with Greek restaurants that wear their Greekness on their sleeves (who doesn't like a touch of island-taverna charm?), Aphrodite stands out for putting more emphasis on taste and less on dazzling Aegean colors, fishing nets, and the lords and ladies of Olympus. Its single room is modern, restrained in its decor, and softly lit. The specialties—afelia (cubes of lamb meat in a coriander-and-wine sauce), moussaka, kleftiko (oven-baked lamb), and others—are not much different in principle from those of other Greek restaurants in the area, but are generally better prepared and served—which, after all, is difference enough.

Bistro La Forge. Korte Leidsedwarsstraat 26 (off Leidseplein, next to the Black Sheep). ☎ **020/624-0095.** Main courses Dfl 22.50–39.50 ($9.55–$16.80); fixed-price menu Dfl 45 ($19.15). AE, DC, MC, V. Daily noon–2pm lunch (pancakes only), 5–11pm dinner. Tram: 1, 2, 5, 6, 7, 10, or 20 to Leidseplein. BISTRO.

Bistro La Forge serves a fairly traditional French/continental menu of meats and fish at moderate prices. The big attraction here is the open fireplace. Starters include escargots or frog's legs. The à la carte menu has a variety of fish dishes, including salmon in puff pastry, and such meat dishes as fillet of rabbit or fillet of beef with sweet-pepper sauce. The dessert menu includes a cheese plate, sorbet, crepes, and cherries flambé served with vanilla ice cream. There's an extensive wine list.

De Balie. Kleine Gartmanplantsoen 10 (off Leidseplein). ☎ **020/553-5131.** Main courses Dfl 20–30 ($8.50–$12.75); fixed-price menus Dfl 36–48 ($15.30–$20.45). No credit cards. Cafe, daily 11:30am–10pm; restaurant, daily 6–10pm. Tram: 1, 2, 5, 6, 7, 10, or 20 to Leidseplein. GRAND CAFE/CONTINENTAL.

This chic theater cafe-restaurant, practically on the Leidesplein, serves great snacks on the ground floor and fine meals upstairs. The cafe part offers an inexpensive lunch 11:30am to 5pm and snacks 5 to 10pm. De Balie is well placed for a dinner before or after a visit to its own theater, one of the multiscreen cinemas around Leidseplein, or the Stadsschouwburg.

De Blauwe Hollander. Leidsekruisstraat 28 (off Leidseplein). ☎ **020/623-3014.** Main courses Dfl 15–30 ($6.40–$12.75); budget plate Dfl 18 ($7.65). No credit cards. Daily 5–10pm. Tram: 1, 2, 5, 6, 7, 10, or 20 to Leidseplein. DUTCH.

If you'd like a taste of sociable Dutch life, sitting shoulder to shoulder with the natives, the handful of big communal tables at this restaurant should fit the bill perfectly. De Blauwe Hollander can be considered either a best buy as a moderate restaurant or a step-up alternative in the budget category. From a small sidewalk gallery you have a good view of the passing parade in this busy area of town, but the menu has very little that's more imaginative than roast beef, spareribs, and chicken. Everything is served with fries and a salad or vegetable.

De Boemerang. Weteringschans 171 (near the Rijksmuseum). ☎ **020/623-4251.** Main courses Dfl 17.50–40 ($7.45–$17). AE, DC, MC, V. Mon–Tues and Thurs–Fri noon–11pm, Sat–Sun 4–11pm. Tram: 6, 7, or 10 to Weteringschans. DUTCH.

This restaurant, which opened in 1915, is the place to go for mussels. The original owner named it Boemerang because he hoped his customers would return—and that they have. The decor is old and eclectic and includes hundreds of pieces of paper currency hanging from the ceiling, a jukebox with 40-year-old golden oldies, and old copper kettles and pans. But it's not the atmosphere that attracts customers—it's the most succulent mussels (from Zeeland) you've ever tasted, served in large pots with a variety of dipping sauces, in such huge quantities that they're almost impossible to finish. People also come here for the juicy steaks served with fries.

Manchurian. Leidseplein 10a. ☎ **020/623-1330.** Main courses Dfl 32.50–42.50 ($13.85–$18.10); rijsttafel Dfl 42.50–79 ($18.10–$33.60). AE, DC, MC, V. Daily noon–2:45pm and 5–10:45pm. Tram: 1, 2, 5, 6, 7, 10, or 20 to Leidseplein. ASIAN.

Apart from the lucky color red, the decor is minimal at this trilevel restaurant. The cuisine ranges from Cantonese, Szechuan, Beijing, and Shanghai to Thai dishes and Indonesian rijsttafels—and the Manchurian actually does a fair job of juggling these diverse types. The house specialty is crispy duck with pancakes, but also try scallion lobster or Siam prawns, Szechuan beef, or any of the sweet-and-sour dishes.

INEXPENSIVE

Sherpa. Korte Leidsedwarsstraat 58 (off Leidseplein). ☎ **020/623-9495.** Fixed-price menus Dfl 15.50–27.50 ($6.60–$11.70). AE, DC, MC, V. Daily 5–11pm. Tram: 1, 2, 5, 6, 7, 10, or 20 to Leidseplein. NEPALESE/TIBETAN.

Sherpa may be a little short on the mystical tranquillity that characterizes its Himalayan homeland, but that's to be expected—it's hard for tranquillity to survive in this brash restaurants-and-bars district. Anyway, Sherpa adds a bit of culinary diversity to the area and its prices are reasonable. What's more, it's the only restaurant of its kind in Holland. You can eat "Yeti's food" (fried noodles with fried chicken and sautéed vegetables), or sample various other traditional Nepalese and Tibetan favorites.

7 Around Rembrandtplein

MODERATE

Brasserie Schiller. In the Hotel Schiller, Rembrandtplein 26–36. ☎ **020/554-0700.** Main courses Dfl 29.50–35 ($12.55–$14.90); fixed-price menu Dfl 49.50 ($21.05). AE, DC, MC, V. Daily 7am–11pm. Tram: 4, 9, 14, or 20 to Rembrandtplein. CLASSICAL FRENCH/DUTCH.

Beamed and paneled in well-aged oak and graced with etched-glass panels and stained-glass skylights, this 100-plus-year-old jugendstil landmark (not to be mistaken for the equally notable Café Schiller next door) is a splendid sight. Paintings by the artist who built the hotel, Frits Schiller, adorn the walls. Former chefs supplied the restaurant with the exact recipes and techniques used in the old days. On the classic menu you find everything from stewed eel and potato-and-cabbage casserole to T-bone steak, roast leg of lamb with mint sauce, and spaghetti bolognese.

Grand Café l'Opéra. Rembrandtplein 27–29. ☎ **020/620-4754.** Lunch Dfl 11.50–19.50 ($4.90–$8.30); main courses Dfl 24.50–34.50 ($10.45–$14.70). AE, DC, JCB, MC, V. Sun–Thurs 10am–1am, Fri–Sat 10am–2am. Tram: 4, 9, 14, or 20 to Rembrandtplein. GRAND CAFE.

The main advantage of l'Opéra is that beyond its beautiful jugendstil facade it has probably the best and most restrained terrace in Rembrandtplein, though others are more centrally located on the square. On busy days in good weather, the art deco interior is a cool and quiet brasserie-style retreat, but of course on such days no one wants to go inside. The food in this cafe-restaurant is fine, if nothing to write home about. The menu items include such standards as salads, steak and mushrooms, croquettes, and mussels, and even Thai chicken curry for variation. Service, though friendly, is at times a little erratic.

Memories of India. Reguliersdwarsstraat 88. ☎ **020/623-5710.** Main courses Dfl 28.50–38 ($12.15–$16.15); fixed-price menus Dfl 30–42.25 ($12.75–$18). AE, DC, MC, V. Daily 5–11:30pm. Tram: 4, 9, 14, or 20 to Rembrandtplein. INDIAN.

The owner earned his spurs in the crowded London market for Indian cuisine and then brought his award-winning formula to Amsterdam. That formula is simple, really: Serve top-flight Indian cuisine in a setting that gives traditional Indian motifs a modern slant, charge moderate prices, and employ an attentive staff. Memories has won plenty of friends since it opened its doors a few years ago. The restaurant somehow manages to combine the hallowed silence of diners intent on their plates with a buzz of friendly conversation. Takeout service is available.

✪ **Royal Café de Kroon.** Rembrandtplein 17. ☎ **020/625-2011.** Snacks Dfl 7.50–22.50 ($3.20–$9.55); fixed-price menu Dfl 60 ($25.55). AE, MC, V. Sun–Thurs 10am–1am, Fri–Sat 10am–2am. Tram: 4, 9, 14, or 20 to Rembrandtplein. GRAND CAFE.

The "Royal Café" tag may be a tad overdone, but de Kroon comes close to justifying it. Along with the Café Schiller opposite, it has gone a long way toward raising the often tacky standards of Rembrandtplein. A fanciful mix of Louis XVI–style and tropical decor makes an eclectic but restful setting for the palm court orchestra that plays here on Sunday. De Kroon also has a superb enclosed balcony overlooking the bustling square. The diverse, international menu choices range from snacks to three-course meals.

INEXPENSIVE

Falafel Koning. Reguliersteeg 2 (off Reguliersstraat, down a small alley directly across from the Tuschinski Cinema). No phone. Snacks Dfl 6–10 ($2.55–$4.25). Daily 10am–1am. Tram: 4, 9, 14, or 20 to Rembrandtplein. ISRAELI.

This tiny gem of a restaurant really needs a category all to itself: "Almost Cost-Free" comes to mind. The specialty of the house will set you back a mere Dfl 6 ($2.55). It's falafel, but don't laugh—it's probably the best falafel this side of the River Jordan: mashed chick peas mixed with herbs, rolled in a ball along with what must be some magic ingredient, fried, and served in pita bread with salad. The snack bar is capable of seating about eight people at a push, plus more at a few tables outside when the sun shines, and is tastefully decorated with an Israeli billboard and a poster for an exhibition on Hebraic script in Zurich that probably happened about 20 years ago.

8 In the Jordaan

EXPENSIVE

Bordewijk. Noordermarkt 7 (at Prinsengracht). ☎ **020/624-3899.** Main courses Dfl 42.50–47.50 ($18.10–$20.20); fixed-price menu 63.50–84.50 Dfl ($27.50–$37). AE, MC, V. Tues–Sun 6:30–10pm. Bus: 18 or 22 to Haarlemmer Houttuinen. FRENCH.

This pleasantly located restaurant is often regarded as one of the best in the city. The decor is tasteful, with green potted plants offsetting the severity of the white walls and metallic black tables. Service is relaxed yet attentive, and on mild summer evenings you can't beat dining alfresco on the canal-side terrace. But the real treat is the food. An innovative kitchen staff uses Italian and Asian flourishes to accent French standards. The menu changes often, but might include salted rib roast with bordelaise sauce, serrano ham marinated in wine and vinegar and served with fresh pasta, pigeon cooked in the style of Bresse, or even Japanese-style raw fish. Dinner is followed by a fine selection of cheeses. The wine list is superb.

MODERATE

At Mango Bay. Westerstraat 91 (off Prinsengracht). ☎ **020/638-1039.** Reservations recommended on weekends. Main courses Dfl 23.50–28.50 ($18.10–$12.15); fixed-price menus Dfl 32.50–39.50 ($13.85–$16.80). AE, DC, MC, V. Daily 6pm–midnight. Tram: 3 or 10 to Marnixstraat. FILIPINO.

There used to be four Filipino restaurants in Amsterdam, but now only At Mango Bay remains—a clear case of survival of the fittest. This slice of the Philippines occupies the front room of a canal house in the heart of the Jordaan. Diners enjoy delicately flavored dishes amid festive and colorful surroundings, with tropical flowers and a mural depicting an island paradise. The food also evokes the south Pacific: Entrees include prawns simmered in coconut milk with hints of ginger, coriander, and lemongrass; and beef marinated in honey and soy sauce. Cocktails are equally exotic. One favorite, a dangerous but tasty mixture of mango, passion fruit, lemon juice, and brandy, is humorously titled "Imelda's Shoes Plus or Minus 3,000 Ingredients."

Cyrano. Westerstraat 200 (off Prinsengracht). ☎ **020/623-4270.** Main courses Dfl 22.50–34 ($9.55–$14.45). AE, DC, MC, V. Mon 9am–3pm, Tues–Fri 6pm–1am, Sat–Sun 6pm–3am. Tram: 3 or 10 to Marnixstraat. FRENCH.

The decor of this pastoral restaurant features wooden tables, a beamed ceiling, and whitewashed walls. Here you can get a taste of French regional dishes, such as lamb with thyme blossoms or prawns flambéed with pastis, and the ubiquitous escargots (snails). There's also a rustic bar where you can wait for an empty table, sipping kir or a Dubonnet, in a generally warmer atmosphere. Monday's unusual hours coincide with the Monday morning flea market on Noordermarkt.

Het Stuivertje. Hazenstraat 58 (off Lauriergracht). ☎ **020/623-1349.** Reservations required. Main courses Dfl 18–30 ($7.65–$12.75). AE, MC, V. Tues–Sun 5:30–11:30pm. Tram: 7, 10, or 20 to Marnixstraat. DUTCH/FRENCH.

This traditional restaurant is always crowded with people enjoying either the seasonal menu of the month or the regular menu. The latter features everything from vegetarian dishes such as broccoli soufflé to goat stew with fennel and thyme, plus more traditional items like salmon with hollandaise and breast of veal stuffed with vegetables.

Hostaria. Tweede Egelantiersdwarsstraat 9 (off Egelantiersgracht). ☎ **020/626-0028.** Main courses Dfl 29.50–34.50 ($12.55–$14.70). No credit cards. Tues–Sun 6–10:30pm. Tram: 13, 14, 17, or 20 to Westermarkt. ITALIAN.

This lively street lined with cafes and restaurants might remind you of Italy. On long summer evenings, even the ubiquitous Amsterdam cyclists have trouble picking their way through the many pedestrians out for a stroll. The Hostaria adds a little piece of authentic Italy to the scene, serving delicate homemade pasta and *secondi piatti* such as veal stuffed with Italian sausage, or duck cooked Roman style.

Rakang Thai. Elandsgracht 29–31 (off Prinsengracht). ☎ **020/620-9551.** Main courses Dfl 25.50–38.50 ($10.85–$16.40); fixed-price menus Dfl 52.50–75.50 ($22.35–$32.10). AE, DC, MC, V. Daily 6pm–midnight. Tram: 7, 10, 17, or 20 to Marnixstraat. THAI.

A meal in this restaurant is a delight to all the senses. The dishes, many of them authentic regional specialties, are prepared with Thai spices, blending fierce chile peppers with more delicate flavors like ginger, coriander, and Thai basil. Bowls of delicately perfumed pandang rice accompany meals. Printed fabrics are draped along the walls and chairs are swathed in soft cottons.

✪ **Spanjer & Van Twist.** Leliegracht 60 (off Keizersgracht). ☎ **020/639-0109.** Reservations not accepted. Main courses Dfl 22.75–28.75 ($9.70–$12.25). MC, V. Daily 10am–1am (only light snacks after 11pm). Tram: 13, 14, 17, or 20 to Westermarkt. CONTINENTAL.

This place would almost be worth the visit for its name alone, so it's doubly gratifying that the food is good, too. The interior is typical *eetcafé* style, with the day's specials chalked on a blackboard, a long table with newspapers at the front, and the kitchen visible in back. High standards of cooking, however, put this place above others of the kind. The eclectic menu changes seasonally, but to give an idea of its range, I've come fork-to-face in the past with Thai fish curry and *pandan* rice; *saltimbocca* of trout in white-wine sauce; and artichoke mousseline with tarragon sauce and green asparagus. In fine weather, you can eat on an outdoors terrace beside the tranquil Leliegracht canal.

Speciaal. Nieuwe Leliestraat 140–142 (off Prinsengracht). ☎ **020/624-9706.** Main courses Dfl 21.50–27.50 ($9.15–$11.70); rijsttafel Dfl 60 ($25.55). AE, MC, V. Daily 5:30–11pm. Tram: 13, 14, 17, or 20 to Westermarkt. INDONESIAN.

Special is the perfect word to describe Speciaal if you're a devoted fan of Amsterdam's finest rijsttafel restaurants. This cozy little place is owned and operated by a young Indonesian. Its walls are adorned with the mats that traditionally covered the spice crates that were sent to Speciaal from the East Indies. Equally true to the traditions of those islands is the cooking. The saté, or kabobs, of goat meat are charcoal roasted to perfection. The specialty of the house is the multilayered Indonesian cake called spekkoek.

Toscanini. Lindengracht 75 (off Brouwersgracht). ☎ **020/623-2813.** Reservations required. Main courses Dfl 24–27 ($10.20–$11.50). AE, DC, MC, V. Daily 6–10:30pm. Tram: 3 or 10 to Marnixplein. SOUTH ITALIAN.

This small Jordaan restaurant has a warm and welcoming ambience and excellent southern Italian food. It's popular with the artists and bohemians who inhabit this neighborhood. Toscanini has the type of unembellished country-style decor that speaks of authenticity, as does the fresh homemade food. Service is congenial but can be slow, though that doesn't seem to deter the loyal regulars, who clamor for such specialties as the delicious veal lasagna and fazzoletti, green pasta stuffed with ricotta, mozzarella, and mortadella.

INEXPENSIVE

Duende. Lindengracht 62 (off Prinsengracht). ☎ **020/420-6692.** Tapas dishes Dfl 3.50–9.50 ($1.50–$4.05). No credit cards. Daily 5pm–1am. Bus: 18 or 20 to Haarlemmerstraat. SPANISH TAPAS BAR.

Dark, smoky, atmospheric, friendly—there's no better place than Duende to experience the varied palette of little dishes that are Spanish *tapas.* Take just one or two and you have a nice accompaniment to a few drinks; put five, six, or more together and you have a full-scale meal on your hands. You can pick from dozens of choices, including *tortilla Española, champiñones al ajillo* (garlic mushrooms), and *calabacín a la marmera* (eggplant with seafood). Accompany them with sangria, jump into the arena of friendly conversation, and you'll be clapping your hands and stamping your feet before long. But bear in mind that though the tapas dishes are cheap individually, their cost soon adds up.

9 Around Museumplein & Vondelpark

EXPENSIVE

✪ **Bodega Keyzer.** Van Baerlestraat 96 (beside the Concertgebouw). ☎ **020/671-1441.** Main courses Dfl 39.50–67.50 ($16.80–$28.70); fixed-price menu Dfl 65 ($27.65). AE, DC, MC, V. Mon–Sat 9am–midnight, Sun 11am–midnight. Tram: 2 to Willemsparkweg; 3, 5, 12, or 20 to Van Baerlestraat; 16 to De Lairessestraat. CONTINENTAL.

Museumplein Area & Amsterdam South Dining

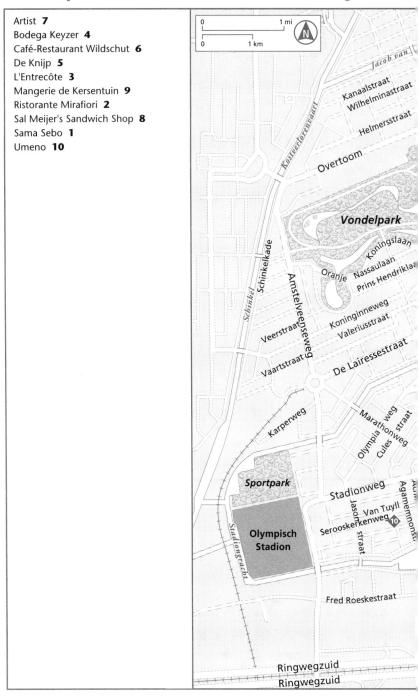

Helmersstraat
Overtoom
Vondelstr.

1e Constantijn Huygensstraat

Stadhouderskade

Singelgracht

Van nnepkanaal

Vondelpark

P. C. Hooftstraat **2** **1**

3

Jan Luykenstraat
Paulus Potterstraat

Museumstraat

Horststraat

Hobbemakade

Van Eeghenstraat
Willemsparkweg
Van Breestraat
Valeriusstraat
Johannes Verhulststraat

Jacob Obrechtstraat

Museumplein

Museumplein

4

Vermeerstraat

Pieter de Hoochstraat

Halsstraat
Quellijnstraat
Daniel Stalpertstraat

Frans

De Lairessestraat

Emmastraat

Van Baerlestraat

Nicolaas Maesstraat

5

Frans van Mierisstraat

Ruysdael straat

straat

6

Ruysdaelkade

Boerenwetering

Govert Flinckstraat
1e Jan Steenstraat

7

Ceintuurbaan
Van Ostadestraat
Rustenburgerstraat

an van Goyenkade

Reijner Vinkeleskade

Noorder Amstel Kanaal

Hobbemakade

Ferdinand Bolstraat

Apollolaan
Titiaanstraat

Jan van Eijckstraa

Apollolaan

Jozef Israelskade
Amstel Kanaal
Amstelkade

Olympiaplein
Sportpark
Olympiaplein
plein

Gerrit v. d. Veenstraat

9

Michelangelostraat

Minervalaan

Ruebensstraat

Beethovenstraat

Schubert straat

Richard Wagnerstraat

Stadionweg

Diepenbrockstraat

Heijermansweg

Overtoom

Haringvlietstraat

Herman

Churchilllaan
Deurloostraat

Scheldestraat

8

Stadionweg

Watteaustr

Parnassus

weg

Stadionkade

Zuider Amstel Kanaal

Minervalaan

Beatrixpark

Prinses Irenestraat

Ringwegzuid
Ringwegzuid

| Railroad ┼┼┼┼┼ |

Whether or not you attend a concert at the Concertgebouw, you may want to visit its next-door neighbor, Bodega Keyzer. An Amsterdam landmark since 1903—old-timers say it hasn't changed a whit through the years—the Keyzer has enjoyed a colorful joint heritage with the world-famous concert hall. Among the many stories still told here is the one about the night a customer mistook a concert soloist for a waiter and tried to order some whisky from him. The musician, not missing a beat, lifted his violin case and said graciously, "Would a little Paganini do?" The traditional dark-and-dusky decor and highly starched pink linens add elegance to the place. The menu leans heavily to fish from Dutch waters and, in season, to game specialties, such as hare and venison.

Ristorante Mirafiori. Hobbemastraat 2 (between Leidseplein and the Rijksmuseum). ☎ **020/662-3013.** Main courses Dfl 22–36 ($9.35–$15.30); fixed-price menu Dfl 90 ($38.30). AE, DC, MC, V. Wed–Mon noon–3pm and 5–11pm. Tram: 2, 5, or 20 to Hobbemastraat. ITALIAN.

This typical Italian restaurant has welcomed many famous guests to its three intimate dining rooms—the late Sammy Davis Jr., Liza Minnelli, and Eddie Murphy, to name just a few. Soups and 13 pasta dishes are on the menu, which also features *cotoletta alla milanese* (breaded veal cutlets Milanese style), *osso bucco* (beef-on-the-marrowbone), and *pollo cacciatora* (chicken in tomato sauce). For dessert, try the luscious zabaglione or the *banana al fiamma*.

MODERATE

Café-Restaurant Wildschut. Roelof Hartplein 1–3 (off Van Baerlestraat). ☎ **020/676-8220.** Main courses Dfl 16–27.50 ($6.80–$11.70); fixed-price menu Dfl 50 ($21.30). MC, V. Mon–Thurs 9am–1am, Fri 9am–3am, Sat 10:30am–3am, Sun 9:30am–midnight. Tram: 3, 12, 20, or 24 to Roelof Hartstraat; 5 to Joh. M. Coenenstraat. GRAND CAFE.

Wildschut is one of those places that keeps its chic reputation through thick and thin. It occupies a curved dining room at the junction of Van Baerlestraat and Roelof Hartstraat. Amsterdam's bold and beautiful like to see and be seen on the fine terrace in summer or amid the smoke in the brasserie-style interior in winter. It gets crowded here on Friday and Saturday evenings, so be prepared to join the standing throng while waiting for a table. The food is straightforward but good, ranging from BLTs, to vegetarian lasagna, to American rib-eye with green pepper sauce. If at all possible, try to wear something that gets you noticed—but not too much, if you get the idea.

✪ **De Knijp.** Van Baerlestraat 134 (near the Concertgebouw). ☎ **020/671-4248.** Reservations required for lunch and for more than 5 people. Main courses Dfl 29.50–39.50 ($12.55–$16.80); fixed-price menus Dfl 47.50–67.50 ($20.20–$28.70). AE, DC, MC, V. Mon–Fri noon–3pm; daily 5:30pm–1:30am. Tram: 3, 5, 12, 20, or 24 to Van Baerlestraat; 16 to De Lairessestraat. DUTCH/FRENCH.

One of the advantages of this fine restaurant is that it's open late—its kitchen is still taking orders when chefs at many other Amsterdam restaurants are sound asleep back home. This would not count for much, of course, if the food weren't good, but De Knijp is definitely worth staying up late for, or worth stopping by for after a performance at the nearby Concertgebouw. The menu is not wildly inventive, but you might try such specialties as carpaccio with pesto, poached salmon with tarragon sauce, and goose breast with pink pepper sauce. Look also for friendly, if sometimes a little worn-out, service (this is a hardworking place), and an intimate bistro ambience, with lots of wood and tables on two levels.

L'Entrecôte. P. C. Hooftstraat 70 (near the Rijksmuseum). ☎ **020/673-7776.** Main courses Dfl 35–50 ($14.90–$21.30). AE, DC, MC, V. Mon–Sat 5:30–11pm. Tram: 3, 12, or 20 to Van Baerlestraat; 2 or 5 to Paulus Potterstraat. FRENCH/AMERICAN.

This small, art deco–style, bilevel restaurant is famous for its sirloin steak dinners. Beef and veal steaks served with french fries and a salad are favorite choices, too. The upholstered chairs are comfortable, and some of the decor is quite dramatic. Service is swift, making this an ideal pre-Concertgebouw concert dining spot.

Sama Sebo. P. C. Hooftstraat 27 (at Hobbemastraat, near the Rijksmuseum). ☎ **020/ 662-8146.** Main courses Dfl 27.50–28.50 ($11.70–$12.15); rijsttafel Dfl 50 ($21.30). AE, DC, MC, V. Mon–Sat noon–2pm and 6–10pm. Tram: 3, 12, or 20 to Van Baerlestraat; 2 or 5 to Paulus Potterstraat. INDONESIAN.

Many Amsterdammers consider Sama Sebo the best Indonesian restaurant in town. Here a 17-dish rijsttafel is served in a small but very Indonesian environment of rush mats and batik. You can also put together your own selection of dishes—prices range from Dfl 3.50 to Dfl 12.50 ($1.50 to $5.30)—to make your own minirijsttafel.

✪ **Vertigo.** Vondelpark 3 (at the Film Museum). **020/612-3021.** Reservations recommended on weekends. Main courses Dfl 28.50–41 ($12.15–$17.45). AE, MC, V. Daily 10am–1am. Tram: 1 or 6 to 1e Constantijn Huygensstraat; 2, 3, 5, 12, or 20 to Van Baerlestraat. MEDITERRANEAN.

If the name of this animated cafe/restaurant suggests a high location, the reality is far less giddy—in terms of altitude, at least. The reference is to Hitchcock's classic movie. In the vaulted basement of a monumental, late 19th-century villa, Vertigo shares premises with the Film Museum. Hence the portraits of screen legends on the walls and the classic scenes of movie dining on the menu. On summer days, the outside terrace on the edge of Vondelpark is a favored time-out spot for in-line skaters and joggers, and on hot days a restricted menu is served here; you can expect to share your table and make instant acquaintance of just about everyone within earshot. At other times, you can enjoy the southern-European–inspired cuisine in an intimate, candle-lit setting inside. The menu, which changes every 6 to 8 weeks, has a choice of fish, meat, and vegetarian options, plus some fresh pasta varieties. If you see grilled breast of guinea fowl on the menu again, my advice is to go for it!

10 In Amsterdam South

EXPENSIVE

✪ **Mangerie de Kersentuin.** In the Garden Hotel, Dijsselhofplantsoen 7 (off Apollolaan). ☎ **020/664-2121.** Reservations recommended on weekends. Main courses Dfl 42.50–49 ($18.10–$20.85); fixed-price menus Dfl 52.50–72.50 ($22.35–$30.85). AE, DC, MC, V. Mon–Fri noon–2pm; Mon–Sat 6–11pm. Tram: 16 to De Lairessestraat. INTERNATIONAL.

All cherry red and gleaming brass, the spectacular de Kersentuin ("Cherry Orchard") has floor-to-ceiling windows looking onto the residential street outside and partly screened interior windows looking into the glimmering kitchen inside. Attention to detail has made this restaurant a mecca for visiting stars. You eat with Christofle silver-plate flatware and drink wine or champagne that was personally selected by the restaurateur and his chef. From nouvelle cuisine and a strictly French approach to cooking, this place has progressed to its own unique culinary concept, based on regional recipes from around the world, and using fresh ingredients from Dutch waters and farmlands. The menu changes every 2 months, but these samples give some idea of what to expect: lamb filet prepared in goose fat with creamy salsifies, and coriander-scented vanilla sauce; sea bass sautéed with peppers, garlic, sea salt, and sesame seeds, served on stir-fried bok choy and tofu, with lemongrass butter.

MODERATE

Umeno. Agamemnonstraat 27 (off Olympiaplein). ☎ **020/676-6089.** Main courses Dfl 29.50–49.50 ($12.55–$21.05). No credit cards. Tues–Sun noon–2pm and 6pm–midnight. Tram: 24 to Olympiaplein. JAPANESE.

This intimate eatery, somewhat off the beaten track near the Olympic Stadium, is popular with local Japanese residents—you get only chopsticks to eat with. Both the food and the service make the tram ride out here worthwhile. Decor is traditional and delicate, with rice paper–covered windows, and the menu comes in a wooden box. It's generally no problem to find a seat, but as the restaurant seats only 32, it makes sense to call ahead. The sushi and sashimi are always fresh and their quality is high. Other traditional dishes include shabu-shabu, sukiyaki, yakitori, and tonkatsu.

INEXPENSIVE

Artist. Tweede Jan Steenstraat 1 (off Van Woustraat). ☎ **020/671-4264.** Main courses Dfl 9–19 ($3.85–$8.10); fixed-price menu (meze) Dfl 20 ($8.50). AE, DC, MC, V. Daily 5–11pm. Tram: 4 to Van Woustraat. LEBANESE.

Owners Ralfo and Simon have brought a little piece of the eastern Mediterranean to Amsterdam South and presented it in a simple, authentic way at low cost with good taste guaranteed. Members of the city's Lebanese community are often seated at the tables here—always a good sign for an ethnic restaurant. Specialties include Lebanese meze and a selection of small dishes that adds up to a big meal, including falafel, couscous, and even Lebanese pizza. Many of the dishes here are vegetarian.

11 Specialty Dining

LOCAL FAVORITES

To eat a *broodje* (sandwich) in a real *broodjeswinkel* (sandwich shop), go to the ever-crowded **Eetsalon Van Dobben,** Korte Reguliersdwarsstraat 5–9 (☎ **020/624-4200**), off Rembrandtplein; or **Broodje van Kootje,** Leidseplein 20 (☎ **020/623-2036**) and Spui 28 (☎ **020/623-7451**), easily identified by their bright-yellow broodje-shaped signs.

  If the shortage of good pastrami on rye in Amsterdam starts to get to you, take the no. 25 tram out to ✪ **Sal Meijer,** Scheldestraat 45 (☎ **020/673-1313**), off Churchilllaan, a kosher sandwich shop, where members of the city's Jewish community gather each day. Both the sandwiches and the conversation are excellent. Sal also delivers, depending on where you are and how many sandwiches you want.

LIGHT, CASUAL & FAST FOOD

Croissanteries have popped up all over town to offer the Dutch an alternative to their traditional broodje. For a quick breakfast of croissant, coffee or tea, and orange juice, try **Délifrance,** Damrak 83 (☎ **020/622-2884**).

  Lovers of fresh-baked goodies will appreciate **Paul Kaiser,** Wijde Heisteeg 3–5 (☎ **020/638-6595**), between Singel and Herengracht, a bakery/coffee shop where

---

Student Tips

Since part of the main university has moved outside the city of Amsterdam, it's no longer really a convenient resource for students in the city. Students tend to congregate in the cafeteria-style **Atrium** restaurant, at Grimburgwal 237 (☎ **020/525-3999**), open daily noon to 7pm; and nearby at the cafe **'t Gasthuys,** Grimburgwal 7 (☎ **020/624-8230**), which serves good, inexpensive food.

You Paid What?

47,000 hotels, 700 airlines, 50 rental car companies. And a few million ways to save money.

Travelocity.com
A Sabre Company

Go Virtually Anywhere.

Will you have enough stories to tell your grandchildren

Yahoo! Travel

your roll comes fresh from the oven. It has a tearoom annex (entrance at Singel 385), that serves delicious fruit pies and cakes.

If you thought Amsterdam was a bagel-free zone, think again. Some of the best bagels come from the **Gary's Muffins** chain. You can have plain, sesame, whole wheat, poppy, pumpernickel, cinnamon raisin, onion, and garlic bagels. The 20 different kinds of toppings include pesto cream cheese and tomato, and goat cheese, honey, and walnuts; the bagels range in price from Dfl 2.50 to Dfl 7.50 ($1.05 to $3.20). Gary's also does a takeout service. There are four Gary's Muffins: Prinsengracht 454 (☎ 020/420-1452); Marnixstraat 121 (☎ 020/638-0186); Jodenbreestraat 15 (☎ 020/421-5930); and Reguliersdwarsstraat 53 (☎ 020/420-2406). The first three are open daily 8:30 to 6 or 7pm; the fourth is open daily noon to 3 or 4am.

CAFES, TEAHOUSES & COFFEE HOUSES

There are two sorts of cafes in Amsterdam: the museum or department-store lunch-room type and the Parisian people-watching type (the city's brown cafes are more like bars or pubs than cafes in the French or American sense). In the first category, four of the best are **La Ruche,** in De Bijenkorf department store, Dam 1 (☎ 020/621-8080), a Rietveld-style cafeteria/restaurant on the second floor with a view of the Dam from its big windows; or try the same store's more intimate **Literair Café** on the fourth floor, beside the book department, where you can have sushi, sandwiches, and light snacks. **Metz,** in Metz & Co department store, Leidsestraat 34–36 (☎ 020/520-7020), at the corner of Keizersgracht, is a rooftop glass cupola cafe by Gerrit Rietveld that offers a spectacular panorama across the rooftops of Amsterdam; people drop in often for tea, which is served all day and consists of a pot of tea and a choice of cakes and sandwiches. Various one-plate meals, such as grilled chicken and vegetable stew, are also available.

The chic **David & Goliath,** in Amsterdams Historisch Museum, Kalverstraat 92 (☎ 020/623-6736), has a high-beamed ceiling and lofty wooden statues of David and Goliath, salvaged from an amusement park that was a feature of Amsterdam's landscape for nearly 250 years (1625–1862). Another good stopping place in the Center is **Espresso Corner Baton,** Herengracht 82 (☎ 020/624-8195), at Herenstraat, which seats 100 people and serves salads, quiches, a choice of 30 hot or cold sandwiches, plus pastries and desserts such as tiramisu. Near the Town Hall–Muziektheater complex, **Puccini,** Staalstraat 17 (☎ 020/427-8341), is renowned for its coffee and homemade fruit tarts, cakes, and pastries.

Among cafes and tearooms convenient for shoppers is the **Berkhoff Tearoom,** Leidsestraat 46 (☎ 020/624-0233). Outside Centraal Station, overlooking the inner harbor, **Smits Coffee House NZH,** Stationsplein 10 (☎ 020/623-3777), has a pleasant waterside terrace in the summer, from where you can watch the canal boats float by. **Greenwood's,** Singel 103 (☎ 020/623-7071), brings English ambience to its tea, homemade scones with jam and clotted cream, and lemon meringue pie.

For an overview of Amsterdam's "smoking coffeeshops," which sell marijuana and hashish, see chapter 9.

FAST FOOD

No matter how determined we may be to eat well or eat native whenever we travel, a glimpse of the Golden Arches can occasionally be a welcome sight. For fast food in Amsterdam, you find **McDonald's** at, among other places, Muntplein 9 (☎ 020/622-4087), Leidsestraat 95–97 (☎ 020/626-0136), Kalverstraat 45–47 (☎ 020/623-6855), and Damrak 92 (☎ 020/624-9147) and **Burger King** at Leidseplein 7 (☎ 020/622-4047), Nieuwendijk 218 (☎ 020/620-8048), and Centraal Station, Platform 2b (☎ 020/423-4888).

New York Pizza, Amsterdam's answer to Pizza Hut, is bright, clean, and decorated in Italy's national colors—red, white, and green. Branches are at Spui 2 (☎ **020/ 420-3538**); Reguliersbreestraat 15–17 (☎ **020/420-5585**); Damstraat 24 (☎ **020/ 422-2123**); and Leidsestraat 23 (☎ **020/622-8689**).

If you're a homesick Brit or just an admirer of traditional British fish-and-chips, head straight for **Al's Plaice** (get it?), Nieuwendijk 10 (☎ **020/427-4192**), where the business gets done with the requisite amounts of salt and vinegar, the pickled onions are big and juicy, and the paper wrappers all you could hope for; there's takeout service and seats for 24 inside. Al's is open Monday 5 to 10pm, and Wednesday to Sunday noon to 10pm.

Another quick-bite alternative, particularly for seriously cash-strapped budget travelers, are the branches of **Febo Automatiek** that you find all around town. They open directly on the sidewalk and look like giant streetside vending machines. Drop your guilder coins in the appropriate slots and—voilà!—you have a lunch of Indonesian *nasi* or *bami goreng,* hamburger, fries, and a milk shake—I wouldn't say the portions are small, but they do have a compact form factor.

DESSERTS

A crowded spot on Saturday morning is **Kweekboom,** Reguliersbreestraat 36 (☎ **020/623-1205**), between Muntplein and Rembrandtplein. It's a coffee shop/ candy store/pastry shop/ice-cream stand, where everything is freshly made and the management proudly displays awards won for everything from tarts, bonbons, and butter cookies to fantasy cakes (whatever they may be). You may have to push your way to the back and wait for a table.

The best ice-cream source in town (now *there's* a statement that could cause trouble) is **Gelateria Italiana Peppino,** Eerste Sweelinckstraat 16 (☎ **020/676-4910**), near the Albert Cuyp market. Run by second- and third-generation Italian immigrants, this parlor serves up almost 100 different flavors of homemade ice cream, and great cappuccino. It's only open from March to October. Also notable is **Gelateria Jordino,** Haarlemmerdijk 25 (☎ **020/420-3225**), whose 30 flavors of Italian ice cream, plus chocolate cake and desserts, ought to appeal to someone.

TAKEOUT

Sabrina and Denise at **Basilico,** Willemstraat 29a (☎ **020/627-2685**), in the Jordaan, do great homemade Italian food—but only for takeout. Main dishes run Dfl 6 to Dfl 12.50 ($2.55 to $5.30). The place is open Monday to Friday 10:30am to 8pm, Saturday 10am to 6pm. If you have a place to heat and eat an Italian meal, go for it.

BREAKFAST

Should you sleep late, keep in mind that the **Café Barbizon,** Golden Tulip Barbizon Palace Hotel, Prins Hendrikkade 59–72 (☎ **020/556-4564**), serves late breakfast from 10:30am to noon. The cost is Dfl 29.50 ($12.55) for juice, two eggs, a *broodje,* and coffee or tea.

In addition to the **Pancake Bakery** (see the main restaurant listing above), another good pancake house is **Bredero,** Oudezijds Voorburgwal 244 (☎ **020/622-9461**), on the canals east of the Dam.

Also try **Café Luxembourg** for a smart breakfast with the day's papers and **Royal Café de Kroon** on Rembrandtplein for a continental breakfast with a great view on the square (see the main restaurant listing above for both of these); and **Gary's Muffins** for a bagel (see "Light, Casual & Fast Food," above).

LATE-NIGHT EATERIES

Since the majority of restaurant kitchens in Amsterdam are closed by 10:30pm, it's good to keep these late-night addresses handy in case the munchies strike. **Bojo,** Lange Leidsedwarsstraat 51 (☎ **020/622-7434**), puts Indonesian snacks on the table from Sunday to Thursday 5pm to 2am, Friday and Saturday 5pm to 5:30am. **Saturnino,** Reguliersdwarsstraat 5 (☎ **020/639-0102**), serves great homemade pizzas and pasta until after midnight. For French specialties in the same neighborhood, **Korte,** Leidsedwarsstraat 26 (☎ **020/624-0095**), takes orders until midnight.

In addition, there's **Bistro La Forge, De Knijp,** and **Sluizer** (see the main restaurant listings above); and **Gary's Muffins,** Reguliersdwarsstraat 53 (see "Light, Casual & Fast Food," above).

6

Exploring Amsterdam

Amsterdam offers sightseers an almost bewildering embarrassment of riches. There are miles and miles of canals to cruise and hundreds of narrow streets to wander, almost 8,000 historic buildings to see in the city center, more than 40 museums of all types to visit, diamond cutters and craftspeople to watch as they practice generations-old skills—the list is as long as every tourist's individual interests, and then some.

The city has 160 canals, with a combined length of 75.5km (47 miles), spanned by 1,281 bridges. So the first thing you should do is join the 2½ million people every year who take a ride around the canals on one of the 70 canal tour-boats. Why? Because the water-level view of those gabled canal houses and the picturesque bridges lends meaning and color to everything else you do during your stay. Amsterdam's 17th-century Golden Age becomes a vivid reality as you glide through the waterways that were largely responsible for those years of prosperity. You view the canal houses from canal level, just as they were meant to be seen. This is also the best way to see Amsterdam's large and busy harbor. (See "Organized Tours," later in this chapter.)

Suggested Itineraries

If You Have 1 Day

If you have only 1 day in Amsterdam, limit yourself in what you attempt. It's better to come away with a few good memories than to run around trying for a quick glimpse of everything. That doesn't mean you can't see a lot, however. The first thing you should do is invest an hour in a canal-boat trip. Don't worry for one minute about anyone who sniffs at this idea and mutters something about canal-boat tours being tourist traps. Maybe they are, but who cares? The view of Amsterdam from the water is the best you can get, and cruising is faster and a lot easier on your feet than walking.

After the boat tour, you should grab a quick lunch. How about a *broodje* at a *broodjeswinkel,* or, if you're ready to jump in with both feet, a raw herring with onions from one of the many roadside stalls?

Next you might want to do at least part of one of the walking tours listed in chapter 7. You could start with The Golden Age Canals tour, along Prinsengracht, Herengracht, and Keizersgracht, lined by stunning canal houses topped by step, bell, and other decorative gables, and crisscrossed by smaller canals with colorful houseboats anchored along their banks. Since you will have seen some of the main canals on your boat tour, you could instead try either the Old Center tour or the Jordaan tour. When you're finished with that, head for one of the "big four" museums: Rijksmuseum, Van Gogh Museum, Stedelijk Museum, and the Anne Frankhuis. Take a tram if you're running short on time.

After the museum, it will probably be late afternoon and you'll be pretty exhausted, so I'd suggest returning to the hotel for a drink at the bar before dinner or a nap. Since you probably had a Dutch breakfast and a Dutch lunch, you might consider going for an Indonesian rijsttafel at dinner.

Afterward, if you're still up for it, you really shouldn't miss having a drink in a brown cafe—your Amsterdam experience won't be complete without it.

If You Have 2 Days

Follow the first part of the itinerary above at a more relaxed pace. Take some notes while you're on the canal-boat tour about things you'd like to see up close later. Go for a short stroll along your favorite canal before lunch. Do the whole of one of the walking tours, visiting some of the shops and bookstores that you see along the way. Save the big museums for your second day.

On the second day, you can sleep in a little because the museums don't open until later in the morning, then spend the day museum hopping. Before you leave the hotel you might want to try getting tickets to a concert, the ballet, or the opera, so you can attend a show in the evening. You should still be realistic about what's possible. Visiting one museum in the morning and one in the afternoon is enough. If you are keen to see the Anne Frankhuis, you should do that first and go early in the morning (so much for sleeping late!), because there's always a line. After lunch, maybe in a grand cafe, take a tram to your second museum choice. Pick a place for dinner; this time have a Dutch meal. Finally, go see that show.

If You Have 3 Days

Enough museums already! Today is a fresh-air day. If you want to visit the Red Light District, but not at night, morning is the best time to do it. Most of the weird folks have turned in for the day, and there's almost an air of innocence to the place, which actually occupies one of the prettiest parts of the old city.

Otherwise, I suggest you spend the day shopping, sightseeing, and gallery hopping. Walk along Kalverstraat (the more modern shopping street), then perhaps stroll along Spiegelgracht and Nieuwe Spiegelstraat (antiques). Take a walk through the Jordaan, a lively former working-class area now filled with cafes, restaurants, and interesting little boutiques. Or take the tram to Waterlooplein for the flea market, or to Albert Cuypstraat for the great street market there. It would also be a good time to go to the Looiersgracht Market on an antiques hunt. If the weather is fine, have lunch on an open-air terrace and work in some people-watching.

Later, after you've had dinner take a leisurely stroll along the canals, which are particularly beautiful at night when they're lit up. A visit to a jazz club or music bar is a good way to round off your day.

If You Have 4 Days or More

You'll notice I haven't suggested a single side trip yet, even though there's an entire chapter devoted to side trips in this book (chapter 10). That's because 3 days is barely enough to do justice to Amsterdam. With 4 or more days, though, the environs start to come within range.

On your first day of touring, I suggest you travel from Amsterdam to Haarlem, and maybe squeeze into the same day a visit to the North Sea coast at nearby Zandvoort,

> **❷ Did You Know?**
>
> - If Holland's dike defenses against the North Sea ever give way, most of Amsterdam will vanish beneath the waves.
> - About 2,400 legally occupied houseboats float on the city's canals.
> - The Royal Palace on the Dam was built on 13,659 timber piles—a figure all Dutch schoolchildren learn.
> - Rembrandt's famous painting *The Night Watch* actually shows a daytime scene. Centuries of grime dulled its luster until restoration revealed sunlight glinting on the militia company's arms and accouterments. Any votes for *The Day Watch?*
> - More than 550,000 bicycles are in use in the city and more than 150,000 of them are stolen every year.
> - Amsterdam gets a 1½ hour "enema" every day. Between 7 and 8:30pm, 600,000 cubic meters of IJsselmeer water is pumped through the canal system to keep the water from becoming stagnant.
> - Rope and pulleys are still used to get furniture into homes where the staircases are too narrow and steep.
> - Berliner Klaus-Günter Neumann wrote the classic "Dutch" song *Tulips From Amsterdam*—in German.
> - In 1997–98, a German company specializing in conserving natural stone renovated the Nationaal Monument on the Dam, which commemorates victims of Holland's occupation by Nazi Germany during World War II.
> - Before Napoléon's occupation, engraved cartouches served as numbers for address identification purposes. You can still see many of them today.

which has a beach, racetrack, and casino. On your second day, head to Hoorn on the IJsselmeer shore. If you're driving, take in Volendam and Marken along the way, and from Hoorn you can continue on to Enkhuizen and the Afsluitdijk (Enclosing Dike), before returning to Amsterdam.

With more time, you can alternate days spent in the city with visits to, for example, the Bulb Fields and Keukenhof Gardens if it's tulip time; Zaanse Schans for windmills; Leiden for the Pilgrim Fathers; Delft for Holland's royal city; The Hague for the seat of government; and Rotterdam for the world's busiest port.

1 Canal Tours

CANAL BOATS

A typical canal-boat itinerary includes Centraal Station, the Harlemmersluis floodgates (used in the nightly flushing of the canals), the Cat Boat (a houseboat with a permanent population of more than 100 wayward felines), and both the narrowest building in the city and one of the largest houses still in private hands and in use as a single-family residence. Plus, you will see the official residence of the *burgomaster* (mayor), the "Golden Bend" of the Herengracht (traditionally the best address in the city), many picturesque bridges, including the famous Magere Brug (Skinny Bridge) over the Amstel, and the harbor.

Trips last approximately an hour and leave at regular intervals from *rondvaart* (excursion) piers in key locations around town. The majority of launches are docked along Damrak and Prins Hendrikkade near Centraal Station, on Rokin near Muntplein, and at Leidseplein. Tours leave every 15 to 30 minutes during the summer season (9am to 9:30pm), every 45 minutes in winter (10am to 4pm). The average fare is Dfl 12 to Dfl 18 ($5.10 to $7.65) for adults, Dfl 10 to Dfl 12 ($4.25 to $5.10) for children ages 4 to 13.

Operators of canal-boat cruises include **Amsterdam Canal Cruises** (☎ 020/626-5636); **Holland International** (☎ 020/622-7788); **Meijers Rondvaarten** (☎ 020/623-4208); **Rederij Boekel** (☎ 020/612-9905); **Rederij Hof van Holland** (☎ 020/623-7122); **Rederij Lovers** (☎ 020/622-2181)—despite its heart-shaped logo, Lovers is not necessarily for lovers, but is named after the man who started the company; **Rederij Noord-Zuid** (☎ 020/679-1370); **Rederij P. Kooij** (☎ 020/623-3810); and **Rederij Plas** (☎ 020/624-5406). See "More Evening Entertainment" in chapter 9 for information on after-dark cruises.

SALOON BOATS

The *salonboten* (**saloon boats**) date from the early 1900s and were used by doctors, lawyers, and other professionals who needed to move around town a lot. These launches have been lovingly restored and can be booked by groups of 6 to 12 people. For further information, contact **Oudhollandsche Vervoer Maatschappij** (☎ **020/612-9888**).

Catching the Museum Boat

Ever resourceful and ever aware of the transportation resource their canals represent, Amsterdammers have introduced the **Museumboot (Museum Boat),** Stationsplein 8 (☎ **020/530-5412**), to carry weary tourists on their pilgrimages from museum to museum. It's an easy way to travel and, for those with limited time, provides some of the advantages of a canal-boat cruise. Boats depart every 30 minutes (every 45 minutes in winter) 10am to 5pm from Centraal Station (Stop 1) and stop at seven key spots around the city, providing access to museums and other sights. These are:

Stop 1   Museum Amstelkring, Madame Tussaud Scenerama.

Stop 2   Anne Frankhuis, Theatermuseum.

Stop 3   Leidseplein, Vondelpark.

Stop 4   Rijksmuseum, Van Gogh Museum, Stedelijk Museum.

Stop 5   Amsterdams Historisch Museum, Bijbels Museum, Floating Flower Market.

Stop 6   Museum Het Rembrandthuis, Jewish Historical Museum, Artis, Muziektheater, Tropenmuseum.

Stop 7   Netherlands Maritime Museum, newMetropolis.

The day ticket for the Museum Boat, which includes a discount on museum admissions of up to 50%, costs Dfl 25 ($10.65) for adults and Dfl 20 ($8.50) for children age 13 and under; after 1pm, you can buy "stop-tickets," the cost of which depends on the number of stops you plan to disembark at.

Canal Bikers Do It on the Water

A suggested tour by water-bike: Start at the Canal Bikes mooring on Prinsengracht (at Westermarkt). Pedal south along Prinsengracht, past Lauriergracht, Looiersgracht, and Passeerdersgracht, maybe diverting into one or more of these quiet side canals if you fancy. At Leidsegracht, go straight ahead under the Leidsestraat bridge until you come to Spiegelgracht, where you turn right. Continue to the end, then left under the bridge into Lijnbaansgracht.

Turn right at the first corner into a narrow connecting canal that merges with Singelgracht in front of the Rijksmuseum. Go right along this canal, which is bordered by overhanging trees and the back gardens of waterside villas. You pass the Lido Casino and its waterfront cafe terrace, then Leidseplein and the American Hotel.

Keep going, past the Bellevue Theater and De la Mar Theater, and turn right into Leidsegracht, which brings you back to Prinsengracht and the home stretch back to Westermarkt.

CANAL BIKES

If the canal-boat cruise simply whets your appetite to ramble the canals under your own steam, there are sturdy pedal boats, called canal bikes, which (by a strange coincidence) you rent from **Canal Bike,** Weteringschans 24 (☎ **020/626-5574**). Amsterdammers look down their tolerant noses at canal bikers. On the other hand, tourists love the things. No prizes for guessing who has the most fun. Canal bikes seat two or four and come with a detailed map, route suggestions, and a bit about the places you pedal past. It's great fun in sunny weather, and still doable when it rains and your boat is covered with a rain shield. You can also rent a canal bike for evening rambles, when the canals are illuminated and your bike comes with a Chinese lantern. Moorings are at Leidseplein, Prinsengracht at the Anne Frank House, Leidseplein, and on Keizersgracht at Leidsestraat. The canals can get busy with tour boats and other small craft, so watch out, particularly when going under bridges. Rental is Dfl 12.50 ($5.30) per person hourly for one or two people; Dfl 10 ($4.25) per person hourly for three or four people.

2 The Big Four Museums & Galleries

✪ **Rijksmuseum.** Stadhouderskade 42 (behind Museumplein, halfway between Leidseplein and Weteringplantsoen). ☎ **020/673-2121,** or 020/674-7047 for taped information in Dutch and English. Admission Dfl 17.50 ($7.45) adults, free for children under 18. Daily 10am–5pm. Tram: 2, 5, or 20 to Hobbemastraat; 6, 7, or 10 to Weteringschans.

The most significant and permanent outgrowth of Holland's 17th-century Golden Age was its magnificent body of art. Many of these works are now housed in the 260 rooms of the Rijksmuseum, which ranks with the Louvre, the Uffizi, and the Hermitage among major museums of European painting and decorative arts. Architect Petrus Josephus Hubertus Cuypers (1827–1921) designed the core of the present museum; his monumental neo-Gothic building opened in 1885. Since then, many additions have been made to the collections and the building so that the museum now encompasses five departments: Painting, Print Room, Sculpture and Decorative Arts, Dutch History, and Asiatic Art. The collection totals some 7 million individual objects, only a small fraction of which are displayed at any given time.

The museum was founded in 1798 as the National Art Gallery, in The Hague. The steady growth of the collection of paintings and prints necessitated several moves: In 1808 King Louis Napoléon had it moved to his Royal Palace in Amsterdam and renamed it the Royal Museum (the name Rijksmuseum—State Museum—dates from 1815). Then, in 1816 it was moved to a large patrician residence called the Trippenhuis. However, this building soon proved too small and another was sought.

The Rijksmuseum contains the world's largest collection of paintings by the Dutch masters, including the most famous of all, a single work that all but defines the Golden Age and has its own direction-indicator arrows inside the museum. Traffic on that busy route leads to a rectangular gallery containing a painting flanked by a guard, two marble Corinthian columns, and three fire extinguishers. The painting is ***The Shooting Company of Captain Frans Banning Cocq and Lieutenant Willem van Ruytenburch,*** 1642, better known as ***The Night Watch,*** by Rembrandt. The scene it so dramatically depicts is surely alien to most of the people who flock to see it: gaily uniformed militiamen checking their weapons and accouterments before moving out on patrol. Captain Cocq, Lieutenant van Ruytenburch, the troopers, and observers (including Rembrandt himself) gaze down at us through the corridor of time, and we are left to wonder what is going on underneath the paint, inside their minds. This masterpiece was restored after having been attacked and slashed in 1975.

Rembrandt, van Ruisdael, van Heemskerck, Frans Hals, Paulus Potter, Jan Steen, Vermeer, de Hooch, Terborch, and Gerard Dou are also represented in this magnificent museum, as are Fra Angelico, Tiepolo, Goya, Rubens, Van Dyck, and later Dutch artists of The Hague school and the Amsterdam impressionist movement. There are individual portraits and guild paintings, landscapes and seascapes, domestic scenes and medieval religious subjects, allegories, and the incredible (and nearly photographic) Dutch still lifes; plus prints and sculptures, furniture, a collection of 17th-century dollhouses, Asian and Islamic art, china and porcelain, trinkets and glassware, armaments and ship models, costumes, screens, badges, and laces.

To get to the heart of the Golden Age, head for Rooms 207 to 236, where you will find many works by Rembrandt, such as *The Jewish Bride* (ca. 1665) and *The Syndics* (1662), and a great many by other masters such as Gerard Dou, Jan Vermeer, Frans Hals, Jan Steen, Jacob van Ruisdael, and Willem van de Velde.

The New Wing (formerly the South Wing) houses Asiatic Art and works by the 18th-century painters of The Hague school, such as Jozef Israëls and Anton Mauve.

In Rooms 101 to 112, you find exhibits on Dutch history, including beautifully realized model ships, weaponry, paintings of sea battles, trophies of war, paintings of scenes from the Dutch colonies, and similar such items. The ARIA interactive multimedia information center helps you learn more about this enormous museum's collections. By touching a screen, you can access information, including text, illustrations, video, and animation, about more than 1,200 artworks.

You can rest weary feet at the museum's fine Café Cuijpers.

Agenda for Youth

The monthly publication ***Agenda*** lists current events and information on various services available to students. If you're interested in cultural events and are under 26, go by the **Amsterdam Uit Buro (AUB),** at Leidseplein 26 (☎ **020/621-1211**), and pick up a CJP (Cultural Youth Pass), which costs Dfl 20 ($8.50) and grants free admission to most museums and discounts on many cultural events. The AUB is open Monday to Saturday from 10am to 6pm.

The Rijksmuseum

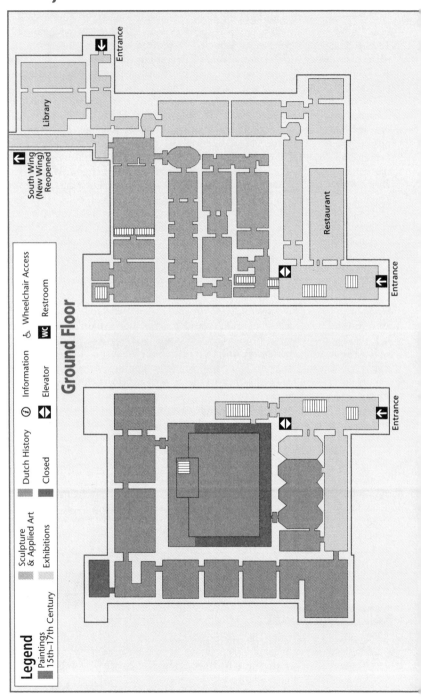

Legend

Paintings
15th–17th Century

Sculpture
& Applied Art

Exhibitions

Dutch History

Closed

Information

Elevator

Wheelchair Access

Restroom

WC

Ground Floor

Library

South Wing
(New Wing)
Reopened

Entrance

Restaurant

Entrance

Entrance

Entrance

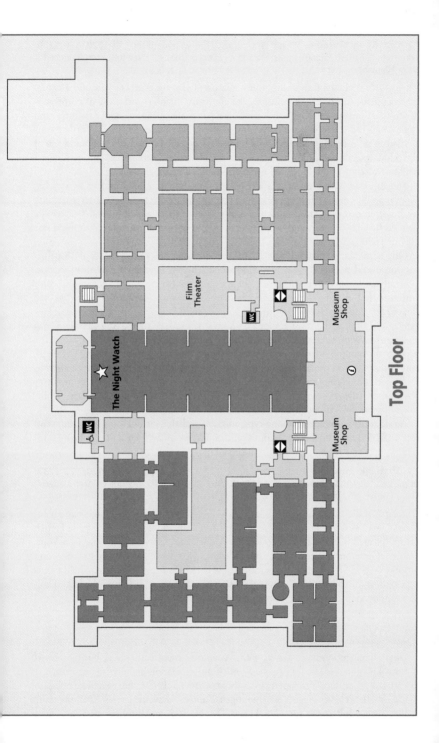

Top Floor

The Night Watch

Film Theater

Museum Shop

Museum Shop

WC

WC

✪ **Van Gogh Museum.** Paulus Potterstraat 7 (at Museumplein). ☎ **020/570-5200.** Admission Dfl 15.50 ($6.60) adults, Dfl 5 ($2.15) children 13–17, free for children under 13. Daily 10am–6pm. Tram: 2, 5, or 20 to Van Baerlestraat; 3, 5, or 12 to Museumplein.

Thanks to the chauvinism of his family—in particular, his brother's wife and a name-sake nephew—nearly every painting, sketch, print, etching, and piece of correspondence that Vincent van Gogh ever produced has remained in his native country, and since 1973 the collection has been housed in its own museum. To the further consternation of Van Gogh admirers and scholars elsewhere in the world, all but a few of the drawings and paintings that are not in the museum's keeping hang at the Kröller-Müller Museum in the Hoge Veluwe National Park near Arnhem.

You can trace this great artist's artistic and psychological development by viewing more than 200 of his paintings displayed simply and in chronological order according to the seven distinct periods and places of residence that defined his short career (he painted for only 10 years and was on the threshold of success when he committed suicide in 1890, age 37).

One particularly splendid wall, on the second floor, has a progression of 18 paintings produced during the 2-year period when Vincent lived in the south of France, generally considered to be his artistic high point. It's a symphony of colors and color contrasts that includes *Gauguin's Chair; The Yellow House; Self-Portrait with Pipe and Straw Hat; Vincent's Bedroom at Arles; Wheatfield with Reaper; Bugler of the Zouave Regiment;* and one of the most famous paintings of modern times, *Still Life Vase with Fourteen Sunflowers,* best known simply as *Sunflowers.* By the time you reach the vaguely threatening painting of a flock of black crows rising from a waving cornfield, you can almost feel the mounting inner pain that the artist was finally unable to bear.

A new wing, elliptical and partly underground, designed by Japanese architect Kisho Kurokawa, opened on Museumplein in June 1999 to house temporary exhibitions of work by Van Gogh and other artists.

Audio tours with mobile phone-type units are available for Dfl 7 ($3) for adults and Dfl 6 ($2.55) for students and groups, and children can try their hands at being budding Van Goghs in the kids' studio in the lobby.

✪ **Stedelijk Museum.** Paulus Potterstraat 13 (at Museumplein). ☎ **020/573-2737.** Admission Dfl 10 ($4.25) adults, Dfl 4.50 ($1.90) children 7–16, free for children under 7. Daily 11am–5pm. Tram: 2, 5, or 20 to Paulus Potterstraat; 3, 12, or 16 to Museumplein.

The city's modern art museum is the place to see works by such Dutch painters as Karel Appel, Willem de Kooning, and Piet Mondrian, alongside works by the French artists Chagall, Cézanne, Picasso, Renoir, Monet, and Manet and by the Americans Calder, Oldenburg, Rosenquist, and Warhol. The Stedelijk centers its collection around the De Stijl, Cobra, post-Cobra, nouveau réalisme, pop art, color-field painting, zero, minimalist, and conceptual schools of modern art. It houses the largest collection outside Russia of the abstract paintings of Kasimir Malevich.

What's in a Name?

Gogh is not pronounced *Go,* as many Americans incorrectly say it, but like *Khokh* (the "kh" sound is like "ch" in the Scottish pronunciation of "loch"—not "lock"). If you can pronounce Van Gogh correctly, you should also be able to handle Schiphol (*Skhip*-ol), Scheveningen (*Skheven*-ingen), and 's-Gravenhage (ss-*Khraven*-hakhe; the correct full name for Den Haag: The Hague), and impress all your Dutch friends.

A New Museumplein

Three of the big four—Rijksmuseum, Van Gogh Museum, and Stedelijk Museum—are conveniently clustered around Museumplein, a big open square just south of the old city. The square has been totally transformed in recent years, and motorized through-traffic has been abolished.

Most of the rebuilt square consists of open green areas bordered by avenues of linden trees and gardens, which can be used for major outdoor events. Walkways and bicycle paths pass through. At the north end are sports and play areas, and a long pond that serves as an ice-skating rink in winter.

I have to say that, compared to the old Museumplein's raggedy appeal, I find the new model to be a charm-free zone, something from the Antiseptic School of urban design.

Architect Alvaro Siza has drawn up plans for restoring the old building as closely as possible to its original 1895 neo-Renaissance appearance, and constructing an extension on Museumplein, but no start date for the project has been announced.

In the museum cafe is a giant Appel mural. Mondrian is represented by, among other works, his *Composition in Red, Black, Blue, Yellow, and Gray* (1920), and, by way of variation, *Composition in Blue, Red, Black, and Yellow* (1922)—the gray's still there, in fact, but he chose not to mention it in the title.

✪ **Anne Frankhuis.** Prinsengracht 263 (beside Westermarkt). ☎ **020/556-7100.** Admission Dfl 12.50 ($5.30) adults, Dfl 5 ($2.15) children 10–17, free for children under 10. Apr–Aug, daily 9am–9pm; Sept–Mar, daily 9am–7pm. Tram: 13, 14, or 17 to Westermarkt.

In summer you may have to wait an hour or more to get in, but no one should miss seeing and experiencing this house, where eight people from three separate families lived together in near total silence for more than 2 years during World War II. The hiding place Otto Frank found for his family and friends kept them safe until, tragically close to the end of the war, it was raided by Nazi forces, and its occupants were deported to concentration camps. It was here that Anne kept her famous diary as a way to deal with the boredom and her youthful jumble of thoughts, which had as much to do with personal relationships as with the war and the Nazi terror raging outside her hiding place. Visiting the rooms where she hid is a moving and eerily real experience.

The rooms of this building, which was an office and warehouse at that time, are still as bare as they were when Anne's father returned, the only survivor of the eight *onderduikers* (divers, or hiders). Nothing has been changed, except that protective Plexiglas panels have been placed over the wall where Anne pinned up photos of her favorite actress, Deanna Durbin, and of the little English princesses Elizabeth and Margaret. As you tour the small building, it's easy to imagine Anne's experience growing up in this place, awakening as a young woman, and writing down her secret thoughts in a diary.

Get there as early as you can to avoid the lines—this advice isn't as useful as it used to be, because everybody is giving it and heeding it, but it will still save you some waiting time.

You can see a bronze sculpture of Anne at nearby Westermarkt.

Central Amsterdam Attractions

3 More Museums & Galleries

Allard Pierson Museum Amsterdam. Oude Turfmarkt 127 (facing Rokin). ☎ **020/ 525-2556.** Admission Dfl 9.50 ($4.05) adults, Dfl 7 ($3) seniors, Dfl 3 ($1.30) children 12–15, Dfl 1 (45¢) children under 12. Tues–Fri 10am–5pm, Sat–Sun 1–5pm. Tram: 4, 9, 14, 16, 20, 24, or 25 to Spui.

The archaeological collection of the University of Amsterdam is permanently on view here, though the frequent temporary and visiting exhibitions are more likely to have truly memorable pieces. In the recently installed Egyptian department you can see a model of the Pyramid of Cheops and other pyramids at Giza, and mummies and funerary and ritual objects; a computer prints out your name in hieroglyphics. Ancient Greece, Rome, Etruria, and Cyprus are among the best represented of other cultures, with pottery, sculpture, glassware, jewelry, coins, and household objects.

✪ **Amsterdams Historisch Museum (Amsterdam Historical Museum).** Kalverstraat 92 and Nieuwezijds Voorburgwal 359 (next to the Begijnhof). ☎ **020/523-1822.** Admission Dfl 12 ($5.10) adults, Dfl 6 ($2.55) children 6–15, free for children under 6. Mon–Fri 10am–5pm, Sat–Sun 11am–5pm. Tram: 1, 2, 4, 5, 9, 16, 20, 24, or 25 to Spui.

Few cities in the world have gone to as much trouble and expense to display and explain its history, and few museums in the world have found as many ways to make such dry material as population growth and urban development as interesting as the latest electronic board game. Don't say you have little interest in Amsterdam's history. This fascinating museum, in the restored 17th-century former city orphanage, gives you a better understanding of everything you see when you go out to explore the city on your own. Gallery by gallery, century by century, you see how a small fishing village became a major world power; you can also view many of the famous paintings by the Dutch masters in the context of their time and place in history.

When you leave the Historical Museum, cut through the Civic Guard Gallery, a narrow, two-story skylit chamber bedecked with a dozen large, impressive 17th-century group portraits. This gallery is the back entrance to the Begijnhof (see "Sights of Religious Significance" later in this chapter).

Bijbels Museum (Biblical Museum). Herengracht 366–368 (near Spui). ☎ **020/ 624-2436.** Admission Dfl 8 ($3.40) adults, Dfl 5.50 ($2.35) children 16 and under. Mon–Sat 10am–5pm, Sun 1–5pm. Tram: 1, 2, or 5 to Spui.

Taking the Good Book as a starting point, you move on to explore biblical history and geography in objects, images, and installations. The setting—twin patrician canal houses from 1662, designed by noted architect Philips Vingboons, and with a lovely courtyard garden—would be worth visiting for its historical interest alone. In 1717, Jacob de Wit painted its main ceiling with mythological scenes. The museum collection includes models of ancient Jerusalem, the Temple of Solomon, and the Tabernacle; archaeological finds from Israel, Palestine, and Egypt; and paintings of biblical scenes. Among the Bibles on display are the first Bible printed in the Low Countries, dating from 1477, and the first edition of the authorized Dutch translation, from 1637.

Small Is Beautiful

The world's smallest art museum, **Reflex** (☎ **020/627-28-32**), is at Weteringschans, opposite the Rijksmuseum. Only 13.2 square meters large, it displays 1,500 miniature paintings, graphics, sculptures, and pictures, including works by Picasso, Lichtenstein, Oldenburg, and Christo. Admission is free, and it's open Tuesday to Saturday 10am to 6pm.

Cultured Money-Savers

One way to save money is to buy the VVV Amsterdam tourist office's **Amsterdam Culture Pass** (see "Your Passport to Culture" in chapter 2).

You can also buy a **Museumjaarkaart (Museum Year Pass)** costing Dfl 60 ($25.55) adults, Dfl 50 ($21.30) adults 55 and over, and Dfl 30 ($12.75) for those 24 and under. The pass gives a year's free admission to some 350 museums throughout Holland and can be bought from the VVV, and from most museums. If museums are high on your sightseeing agenda, it's a good investment even if Amsterdam is your only stop in Holland.

In mid-April, there's no admission fee at most Amsterdam museums during National Museum Weekend, and others charge greatly discounted fees.

Cobra Museum of Modern Art. Sandbergplein 1–3, Amstelveen. ☎ **020/547-5050.** Admission Dfl 8 ($3.40) adults, Dfl 4 ($1.70) children 16 and under. Tues–Sun 11am–5pm. Tram: 5 to Binnenhof; light rail 51 to Beneluxbaan.

You have to head out to the frankly dull dormitory suburb of Amstelveen south of Amsterdam to find one of the most exciting new museums in the country. Exciting, that is, if you like the post–World War II art of the Cobra group, who took their name from the initials of the original players' home cities: Copenhagen, Brussels, and Amsterdam. Folks like Asger Jorn, Karl Appel, and Lucebert weren't instantly popular in their day, and it's probably still stretching the term to describe them so today, but they undoubtedly changed the face of art, and here you can see how.

Joods Historisch Museum (Jewish Historical Museum). Jonas Daniël Meijerplein 2–4 (facing Waterlooplein). ☎ **020/626-9945.** Admission Dfl 10 ($4.25) adults, Dfl 5.50 ($2.35) seniors, Dfl 4 ($1.70) children 13–18, Dfl 2.50 ($1.05) children 6–13, free for children under 6. Daily 11am–5pm. Tram: 9, 14, or 20 to Waterlooplein.

In 1987, this museum opened in the restored Ashkenazi Synagogue complex, a cluster of four former synagogues, in the heart of what was once Amsterdam's thriving Jewish Quarter (see below). It's home to a collection of paintings, decorations, and ceremonial objects confiscated during World War II and patiently reestablished in the postwar period. Through its objects, photographs, artworks, and interactive displays, the museum tells three intertwining stories—of Jewish identity, Jewish religion and culture, and Jewish history in the Netherlands. It presents the community in both good times and bad and provides insights into the Jewish way of life over the centuries. Leave time to appreciate the beauty and size of the buildings themselves, which include the oldest public synagogue in Europe. This is a museum for everyone—Jewish or otherwise. There are frequent temporary exhibitions of international interest.

Madame Tussaud Scenerama. Dam 20. ☎ **020/622-9949.** Admission Dfl 22.50 ($9.55) adults, Dfl 17.50 ($7.45) seniors and children 14 and under. July–Aug, daily 9:30am–5:30pm; Sept–June, daily 10am–5:30pm. Tram: 1, 2, 4, 5, 9, 13, 14, 16, 17, 20, 24, or 25 to the Dam.

If you like your celebrities with a waxen stare, don't miss Madame Tussaud's. This is a uniquely Amsterdam version of the London attraction, with its own cast of Dutch characters (Rembrandt, Queen Wilhelmina, Erasmus, and Mata Hari) among the usual cast of international favorites (Churchill, Kennedy, Gandhi, and Pope John XXIII).

Museum Amstelkring (Ons' Lieve Heer op Solder: Our Lord in the Attic). Oudezijds Voorburgwal 40 (near the Oude Kerk). ☎ **020/624-6604.** Admission Dfl 10 ($4.25) adults, Dfl 6 ($2.55) children and seniors. Mon–Sat 10am–5pm, Sun and holidays 1–5pm. Tram: 1, 2, 4, 5, 9, 13, 16, 17, 20, 24, or 25 to Centraal Station.

Museumplein Area & Amsterdam South Attractions

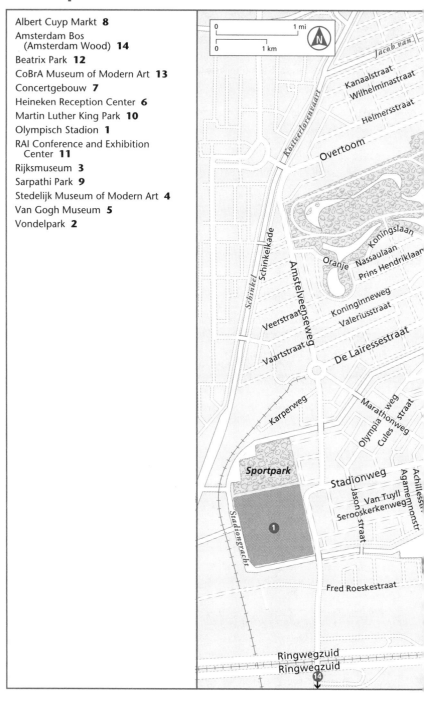

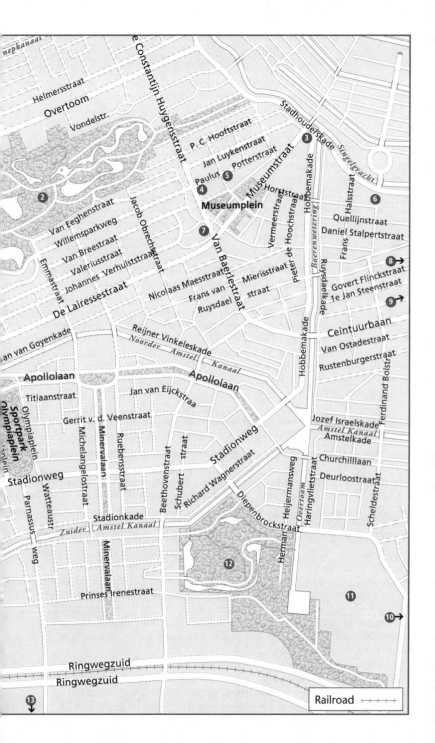

nepkanaal

Helmersstraat

Overtoom

Vondelstr.

e Constantijn Huygensstraat

P. C. Hooftstraat

Jan Luykenstraat

Potterstraat

Paulus **5**

4

Museumstraat

Horststraat

Stadhouderskade

Singelgracht

3

2

Van Eeghenstraat

Willemsparkweg

Van Breestraat

Valeriusstraat

Johannes Verhulststraat

Jacob Obrechtstraat

Museumplein

7

Vermeerstraat

Van Baerlestraat

Hobbemakade

Baerenwetering

Halsstraat

6

Quellijnstraat

Daniel Stalpertstraat

Frans

8 →

Emmastraat

De Lairessestraat

Nicolaas Maesstraat

Frans van Mierisstraat

Ruysdael straat

Pieter de Hoochstraat

Ruysdaelkade

Govert Flinckstraat

1e Jan Steenstraat

9 →

an van Goyenkade

Reijner Vinkeleskade

Noorder Amstel Kanaal

Apollolaan

Ceintuurbaan

Van Ostadestraat

Rustenburgerstraat

Ferdinand Bolstraat

Apollolaan

Titiaanstraat

Jan van Eijckstraa

Hobbemakade

Sportpark
Olympiaplein
Olympiaplein

Gerrit v. d. Veenstraat

Michelangelostraat

Minervalaan

Ruebensstraat

Beethovenstraat

Schubert straat

Stadionweg

Richard Wagnerstraat

Jozef Israelskade

Amstel Kanaal

Amstelkade

Churchilllaan

Deurloostraat

Scheldestraat

Stadionweg

Watteaustr.

Parnassus weg

Stadionkade

Zuider Amstel Kanaal

Minervalaan

Diepenbrockstraat

Herman Heijermansweg

Overtoom Haringvlietstraat

12

11

10 →

Prinses Irenestraat

Ringwegzuid

Ringwegzuid

13 ↓

Railroad ┼┼┼┼┼

137

The Jewish Quarter

For more than 350 years Amsterdam was a center of Jewish life, and its Jewish community was a major contributor to the city's vitality and prosperity. The Waterlooplein area was their neighborhood, where they held their market and built their synagogues. Of the five synagogues built in the 17th and 18th centuries, only the Portuguese Synagogue (see below) continued to serve as a house of worship after the devastating depletion of the Jewish population in World War II. The other buildings, sold to the city in 1955, stood unused and in great need of repair for many years. During those years, the city authorities and the curators of the Jewish Historical Collection of the Amsterdam Historical Museum were patiently reestablishing the collection of paintings, decorations, and ceremonial objects that had been confiscated during World War II.

One of history's quirks is that this tolerant city had a law for more than 200 years, from 1578, prohibiting religious services other than those of the officially favored Dutch Reformed Church. As a result, the city's Catholics, Mennonites, Lutherans, and Jews were forced to hold services in private homes and other secret locations. This museum incorporates the best preserved of these clandestine places of worship. The Catholic church is in the attic of one of the oldest canal houses you can visit, built during 1661–63 for the merchant Jan Hartman. Worshipers entered by a door on a side street and climbed a narrow flight of stairs to the hidden third-floor church. Following Hartman's death in 1668, his house was bought by Jan Reynst, a Protestant merchant. Reynst planned to rent the attic as storage space, but soon realized he could make more money by charging Catholic worshipers for continued use of their "secret" church. An 18th-century redecoration created the chapel-size church you see now, with a baroque altar, spinet-sized pipe organ, and two narrow upper balconies. It's still in use for services and concerts.

Museum Het Rembrandthuis. Jodenbreestraat 4 (behind Waterlooplein). ☎ **020/ 520-0400.** Admission Dfl 12.50 ($5.30) adults, Dfl 2.50 ($1.05) children 6–15, free for children under 6. Mon–Sat 10am–5pm, Sun and holidays 1–5pm. Tram: 9, 14, or 20 to Waterlooplein.

To view the greatest masterpieces by Rembrandt van Rijn you must visit the Rijksmuseum, but in this house you find a more intimate sense of the artist himself. Bought by Rembrandt in 1639 when he was Amsterdam's most fashionable portrait painter, the house, which has 10 rooms, is a shrine to one of the greatest artists the world has ever known. In this house, Rembrandt's son Titus was born and his wife, Saskia, died. The artist was bankrupt when he left it in 1658 (the militia company of Captain Frans Banning Cocq portrayed in *The Night Watch* hated the artistic freedom Rembrandt had exercised on their group portrait and this helped to ruin his previously brilliant career). Not until 1906 was the building rescued from a succession of subsequent owners and restored as a museum.

In 1998, a modern wing for temporary exhibitions was added; restoration completed in 1999 has returned the old house to the way it looked when Rembrandt lived and worked there. Further work in 2000 has restored the artist's cabinet of art and curiosities and the studio he and his pupils used. The rooms are furnished with 17th-century objects and furniture that, as far as possible, match the descriptions in Rembrandt's 1656 petition for bankruptcy. His printing press is back in place, and you can view 250 of his etchings and drawings hanging on the walls. These include self-portraits and landscapes; several relate to the traditionally Jewish character of the neighborhood, such as the portrait of Rabbi Menassah ben Israel, who lived across the street and was an early teacher of another illustrious Amsterdammer, Baruch Spinoza. Opposite Rembrandthuis, appropriately, stands the Amsterdamse Hogeschool voor de Kunsten (Amsterdam High School for the Arts).

Museum van Loon. Keizersgracht 672 (near Vijzelstraat). ☎ **020/624-5255.** Admission Dfl 12 ($5.10) adults, Dfl 7.50 ($3.20) students, free for children 12 and under. Fri–Mon 11am–5pm. Tram: 16, 24, or 25 to Keizersgracht.

The history of this magnificent patrician house, one of a matched pair dating from 1672, is a long saga of ne'er-do-well spouses and ailing orphans, of misguided inheritances and successive bankruptcies. The elegant home was owned by the Van Loon family from 1884 to 1945. On its walls hang more than 80 family portraits, including those of Willem van Loon, one of the founders of the Dutch East India Company; Nicolaes Ruychaver, who liberated Amsterdam from the Spanish in 1578; and another, later, Willem van Loon, who became mayor in 1686. Among other treasures are a family album in which you can see tempera portraits of all living Van Loons painted at two successive dates (1650 and 1675), and a series of commemorative coins struck to honor seven different golden wedding anniversaries celebrated between the years 1621 and 1722. The house's completely restored period rooms are filled with richly decorated paneling, stucco work, mirrors, fireplaces, furnishings, porcelain, medallions, chandeliers, rugs, and more. The garden has carefully tended hedges and a coach house modeled on a Greek temple.

Museum Willet-Holthuysen. Herengracht 605, near Amstel. ☎ **020/523-1870.** Admission Dfl 8 ($3.40) adults, Dfl 4 ($1.70) children 16 and under. Mon–Fri 10am–5pm, Sat–Sun 11am–5pm. Tram: 4 to Utrechtsestraat.

This museum offers another rare opportunity to visit an elegant 17th-century canal house. This particular house, built in 1687, was renovated several times before its last inhabitant gave it and its contents to the city in 1889. Among the most interesting rooms are a Victorian-era bedroom on the second floor, a large reception room with tapestry wall panels, and an 18th-century basement kitchen that's still so completely furnished and functional you could swear the cook had merely stepped out to go shopping.

✪ Nederlands Scheepvaartmuseum (Netherlands Maritime Museum). Kattenburgerplein 1 (in the Eastern Dock). ☎ **020/523-2222.** Admission Dfl 12.50 ($5.30) adults, Dfl 8 ($3.40) children 17 and under. Tues–Sat 10am–5pm (also Mon mid-June to mid-Sept), Sun noon–5pm. Bus: 22 or 32 to Kattenburgerplein.

A bonanza for anyone who loves ships and the sea, the museum overlooks the busy harbor, and is appropriately housed in a former Amsterdam Admiralty arsenal, from 1656. Room after room is filled with boats and ship models, seascape and ship paintings, navigational instruments, prints, and old maps, including a 15th-century Ptolemaic atlas and a sumptuously bound edition of the *Great Atlas, or Description of the World,* produced over a lifetime by Jan Blaeu, the master cartographer of Holland's Golden Age. All the exhibits chronicle the country's abiding ties to the sea through commerce, fishing, yachting, exploration, and war. Among the important papers on

A Familiar Face

Rembrandt painted about 100 self-portraits, more than any other great artist.

display are several pertaining to the Dutch colonies of Nieuwe Amsterdam (New York City) and Nieuwe Nederland (New York State), including a receipt for the land that now surrounds the New York State capital at Albany.

A full-size replica of the Dutch East India Company ship *Amsterdam,* which foundered off Hastings, England, in 1749 on her maiden voyage to the fabled Spice Islands (Indonesia), is moored at the wharf, as is a replica of the *Stad Amsterdam,* a three-masted iron clipper from 1854 (it may eventually be moved to Java Island in the harbor). Other ships that you can see are a steam icebreaker, a motor lifeboat, and a herring lugger; the historic Royal Barge and two towing barges are housed indoors.

You can reach the museum by taking a 20-minute walk along the historical waterfront, the Nautisch Kwartier.

Theatermuseum. Herengracht 168 (at Leliegracht). ☎ **020/551-3300.** Admission Dfl 8.50 ($3.60) adults, Dfl 6.50 ($2.75) seniors and children 7–16, free for children under 7. Tues–Fri 11am–5pm, Sat–Sun 1–5pm. Tram: 13, 14, 17, or 20 to the Dam.

The Netherlands Theater Institute occupies a group of adjoining 17th-century canal houses, two of which house this imaginative museum. No. 168, known as Het Witte Huis (the White House) for its whitish-gray, neoclassical sandstone facade, was built in 1638 by Philips Vingboons and sports the city's first neck gable. Dazzling 18th-century interior ornamentation includes a spiral staircase, intricate stuccowork, and painted ceilings by Jacob de Wit. The elaborate Bartolotti House at No. 170–172, built in 1617–18 by Hendrick de Keyser, famous for its ornate redbrick gable and Dutch Renaissance facade, has 18th-century illuminated ceilings and other interior decoration by Jacob de Wit. In the museum, you find costumes, maquettes, masks, puppets, photographs, paintings, miniature theaters, and theatrical backdrops, covering all forms of theater, including opera and children's theater. Hands-on experience includes creating your own stage and sound effects. Book ahead for hands-on workshops for children (age 7 to 12) on Wednesday, Saturday, and Sunday afternoons.

✪ **Tropenmuseum (Tropical Museum).** Linnaeusstraat 2 (at Mauritskade). ☎ **020/ 568-8215.** Admission Dfl 15 ($6.40) adults, Dfl 12.50 ($5.30) children 18 and under. Daily 10am–5pm. Tram: 9 or 14 to Linnaeusstraat; 7 or 10 to Mauritskade.

One of the city's more intriguing museums belongs to the Royal Tropical Institute, a foundation devoted to the study of the cultures of tropical areas around the world. Its focus reflects Holland's centuries as a landlord in such areas as Indonesia; Surinam (on the northern coast of South America); and the islands of St. Maarten, Saba, St. Eustatius, Aruba, Bonaire, and Curaçao in the West Indies. The Tropical Institute building complex alone is worth the trip to Amsterdam East; its heavily ornamented 19th-century facade is an amalgam of Dutch architectural styles: turrets, stepped gables, arched windows, delicate spires, and the monumental galleried interior court (a popular spot for concerts).

Of the exhibits, the most interesting are the walk-through model villages and city-street scenes that, except for the lack of genuine inhabitants, seem to capture a moment in the daily life of such places as India and Indonesia; the displays of tools and techniques used to produce *batik,* the distinctively dyed Indonesian fabrics; and displays of the tools, instruments, and ornaments that clutter a tropical residence. There's a permanent exhibition on people and environment in West Asia and North Africa.

Part of the premises is given over to the children-only Kindermuseum TM Junior (see "Cool for Kids," later in this chapter, for more details).

Woonboot Museum (Houseboat Museum). Opposite Prinsengracht 296 (at Elandsgracht). ☎ **020/427-0750.** Admission Dfl 4.75 ($2) adults, Dfl 3.50 ($1.50) children size 152cm (5 feet) and under. Tues–Sun 10am–5pm. Tram: 13, 14 17, or 20 to Westermarkt.

Impressions

This city seems to be double: one can also see it in the water; and the reflection of these distinguished houses in these canals makes this spot a fairyland.
—Jean-François Regnard, French writer (1681)

In Amsterdam, no one ever tosses away an old boat. You see many houseboats moored along the canals, on the river, and in the harbor of Amsterdam, but you won't be able to get aboard most of them unless you know the owner. The *Hendrika Maria*, a former commercial sailing ship built in 1914, is an exception. You can visit the original deckhouse where the skipper and his family lived, the cupboard bed in which they slept, and the cargo hold, now equipped as remarkably spacious and comfortable living quarters. How do you get the boat's bottom cleaned? Might you sink? What happens in winter? These and other questions are answered in models, photographs, and books.

4 Offbeat & Alternative Amsterdam
RED LIGHT DISTRICT
This warren of streets and old canals (known as De Rosse Buurt or De Wallen in Dutch) around Oudezijds Achterburgwal and Oudezijds Voorburgwal by the Oude Kerk, a testament to the city's tolerance and pragmatism, is on most people's sightseeing agenda. However, a visit to this area is not for everyone, and if you're liable to be offended by the sex industry exposed in all its garish colors, don't go. If you do choose to go, you need to exercise some caution, because the area is a center of crime, vice, and drugs. As always in Amsterdam, there's no need to exaggerate the risks; and in fact the nightclubs' own security helps keep the brightly lit areas quite safe. Plenty of tourists visit the Rosse Buurt and suffer nothing more serious than a come-on from one of the prostitutes.

At night especially, however, stick to the crowded streets and be wary of pickpockets at all times. There can be a sinister air to the bunches of often weird-looking men who gather on the bridges; and there is a sadder aura around the "heroin-whores" who wander the darker streets. Finally, do not take photographs of the women in the windows, many of whom don't want Mom and Dad to know how they earn a living. Men are always on the lookout, and they won't hesitate to throw your camera (and maybe your person) into the canal. (George Michael seems to have had no trouble filming the video here for his risqué 1999 cover of The Police's seventies classic "Roxanne.")

Still, it's extraordinary to view the prostitutes in leather and lace sitting in their storefronts with their radios and TVs blaring as they do their knitting or adjust their makeup, waiting patiently for customers. The district seems to reflect Dutch pragmatism; if you can't stop the oldest trade in the world, you can at least confine it to a particular area and impose health and other regulations on it. And the fact is that underneath its tacky glitter, the Red Light District contains some of Amsterdam's prettiest canals and loveliest old architecture, plus some excellent bars and restaurants, secondhand bookshops, and other specialty shops (not all of which work the erogenous zones). For more information on the Red Light District, see also chapter 9. To get there, take tram 4, 9, 14, 16, 20, 24, or 25 to the Dam, then pass behind the Grand Hotel Krasnapolsky.

A House of Ill Repute with a Great Reputation

In Amsterdam, streetwalkers are illegal. Bordellos are not. The most celebrated one is **Yab Yum,** Singel 295 (☎ **020/624-9503;** open daily 8am to 4am), in a 17th-century mansion on Singel. Taxi drivers, who get a hefty tip if they deposit you there, love Yab Yum (the name is that of a goddess of love from the *Kama Sutra*).

The women, 20 each evening, all Dutch, well educated, well spoken, gorgeous, and between ages 18 and 24, are strictly moonlighting; no one is twisting their arms. Most are reportedly flight attendants, nurses, students, and housewives. The clientele: businessmen, jet-setters, and kinky couples into threesomes or orgies. A muscle-bound bouncer leads you up the stairs and rings a buzzer. An elegant man shakes your hand and initiates you into the establishment's mysteries.

The decor is quintessential cathouse. There are stalagmite chandeliers, pincushion red-velvet walls, gold encrustations, etched-glass nudes, a lounge with a splashing Venus fountain, and a U-shaped bar where the ladies perch on stools. The price: Dfl 200 ($85) to get in; Dfl 400 to Dfl 1,200 ($170 to $510.65) for champagne while you chat. Innocent entertainment, and expense, can stop there. If it doesn't, you follow a faux leopard-skin carpet leading to 11 luxury bedrooms, which are fitted out like the extravagant whorehouses of Hollywood Westerns but have whirlpool tubs.

OFFBEAT MUSEUMS

Erotic Museum. Oudezijds Achterburgwal 54 (Red Light District). ☎ **020/624-7303.** Admission Dfl 6 ($2.55). Daily noon–midnight. Tram: 4, 9, 14, 16, 20, 24, or 25 to the Dam.

As its name suggests, this museum presents an allegedly artistic vision of eroticism; it focuses on prints and drawings, including some by John Lennon. There is a re-creation of a Red Light alley and an extensively equipped S&M playroom, both of which are rather antiseptic and serious. The only humorous note is an X-rated cartoon depicting some of the things Snow White apparently got up to with the Seven Dwarfs that Walt never told us about.

Hash Marihuana Hemp Museum. Oudezijds Achterburgwal 148 (Red Light District). ☎ **020/623-5961.** Admission Dfl 12.50 ($5.30). Daily 10am–5:30pm. Tram: 4, 9, 14, 16, 20, 24, or 25 to the Dam.

Well, it wouldn't really be Amsterdam, would it, without its fascination with intoxicating weeds. This museum will teach you everything you ever wanted to know, and much that you maybe didn't, about hash, marijuana, and related products. The museum does not promote drug use but aims to make you better informed before deciding whether to light up and, of course, whether to inhale. One way it does this is by having a cannabis garden in the joint (sorry) on the premises. Plants at various stages of development fill the air with an unmistakable, heady, resinous fragrance. And hemp, not plastic, could be the future if the exhibition on the multifarious uses of the fiber through the ages is anything to go by.

Sexmuseum Amsterdam Venustempel. Damrak 18 (near to Centraal Station). ☎ **020/ 622-8376.** Admission Dfl 6 ($2.55) age 16 and over only. Daily 10am–11:30pm. Tram: 1, 2, 4, 5, 9, 13, 16, 17, 20, 24, or 25 to Centraal Station.

Behind its faux-marble facade, this museum is not as sleazy as you might expect, apart from one room covered with straight-up pornography. Otherwise the presentation tends toward the tongue-in-cheek. Exhibits include erotic prints and drawings, and trinkets like tobacco boxes decorated with naughty pictures. Teenage visitors seem to find the whole place vastly amusing, judging by the giggling fits at the showcases. Spare a thought for the models of early erotic photography—slow film speeds in those days made for uncomfortably long posing times!

Tattoo Museum. Oudezijds Achterburgwal 130 (Red Light District). ☎ **020/625-1565.** Admission Dfl 8 ($3.40). Summer, daily noon–6pm; closed Mon the rest of the year. Tram: 4, 9, 14, 16, 20, 24, or 25 to the Dam.

President and curator Henk Schiffmacher (aka Hanky Panky) is a tattoo enthusiast of long standing and has his own suite of personal decorations peeking out from bare arms to prove it. His museum chronicles the history and practice of tattooing around the world, not just in its modern Western variations, and includes exhibits he has gathered himself over the years. There's a library and archive for researchers and regular demonstrations of the tattooist's art.

Torture Museum. Damrak 20–22 (near to Centraal Station). ☎ **020/639-2027.** Admission Dfl 8 ($3.40) adults, Dfl 4 ($1.70) children 12 and under. Daily 10am–11pm. Tram: 1, 2, 4, 5, 9, 13, 16, 17, 20, 24, or 25 to Centraal Station.

You enter through an appropriately long and gloomy tunnel, and emerge with a new appreciation of why the framers of the U.S. Constitution outlawed cruel and unusual punishment. Yet one suspects that the motives of the Torture Museum—and its visitors?—are not purely educational. There is a horrible fascination about devices such as the Inquisition chair, the guillotine, and assorted grotesque implements of torture, punishment, and "redemption" favored by the civil and ecclesiastic authorities in times not so far past.

5 Historic Buildings & Monuments

Beurs van Berlage (Old Stock Exchange). Beursplein 7 (near the Dam). ☎ **020/626-8936.** Admission Dfl 7.50 ($3.20) adults, Dfl 5 ($2.15) children 5–16, free for children under 5. Mon–Fri 9am–5pm. Tram: 4, 9, 14, 16, 20, 24, or 25 to the Dam.

Designed by architect Hendrik Petrus Berlage and built between 1896 and 1903, the Stock Exchange, a massive edifice of colored brick and stone enclosing three arcades roofed in glass and iron, represented a revolutionary break with 19th-century architecture. Though it's no longer the stock exchange, it's still well worth visiting as the prime example of Amsterdam School architecture, which was contemporaneous with the work of Frank Lloyd Wright in America. Note the gable relief of two fishermen with a dog in a boat, depicting a legend of Amsterdam's foundation. Today the building is used as a space for conferences, concerts, and exhibitions.

De Waag (Weigh House). Nieuwmarkt. ☎ **020/557-9898.** Free admission (but some exhibitions charge admission). Sun–Thurs 10am–1am, Fri–Sat 10am–2am. Metro: Nieuwmarkt.

Built in the 14th century, the city's only surviving medieval fortified gate later became a guild house. Among the guilds lodged here was the Surgeon's Guild, immortalized in Rembrandt's painting *The Anatomy Lesson* (1632), which depicts a dissection in the upper-floor Theatrum Anatomicum. Today the Waag is a multimedia center for exhibitions, theater, and music performances. The reading table in its cafe features not only newspapers, as is common in Amsterdam, but also Internet access and a selection of CD-ROMs.

The City of 7,000 Gables

Most of Amsterdam's 7,000 landmark buildings have gables. These hide the pitched roofs (like the false fronts of a town center in the American Old West) and demonstrate the architect's vertical showmanship in a city where tax laws encouraged thin buildings. If you can pick out Amsterdam's various gable styles without developing Sistine Chapel neck syndrome, you can date the buildings fairly accurately. The neck gable, for example (about 1660–1790), looks like a headless neck, with curlicues on the shoulders. Look for the first one at Herengracht 168 (the Netherlands Theater Institute), a 1638 mansion. The earliest type is the wooden, triangular gable (circa 1250–1550). Only two remain, in the Begijnhof and at Zeedijk 1.

Walls in the Begijnhof and on Sint Luciensteeg at the Amsterdam Historical Museum have some good gable stones, including the oldest-known stone, from 1603, showing a milkmaid balancing her buckets.

Incidentally, though the *hijsbalk*—the hook you see on many gables—looks to be ideal for a hanging (the kids maybe), it's actually used for hauling furniture. Rope and pulleys are used to get furniture into and out of homes where the staircases are too narrow and steep.

✪ **Koninklijk Paleis (Royal Palace).** Dam. ☎ **020/620-4060.** Admission Dfl 8 ($3.40) adults, Dfl 6 ($2.55) children 5–12, free for children under 5. Easter and June–Oct, daily 11am–5pm; Nov to mid-Dec and mid-Feb to May, generally Tues–Thurs 12:30–5pm (opening days and hours are highly variable; check before going). Closed mid-Dec to mid-Feb. Tram: 1, 2, 4, 5, 9, 13, 14, 16, 17, 20, 24, or 25 to the Dam.

One of the heavier features of the Dam is the solid, neoclassical facade of the Royal Palace (1648–55). Designed by Jacob van Campen—the Thomas Jefferson of the Dutch Republic—as a Stadhuis (Town Hall) to replace the frumpy and decayed old Gothic one that in 1652 did everyone a favor by burning down, it was designed to showcase the city's burgeoning prosperity; its interior is replete with white Italian marble. Poet Constantijn Huygens called the new Town Hall the "Eighth Wonder of the World."

Not until 1808, when Napoléon Bonaparte's younger brother Louis reigned as king of the Netherlands, did it become a palace, filled with Empire-style furniture courtesy of the French ruler. Since the return to the throne in 1813 of the Dutch House of Orange, this has been the official palace of the reigning king or queen of the Netherlands. Few of them, however, have used it for more than an occasional state reception or official ceremony (such as the inauguration of Queen Beatrix, who prefers living at Huis ten Bosch in The Hague), or as their pied-à-terre in the capital.

In the Vierschaar (Tribunal), magistrates pronounced death sentences watched over by images of Justice, Wisdom and Mercy. Atlas holds up the globe in the high-ceilinged Burgerzaal (Citizen's Chamber), and maps inlaid on the marble floor show Amsterdam as the center of the world. Ferdinand Bol's painting *Moses the Lawgiver* hangs in the Schepenzaal (Council Chamber), where the aldermen met. On the pediment overlooking the Dam, Flemish sculptor Artus Quellien carved a baroque hymn in stone to Amsterdam's maritime pre-eminence, showing figures symbolizing the oceans paying the city homage. The weathervane on the cupola takes the form of a Dutch sailing ship.

Piles of Pilings

The Royal Palace rests on 13,659 timber pilings—a figure that all Dutch school-children are supposed to learn.

OTHER HISTORIC SIGHTS

You may come away thinking that Amsterdam is one big historic monument. Still, some buildings are more historic and monumental than others and therefore more worth going out of your way for. You won't have to go far out of your way to see **Centraal Station.** Built on an artificial island in the IJ inlet of the Zuiderzee (now the IJsselmeer), the station opened in 1889 and was thoroughly disliked by Amsterdammers at the time. Now it's an attraction in its own right, partly for its extravagant Dutch neo-Renaissance facade (architect P. J. H. Cuypers, a Catholic, tossed in a dab of neo-Gothic, too, leading the thoroughly Protestant King William III to scorn "that cathedral"), partly for the liveliness that permanently surrounds it. The left one of the two central towers has a gilded weathervane; on the right one there's a clock.

Not far away, across Prins Hendrikkade at the corner of Geldersekade, is the **Schreierstoren (Tower of Tears),** from 1480, once a strong point in the city wall bristling with cannon. Its name comes from the tears allegedly shed by wives as their menfolk sailed away on voyages from which they might never return. A stone tablet on the wall shows a woman with her hand to her face. She might be weeping, but who knows what emotion that hand is really covering up?

NEW YORK LOVES YA, HENRY

In 1609, Henry Hudson set sail from the Tower of Tears aboard the *Halve Maen* (Half Moon). He "discovered" Long Island, the Hudson River, and the future site of Nieuw Amsterdam, which would become New York City. The Greenwich Village Historical Society pinned a memorial marker to the tower in 1927.

No ambiguity surrounds the **Munttoren (Mint Tower),** at the juncture of Rokin and the Singel. The base of the tower used to be part of the Reguliers Gate in the city wall. In 1620 Hendrick de Keyser topped it with an ornate, lead-covered tower, whose carillon bells sing out gaily every hour and play a full-scale carillon concert on Tuesday and Friday at 12:30 and 1pm.

A monument of a different temper is the sad remains of the **Hollandse Schouwburg,** on Plantage Middenlaan. Not far from the Jewish Historical Museum and Portuguese Synagogue, this is "the place where we commemorate our compatriots who were deported between 1940 and 1945 and did not return." All that remains of the former Yiddish Theater is its facade, behind which is a simple memorial plaza of grass and walkways.

Most of Golden Age Amsterdam's wealth was generated by trade, and most of that trade was organized by the Verenigde Oostindische Compagnie (V.O.C.), based at **Oost Indisch Huis (East India House)** on Oude Hoogstraat, off Kloveniersburgwal. Dating from 1606, this former headquarters of the first multinational corporation now belongs to the University of Amsterdam, but you can stroll into the courtyard.

You might also be interested in **West Indisch Huis (West India House),** at Herenmarkt, off Brouwersgracht. On the north side of this little square is a red-brick building, built as a meat-trading hall in 1615, that in 1623 became headquarters of the Dutch West India Company, which controlled trade with the Americas. It now houses educational organizations, including the John Adams Institute, an American-oriented philosophical and literary society. In the courtyard is a statue of Peter

---

If I Can Make It There . . .

In 1624, the Dutch West India Company built a fortified trading post on the tip of Manhattan Island, naming the settlement that grew up around it Nieuw Amsterdam. Two years later the company's Peter Minuit bought Manhattan Island from the Manhattoes Indians for the equivalent in cloth and trinkets of 60 guilders—surely history's smartest ever real-estate deal. Peter Stuyvesant, a stern ruler who opposed political and religious pluralism, was appointed governor in 1646. Eighteen years later he surrendered Nieuw Amsterdam to the English, who renamed it New York.

Echoes of the Dutch period remain, in Harlem, named after Haarlem, a town west of Amsterdam; Brooklyn, named after Breukelen, a village southeast of Amsterdam; Staten Island, named after the Dutch parliament, the Staten-Generaal; even the notorious Bowery, which began as the *bouwerie,* a road leading to Peter Stuyvesant's farm.

Not far from West India House is Amsterdam's first university, the **Athenaeum Illustre,** at Oudezijds Voorburgwal 231. Founded in 1631, the Athenaeum moved here in 1632, to occupy the 15th-century Gothic Agnietenkapel (Church of St. Agnes) and convent of the Order of St. Francis, whose nuns lost their place to the Dutch Admiralty after the religious upheaval of 1578. The building is now the University of Amsterdam Museum.

Stuyvesant, one-legged governor of Nieuw Amsterdam (later New York) from 1647 until the British took over in 1664. There's a sculpture depicting the first Dutch settlement on Manhattan island, founded in 1626.

SMALLEST HOUSES

The **narrowest house** in Amsterdam (and who knows, maybe even the world) can be seen at **Singel 7.** It's just 1 meter wide, barely wider than the front door. It is, however, a cheat. Only the front facade is really so narrow; behind that it broadens out to more normal proportions. The genuine narrowest house is at **Oude Hoogstraat 22,** between the Dam and Nieuwmarkt. It has a typical Amsterdam bell gable and is 2.02 meters wide and 6 meters deep. A close rival, 2.44 meters wide, can be seen nearby, at **Kloveniersburgwal 26;** this is the cornice-gabled **Klein Trippenhuis,** also known as Mr. Trip's Coachman's House. It faces the elegant Trippenhuis at No. 29, which at 22 meters is the widest Old Amsterdam house, and was built in 1660 for the wealthy merchant Trip brothers. The story goes that the coachman exclaimed one day: "Oh, if only I could be so lucky as to have a house as wide as my master's door." His master overheard this, and the coachman's wish was granted. Nice work if you can get it.

FLOATING CAT HOUSE

No, this is not another Yab-Yum–style paean of praise to a house of ill repute (see above). The **Cat Boat,** one of the city's 2,400 houseboats, on Singel near the Old Lutheran Church, is home to more than 100 stray cats.

OTHER MONUMENTS & SIGHTS

The **Homomonument,** on Westermarkt beside the Westerkerk church, is three granite blocks in the shape of pink triangles (the shape of the Nazi badge for homosexuals), forming a larger triangular outline. One block, a symbol of the future, points into the Keizersgracht; one, at ground level, points toward the nearby Anne Frank House; the other, a sort of plinth about 50cm high, points toward the offices of COC, a gay political organization). Designed by Karin Daan, the monument memorializes gays and lesbians killed during World War II and persecuted throughout the ages.

Magna Plaza, behind the Dam and the Royal Palace, was formerly the main Post Office and is now a shopping mall with an icky Latin name. The elegant, arcaded building dates from the 19th century, when it was nicknamed Perenberg (Pear Mountain) because of its pear-shaped tower decorations.

The precariously tilting **Montelbaanstoren,** the "leaning tower of Amsterdam," a fortification at the juncture of the Oude Schans and Waals-Eilandsgracht canals, dates from 1512. It is one of few surviving elements of the city's once powerful defensive works. In 1606, Hendrick de Keyser added an octagonal tower and spire.

Made of African azobe wood, the famous **Magere Brug (Skinny Bridge),** a double-drawbridge, spans the Amstel between Kerkstraat and Nieuwe Kerkstraat. This is the latest successor, dating from 1969, to the 1672 original, which legend says was built to make it easier for the two wealthy Mager sisters, who lived on opposite banks of the river, to visit each other. The footbridge, one of the city's 60 drawbridges, is itself a big draw, especially after dark, when it is illuminated by hundreds of lights. A bridge master who gets around by bicycle raises it to let boats through.

Though most of the **Blauwbrug (Blue Bridge)** over the Amstel at Waterlooplein looks gray to me, since a recent renovation its lanterns are once again as blue as when Impressionist artist George Hendrik Breitner painted the scene in the 1880s. The cast-iron bridge, inspired by Paris's Pont Alexandre III and opened in 1884, is named after a 16th-century timber bridge that was painted Nassau blue following the 1578 Protestant takeover.

6 Sights of Religious Significance

Religion has always played an important part in Amsterdam's history, and hundreds of churches are testimony to the great variety of religious beliefs still alive—if not always well—in the city. Most can be visited during regular services; some have open doors during weekdays so that visitors may have a look around.

✪ **Begijnhof.** Gedempte Begijnensloot (at Spui). ☎ **020/625-8853.** Free admission. Daily until sunset. Tram: 1, 2, or 5 to Spui.

This 14th-century cluster of small homes around a garden courtyard is one of the best places to appreciate the earliest history of the city, when Amsterdam was a destination for religious pilgrims and an important center of Catholic nunneries. The Begijnhof itself was not a convent (that was located next door, where the Amsterdams Historisch Museum now stands); it was an almshouse for pious lay women—*begijnen*—involved in religious and charitable work for the convent. It remained in operation even after the about-face changeover of the city from Catholicism to Protestantism in the late 16th century. The last of the *begijnen* died in 1971, but you can still pay homage to these pious women by pausing for a moment at the small flower-planted mound that lies just at the center garden's edge across from the English Reformed Church. Opposite the front of the church is a secret Catholic chapel built in 1671 and still in use. Only one of the old wooden houses from the early period remains. You're welcome to visit the Begijnhof during daylight hours (the city's low-income senior citizens now reside in the old homes, and their privacy is respected after sunset).

Nieuwe Kerk (New Church). Dam (beside the Royal Palace). ☎ **020/638-6909.** Admission and opening hours vary with different events. Tram: 1, 2, 4, 5, 9, 13, 14, 16, 17, 20, 24, or 25 to the Dam.

Many of this originally Catholic church's priceless treasures were removed and its colorful frescoes painted over in 1578 when it passed into the hands of Protestants, but since 1814 (when the king first took the oath of office and was inaugurated here—Dutch royalty are not crowned; Queen Beatrix, too, was inaugurated here in 1980), much of its original grandeur has been restored. The church boasts a stately arched nave, an elaborately carved altar, a great pipe organ that dates from 1645, and several noteworthy stained-glass windows. It also holds sepulchral monuments for many of Holland's most revered poets and naval heroes. A sculpture depicting the 17th-century Dutch Admiral Michiel De Ruyter amidst the wreckage of a great sea battle at the Nieuwe Kerk in Amsterdam. Afterwards, take the weight off your feet on the sidewalk terrace of the fine cafe, the Nieuwe Café, attached to the church.

Noorderkerk (North Church). Noordermarkt 44–48 (off Prinsengracht). ☎ **020/626-6436.** Free admission. Mon 10:30–12:30, Sat 11am–1pm, Sun (services) 10am and 7pm. Tram: 1, 2, 5, 13, 17, or 20 to Martelaarsgracht.

Recently restored, the city's first Greek cross-shaped church with central pulpit, designed by Hendrick de Keyser and dating from 1620–23, was built for the poor Calvinist faithful of the Jordaan. The four triangular houses tucked into the angles of the cross weren't part of De Keyser's original plan; architect Hendrick Staets, unwilling to see so much useful space go to waste, added them after De Keyser's death in 1621. This is still a working church, with an active congregation. A plaque on the facade recalls the February 1941 strike in protest of Nazi deportation of the city's Jewish community. From May to September, a classical music recital takes place every Saturday at 2pm; admission costs Dfl 10 ($4.25).

Oude Kerk (Old Church). Oudekerksplein 23 (off Oudezijds Voorburgwal). ☎ **020/625-8284.** Admission Dfl 7.50 ($3.20) adults, Dfl 5 ($2.15) students/seniors. Mon–Sat 11am–5pm, Sun 1am–5pm. Tram: 4, 9, 14, 16, 20, 24, or 25 to the Dam.

This late-Gothic church was begun in 1250. On its southern porch, to the right of the sexton's house, you will see a coat of arms belonging to Maximilian of Austria, who, with his son Philip, contributed to the porch's construction. Rembrandt's wife Saskia is buried here. The church contains a magnificent organ from 1724 and is regularly used for organ recitals. Nowadays, the pretty little gabled almshouses around the Oude Kerk feature red-fringed windows through which can be seen the scantily dressed ladies of the Red Light District.

Portuguese Synagogue. Mr. Visserplein 3. ☎ **020/624-5351.** Admission Dfl 7.50 ($3.20) adults, Dfl 5 ($2.15) children 10–15. Apr–Oct, Sun–Fri 10am–12:30pm and 1–4pm; Nov–Mar, Mon–Thurs 10am–12:30pm and 1–4pm, Fri 10am–3pm, Sun 10am–noon. Closed Jewish holidays. Tram: 9, 14, or 20 to Waterlooplein.

Sephardic Jews fleeing Spain and Portugal during the 16th and early 17th centuries established a neighborhood east of the center known as the Jewish Quarter. In 1665 they built an elegant Ionic-style synagogue within an existing courtyard facing what is now a busy traffic circle. The total cost of the magnificent building was 186,000 florins, a king's ransom in those days but a small price to pay for the city's Jewish community, whose members could worship openly for the first time in 200 years. The building was restored in the 1950s. Today it looks essentially as it did 320 years ago, with its women's gallery supported by 12 stone columns to represent the Twelve Tribes of Israel, and the large, low-hanging brass chandeliers that together hold 1,000 candles, all of which are lighted for the private weekly services.

Westerkerk (West Church). Prinsengracht 279–281 (at Westermarkt). ☎ **020/624-7766.** Free admission to church; to tower Dfl 3 ($1.30) adults, Dfl 2 (85¢) children. Church: Mon–Sat 11am–3pm; tower: June–Sept, daily 10am–6pm. Tram: 13, 14, 17, or 20 to Westermarkt.

The Renaissance-style Westerkerk holds the remains of Rembrandt and his son, Titus, and is where in 1966 Princess (now Queen) Beatrix and Prince Claus said their marriage vows. The church was begun in 1620, at the same time as the Noorderkerk, and opened in 1631. The initial designer was Hendrick de Keyser, whose his son Pieter took over after his father's death in 1621. The church's interior, light and spacious, has a fine organ. The 85-meter-high (277 feet) tower, the Westertoren, is Amsterdam's tallest, providing a spectacular view of the city; on its top is the blue, red, and gold crown of the Holy Roman Empire, a symbol bestowed by the Austrian emperor Maximilian.

Zuiderkerk (South Church). Zuiderkerkhof 72 (between Nieuwmarkt and Waterlooplein). ☎ **020/622-2962.** Free admission. Mon–Wed and Fri noon–5pm, Thurs noon–8pm. Metro: Nieuwmarkt. Tram: 9, 14, or 20 to Waterlooplein.

The Zuiderkerk, the city's first Protestant church, designed by Hendrick de Keyser and built between 1603 and 1614, has since succumbed to a shortage of worshipers. Today the building houses a permanent exhibition on modern town planning in Amsterdam. From June to September the church tower can be visited and climbed on a free guided tour; these leave on the hour, 2 to 4pm Wednesday to Saturday.

7 Other Attractions

Heineken Reception Center. Stadhouderskade 78 (on the Singelgracht, near the Rijksmuseum). ☎ **020/523-9666.** Admission Dfl 2 (85¢) donated to charity. Guided tours Mon–Fri 9:30 and 11am; June to mid-Sept, also 1 and 2:30pm; July–Aug, also Sat 11am, 1, and 2:30pm. Tram: 25 to Stadhouderskade.

You can take a tour of the former Heineken brewing facilities, which date from 1868. Before the brewery stopped functioning in 1990, it was producing more than a million hectoliters annually. The fermentation tanks, each capable of holding a million glassfuls of Heineken, are still there for visitors to see. Guides explain the brewing process and show a film about the company's history on a multiscreen video wall; you go through 5,000 years of brewing history in 5 minutes flat. Heineken's hospitality extends to two complimentary glasses per person—enough to cast a warm glow of appreciation over the visit, and not enough to spoil it.

Holland Experience. Waterlooplein 17. ☎ **020/422-2233.** Admission Dfl 19.50 ($8.30) adults, Dfl 16 ($6.80) seniors and children 12 and under. Daily 10am–10pm. Tram: 9, 14, or 20 to Waterlooplein.

This multidimensional film and theater show takes you through the landscapes and culture of Holland at different periods of its history and today. If you've ever nervously wondered what would happen to the city if all that seawater should ever break through the defensive dikes, Holland Experience will give you a taste; in its simulated dike collapse, 80,000 liters of water pour toward you. Other exhibitions include farming and fishing scenes. The toilets here (I can only vouch for the men's) are themselves of interest; they're designed to look like the deck of a ship passing along the Dutch coast, and come complete with marine sound effects and salt-air breeze.

✪ **newMetropolis Science and Technology Center.** Oosterdok 2 (above the IJ tunnel in the eastern harbor). ☎ **0900/919-1100.** Admission Dfl 22.50 ($9.55) adults, Dfl 15 ($6.40) children 4–16, free for children under 4. July–Aug, daily 10am–9pm; Sept–June, Mon–Thurs 10am–6pm, Fri–Sun 10am–9pm. Bus: 22 to Kadijksplein.

newMetropolis is a paean of praise to science and technology. It's located in a strikingly modern building (designed by Italian architect Renzo Piano), which seems to reproduce the graceful lines of an ocean-going ship. The center is a hands-on experience as much as a museum, with games, experiments, demonstrations, workshops, and theater and film shows. You learn how to steer a supertanker safely into port, boost your earnings on the floor of the New York Stock Exchange, and execute a complicated surgical procedure. One exhibit will even try to make you understand the basis of sexual attraction. Internet-linked computers on every floor help provide insights.

EXHIBITIONS

If you're lucky, you might just be in town when one of the big shows, or one that interests you personally, is on at the giant **RAI Conference and Exhibition Center,** Europaplein (☎ 020/549-1212), in the southern outskirts. Events might include the Home Interiors Exhibition, the Dutch Art and Antiques Fair, the Love & Marriage Show (a fair exhibiting everything from wedding dresses to his 'n' hers towels), the Car Show, and (this being Holland) the Bicycle Show.

MARKETS

There are more than 50 outdoor markets every week in Amsterdam, some of them permanent or semipermanent, and others just passing through. For more details, see "Markets" in chapter 8, but here are three that you shouldn't miss.

The ✪ **Floating Flower Market** on Singel is a stunning mass of flowers strung along the canal. Awnings stretch to cover stall after stall of brightly colored blossoms, bulbs, and potted plants. A stroll down that fragrant line is surely one of Amsterdam's most heart-lifting experiences. Looking for a bargain-basement souvenir is made easy at the ✪ **Waterlooplein Flea Market,** on Waterlooplein, naturally enough. You find all kinds of stuff here, not all of it junk, and a constant press of people with good buys on their mind. The **Albert Cuyp Markt,** on Albert Cuypstraat, is more of an everyday market for food, clothes, and other things, but is almost as colorful as the other two.

8 Green Amsterdam

Amsterdam is not a notably green city, particularly in the Old Center, where the canals are the most obvious and visible encroachment of the natural world. Still, the city as a whole has plenty of parks, including the famous ✪ **Vondelpark.** Just watch out for the tasty-looking "gateau" that they sell there, or you may find yourself floating above the trees: Drug-laced space-cake is an acquired taste, and not everyone is ready to acquire it.

Otherwise, the Vondelpark is a fairly standard park, the site of skateboarding, Frisbee-flipping, in-line skating, model-boat sailing, soccer, softball and basketball games, open-air concerts, open-air theater performances, smooching in the undergrowth, parties, picnics, arts-and-crafts markets, and, perhaps not-so-standard, topless sunbathing. Best of all, it's free, or as the Dutch say, gratis. The Vondelpark lies generally southwest of Leidseplein, with entrances all around; the most popular is adjacent to Leidseplein, on Stadhouderskade.

You can rent in-line skates from **Rent A Skate,** Damstraat 21 (☎ 020/664-5091), and tour the park in style. Including protective gear, it costs Dfl 10 ($4.25) an hour for adults, or Dfl 15 ($6.40) for a half day and Dfl 25 ($10.65) for a full day; for children 10 and under, Dfl 5 ($2.15) an hour, Dfl 10 ($4.25) for a half day, and Dfl 17.50 ($7.45) for a full day.

After Vondelpark, the city's other parks are fairly tame, but the following still make pleasant escapes on a warm summer day: **Sarphati Park,** 2 blocks behind the Albert Cuyp Markt in South Amsterdam; **Beatrix Park,** adjacent to the RAI Convention and Exhibition Center; **Rembrandt Park** and **Erasmus Park** in the west of the city; **Martin Luther King Park,** beside the River Amstel; and the **Oosterpark,** in East Amsterdam.

TIMBUKTU   KALAMAZOO

AT&T Direct® Service

The easy way to call home from anywhere.

Global
connection
with the AT&T
Network

AT&T
direct
service

or the easy way to call home, take the attached wallet guide.

Amsterdam East Attractions

Artis Zoo **7**

Hollandse Schouwburg **6**

Hortus Botanicus **5**

Joods Historisch Museum **4**

Museum Het Rembrandthuis **2**

Nederlands Scheepvaartmuseum **1**

Portuguese Synagogue **3**

Tropenmuseum **8**

To enjoy scenery and fresh air, you should head out to the giant **Amsterdamse Bos (Amsterdam Wood),** whose main entrance is on Amstelveenseweg, in the southern suburb of Amstelveen. This is nature on the city's doorstep. The park was laid out during the Depression years as a public works project. By now the trees, birds, insects, and small animals are firmly established. From the entrance, follow the path to the Roeibaan, a 2-kilometer rowing course. Beyond the western end of the Roeibaan is the Bosmuseum (☎ 020/676-2152), where you can trace the park's history and learn about its wildlife. This free museum is open daily 10am to 5pm. Nearby is a big pond called the **Grote Vijver,** where you can rent boats (☎ 020/644-5119), and the Openluchttheater (Open-Air Theater), which often has performances on summer evenings. In 2000, the **Kersenbloesempark (Cherry Blossom Park)** opened in the Amsterdamse Bos, its 400 cherry trees donated by the Japan Women's Club to mark 400 years of cultural ties between the Netherlands and Japan. The best way to the Amsterdamse Bos from the city center is to take tram 6, 16, or 24 to Stadionplein and then to take any bus, except the No. 23, along Amstelveenseweg to the entrance.

✪ **Hortus Botanicus (Botanical Garden).** Plantage Middenlaan 2a (near Artis Zoo). ☎ **020/625-9021.** Admission Dfl 10 ($4.25) adults, Dfl 6 ($2.55) children 5–14, free for children under 5. Apr–Sept, Mon–Fri 9am–5pm, Sat–Sun 11am–5pm; Oct–Mar, Mon–Fri 9am–4pm, Sat–Sun 11am–4pm. Tram: 9, 14, or 20 to Plantage Middenlaan.

The Botanical Garden, which was established here in 1682, is a medley of color and scent, with some 250,000 flowers and 115,000 plants and trees, from 8,000 different varieties. It owes its origins to the treasure trove of tropical plants the Dutch found in their colonies of Indonesia, Surinam, and the Antilles, and its contemporary popularity to the Dutch love affair with flowers. Among its highlights are the Semicircle, which reconstructs part of the original design from 1682; the Mexico–California Desert House; the Palm House, with one of the world's oldest palm trees; and the Tri-Climate House, which displays tropical, subtropical, and desert plants.

9 Organized Tours

BY BICYCLE

You're going to look pretty conspicuous taking one of the guided tours offered by **Yellow Bike,** Nieuwezijds Kolk 29, off Nieuwezijds Voorburgwal (☎ 020/620-6940). Why? Because you're going to be cycling on a yellow bicycle along with a dozen other people also on yellow bicycles, that's why. In partial compensation, you have a close encounter with Amsterdam or the nearby countryside.

Two easy-ish, 6½-hour guided bike tours outside Amsterdam are offered by **Let's Go!** (☎ 020/600-1809). Just call the reservation number and leave your booking on the answering machine. One tour, 30km (19 miles), goes north to the IJsselmeer shore at Edam, Volendam, and Monnickendam; the other, 24km (15 miles), goes east to the castles, windmills, and fortifications of the Gooi and Vecht districts. Each tour costs Dfl 45 ($19.15), discount of Dfl 2.50 ($1.05) with a student card; return ticket by train is not included.

BY BOAT

The **Historic Ferry** (☎ 0900/9292) plies a 2-hour furrow around the harbor and along the IJ from behind Centraal Station. It operates on Sunday from Easter to mid-October at noon, 2, and 4pm; tickets cost Dfl 10 ($4.25) for adults, Dfl 6 ($2.55) for children.

Get closer to nature with **Wetlands Safari** (☎ 020/686-3445), who will take you on boat tours of the watery landscapes and villages around the city. You can also board a flat-bottomed boat in the **Amsterdamse Bos (Amsterdam Woods)** on the southern edge of town.

BY BUS

For many travelers, a quick bus tour is the best way to launch a sightseeing program in a strange city, and though Amsterdam offers its own unique alternative—a canal-boat ride—you might want to get your bearings on land as well. A 3-hour tour costs Dfl 37.50 to Dfl 52.50 ($15.95 to $22.35); on most tours children 4 to 13 are charged half price. Major companies offering these and other motor-coach sightseeing trips are **The Best of Holland,** Damrak 34 (☎ 020/623-1539); **Holland International,** Dam 6 (☎ 020/625-3035); **Keytours,** Dam 19 (☎ 020/624-7304); and **Lindbergh Excursions,** Damrak 26 (☎ 020/622-2766).

ON FOOT

Amsterdam Walking Tours (☎ 020/640-9072) leads guided strolls through historic Amsterdam on Saturday and Sunday at 11am. If you'd rather guide yourself around, try **Audio Tourist,** Oude Spiegelstraat 9 (☎ 020/421-5580), whose map-and-cassette packages allow you to "see Amsterdam by your ears." You can choose different tours lasting from 2 to 3 hours. Renting the cassette player, tape, and map costs Dfl 15 ($6.40) for adults, Dfl 7.50 ($3.20) for children 13 and under, and seniors and holders of an Under-26 Pass get a 20% discount. Audio Tourist operates April to September daily from 9am to 6pm; October to March Tuesday to Sunday 10am to 5pm.

BY AIRPLANE

A 30-minute bird's-eye view of Amsterdam, the tulip fields, the beaches, and nearby Volendam helps you fix the city firmly in its environs and presents quite graphically its all-important relationship with the sea. During summer months, **KLM Cityhopper,** KLM's domestic affiliate, offers Saturday- and Sunday-afternoon sightseeing flights from Schiphol Airport. For details, fares, and booking, call ☎ **020/474-7747.** If money is no object, you can also charter a chopper for an aerial tour of Amsterdam from **KLM Helikopters,** which operates big birds that usually do stuff like servicing North Sea oil rigs. For details, fares, and booking, call ☎ **020/474-7747.**

DIAMOND TOURS

Visitors to Amsterdam during the 1950s and 1960s, when the diamond business was booming, were able to go to the diamond-cutting factories of Amsterdam and take tours through their workrooms. Now you'll be lucky to see one lone polisher working at a small wheel set up in the back of a jewelry store or in the lobby of a factory building. Never mind, you still can get an idea of how a diamond is cut and polished. You need no special directions or instructions to find this sightseeing activity; you see signs all over town for diamond-cutting demonstrations. You're also on your own if you decide to buy.

The major diamond factories and showrooms in Amsterdam are the **Amsterdam Diamond Center,** Rokin 1, just off the Dam (☎ **020/624-5787**); **Coster Diamonds,** Paulus Potterstraat 2–6, near the Rijksmuseum (☎ **020/676-2222**); **Gassan Diamonds,** Nieuwe Uilenburgerstraat 173–175 (☎ **020/622-5333**); **Holshuijsen Stoeltie,** Wagenstraat 13–17 (☎ **020/623-7601**); **Van Moppes Diamonds,** Albert Cuypstraat 2–6, at the daily street market (☎ **020/676-1242**); and **Reuter Diamonds,** Kalverstraat 165 or Singel 526 (☎ **020/623-3500**).

The Guide

"My guides are interesting people, not faceless tour operators," says René Dessing, a suave, bespectacled historian-turned-tour-operator. If you're finicky about your culture, Dessing is the man to go to. He offers everything from architecture walks to painting classes on canal boats. The long list of VIPs who have bought Dessing's pitch, at dizzying rates of Dfl 350 ($148.95) per half day, plus 17.5% VAT, includes Boris Yeltsin and other Russian heads of state. Why bother? Access. Dessing's multilingual freelance guides—trained art historians—can get you into private collections, the Royal Palace even when it's closed to the public, the magnificent Amsterdam school of Scheepvaarthuis (never open to the public), and just about anywhere else you could want to go. Trips to clog-makers and tulip fields, though heavily discouraged, are given a highbrow spin. Some clients wind up spending half their day in a cozy brown cafe. "The idea," says Dessing, "is to make new friends." His company, **Artifex,** Herengracht 342, 1016 CG Amsterdam (☎ **020/620-8112;** fax 020/620-6908), can plan your entire trip to Amsterdam, from air tickets on up, or escort you à la carte. The further ahead you reserve, the more thorough the scheduling.

10 Especially for Kids

Kids may get a little bored at the Amsterdam art museums, but they're more likely to be interested in the **Anne Frankhuis** (see "The Big Four Museums & Galleries" above). There's a section of the Tropenmuseum (see "More Museums & Galleries" above) open only to children ages 6 to 12 (one adult per child is allowed); it's called **Kindermuseum TM Junior** (☎ 020/568-8300 for information). The Vincent van Gogh Museum (see "The Big Four Museums & Galleries" above) has a children's painting area on the ground floor, where budding van Goghs can get in some supervised practice. **Madame Tussaud Scenerama** (see "More Museums & Galleries" above) is always fun for kids, though if they're too small they might be a little frightened by the wax statues. If all else fails, take them to **Intersphere Lasergames,** Prins Hendrikkade 194 (☎ 020/622-4809), where in a gloomy mist-suffused futuristic world they can zap each other until the electric sheep come home. There are theater workshops at the Theatermuseum (see above) for children ages 7 to 12 on Wednesday, Saturday, and Sunday afternoons.

Older kids might appreciate the sheer white-knuckle excitement of—well, **chess,** actually. It's played with giant plastic pieces on an open-air board at Max Euweplein, next to the Casino behind Leidseplein. They can even challenge one of the minor masters who hang around there. Finally, there are the **carillons:** Church belfries and towers throughout the city break into pretty melodies at every possible opportunity—that should hold their attention for around 30 seconds, the first time anyhow.

✪ **Artis Zoo.** Plantage Kerklaan 38–40. ☎ **020/523-3400.** Admission Dfl 25 ($10.65) adults, Dfl 17.50 ($7.45) children 4–11, free for children under 4. Daily 9am–5pm. Tram: 9 or 14 to Plantage Middenlaan.

If you're at a loss for what to do with the kids, the Artis Zoo is a safe bet. Established in 1838, the oldest zoo in the Netherlands houses more than 6,000 animals. Of course, you find the usual tigers, leopards, elephants, camels, and peacocks that no self-respecting zoo can do without. Yet there's also much more, for no extra charge. There's the excellent Planetarium (closed Monday morning), and a Geological and Zoological Museum. The Aquarium, built in 1882 and recently fully renovated, is superbly presented, particularly the sections on the Amazon River, coral reefs, and Amsterdam's own canals, with their fish population and burden of urban detritus. Finally, there's a children's farm, where kids help tend to the needs of resident sheep, goats, chickens, and cows. You can rest for a while and have a snack or lunch at Artis Restaurant. Artis gets 1.2 million visitors yearly.

11 Free Amsterdam

The words *free* and *Dutch* are generally thought to mix together about as well as oil and water. Perhaps rattled by accusations that Amsterdam has grown too expensive, and by stiff competition from Prague in the young-and-alternative market, the VVV tourist office has drawn up a list of free things to see and do in the city. Here are some highlights:

- Admire 15 enormous 17th-century paintings of the Amsterdam Civic Guards, in the **Schuttersgalerij,** a covered passageway between the Begijnhof and the Amsterdams Historisch Museum.
- Visit the **Begijnhof** itself (see "Sights of Religious Significance," earlier in this chapter).
- Judge horseflesh at the **Hollandsche Manège (Dutch Stables),** at Vondelstraat 140, built in 1882 and inspired by the Spanish Riding School in Vienna.

- Cross the bridge over Reguliersgracht at Herengracht, from which you can see no fewer than **15 bridges.**
- Breathe scented air in the **Rijksmuseum Garden** and see fragments from ruined old buildings that are stored there.
- Find out where Amsterdam is going as a city at the permanent town planning exhibition in the **Zuiderkerk.**
- Assess the chance of getting your feet wet, at the **Normaal Amsterdams Peil (Normal Amsterdam Level),** a fixed point against which measurements of sea level are made. Beside a bronze plaque in the passageway between the Muziektheater and the Stadhuis (Town Hall) in Waterlooplein are three glass columns filled with water. The first two show the current sea level at Vlissingen and IJmuiden; the third, 5m (15 feet) above your head, shows the high-water mark during the disastrous floods in Zeeland in 1953. The NAP sets the standard for altitude measurements in Europe.
- Hear the **lunchtime concerts,** 12:30 to 1pm, at the Muziektheater (Tuesday) and the Concertgebouw (Wednesday) every week from October to June.
- Sail on the **IJ ferry** across the channel from behind Centraal Station to North Amsterdam (see "Getting Around" in chapter 3).
- Visit the **Floating Flower Market** on the Singel (see "Markets" in chapter 8)—the flowers, however, are not free.
- Tour Europe in a single street, Roemer Visscherstraat 20–30, where the **Seven Countries Houses** were built in 1894 in the styles of Germany, France, Spain, Italy, Russia, Holland, and England.
- Stand on the **Magere Brug (Skinny Bridge)** over the River Amstel between Kerkstraat and Nieuwe Kerkstraat.
- Check out the **narrowest houses** (see "Historic Buildings & Monuments," earlier in this chapter).
- Hear the music from four **17th-century carillons:** Westertoren (Tuesday noon to 1pm); Zuidertoren (Thursday noon to 1pm); Munttoren (Friday noon to 1pm); and Oude Kerkstoren (Saturday 4 to 5pm).
- Listen to the earthier performances of the **barrel organs** in the street (mixed with the rattle of money as the organ-grinder tries to persuade you to make a donation).

As well as the preceding list, the streets of Amsterdam are so filled with spectacle that they constitute an ongoing, 24-hour special event all by themselves. They do, however, come into full bloom at such times as the **Spui Art Market,** from March to December, when local artists mount outdoor exhibitions along the Spui. On April 30, Amsterdam, along with the rest of the country, holds a gigantic dawn-to-dawn street carnival in celebration of **Queen's Day.** In the last two weeks in May, **Floating Amsterdam** transforms the Amstel River into an outdoor theater, with performances near the Muziektheater. In August, the Prinsengracht concerts set the air ringing with music from flat-bottomed boats up and down the canal; late August, when there are folk dances on Dam Square with participants from around the world performing their own native dances; and early September, when there's a spectacular floral parade from the flower market at Aalsmeer to Amsterdam. There are ✪ free lunchtime concerts at 12:30pm on Tuesdays at the Muziektheater, and on Wednesdays in the Concertgebouw that are quite special. The program may feature chamber music, symphonic performances, or abbreviated previews of a full concert to be played to paying guests that same evening by local or visiting musical groups. In mid-April, there's no admission fee at most Amsterdam museums during National Museum Weekend, while a few charge greatly discounted fees.

12 Sports & Recreation

RECREATION, LEISURE & OUTDOOR ACTIVITIES

BEAUTY SALONS   The **Body Tuning Clinic,** Jan Luykenstraat 40 (☎ **020/ 662-0909**), and **Vitalitae,** Nieuwezijds Voorburgwal 301 (☎ **020/624-4441**), will both take excellent care of the outer you.

BOATING & CANOEING   From March 15 to October 15, you can go to Loosdrecht, outside Amsterdam, to rent sailing equipment at **Ottenhome** (☎ **035/ 582-3331**). **Yacht Haven Robinson,** Dorpstraat 3, Landsmeer (☎ **020/482-1346**), rents rowing equipment. Canoes can be rented in the **Amsterdamse Bos,** south of the city, for use in the park only.

BOWLING   If you find you just have to knock down a few pins, try **Knijn Bowling,** Scheldeplein 3 (☎ **020/664-2211**).

CYCLING   South of the city is Amsterdamse Bos, where you can rent bicycles (☎ **020/644-5473**) for touring the woodland's paths. Of course, you can always do as Amsterdammers do and explore all those city bridges and canals by bike (see "By Bicycle & Moped," under "Getting Around" in chapter 3 for rental information).

FISHING   Anglers should try the **Bosbaan** artificial pond in Amsterdamse Bos, south of the city. You can get a license there at Nikolaswetsantraat 10 (☎ **020/ 626-4988**), open Tuesday to Friday, or at any fishing supply store in the area.

FITNESS CENTERS   If don't want to neglect your exercise routine, there are several centers you can try, including **Fitness Aerobic Center Jansen,** Rokin 109–111 (☎ **020/626-9366**); **Sporting Club Leidseplein,** Korte Leidsedwarsstraat 18 (☎ **020/620-6631**); **Garden Gym,** Jodenbreestraat 158 (☎ **020/626-8772**); and **Splash,** Looiersgracht 26 (☎ **020/624-8404**).

GOLF   There are public golf courses in or near Amsterdam at the **Golf en Conference Center Amstelborgh,** Borchlandweg 6 (☎ **020/697-5000**); **Sloten,** Sloterweg 1045 (☎ **020/614-2402**); **Waterland Golf Course,** Buikslotermeerdijk 141 (☎ **020/636-1010**); and **Spaarnwoude Golf Course,** Het Hogeland 2, Spaarnwoude (☎ **020/538-5599**). Call ahead for greens fees and tee times.

HORSEBACK RIDING   Riding, both indoor and outdoor, is offered at **Amsterdamse Manege,** Nieuwe Kalfjeslaan 25 (☎ **020/643-1342**); indoor riding only is available at **Nieuw Amstelland Manege,** Jan Tooropplantsoen 17 (☎ **020/643-2468**). Horses rented at **De Ruif Manege,** Sloterweg 675 (☎ **020/615-6667**), can be ridden in Amsterdamse Bos.

ICE SKATING   All those Dutch paintings of people skating and sledding—not to mention the story of Hans Brinker and his silver skates—will surely get you thinking about skating on Amsterdam's ponds and canals (see the box "Skating on the Dutch Canals"). However, doing this won't be easy unless you're willing to shell out for a new pair of skates, since very few places rent them. One that does is **Jaap Eden Baan,** Radioweg 64 (☎ **020/694-9894**), where you can rent skates from November to February, and they even allow you to take them out of the rink. The Jaap Eden Baan's marvelous outdoor rink is popular in wintertime, but unless you're highly competent, watch out for the long lines of speed skaters practicing for the next Eleven Cities Race inn Friesland.

JOGGING   The two main jogging areas are Vondelpark in the Center and Amsterdamse Bos on the southern edge of the city. You can also run along the Amstel River.

Skating on the Dutch Canals

In winter, the Dutch watch the falling thermometers with the same focus as people in Aspen and Chamonix. When the temperature drops low enough for long enough, the landscape becomes a big ice-maker, and rivers, canals, and lakes become sparkling highways through the countryside. If you're here at such a time, the best experience of all may be skating on the canals of Amsterdam to the strains of classical music. Little kiosks are set up on the ice to dispense heart-warming liqueurs. Just be cautious when skating under bridges, and in general don't go anywhere that the Dutch themselves don't.

If you choose to run along the canals, as many do, watch out for uneven cobbles, loose paving stones, and dog poop.

SAILING   Sailboats and sailboards can be rented at **Duikelaars** on the Sloterplas Lake, Sloterpark, Noordzijde 41 (☎ **020/613-8855**).

SAUNA & MASSAGE   Sauna Deco, Herengracht 115 (☎ **020/627-1773**), and **Oibibio Thermen,** Prins Hendrikkade 20–21 (☎ **020/553-9311**), are two places where, in Dutch style, you get down to the altogether in mixed facilities. At **Koan Float,** Herengracht 321 (☎ **020/625-4970**), you can float away the stress of a hard day's sightseeing.

SWIMMING   Amsterdam's state-of-the-art swimming facility is **De Mirandabad,** De Mirandalaan 9 (☎ **020/642-8080**). This ultramodern complex features indoor and outdoor pools with wave machines, slides, and other amusements. **The Marnixbad,** Marnixplein 5 (☎ **020/625-4843**), is a glass-enclosed public pool. The **Zuiderbad,** Hobbemastraat 26 (☎ **020/679-2217**), dates from 1911. Other public pools are the **Floralparkbad,** Sneeuwbalweg 5 (☎ **020/636-8121**), and the **Sloterparkbad,** Slotermeerlaan 2 (☎ **020/611-4565**).

TABLE TENNIS   Ping-Pong to your heart's content at **Tafeltennis Centrum Amsterdam,** Keizersgracht 209 (☎ **020/624-5780**).

TENNIS & SQUASH   You find indoor courts at **Frans Otten Stadion,** Stadionstraat 10 (☎ **020/662-8767**). For both indoor and outdoor courts, try **Gold Star,** Karel Lotsylaan 20 (☎ **020/644-5483**), and **Amstelpark Tenniscentre,** Koenenkade 8, Amsterdamse Bos (☎ **020/644-5436**), which has a total of 36 courts.

Squash courts can be found at **Squash City,** Ketelmakerstraat 6 (near Centraal Station) (☎ **020/626-7883**).

SPECTATOR SPORTS

AMERICAN FOOTBALL   Yes, there's an American football league in Europe, and Amsterdam has its own franchise. The Amsterdam Admirals, complete with cheerleaders, is based at the Amsterdam ArenA (see "Soccer," below).

BASEBALL   Honk if you like baseball (the game is called *honkbal* in Holland). The Amsterdam Pirates aren't the greatest practitioners of the art, but they have their moments, as you can see at the **Sportpark,** Jan van Galenstraat 16 (☎ **020/684-8143**).

SOCCER   Soccer (called football in Europe) is absolutely the biggest game in Holland. Amsterdam's world-famous team, Ajax, is the best in Holland, and quite often the best in Europe as well. Ajax plays its home matches in a fabulous new stadium, the **Amsterdam ArenA,** in Amsterdam Zuidoost (☎ **020/311-1333**).

7

Strolling & Biking in Amsterdam

The best way to discover Amsterdam is on foot. The first tour described here picks a way among the essential sights of the horseshoe of 17th-century, Golden Age canals. Tours 2, 3, and 4 focus on the Old Center, the Jordaan, and Jewish Amsterdam, respectively.

Our fifth tour is no leisurely stroll, but a taste of that essential Amsterdam experience: cycling. Bicycles are a key part of the mechanism that makes Holland tick, and no trip to Amsterdam can be considered complete without some time spent in the saddle. This tour whisks you out from the Center, along the Amstel River, for a breath of fresh country air a few miles beyond, at the historic riverside village of Ouderkerk aan de Amstel.

Walking Tour 1: The Golden Age Canals

Start: Herenmarkt (off Brouwersgracht).
Finish: River Amstel.
Time: 3 hours to all day, depending on how long you linger in museums and shops along the way.
Best Times: Begin in the morning.

The three 17th-century canals you explore on this tour—Herengracht (Gentlemen's Canal), Keizersgracht (Emperor's Canal), and Prinsengracht (Princes' Canal)—are the very heart of Golden Age Amsterdam, emblems of the city's wealth and pride in the heyday of its expansion. Each one deserves at least a morning or afternoon all to itself. Time being limited, we're going to combine them in one monumental effort; if you're not so rushed, by all means slice the tour up into two or three segments for a more leisurely experience.

You stroll along miles of tree-lined canals and pass innumerable old canal houses with gables in various styles (bell, step, neck, and variations), classical facades, warehouses converted to apartments, houseboats, bridges, museums, cafes, restaurants, boutiques and offbeat shops, seagulls and herons. I'm only going to mention the most special sights and point out some insider tips along the way. This should leave you with plenty of space for making your own discoveries along the way.

The jump-off point, which is within easy walking distance of Centraal Station (tram: 1, 2, 5, 9, 16, 17, 20, 24, or 25), is:

1. **West-Indisch Huis (West India House),** at Herenmarkt, just off Brouwersgracht (see "Historic Buildings & Monuments" in

Walking Tour: The Golden Age Canals

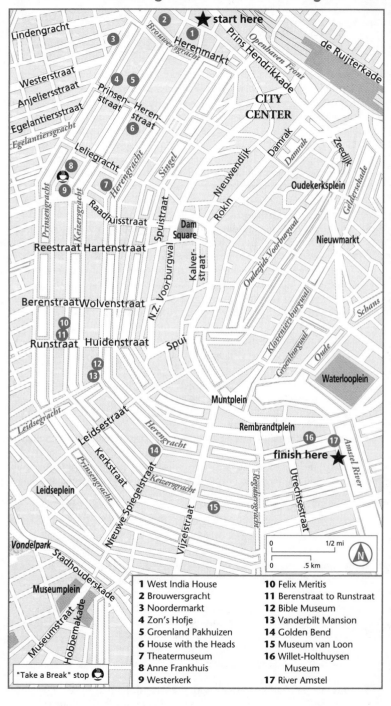

start here

Lindengracht

Brouwersgracht

2

1

Herenmarkt

Prins Hendrikkade

Openhaven Front

de Ruijterkade

3

Westerstraat

Anjeliersstraat

4 **5**

Prinsen-
straat

Heren-
straat

**CITY
CENTER**

Egelantiersstraat

6

Egelantiersgracht

Nieuwendijk

Damrak

Damrak

Zeedijk

Leliegracht

Herengracht

Singel

Oudekerksplein

Geldersekade

8

7

Prinsengracht

Keizersgracht

Raadhuisstraat

Spuistraat

Rokin

Nieuwmarkt

9

**Dam
Square**

Reestraat Hartenstraat

N.Z. Voorburgwal

Oudezijds Voorburgwal

Kalver-
straat

Schans

BerenstraatWolvenstraat

Kloveniersburgwal

Groenburgwal

Oude

10

11

Runstraat   Huidenstraat

Spui

Waterlooplein

12

13

Muntplein

Leidsegracht

Leidsestraat

Herengracht

Rembrandtplein

16 **17**

Amstel River

Kerkstraat

Prinsengracht

14

Keizersgracht

finish here

Leidseplein

Nieuwe Spiegelstraat

Vijzelstraat

Reguliersgracht

Utrechtsestraat

15

Vondelpark

Stadhouderskade

| 0 | | 1/2 mi |
| 0 | | .5 km |

N

Museumplein

Museumstraat

Hobbemakade

"Take a Break" stop

1 West India House
2 Brouwersgracht
3 Noordermarkt
4 Zon's Hofje
5 Groenland Pakhuizen
6 House with the Heads
7 Theatermuseum
8 Anne Frankhuis
9 Westerkerk

10 Felix Meritis
11 Berenstraat to Runstraat
12 Bible Museum
13 Vanderbilt Mansion
14 Golden Bend
15 Museum van Loon
16 Willet-Holthuysen
     Museum
17 River Amstel

chapter 6). The 17th-century headquarters of the Dutch company that handled trade with the Americas and Africa later became offices of a social-welfare organization, a Lutheran orphanage, and now houses educational institutes.

Walk up the tranquil, residential:

2. Brouwersgracht (Brewers' Canal) to the point where it joins Prinsengracht. Thanks to its humpback bridges, moored houseboats, and 17th- and 18th-century brewery *pakhuizen* (warehouses), this is one of Amsterdam's most photogenic corners. Most warehouses have been turned into apartments. Worth special attention are nos. 204 and 206, "Het Kleine Groene Hert" (the Little Green Deer) and "Het Groote Groene Hert" (the Big Green Deer)—each building has a gable crowned with a sculpted deer painted green. Note two excellent brown cafes: Tabac, Brouwersgracht 101, and Papeneiland, Prinsengracht 2–4, for possible future reference.

On Prinsengracht, which in the 17th century was home to storekeepers and craftsmen, your first stop is:

3. Noordermarkt. On Saturday from 10am to 3pm this old market square hosts a Farmers' Market for "bio" (organic) products and a Bird Market. A popular flea market that overflows onto neighboring Westerstraat takes over on Monday from 7:30am to 1:30pm; clothes that were fashionable a decade and more ago are, for some reason, highly esteemed. Pause for a moment to admire the elaborate gables of the houses at nos. 15–22, each one decorated with an agricultural image—a cow, a sheep, a chicken—from the time when a livestock market was held here.

The Noorderkerk (North Church), the last masterpiece by Hendrick de Keyser, the guiding hand behind many of Amsterdam's historic churches, dominates the square. It's something of a rarity in this nominally Calvinist city, since it has a large and active congregation. A plaque on the facade recalls the February 1941 strike in protest at Nazi deportation of the city's Jewish community (see "Sights of Religious Significance" in chapter 6).

Continue along Prinsengracht to the bridge at Prinsenstraat, and cross over. A few steps back along the canal on this side is:

4. Zon's Hofje, at Prinsengracht 159–171, a hidden almshouse surrounding a garden at the end of the passageway. You can discreetly (people live here) walk through the passageway to the garden, which has a carved plaque from a vanished clandestine church called Kleine Zon (Little Sun) showing animals piling two-by-two onto Noah's Ark.

Farther back along the canal, at nos. 89–133, is another former almshouse, Van Brienen's Hofje, from 1790 (also known as De Ster Hofje after De Ster brewery that once occupied the site). Merchant Jan van Brienen supposedly built it in gratitude for his escape from a vault in which he had accidentally been locked. But I don't want you to have to backtrack too far, and besides, this one is usually closed, so unless you're something of a *hofje* enthusiast you can leave it alone.

Head down Prinsenstraat to Keizersgracht, named after the Austrian Emperor Maximilian, whose crown graces the summit of the Westerkerk's spire. A short detour to the left at this point brings you to the:

5. Groenland Pakhuizen (Greenland Warehouses), at nos. 40–44. Built in 1621 to store whale oil, they are now well-oiled apartments.

Cross the Keizersgracht bridge, noting the houseboats tied up on either side, to Herenstraat, and go right on Keizersgracht, to the:

6. Huis met de Hoofden (House with the Heads), built in 1621–22 by Hendrick de Keyser, at no. 123. The heads in question on the facade represent, from left to right, Apollo, Ceres, Mars, Athena, Bacchus, and Diana.

Turn left along the pretty Leliegracht side canal, then, right onto Herengracht, the ultimate Amsterdam addresses for flourishing bankers and merchants of the 17th century:

7. Theatermuseum, entrance at Herengracht 168, a graceful house built in 1638 for Michiel Pauw, who established a colony in America and named it Pavonia after his august self. It extends into the flamboyant Bartolotti House at nos. 170–172, built in 1617 for Guillielmo Bartolotti, who began life as homely old Willem van den Heuvel and switched to the fancy moniker after he made his bundle in brewing and banking (see "More Museums & Galleries" in chapter 6).

Backtrack to Leliegracht; then, go up onto Prinsengracht—noting on the way, the Greenpeace headquarters at Leliegracht 51, in a rare Amsterdam *jugendstil* house (1905), designed by Gerrit van Arkel—and turn left to visit the:

8. Anne Frankhuis, at Prinsengracht 263, where the young Jewish girl Anne Frank (1929–45) hid from the Nazis and wrote her imperishable diary. The earlier you get to this house the better, because the line to get in grows as the day progresses (see "The Big Four Museums & Galleries" in chapter 6).

Note De Prins at Prinsengracht 124 on the opposite bank; for reasons of time, I'm not proposing this cafe/restaurant for a break on this tour, but it is my Best Value restaurant recommendation and I strongly suggest you keep it in mind for another time (see "Along the Canal Belt" in chapter 5).

At this point, however, you may need a break for lunch, so pop into:

🍵 **TAKE A BREAK   Rum Runners,** Prinsengracht 277 (☎ **020/627-4079**), a Caribbean restaurant where they serve a stiff margarita and a mean guacamole, along with other laid-back drinks and meals (see "Along the Canal Belt," in chapter 5).

Afterward, with miles and miles to go before you sleep, you may be tempted to stow away on a pedal bike from the Canal Bikes moorings outside Rum Runners, but if you're staying with the program, continue a few steps to Westermarkt and its:

9. Westerkerk. The Dutch Renaissance church was begun in 1620, at the same time as the Noorderkerk, and was designed by Hendrick de Keyser. Hendrick's son Pieter took over after his father's death, and the church was opened in 1631 (see "Sights of Religious Significance" in chapter 6). Should you be passing between June and mid-September, from Wednesday to Saturday, you can climb to near the summit of the Westertoren, 85m (277 ft.) high, nicknamed "Lange Jan" (Long John).

At Westermarkt 6 is the house where Descartes lived in 1634, when he wrote his *Treatise on the Passions of the Soul*. At the time, Descartes apparently thought he was in need of some nonphilosophical passion (therefore, he undoubtedly was), so he had an affair with his maid, producing a child. Also on Westermarkt is a bronze sculpture of Anne Frank, and the pink marble triangles of the Homomonument, dedicated to persecuted gays and lesbians.

It's a bit soon for another break, but in case Rum Runners hadn't enough local color for your taste, cross over Westermarkt and try:

🍵 **TAKE A BREAK   De Kalkhoven,** Prinsengracht 283 (☎ **020/624-9649**), which has a satisfactory supply of local color—rugs on the tabletops and serious drinkers at the bar. You can eat plain but hearty Dutch bar food here.

A short westward detour on Rozengracht brings you to the fanciful Blue Gold Fish gift shop at no. 17 (see "Crafts & Curios" in chapter 8). Otherwise, continue along Prinsengracht to Reestraat, where you turn left. At Keizersgracht go right to:

10. **Felix Meritis,** Keizersgracht 324, built in 1788 by Jacob Otten Husly as the headquarters of a Calvinist philosophical society. The name (which was the group's motto) means "Happiness Through Merit," and they invited luminaries such as Czar Alexander 1 and Napoléon to this Palladian setting, complete with Corinthian columns and triangular pediment, to experience the consolations of that philosophy. The building was later the home of the Dutch Communist Party, and today keeps faith with its free-thinking past by hosting avant-garde theater and dance troupes (see "Other Venues" in chapter 9).

Continue along the canal, across Berenstraat, toward Runstraat. On this stretch, we're going to do something different. Instead of standing directly in front of buildings of interest, craning your neck skyward to eyeball the detail, I want you to walk along the near bank of Keizersgracht (the one with even-numbered houses) and look across the water to the other side, so that you can view things in panorama (in summer, leaves on elm trees along the canal screen some facades).

11. **Berenstraat to Runstraat.** The third building along from Wolvenstraat (no. 313), an office block from 1914, is almost modern in Keizersgracht-time.

Two houses along (no. 317), the stately canal-side home belonged to one Christoffel Brants, who counted Peter the Great among his acquaintances. A story goes that Peter sailed into Amsterdam in 1716, planning to stay a night here. The Czar of All the Russias got royally drunk, kept the mayor waiting at a reception in his honor, and then removed to the Russian ambassador's residence at Herengracht 527 to sleep off his hangover.

Next door (no. 319), is a work by Philips Vingboons from 1639. You can compare its ornate neoclassical facade to the Theatermuseum building by the same architect, at Herengracht 168 (see above).

Note how narrow is the facade of the seventh building before Huidenstraat (no. 345a), and run your eyes over the trio of graceful neck gables on the last three houses (nos. 353–357).

At Runstraat, cross over to Huidenstraat and go along it to Herengracht. Turn right to the:

12. **Bijbels Museum (Biblical Museum),** at Herengracht 366–368, in one of a group of four 1660s houses (364–370) with delicate neck gables, built by Philips Vingboons for timber merchant Jacob Cromhout. These houses are known as the "Father, Mother, and Twins." The museum, naturally enough, features Bibles and things biblical, but its canal house setting and painted ceilings from 1717 by Jacob de Wit are at least as interesting (see "More Museums & Galleries" in chapter 6).

Continuing a few doors farther along Herengracht, to:

13. **The Vanderbilt Mansion,** at nos. 380–382. Well, it's not the Fifth Avenue mansion built for U.S. tycoon William H. Vanderbilt in New York, but a replica (and, as the original no longer exists, the only example) constructed in 1889 for Dutch tobacco mogul Jacob Nienhuijs.

Cross elegant Leidsegracht, dug in 1664 for barge traffic to and from Leiden, and cross busy Leidsestraat to the:

14. **Gouden Bocht (Golden Bend).** You can trace the development of the rich folk's wealth and tastes as you progress up the house numbers on Herengracht, and this

section, so named because of its opulent palaces, is the top of the heap. Built with old money around the 1670s, in the fading afterglow of the Golden Age, when French-influenced neoclassicism was all the rage, they are on double lots with double steps and central entrances. Compare the sober baroque facades here with the exuberant gabled houses from half a century earlier, back along the canal.

Turn right onto Nieuwe Spiegelstraat, a street lined with expensive antiques shops (at its end you can see the Rijksmuseum). Go left on the far bank of Keizersgracht to the:

15. Museum Van Loon, at no. 672. This museum gives you a rare glimpse behind the gables at a patrician house of the post-Golden Age (see "More Museums & Galleries" in chapter 6).

Cross Reguliersgracht and return to Herengracht, passing through neat little Thorbeckeplein (with some not-so-neat little sex clubs behind it), and go right, across Utrechtsestraat, which is a cornucopia of good restaurants and variegated stores, to the:

16. Museum Willet-Holthuysen, at Herengracht 605, a patrician canal house dating from 1687, richly decorated in Louis XIV style. The table under a big chandelier in the dining salon, is set for a meal being served more than 300 years late (see "More Museums & Galleries" in chapter 6).

Stroll to the end of Herengracht and finish your trek at the:

17. Amstel River, which at this point is thick with houseboats and canal barges. To your left is the recently refurbished Blauwbrug (Blue Bridge) over the Amstel, built in 1884 on the lines of Paris's Pont Alexandre III that spans the Seine; to your right, the famous Magere Brug (Skinny Bridge) double drawbridge.

Walking the short distance along the river to Waterlooplein, or backtracking to Utrechtsestraat, puts you on the tram net for return to your hotel. Maybe you're footsore and hungry, though, and want to eat *right now.* If the weather is fine, you can do no better than to hobble a short distance to Prinsengracht, to:

🌀 **WINDING DOWN   Kort,** Amstelveld 12 (☎ **020/626-1199**), which is my best al fresco dining recommendation, thanks to great food and a big sidewalk terrace beside the canal (see "Along the Canal Belt" in chapter 5).

Walking Tour 2: The Old Center

Start: The VVV office at Stationsplein, in front of Centraal Station.
Finish: Oude Brugsteeg.
Time: 2½ to 4 hours, depending on how long you spend in museums or shops.
Best Times: If you want to see the museums, it's best to start just before 10am, when they open. Otherwise, any time is fine.

This tour takes you to some of the main city-center points of interest and then crosses through an area of 16th-century canals to the Red Light District. It ends smack dab in the middle of the district—but I'll point out a fast escape route. Begin beside the VVV office, at:

1. Centraal Station, designed by Petrus Josephus Hubertus Cuypers and built between 1884 and 1889 on an artificial island in the IJ channel (see "Historic Buildings & Monuments" in chapter 6). Walk straight ahead along Damrak. In the 17th century, the adjacent canal was filled with small cargo boats and lined with ships' chandlers and mapmaker shops; today it is a brash street bordered by tourist shops, cafes, the Amsterdam Sex Museum at no. 18, and department stores, such as De Bijenkorf, Amsterdam's answer to Bloomingdale's (at Dam 1, but with entrances on Damrak also). As you go along Damrak, look to your left, past the canal boat moorings, at the houses on the opposite bank, which stand, Venice style, in the water. When you reach:

2. **Damrak 28–30,** look up at the office building and you see 4 baboons and 22 owls peering down at you. These sculptures on the facade are by Joseph Mendes da Costa (1863–1939), who was noted for his animal sculptures and was given an honorary degree in biology by the University of Groningen.

Down Damrak a bit and across the street in Beursplein is the:

3. **Beurs van Berlage (Stock Exchange),** built by Hendrik Petrus Berlage between 1896 and 1903 and now a concert venue (see "Historic Buildings & Monuments" in chapter 6). Also here is:

4. **'y Beursmannetje,** a statue of a man with a folded newspaper under his arm, given to the city by *Financieel Dagblad,* Holland's main business newspaper.

Leading off the other side of Damrak, is:

5. **Zoutsteeg,** a narrow street filled with restaurants and stores; centuries ago, when Damrak was part of the Amstel River, ships unloaded salt here (*zout* means "salt" in Dutch).

Cross Nieuwendijk to Gravenstraat (which is a little to the right). You pass:

6. **De Drie Fleschjes** (at no. 16), a 17th-century *proeflokaal* (tasting house), where merchants sampled liqueurs and spirits. From here you can see the:

7. **Nieuwe Kerk (New Church),** the National Church, where since 1815 all kings and queens of the Netherlands have been crowned (see "Sights of Religious Significance" in chapter 6).

Continuing around the church, you see, across Nieuwezijds Voorburgwal, the:

8. **Koninklijke Paleis (Royal Palace),** built as a town hall between 1648 and 1655 and later chosen as an official residence of the royal family (see "Historic Buildings & Monuments" in chapter 6). A symbolic sculpture on the rooftop depicts Atlas carrying a globe.

Directly across the square from the Royal Palace is the:

9. **National Monument,** built in 1956 to honor the World War II dead. This 72-foot obelisk, designed by J. J. P. Oud, is embedded with three sculptures by J. W. Rädeler: *War,* symbolized by four male figures; *Peace,* represented by a woman and child; and *Resistance,* signified by two men with howling dogs. The monument is the focus of a memorial ceremony every May 4, when the queen places a wreath on the spot. During the rest of the year the monument area is a hangout for teens. To the left, if you're facing the palace, is Kalverstraat, the country's busiest pedestrian shopping street.

Stroll onto Kalverstraat, lined with popular department stores, shops, and boutiques, and look for the:

10. **Amsterdams Historisch Museum,** at Kalverstraat 92. You see a porch dating from 1592 that used to be the entrance to the city orphanage and is now the museum entrance. The outer courtyard was for the boys; to the left are cupboards where they stored their tools. The inner courtyard was for the girls; it's now the museum entrance. The museum itself is fascinating (see "More Museums & Galleries" in chapter 6).

After visiting the museum, pass through a small alleyway, the Schuttersgalerij, a magnificent gallery lined with 16th- and 17th-century militia paintings, to the:

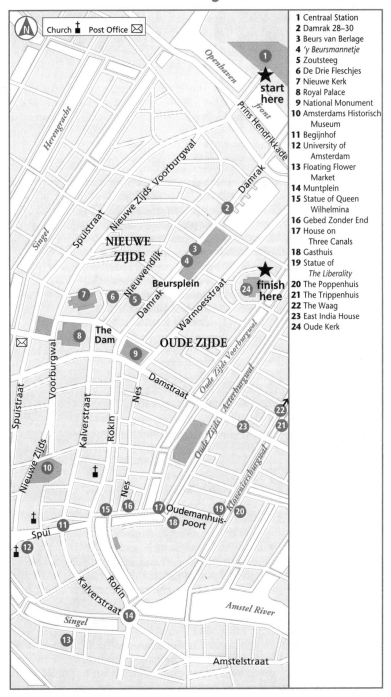

Church ✝ Post Office ✉

start here

finish here

Openhaven

Prins Hendrikkade

Herengracht

Nieuwe Zijds Voorburgwal

Spuistraat

Singel

Damrak

NIEUWE ZIJDE

Nieuwendijk

Beursplein

Warmoesstraat

Damrak

The Dam

Voorburgwal

OUDE ZIJDE

Oude Zijds Voorburgwal

Achterburgwal

Damstraat

Nes

Kalverstraat

Rokin

Nieuwe Zijds

Spuistraat

Oude Zijds

Kloveniersburgwal

Oudemanhuis-poort

Spui

Rokin

Kalverstraat

Singel

Amstel River

Amstelstraat

1 Centraal Station
2 Damrak 28–30
3 Beurs van Berlage
4 'y Beursmannetje
5 Zoutsteeg
6 De Drie Fleschjes
7 Nieuwe Kerk
8 Royal Palace
9 National Monument
10 Amsterdams Historisch Museum
11 Begijnhof
12 University of Amsterdam
13 Floating Flower Market
14 Muntplein
15 Statue of Queen Wilhelmina
16 Gebed Zonder End
17 House on Three Canals
18 Gasthuis
19 Statue of *The Liberality*
20 The Poppenhuis
21 The Trippenhuis
22 The Waag
23 East India House
24 Oude Kerk

11. **Begijnhof,** where devout women lived since the 14th century. No. 34, the oldest house in Amsterdam, was built in 1475 and is one of only two wooden houses remaining in the city (see "Sights of Religious Significance" in chapter 6).

Pass between nos. 37 and 38 into Spui. Opposite is the Maagdenhuis, the main building of the:

12. **University of Amsterdam.** You wouldn't even notice it if you didn't know where to look. Part of the university has been moved outside the city, but some departments remain in Amsterdam, including the literature and history departments on Spuistraat and this main building here. You also see a statue of a small boy, *Het Lieverdje,* supposed to represent a typical Amsterdam kid.

After all that walking you're probably ready to:

☕ **TAKE A BREAK   Café Hoppe,** Spuistraat 18–20 (☎ **020/623-7849**), a brown cafe dating from 1670, is a good place to stop for a drink and a snack. It's often crowded with regulars and adventurous tourists; in good weather, the crowd spills out onto the sidewalk. A convivial atmosphere and authentic brown-cafe decor make it a great place to while away an afternoon. If Hoppe is too crowded, try the equally inviting **Grand-Café Luxembourg,** Spuistraat 24 (☎ **020/620-6264**).

When you're ready to resume your tour, walk up Spui, to the Singel, turn left to the bridge, and cross over to the opposite bank. This brings you to the:

13. **Bloemenmarkt (Floating Flower Market),** one of Amsterdam's great spots. It's like a botanical garden that happened to go adrift on the canal. This is probably the best and certainly the most atmospheric place to buy cut flowers and bulbs. Nearby is:

14. **Muntplein,** which has become a busy tram intersection, and its Munttoren (Mint Tower), whose bells sing out gaily in concert on Tuesday and Friday at 12:30 and 1pm (see "Historic Buildings & Monuments" in chapter 6).

Turn left at Rokin, and pass the:

15. **Statue of Queen Wilhelmina.** Then walk into Lange Brugsteeg. Past Nes is:

16. **Gebed Zonder End (Prayer Without Ending),** an alley, the name of which comes from the convents that used to be here; it's said that you could always hear the murmur of prayers from behind the walls.

Follow Grimburgwal across Oudezijds Voorburgwal and Oudezijds Achterburgwal. Between these canals is the:

17. **House on Three Canals.** From here, cross the bridge to the far side of Oudezijds Achterburgwal (the home of the Erotic Museum, at no. 54, the Tattoo Museum at no. 130, and the Hash Marihuana Hemp Museum at no. 148; (see chapter 6 for all three), where you pass the:

18. **Gasthuis,** once a hospital and now part of the University of Amsterdam campus. Turn into arcaded Oudemanhuispoort, which hosts a secondhand book market popular with students.

At the end of the arcade, turn left on Kloveniersburgwal, having first look above the exterior doorway for the:

19. **Statue of *The Liberality,*** a seated female figure carrying three objects: a cornucopia (horn of plenty), symbolizing abundance; a book, symbolizing wisdom; and an oil lamp, symbolizing enlightenment. An old man and an old woman at her sides represent old age and poverty. The statues were done by the city sculptor A. Ziesenis in 1785.

Continue on Kloveniersburgwal, cross over the canal at the next bridge, and backtrack a short way to:

20. **The Poppenhuis,** at Kloveniersburgwal 95. This lovely canal house in classical mansion style was built in 1642 by the architect Philips Vingboons for Joan Poppen, the dissolute grandson and heir of a rich German merchant. The youth hostel next door at no. 97 was originally a home for retired ships' captains.

Continue on Kloveniersburgwal to:

21. **The Trippenhuis,** at Kloveniersburgwal 29. This was built between 1660 and 1664 by Philips Vingboons for the Trip brothers, who were arms dealers, which accounts for the martial images and emblems dotted about the house. Originally, there were two houses behind a single classical facade, but the two have since been joined.

Continue to Nieuwmarkt and:

22. **De Waag (Weigh House),** originally one of the city's medieval gates, and later the Weigh House and guild offices (see "Historic Buildings & Monuments" in chapter 6). It now houses a multimedia center and a smart cafe-restaurant.

After taking a turn around bustling Nieuwmarkt, come back along the opposite bank of Kloveniersburgwal to Oude Hoogstraat, and turn right to:

23. **East India House (Oostindisch Huis)** and its courtyard, dating from 1606. This was headquarters of the Dutch East India Company, the V.O.C. (Verenigde Oost Indische Compagnie). It now belongs to the University of Amsterdam (see "Historic Buildings & Monuments" in chapter 6).

Continue along Oude Hoogstraat, cross the canal (straight ahead) onto Oude Doelenstraat, and cross the next canal, too. The next step takes you to the heart of the Red Light District (if you don't want to go there, you can make a quick escape along the fringe of the district: Keep straight on through Damstraat and don't stop until you reach the Dam). If you have no objections to viewing the Red Light District in all its tacky glory, turn right onto Oudezijds Voorburgwal, and keep straight on to the:

24. **Oude Kerk,** a late Gothic church begun in 1300. Rembrandt's wife Saskia is buried here (see "Sights of Religious Significance" in chapter 6). Nowadays, the pretty little gabled almshouses around the church feature red-fringed windows through which you can see scantily dressed ladies of the Red Light District.

Finally, turn right through Enge Kerksteeg, right again onto Warmoesstraat, and left onto Oude Brugsteeg. At the end of this small street, to your left you see a gable decorated with a coat of arms protected by two lions. The building was early Amsterdam's customhouse, and the city crest you're looking at is a fitting end to your walk through the old heart of Amsterdam.

Walking Tour 3: The Jordaan

Start: Brouwersgracht.
Finish: Noordermarkt.
Time: Allow between 1½ and 2 hours.
Best Times: Anytime, but if you want to visit one of the Jordaan's lively markets, go either on a Monday morning or on Saturday. On Monday there's a general market at Noordermarkt and along Westerstraat where you find, among other items, fabrics and secondhand clothing. On Saturday, Noordermarkt hosts a bird market and a farmer's market featuring organically grown produce.

There's little in the way of "attractions" in the old working-class district called the Jordaan, but the area has a charm of its own. The neighborhood was originally built for artists, craftsmen, and tradesmen, and the old character still remains, though gentrification has left its mark. Public transportation ranges from sketchy to nonexistent here, so the best way to get at the Jordaan is to walk. The start of this walking tour is:

1. **Brouwersgracht.** Walk along the houseboat-lined canal side, past the statue of the writer Theo Thijssen (1879–1943) to:

2. **Palmgracht.** The house at no. 28–30 hides a small courtyard behind its green door. The turnip on the gable stone is a pun on the name of a former owner, who was called "Raep," which means (you guessed it) turnip. Turn left into Palmdwarsstraat, which leads into Tweede Goudsbloemdwarsstraat and Lindengracht. Turn right and take the first street on the left to:

3. **Karthuizerplantsoen.** Nothing is left of the Carthusian monastery that once occupied this corner and extended toward Lijnbaansgracht. A children's playground now marks the spot where the monastery's cemetery stood. At Karthuizerstraat 11–19 you see a perfect row of neck-gabled houses from 1731, named after the four seasons. Farther down this street, at nos. 69–191, is the Huiszitten Weduwenhof, a peaceful courtyard surrounded by houses that were once the homes of poor widows and are now occupied by students.

Turn left into Tichelstraat, cross Westerstraat, which was once a broad canal, and continue along a string of *dwarsstraten* (side streets) to:

4. **Tweede Anjeliersdwarsstraat, Tweede Tuindwarsstraat, and Tweede Egelantiersdwarsstraat**—it may take you longer to pronounce the names of these lively streets, lined with cafes, restaurants, offbeat stores and boutiques, than to walk through them. At the end you see the tall spire of the Westerkerk (West Church), whose carillon breaks into cheerful song at every opportunity (see "Sights of Religious Significance" in chapter 6).

Turn right along:

5. **Egelantiersgracht,** a quiet canal with interesting 17th- and 18th-century houses. There's a trio of simple bell gables at nos. 61–65, one of which has a falcon carved on the gable stone. If the door is open, you can take a peek into the Andrieshofje at nos. 107–145. A corridor decorated with blue and white tiles leads up to a small courtyard with a beautiful garden.

Retrace your steps, turn right into Tweede Leliedwarsstraat, and continue to:

6. **Bloemgracht,** undoubtedly the grandest Jordaan canal. Three step-gabled houses at 87–91 are absolute gems. Their carved gable stones, which date from 1642, represent a townsman, a countryman, and a seaman. Walk back toward the Prinsengracht, where you see facing you the magnificent tower of the Westerkerk. This church is the symbol of the Jordaan, though it stands just outside the neighborhood. Just as London's Cockneys are not real Cockneys unless they were born "within the sound of Bow Bells," so Amsterdam's Jordaanees are not genuine Jordaanees unless they were born within earshot of the Westerkerk's carillon.

Turn left and walk up to:

7. **Egelantiersgracht.** A hardware store on this corner, at no. 2–6, is an example of Amsterdam School architecture from 1927. Its intricate brickwork and cast-iron ornaments were influenced by art deco. To the left of the store, a step-gabled house from the 1730s is decorated with sandstone ornaments.

Egelantiersgracht is a particularly good place to:

Walking Tour: The Jordaan

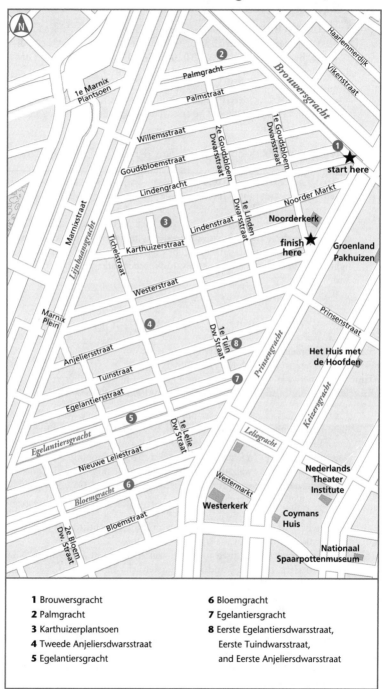

1 Brouwersgracht
2 Palmgracht
3 Karthuizerplantsoen
4 Tweede Anjeliersdwarsstraat
5 Egelantiersgracht

6 Bloemgracht
7 Egelantiersgracht
8 Eerste Egelantiersdwarsstraat,
   Eerste Tuindwarsstraat,
   and Eerste Anjeliersdwarsstraat

☕ **TAKE A BREAK**   Though there are plenty of cafes in the area where you can rest your legs and quench your walker's thirst, the best terrace is at **Café 't Smalle,** Egelantiersgracht 12 (☎ **020/623-9617**), a *gezellig* brown cafe where the air is thick with cigar smoke, jenever vapor, and lively conversation. The place is usually packed with locals, but you can escape the crush on the splendid water-side terrace, a perfect place to watch cyclists and cars rushing past while resting your legs on the terrace railing. The cafe serves snacks like *bitterballen* and cheese, and homemade soup.

When you've finished your break, turn right off of Egelantiersgracht onto another sequence of side streets:

8. **Eerste Egelantiersdwarsstraat, Eerste Tuindwarsstraat, and Eerste Anjeliersdwarsstraat** (by this time you may be better able to deal with the length of the names, if not their pronunciation), to Westerstraat. On the way, between Egelantiersstraat and Tuinstraat, a passage leads to the Claes Claesz Hofje (the entrance is next to a solid brick wall on the right side of Egelantiersdwarsstraat): two minuscule courtyards surrounded by even more minuscule apartments. Turn right onto Westerstraat and walk toward Noordermarkt (see stop 3 on Walking Tour 1).

Walking Tour 4: The Jewish Quarter

Start: Waterlooplein.
Finish: *The Dockworker,* on Jonas Daniël Meijerplein.
Time: Allow between 1½ and 3 hours, not including museum and rest stops.
Best Times: From 10am to 5pm, when the Waterlooplein flea market is open.

This area has changed almost beyond recognition since World War II, but there remain mementos and memorials of Amsterdam's once-thriving Jewish community. Start out at Waterlooplein, where you can enjoy the:

1. **Waterlooplein Flea Market.** If you like flea-market shopping, beware: You may have to continue this walking tour tomorrow. In the middle of the square is the Muziektheater and the new Amsterdam Town Hall. Also on Waterlooplein is the:

2. **Moses and Aaron Church,** which has nothing to do with Jewish history—it started out as a secret church for Catholics who were forbidden to worship in public when the Calvinists rose to power in the 16th century.

Continue to the end of the street, and turn into:

3. **Jodenbreestraat,** which used to be the center of Jewish Amsterdam. Now it's mostly modern buildings, and unfortunately the right side of the street was knocked down in 1965, destroying any distinctive character that was left. At no. 4–6 you find the:

4. **Museum Het Rembrandthuis.** Rembrandt was not Jewish, but because he lived at this house (see "More Museums & Galleries" in chapter 6) in what was then a primarily Jewish neighborhood, he often painted portraits of Jewish people who were his friends and neighbors.

Keeping the water to your right, walk down to the bridge that leads to Staal-straat, and cross over to:

Walking Tour: The Jewish Quarter

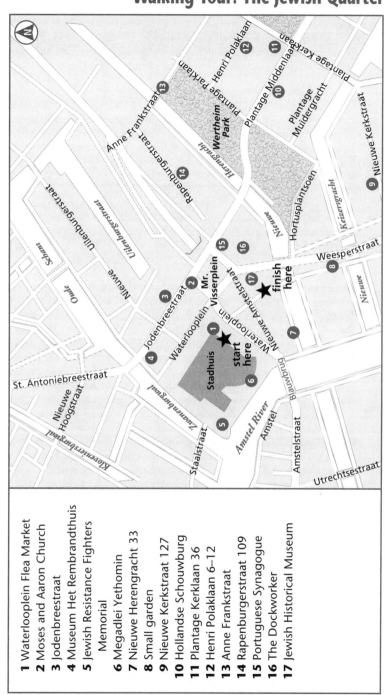

1 Waterlooplein Flea Market
2 Moses and Aaron Church
3 Jodenbreestraat
4 Museum Het Rembrandthuis
5 Jewish Resistance Fighters
   Memorial
6 Megadlei Yethomin
7 Nieuwe Herengracht 33
8 Small garden
9 Nieuwe Kerkstraat 127
10 Hollandse Schouwburg
11 Plantage Kerklaan 36
12 Henri Polaklaan 6–12
13 Anne Frankstraat
14 Rapenburgerstraat 109
15 Portuguese Synagogue
16 The Dockworker
17 Jewish Historical Museum

TAKE A BREAK   **Puccini,** Staalstraat 17 (☎ **020/427-8341**), a delightful place to stop for coffee and homemade desserts (fruit tarts, cakes, and luscious
pastries), which you can watch them prepare before your very eyes.

Go back over the bridge and turn right, to see the:

5. **Jewish Resistance Fighters Memorial,** a black marble monument to Jews who
tried to resist or escape Nazi oppression and to the people who helped them.

Turn left at the monument (Grand Café Dantzig is to your left, the Amstel
River to your right), and walk about 200 yards toward the Blauwbrug (Blue
Bridge). Just before the bridge, look for the outline of:

6. **Megadlei Yethomin,** which, starting in 1836, was an orphanage for German and
Eastern European Jewish boys. During World War II, the boys were taken to
Sobibor concentration camp. After the war, the orphanage reopened, this time as
a home for boys who wanted to get to Israel; it successfully placed many orphans
in Israel before closing in 1955. Only the outline of the building remains today,
as a memorial to the orphans and the caretaker who died in Sobibor; the rest was
demolished in 1977 to make way for the metro and later for the new Town Hall
and the Muziektheater.

Continue to the Blauwbrug. Don't cross, however; instead, continue along
with the river to your right. Then turn left into Nieuwe Herengracht just before
the drawbridge and walk to:

7. **Nieuwe Herengracht 33,** which used to be a Portuguese Jewish home for the
elderly. There was room for 10 people, and they had their own synagogue within.

Walk to the end of Nieuwe Herengracht and turn right across Vaz Diasbrug.
Take a look back down the canal as you cross the bridge—there's a picture-perfect
view of canal houses and houseboats that's very typically Amsterdam. Continue
along this road, which is now Weesperstraat, until you reach:

8. **A small garden.** This is a great place to sit and rest for a few minutes. The garden contains a monument to Dutch people who protected the Jews during
World War II. The memorial, unveiled in 1950, takes the shape of a white lime-
stone altar, and has five reliefs of mourning men, women, and children.

Continue along Weesperstraat to Nieuwe Kerkstraat. Go left to:

9. **Nieuwe Kerkstraat 127,** formerly the Metaarhuis, where corpses from the
Nieuwe Keizersgracht hospital were cleansed according to Jewish ritual.

Walk farther along and cross the bridge at the end of Nieuwe Kerkstraat; veer
to the left a bit and you'll be on Plantage Kerklaan. Walk down Plantage
Kerklaan to the traffic lights and take a left onto Plantage Middenlaan. On your
left you see the:

10. **Hollandse Schouwburg,** at Plantage Middenlaan 24. Jews were often ordered to
report to this building, which had been a Jewish theater, before being deported
to Nazi concentration camps. It's said that the children of some of these people
were sent across the street to a kindergarten, where many were saved by being
taken "underground" through the attached houses. A plaque on the school building celebrates the children's escape. Opposite, you see the bright primary colors
of the Moederhuis, a home for single mothers designed by architect Aldo van
Eyck and opened in 1978.

Go back to the traffic lights, turn left, and, continue along Plantage Kerklaan.
Soon you come to:

11. **Plantage Kerklaan 36,** where a plaque commemorates Jewish resistance fighters
who tried to destroy the city registers to prevent the Nazis from discovering how

many Jews were in Amsterdam and where they were living. This might have kept thousands of Amsterdam's Jews from dying in concentration camps. Unfortunately, the attempt failed and 12 people were executed.

Stay on Plantage Kerklaan, then turn on to Henri Polaklaan, where you see:

12. **Henri Polaklaan 6–12,** the former Portuguese Jewish Hospital, built in 1916. The pelican on the facade is a symbol of the Portuguese Jewish community.

Go right at the end of Henri Polaklaan, to Plantage Parklaan, and turn right, then left onto:

13. **Anne Frankstraat** (for more about Anne Frank and the Anne Frankhuis, see "The Big Four Museums & Galleries" in chapter 6). Cross the bridge and go straight on until you get to Rapenburgerstraat. Turn left and walk on until you see:

14. **Rapenburgerstraat 109,** Beth Hamidrash Ets Chaim (now the home of *NIW,* Holland's weekly Jewish newspaper), once a center of Jewish learning, where Amsterdam Jews studied Jewish law and the commentaries. The building dates from 1883; the study hall was founded in 1740.

At the end of Rapenburgerstraat, cross over to Mr. Visserplein. As you cross the road, the:

15. **Portuguese Synagogue** is on your left (see "Sights of Religious Significance" in chapter 6).

Make a left onto Jonas Daniël Meijerplein; in the square you see:

16. *The Dockworker.* Jonas Daniël Meijerplein is where many Jews were forced to wait for their deportation to concentration camps. This bronze statue was erected in 1952 in commemoration of the 1941 February Strike by the workers of Amsterdam to protest the deportation of the city's Jewish population. The strike, one of the biggest collective actions in all of occupied Europe against the Nazi persecution, was ruthlessly suppressed.

Still on Jonas Daniël Meijerplein, visit the:

17. **Joods Historisch Museum (Jewish Historical Museum),** at no. 2–4, in a building that once housed four synagogues built by Jews who fled Germany and Poland in the 17th and 18th centuries (see "More Museums & Galleries" in chapter 6). Across the street from the museum is the Arsenal, which served as a storage space for munitions in the 19th century and is now part of the museum.

Biking Tour: Along the Amstel River

Start: Waterlooplein.
Finish: Amstel Station.
Time: Allow between 3 and 4 hours, not including rest stops.
Best Times: Outside of rush hour (around 8 to 10am and 5 to 7pm).

This cycling route begins in the city center, and follows a scenic and relatively quiet way through the city, finally emerging into the countryside alongside the Amstel River for the short but glorious hop out to Ouderkerk aan de Amstel village.

The nearest place to the starting point to rent a bike is **MacBike,** Mr. Visserplein 2 (☎ **020/620-0985**), facing Waterlooplein. Prices begin at Dfl 12.50 ($5.30) a day. When you've saddled up, head for:

1. The east bank of the **Amstel River** (the left bank as you face the river at Waterlooplein). The Amstel is likely to be fairly busy with waterborne traffic at this point, and there are houseboats moored along both banks.

Continue to the:

2. **Magere Brug,** the "Skinny Bridge" over the Amstel—actually it's an 18th-century replacement for the original 17th-century bridge. Cross to the opposite bank and cycle southward along the Amstel. On the other side of the river, you can see the Theater Carré. Continue over Sarphatistraat, which you can easily recognize by its tram lines. You need to detour around a break in the riverside road now, over busy Stadhouderskade, and back to the river again at:

3. **Amsteldijk.** Keep pedaling south on this road, enjoying the riverside views, until you reach the **Berlage Brug (Berlage Bridge),** where you need to be more careful, as the traffic gets noticeably busier at this point.

Stay on Amsteldijk until you arrive at:

4. **Martin Luther King Park.** Most of the road traffic swings away to the right on President Kennedylaan at this point, but you should stay on Amsteldijk, which gradually becomes almost rural, though with houseboats alongside the road in place of country cottages. Up ahead you'll hear a noise like a substantial storm coming your way, but you're just getting closer to the highway bridge carrying the A10 Ring Road across the river. Pass under the bridge and finally you're in the countryside, passing:

5. **Amstel Park.** Continue to the statue of Rembrandt and a windmill at its end. Around this characteristic old Dutch scene, there'll probably be a characteristic new Dutch scene: busloads of tourists photographing Rembrandt, the windmill, themselves, and everything in sight, probably including you as you glide past. Beyond this is:

Cycling in Amsterdam

What are the rules of the road for cycling in Amsterdam? Apparently, there are none. CYCLISTS RULE OKAY! Cyclists can go anywhere they want, whenever they want, however they want, and do whatever they want when they get there. Or so you would think from the antics of Amsterdam's massed legions of cyclists. They're enough to put a scare into a bunch of Hell's Angels. Particularly terrifying are the mothers with two kids, one on the front handlebars and the other in a kiddies' seat at the back, dicing with the trams at Leidseplein. Cycling is one activity where you should disregard the maxim "When in Amsterdam, do as the Amsterdammers do"—you could end up dead, which will certainly spoil your vacation.

It takes a while to get used to moving smoothly and safely through the whirl of trams, cars, buses, trucks, fellow cyclists, and pedestrians, particularly if you're on a typically ancient and much-battered *stadfiets* (city bike)—the only kind of bike that makes economic sense here, as anything fancier will attract a crowd of people wanting to steal it. It's better to develop your street smarts slowly. I know this sounds like wimpish advice—you might have ridden a mountain bike from one end of the Rockies to another for all I know—but remember that not everyone on the road is as sensible as you are.

The first rule of cycling in Amsterdam: Don't argue with trams—they bite back. The second rule: Cross tram lines at a sharp angle so that your wheels don't get caught in them, which could pitch you out of the saddle. And the third rule: Don't crash into civilians (pedestrians). That's all. Like everyone else, you can make up the rest of the rules as you go along.

Biking Tour: Along the Amstel River

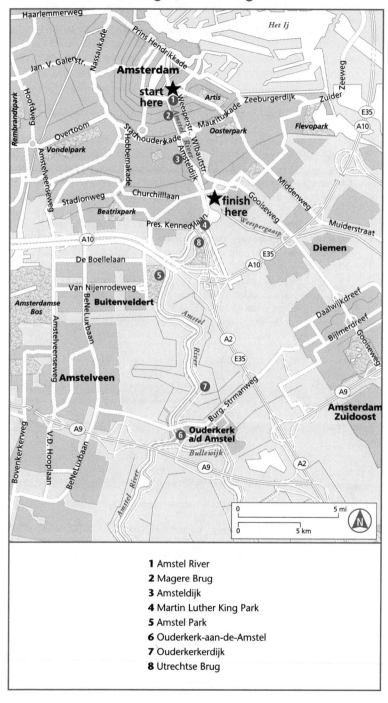

1 Amstel River
2 Magere Brug
3 Amsteldijk
4 Martin Luther King Park
5 Amstel Park
6 Ouderkerk-aan-de-Amstel
7 Ouderkerkerdijk
8 Utrechtse Brug

🍽 **TAKE A BREAK**   **'t Klein Kalfje,** Amsteldijk 355 (☎ **020/644-5338**), an atmospheric little Dutch cafe-restaurant with a riverside terrace and canal barges moored alongside. The terrace is separated from the cafe by the road. There used to be a traffic sign here whose unofficial icon indicated CAUTION: WAITER CROSSING.

The river is tranquil and scenic from now on, as you pass cottages and villas all the way to:

6. **Ouderkerk aan de Amstel.** The little village has an abundance of cafes and restaurants with riverside terraces, several of them owned by Holland's first family of cuisine: the Fagels. The Fagels are a multi-generational family of chefs and restaurateurs with a high reputation in the land. If you've still got some energy left, you can put it to use exploring the village, before settling down on any one of the riverside or sidewalk terraces for something restorative.

For the return trip, change to the right bank of the river, on:

7. **Ouderkerkerdijk,** narrower and quieter than Amsteldijk, and with almost no cars. You pass another windmill and several little hamlets along the way.

Recross the Amstel at the:

8. **Utrechtse Brug.** This marks your return to Amsteldijk and busy city streets. At Berlage Brug you can either recross the river and cycle a few hundred yards to Amstel Station, where you, your bike, and your no-doubt weary legs can board a metro train back to Waterlooplein, or you can cycle back along either bank.

Shopping 8

From its earliest days, Amsterdam has been a trading city. First, trade centered on the fish that the original dammers of the Amstel caught in the rivers and the North Sea; later, during the 17th century, on the spices, furs, flower bulbs, and artifacts carried back to Europe by the ships of the Dutch East and West India Companies.

The fish were sold on the spot where a major department store now stands, and the early townspeople brought calves to market on the same street you will walk along to begin a shopper's walking tour through Amsterdam. The luxury items you buy today are the same sort of goods Dutch merchants sold to each other in the Golden Age of the 17th century, and the junk you buy in the flea market at Waterlooplein is much the same as it has been for hundreds of years.

Adding a modern dimension to this tradition-laden scene are the funky boutiques you find scattered around Amsterdam, and adding sparkle are the diamond cutters. Still, tradition is one thing, modern facilities are another. Amsterdam has the full range of shopping facilities, from small and highly individualistic, not to say eccentric, boutiques whose designers are often small-name, through chains and department stores to shopping malls. The Dutch themselves enjoy shopping and where possible like to take the time to seek out the more offbeat places, though they face the same time constraints as are to be found in most cities and so, more often than not, they fall back on the tried and tested.

For visitors, shopping can be an interesting extension to your experience of Amsterdam, precisely because the city center is small enough that shops and other attractions are often right beside each other. Rather than going on dedicated shopping expeditions, it may make more sense to simply drop into the nearest shops while you're involved in more weighty cultural matters. Whatever kind of shopping you prefer, you're sure to be impressed with the range of shopping possibilities Amsterdam offers.

1 The Shopping Scene

SHOPPING ORIENTATION

HOURS   Regular shopping hours in Amsterdam are Monday from 11am to 6pm; Tuesday, Wednesday, and Friday from 9am to 6pm; Thursday from 9am to 9pm; and Saturday from 9am to 5pm. In recent years there has been something of a revolution in the previously restricted opening hours: Against the wishes of churches and other groups, many shops now stay open on Sunday as well, usually from noon to 5pm, and more and more supermarkets are staying open daily from 8am to 8pm (or even until 10pm).

PRICES   These are fixed in Holland, with all applicable taxes included in the amounts shown on tags and counter display cards. Although end-of-season and other special sales occur from time to time throughout the year, the practice of discounting as we know it is not yet part of the Dutch pricing system, so there's little use running from store to store trying to find a better price on ordinary consumer goods. If you want a bargain, go to the Waterlooplein flea market, though even there you find that the Dutch have much less interest in the sport of haggling—or margin in their prices—than their counterparts in countries farther south. They're simply too practical to quote a ridiculous price in the expectation that it will be cut in half or that you'll be fool enough to pay it.

NIGHT SHOPS   While these fall more into the category of food shops, they are a resource not to be ignored for keeping you stocked with things to munch after normal hours. Suppose you feel like an evening "at home" in your hotel, watching television or whatever, and you either don't fancy the room-service menu or your hotel doesn't provide this service. There is sure to be a night shop close to the hotel (ask at the front desk), and many can prepare take-out meals to about the same standard as you would find in a typical Dutch restaurant for 10% to 20% less than the restaurant price. Many night shops stock fresh delicatessen food. Opening times are usually 5 to 11pm or midnight.

VAT & THE VAT REFUND   If you live outside the European Union (EU), whatever your nationality, you're entitled to a refund of the VAT—value-added tax—you pay on your purchases of Dfl 300 ($127.65) or more in one store in 1 day. On highticket items, the savings of 13.5% can be significant. You must export the purchases within 3 months. To obtain your VAT refund, ask for a **tax-free shopping check** from the store when you make your purchase. When you are leaving the EU, present this check, your purchases, and receipts to Customs. They will stamp the check. You can get the refund in cash at an International Refund Point (in Holland, this is the ABN-AMRO bank in the Schiphol Airport terminal lounge). Otherwise you can return the check to **Europe Tax-Free Shopping,** Leidsevaartweg 99, 2106 AS, Heemstede, Netherlands (☎ **023/524-1909;** fax 023/524-6164), who will refund the tax, minus their commission, to your credit card or by check.

DUTY-FREE ITEMS   Duty-free shopping has been abolished within the European Union. This means that if you are traveling from one member country of the EU to another, you can no longer buy duty-free goods at airports, on ferries, and at border crossings. If, however, you are traveling to or from the EU from a nonmember country, such as the United States, normal duty-free shopping rules apply.

BEST BUYS

If an item in an Amsterdam store window takes your fancy or fills a specific need, buy it, of course. But often both prices and selections in Holland are too close to what you can find at home to justify the extra weight in your suitcase or the expense and trouble of shipping (prices of many consumer items in Holland are in any case often significantly higher than the same or equivalent items in the United States). Exceptions are the special items that the Dutch produce to perfection (delftware, pewter, crystal, and old-fashioned clocks), or commodities in which they have significantly cornered a market, like diamonds. None of these are a cheap commodity, unfortunately, and you'll want to do some homework in order to make canny shopping decisions, but if you know enough and care enough, you can find excellent values and take home beautiful, and in some cases valuable, treasures from Holland that will please you much more and much longer than the usual souvenirs. And if money is a consideration, remember that the Dutch also have inexpensive specialties, such as cheese, flower bulbs, and chocolate.

ANTIQUES   Antiques lovers love Holland! And why not, when you think of all those tankards, pipes, cabinets, clocks, kettles, vases, and other bric-a-brac you see in the old Dutch paintings that still show up among the treasures of shops on Amsterdam's Nieuwe Spiegelstraat. It's the 20th century's good fortune that since the 17th century the Dutch have collected everything—from Chinese urns to silver boxes, from cookie molds to towering armoires—and should you find that while you're in Amsterdam there is a *kijkdag* (looking day) for an upcoming auction, you will realize that antiques still pour forth from the attics of the old canal houses. With 165 antiques shops in the city, there's no lack of choice.

CHEESE   Holland is the Wisconsin of Europe, well known around the world for its butter and cheese. Gouda (correctly pronounced, in Dutch, *how*-duh) and Edam are the two Dutch cheeses most familiar to us because they have been exported from Holland for so long—since the 1700s—but once inside a Dutch cheese store, you quickly realize that there are many other interesting choices, including a nettle cheese that's a specialty of Friesland. Before you simply point to any cheese and say, "I'll take that one," you need to know that in Holland you have the choice of factory cheese, made of pasteurized milk, or *boerenkaas,* which is farm cheese that is produced in the old, careful way with fresh, unpasteurized milk straight from the cow. Boerenkaas is more expensive, of course, but it also can be expected to be more delicious. Look for the boerenkaas stamp. Another choice that you will make is between young and old cheese; it's a difference of sweetness, moistness, and a melting quality in the mouth (*jonge,* or young, cheese) and a sharper, drier taste, and a crumbly texture (*oude,* or old, cheese).

CHOCOLATE   There's little to tell about Dutch chocolate except that it deserves its excellent reputation. Droste, Verkade, and Van Houten are three of the best Dutch brand names to look for, or you can seek out the small specialty chocolate shops that still home-make and hand-fill the boxes of bonbons. (In fact, though no Dutch person would be unhappy to receive chocolates from these manufacturers, they themselves generally prefer handmade Belgian chocolates from such makes as Wittamer, Nihoul, Neuhaus, Godiva, and Leonidas.)

CRYSTAL & PEWTER   Holland is not the only country that produces fine pewter ware and crystal, but the Dutch contribute both a refined sense of design and a respect for craftsmanship that combine to produce items of exceptional beauty and quality. Also, if you remember the classic Dutch still-life paintings and happy scenes of 17th-century family life, pewter objects are part of Holland's heritage. As with hand-painted earthenware, there are Dutch towns associated with each of these crafts and long-established firms whose names are well known as quality producers. Crystal, for example, has long been associated with Leerdam, south of Utrecht, and Maastricht, in Limburg, whose manufacturers have joined together to market under the names of **Royal Netherlands** in the United States and **Kristalunie** in Holland. To spot the genuine article, look for the four triangles of the **Royal Leerdam** label.

Traditionally, pewter was the specialty of the little town of Tiel, near Arnhem in the eastern part of Holland. Gradually, though, the old firms are disappearing, making it more difficult to find fine-spun pewter produced in the old way and in the old molds. An important shopping note on pewter is that though the Dutch government now bans the use of lead as a hardening agent, this assurance only protects you from toxicity in new pewter. Don't buy any antiques for use with food or drink. If you're not sure, look inside the pitcher or goblet; if it's light in color, it's fine; if it's dark and has a blue shine, buy it for decorative purposes only.

DELFTWARE & MAKKUMWARE   There are three types of delftware available in Amsterdam—Delftware, Makkumware, and junk—and since none of it is cheap, you need to know what the differences are among the three types and what to look for to determine quality. But first, a few words of historical background and explanation: delftware (with a lowercase *d*) has actually become an umbrella name for all Dutch hand-painted earthenware pottery resembling ancient Chinese porcelain, whether it is blue and white, red and white, or multicolored, and regardless of the city in which it was produced.

Delftware, or Delft Blue (with a capital *D*), on the other hand, refers to the predominantly blue-and-white products of one firm, **De Koninklijke Porceleyne Fles** of Delft. This is the only survivor of the original 30 potteries in Delft that during the 17th century worked overtime in that small city to meet the clamoring demand of the newly affluent Dutch for Chinese-style vases, urns, wall tiles, and knickknacks—real or reproduced, porcelain or pottery. Originally, pottery made at Delft was white, imitating tin-glazed products from Italy and Spain. During the 16th century, Chinese porcelain was imported to Holland—this was decorated in blue and was of superior quality. The Delftware factories refined their products, using a white tin glaze to cover the red clay and decorating it in blue. This Delft Blue became famous the world over. It was cheaper than Chinese porcelain and it was skillfully made. Polychrome decorations were also used, both on a white and on a black background.

Similarly, the term *makkumware* is becoming synonymous with multicolored—or polychrome—pottery, whereas Makkumware is, in fact, the hand-painted earthenware produced only in the town of Makkum in the northern province of Friesland and only by the 300-plus-year-old firm of **Tichelaars,** which was founded in 1660 and now is in its 10th generation of family management. Makkumware has a similar history to Delft Blue, though it exists only with polychrome decoration.

Delft and Makkumware are for sale in specialized shops all over the country, but it is far more interesting to go to one of the workshops in the towns themselves and see how they are made. Little has changed over the centuries, and all the decorating is still done by hand. This makes it quite pricey, but each piece is a unique product, made by craftsmen.

Copies of the products of both De Porceleyne Fles and Tichelaars are numerous, with some copies nearly equal in quality and others missing by miles the delicacy of the brush stroke, the richness of color, or the sheen of the secret glazes that make the items produced by these two firms so highly prized, and so expensive.

Your eye should tell you which pieces of pottery are worth their prices, but to be sure that yours is a *real* Delft vase, for instance, look on the bottom for the distinctive three-part hallmark of De Porceleyne Fles: an outline of a small pot, above an initial *J* crossed with a short stroke (actually it's a combined initial, *J* and *T*), above the scripted word *Delft,* with the *D* distinctively written like a backward *C.*

To distinguish the products of Tichelaars, look for a mark that incorporates a crown above a shield showing the word *Makkum* and two scripted *T's,* overlapped like crossed swords (or look simply for the crossed *T's,* since the crown is a rather recent addition to their mark, the result of a royal honor bestowed on the company for its 300th anniversary in 1960).

DIAMONDS   Amsterdam has been a major center of the diamond-cutting industry since the 15th century and is one of the best places in the world to shop for diamond jewelry and unmounted stones in all gradations of color and quality. There are still 24 diamond-polishing workshops in the city.

Dutch jewelers generally adhere to the standards of both the Gemological Institute of America and the U.S. Federal Trade Commission, and most will issue a certificate with a diamond they sell that spells out the carat weight, cut, color, and other pertinent identifying details, including any imperfections.

Should you decide to buy a diamond, there are four factors influencing its quality that should be considered. The first is its weight, which will be stated as either points or carats (100 points equals 1 carat equals 200 milligrams, or 3.47 grains troy). Next is the cut, which may be a classic round (brilliant) cut, a pear shape, a rectangular emerald cut, an oval, or a long and narrow double-pointed marquise. This is initially a matter of design preference rather than a factor in a stone's value; it is also, however, the test of the diamond cutter's ability to polish each of 58 facets at an angle that varies no more than half a degree from every other angle. To evaluate a diamond's cut, hold it to the light and look into the table (which is the name of the flattened top and the diamond's largest facet); if you see a dark circle, you know the stone is well cut and is reflecting light to its full capacity; if you don't, expect to pay less and to get less sparkle.

Also expect to pay more or less according to the clarity and color of a diamond. The clarity can be reliably evaluated only by a jeweler, who uses a loupe, or small eyeglass, to magnify the stone 10 times; the fewer the imperfections, the better the diamond and the higher the price (and, by the way, only a stone with *no* visible imperfections at that magnification can be described as "perfect" according to the guidelines of the Gemological Institute). Likewise, the whiter the diamond, the better the quality and the greater its value. To see for yourself whether a stone you are considering is closer to white than yellow or even brown, hold it with tweezers and look at it from the side, against a pure background (do this preferably in daylight through a north window, and never in direct sunlight). But don't expect to see blue unless you're looking at what a diamond dealer calls a "fancy" (a colored diamond), similar to the yellow Tiffany diamond or the deep-blue Hope.

FLOWER BULBS   Nothing is more Dutch than a tulip, and no gift to yourself will bring more pleasure than to take home some bulbs to remind you of Holland all over again when they pop up every spring. You may have a problem making your choices, however, since there are more than 800 different varieties of tulip bulbs available in Holland, not to mention more than 500 kinds of daffodils and narcisci, and 60 different varieties of hyacinth and crocus. Many growers and distributors put together combination packages with various amounts of bulbs that are coordinated according to the colors of the flowers they will produce, but it's great fun—since so many bulbs are named for famous people—to put together your own garden party with Sophia Loren, President Kennedy, Queen Juliana, and Cyrano de Bergerac!

You might not know what kind to buy though, as it is difficult to choose from the incredible variety of shapes and colors offered in Holland. Some bulbs flower early in January; others wait until the warmer months of May or June. Knowing this, you can choose bulbs with different flowering times, so you can enjoy their bloom over a long period in spring. In Amsterdam, you can't do better than to buy them from the Floating Flower market on the Singel Canal (see below).

If you worry about the failure rates or bug-ridden bulbs, don't! The Dutch have been perfecting their growing methods and strengthening their stock for more than 400 years, and as in everything they do, perfection is not simply a standard to strive for, it's an obligation. Do check before buying, however, since not all bulbs are certified for entry into the United States. Packages are marked; look for the numbered phyto-sanitary certificate attached to the label—it allows you to import the bulbs into the United States.

OLD-FASHIONED CLOCKS   It's true that the Swiss make the finest clocks in the world, but what they do well for the inner workings, the Dutch do well for the outside, particularly if you like a clock to be old-fashioned, handcrafted, and highly decorated with figures and mottoes or small peekaboo panels to show you the innards.

There are two types of clocks that have survived the centuries and the shift in Dutch taste to more contemporary timepieces. One is the Zaandam clock, or Zaanseklok, from the small city across the harbor from Amsterdam, which is identified by its ornately carved oak or walnut case and brass panels, its tiny windows on the dial face, and the motto *Nu Eick Syn Sin,* which basically translates from Old Dutch as "To Each His Own." The other popular clock style is the Friese Stoelklok, or Frisian clock, which is even more heavily decorated, customarily with hand-painted scenes of the Dutch countryside or ships at sea (that may even bob back and forth in time with the ticks) or possibly with both motifs and a smiling moon face.

GREAT SHOPPING AREAS

The easiest way to approach shopping in Amsterdam is to devote a day to the project, put on your most comfortable shoes, and walk. You can window-shop all the way from the Dam to the Concertgebouw if you have the stamina, and as long as you remember a few key jogs in the path, you won't even need to consult a map. A few shopping streets are pedestrians-only, some are busy thoroughfares, and others are peaceful canal-side esplanades or fashionable promenades, but each segment in this ever-growing network of commercial enterprises has developed its own identity or predominant selection of goods as a specialty. To get you on your way, here are three suggested shopping walks:

If you're looking for jewelry, trendy clothing, or athletic gear, begin at the department stores at the Dam and follow Kalverstraat to Heiligeweg; turn right there and continue shopping until you reach the Leidseplein. (Heiligeweg becomes Leidsestraat after it crosses the Koningsplein, but it's really one long street, so you can't possibly get lost.)

If you're feeling rich or simply want to feast your eyes on lovely things (fashion, antiques, and art), begin at the Concertgebouw and walk along Van Baerlestraat toward Vondelpark; turn right on the elegant P. C. Hooftstraat. At the end of the street, by the canal, turn right again and walk to the Rijksmuseum, then turn left across the canal. Straight ahead is the Spiegelgracht, a small and quiet bit of canal that's the gateway to the best antiques-shopping street in Amsterdam, if not in all of Europe.

Finally, if your idea of a good day of shopping includes fashion boutiques, funky little specialty shops, and a good browse through a flea market or secondhand store, cut a path from west to east through the old city by beginning at the Westermarkt and crisscrossing among the canals. Reestraat, Hartenstraat, Wolvenstraat, and Runstraat are particularly good choices with lots of fun shops, including one that boasts Europe's largest selection of ribbons and braid, and another with elaborately painted toilet bowls. At the Dam you can take Damstraat and its continuations (Oude Doelenstraat, Hoogstraat, and Nieuwe Hoogstraat) to St. Antoniesbreestraat (and its continuation, Jodenbreestraat) to Nieuwe Uilenburgerstraat to Waterlooplein and the market. Or at the Dam, follow Rokin to the Muntplein and walk from there, or take tram no. 9 or 14 to the stop for the Muziektheater/Waterlooplein.

To plan your own shopping route through Amsterdam, here are brief descriptions of the major shopping streets and what you can expect to find along each of them:

KALVERSTRAAT   This is the busiest stretch of pedestrian shopping in the city. At one end is the Dam with its department stores; at the other end, the Muntplein traffic hub. In between, Kalverstraat is a hodgepodge of shopping possibilities. Punk-tinged boutiques for the young and athletic-shoe emporiums are side-by-side with shops selling dowdy raincoats and conservative business suits, bookstores, fur salons, maternity and baby stores, and record shops.

The big and busy **Vroom & Dreesman** department store has its main entrance on Kalverstraat, as does the elegant **Maison de Bonneterie en Pander;** also along the way are **Benetton** and **Fiorucci,** plus everything in the way of fast food from *frites* to *poffertjes.* The more conservative and well-established fashion shops for men and women on Kalverstraat are **Maison de Vries, Claudia Sträter,** and **Austin Reed;** for leather goods, **Zumpolle** offers elegant and high-quality handbags and leather suitcases. Something big, brash, and new on Kalverstraat is the **Kalvertoren Shopping Center,** a multistory mall with 45 shops, cafes, and restaurants, including the cheap 'n' cheerful department store **Hema.**

ROKIN   Parallel to Kalverstraat and also running from the Dam to the Muntplein is Rokin, one of the busiest tram routes in the city. Along here you will find art galleries and antiques shops, and elegant fashion boutiques such as **Le Papillon** for fitness/dance wear, **Jan Jensen** for shoes, **Emmy Landkroon** and **Sheila** for haute couture, or the straightforward chic of **Agnès B.**

HEILIGEWEG, KONINGSPLEIN & LEIDSESTRAAT   The fashion parade that begins on Kalverstraat continues around the corner on Heiligeweg, across the Koningsplein and along Leidsestraat, all the way to the Leidseplein. But the mood changes: The shops are more elegant, and instead of a sprinkling of fast-food outlets and souvenir shops, you find congenial cafes and airline ticket offices. Along the way, look for **Esprit** and **Khymo** for men's and women's fashion; **Pauw Boutique, Cora Kemperman,** and **Agnès B** for women's fashion; **Smit-Bally** for shoes; the Amsterdam branches of **Studio Haus** for modern china and crystal and **Cartier** for gold and silver; the **Amsterdam Diamond Center** and **Rokin Diamonds** for, guess what? **Metz & Co.,** a dry-goods store at the corner of the Keizersgracht; and for men's and women's fashions, **Meddens** on Heiligeweg. **Morris** has suedes and leather on Leidsestraat; **Crabtree & Evelyn** has its usual array of fragrant soaps, sachets, and cosmetics; and **Shoe-Ba-Loo** has, you guessed it, a choice selection of shoes.

P. C. HOOFTSTRAAT & VAN BAERLESTRAAT   P. C. Hooftstraat (known locally as "the P. C. Hooft," or "pay-say hoaft") is the (diminutive) Madison Avenue of Amsterdam, where well-dressed and well-coiffed Amsterdammers buy everything from lingerie to light bulbs. Along its 3 short blocks you find shops selling furniture, antiques, toys, shoes, chocolates, Persian rugs, designer clothes, fresh-baked bread and fresh-caught fish, china, books, furs, perfume, leather goods, office supplies, flowers, and jewelry. And around the corner on Van Baerlestraat are more boutiques, shoe shops, and enough branches of the major banks to guarantee that you can continue to buy as long as your traveler's checks hold out. Worth special mention are **Edgar Vos, Frans Molenaar, Tim Bonig, Rob Kroner, Jacques d'Ariege, DKNY, Laurèl,** and **Gimmicks, Pauw Boutique,** and at the corner of Van Baerlestraat, **Azurro,** all for women's fashions; **Pauw Junior** on Van Baerlestraat for children's clothes; branches of **Emporio Armani, Hobbit, Rodier Paris, MacGregor,** and **Society Shop** for men's fashions; and **Godiva Chocolatier** for handmade pralines. Van Baerlestraat continues southward onto Beethovenstraat, which is rich in boutiques, delicatessens, cafes, and specialty grocers.

SPIEGELSTRAAT (NIEUWE SPIEGELSTRAAT TO SPIEGELGRACHT)
This is the antiques esplanade of Amsterdam, and though it covers only a short 4-block stretch of street-plus-canal, it's one of the finest antiques-hunting grounds in Europe. No wonder! At one end of this shopping street is the Rijksmuseum; at the other, the Golden Bend of the Herengracht Canal, where Amsterdam's wealthiest burghers once kept house. It seems that, now that these beautiful gabled homes have been turned over to banks and embassies, all the treasures they contained have simply found their way around the corner to the antiques shops. Among the items you might expect to see are dolls with china heads, rare editions of early children's books, Indonesian puppets, Persian tapestries and rugs, landscape paintings, prints, reproductions and modern art, brass Bible stands and candlesticks, copper kettles, music boxes, old Dutch clocks, and, of course, the little *spiegels,* or mirrors, that give this street its name, and which the Dutch use beside upper-story windows to see who's knocking at their door.

AMSTELVEEN   This as an *outsider's* tip. Amstelveen is a new town built around an old village in the polderland south of Amsterdam. Think of modern, clean, efficient living in a garden city. The shopping center here has many of the nonspecialist types of outlets—department stores, boutiques, toy shops, and the like—that you find in Amsterdam. Here, however, they're in an enclosed mall and you can get around them all a lot quicker. So if you don't like shopping, but can just about tolerate it if you get through it quickly, this may be the place for you. Take the no. 5 tram from Centraal Station to the terminus, which is right beside the Amstelveen shopping center; the journey lasts about 25 minutes.

OTHER SHOPPING AREAS
For more antiques shops, look along the Prinsengracht between Leidsestraat and Westermarkt, or visit the **Kunst- & Antiekcentrum de Looier** (see "Shopping A to Z," below). For the up-and-coming funky boutiques of Amsterdam, look among the canals east and west of the Dam, or in the nest of streets beyond the Westermarkt known as the **Jordaan.**

2 Shopping A to Z

Here is a selection of stores in Amsterdam, some of which you might not otherwise have found. It can save you time and trouble with your shopping list or simply provide interesting shops to visit.

ALTERNATIVES
Blame the alphabet, if it seems odd to start with alternative shopping options before going into the mainstream!

Magic Mushroom Gallery. Singel 524 (near Muntplein). ☎ **020/422-7845.** Tram: 4, 9, 14, 16, 20, 24, or 25 to Muntplein.

How to define this place that seems to tread a thin line? It sells "natural drugs" and "psychoactive mushrooms" that are much better for you, apparently, than illegal narcotics. Improve your sex life with Yohimbe Rush and Horn E; boost your energy with Space Liquid and Herbal Booster; grow your own Mexican mushrooms; then unwind with After Glow and Rapture. Open Monday to Saturday 9:30am to 6pm; there's another store at Spuistraat 249 (☎ **020/427-5765**).

Oibibio Department Store. Prins Hendrikkade 20–21. ☎ **020/553-9355.** Tram: 1, 2, 4, 5, 9, 13, 16, 17, 20, 24, or 25 to Centraal Station.

This is part of the New Age Oibibio restaurant, bookshop, cafe, teahouse, dance club complex. If what you want is the ecological seal of approval in fashion, babies and children's wear, interior decoration, homeopathic drugs, cosmetics, bath and bedtime products, food, and stationery, then this is the place. Soft music and delicate scents smooth your path around this other-worldly store, though, strange to relate, just as in mainstream department stores the path leads not so much to enlightenment as to the cash tills. Open Monday noon to 6:30pm, Tuesday and Wednesday 10am to 6:30pm, Thursday and Friday 10am to 9pm, Saturday from 10am to 6pm, and Sunday noon to 6pm.

ANTIQUES

A. van der Meer. P. C. Hooftstraat 112. ☎ **020/662-1936.** Tram: 2, 3, 5, 12, or 20 to Van Baerlestraat.

For more than 30 years, A. van der Meer has been a landmark amid the fashionable shops of P. C. Hooftstraat and a quiet place to enjoy a beautiful collection of antique maps, prints, and engravings. And 17th- and 18th-century Dutch world maps by the early cartographers Blaeu, Hondius, and Mercator are a specialty. Also, there is a small collection of Jewish prints by Picart and 18th-century botanicals (pictures of flowers) by Baptista Morandi and 19th-century works by Jacob Jung, mostly of roses. There are also 19th-century lithographs of hunting scenes by Harris. Open Monday to Saturday 10am to 6pm.

✪ **Kunst- & Antiekcentrum de Looier.** Elandsgracht 109. ☎ **020/624-9038.** Tram: 7, 10, 17, or 20 to Elandsgracht.

This big indoor antiques market spreads through several old warehouses along the canals in the Jordaan. As in New York, London, and other cities, individual dealers rent small stalls and corners to show their best wares. The old armoires and other pieces of heavy Dutch traditional furniture are too large to consider buying, but many dealers also offer antique jewelry, prints and engravings, and the omnipresent Dutch knickknacks. Open Saturday to Wednesday 11am to 5pm, Thursday 11am to 9pm.

Premsela & Hamburger. Rokin 98. ☎ **020/624-9688** or 020/627-5454. Tram: 4, 9, 14, 16, 20, 24, or 25 to Spui.

Opposite the Allard-Pierson Museum, this fine jewelry and antique silver establishment—purveyors to the Dutch court—opened in 1823. Inside their brocaded display cases and richly carved cabinets is a variety of exquisite and distinctive items. You can find decorative modern and antique silver objects and Old Dutch silver fashioned by 17th-century crafters. Feast your eyes on an 18th-century perpetual calendar, a silver plaque depicting the entrance to an Amsterdam hospital, and a variety of sterling silverware. Their workshop designs, makes, and repairs jewelry. Open Monday to Friday 9:30am to 5:30pm.

ART

Galleries abound in Amsterdam, particularly in the canal area near the Rijksmuseum, and a quick look at the listings of their exhibitions proves that Dutch painters are as prolific in the 20th century as they were in the Golden Age. The VVV Tourist Information Office publication *What's On in Amsterdam* is your best guide to who is showing and where; your own eye and sense of value will be the best guide to artistic merit and investment value.

Amsterdam will at least give one's regular habits of thought the stimulus of a little confusion.

—Henry James

On the other hand, posters and poster reproductions of famous artworks are an excellent item to buy in Amsterdam. The Dutch are well known for their high-quality printing and color-reproduction work, and one of their favorite subjects is Holland's rich artistic treasure trove, foreign and domestic. Choose any of the three major art museums as a starting point for a search for an artistic souvenir, but if you like modern art—say, from the impressionists onward—you will be particularly delighted by the wide selection at the **Stedelijk Museum of Modern Art,** Paulus Potterstraat 13 (☎ **020/573-2911**); and if you particularly like Van Gogh, the **Van Gogh Museum,** Paulus Potterstraat 13 (☎ **020/570-5200**), is another good source of reproductions. And at **Museum Het Rembrandthuis,** Jodenbreestraat 4 (☎ **020/624-9486**), you can buy a Rembrandt etching for Dfl 30 ($12.75) or Dfl 40 ($17) mounted; it's not an original, of course, but it is a high-quality modern printing produced individually, by hand, in the traditional manner from a plate that was directly and photographically produced from an original print in the collection of Rembrandthuis. Or for something simpler and cheaper to remind you of the great master, Het Rembrandthuis also sells mass-printed reproductions of the etchings, or small packets of postcard-sized reproductions in sepia or black and white on a thick, fine-quality paper stock (including a packet of self-portraits).

Perhaps you're more interested in an artistic, rather than photographic, view of Amsterdam or the Dutch countryside. **Mattieu Hart,** which has been in its location on the Rokin since 1878, sells color etchings of Dutch cities.

Here are just a few of Amsterdam's 140 or so galleries that hold contemporary and modern art, photography, sculpture, and African art.

✪ **Animation Art.** Berenstraat 19 (between Keizersgracht and Prinsengracht). ☎ **020/627-7600.** Tram: 1, 2, or 5 to Spui.

Got a favorite cartoon character? Well, Animation Art has original drawings and cell-paintings of all different kinds of cartoons. A fun place for the kid in everyone. Open Tuesday to Friday 11am to 6pm, Saturday 11am to 5pm, and Sunday (not in January or February) 1 to 5pm.

Art Rages. Spiegelgracht 2a. ☎ **020/627-3645.** Tram: 6, 7, or 10 to Spiegelgracht.

You find some interesting contemporary ceramics, glass, jewelry, and mixed-media pieces from all over Europe, and the United States and Canada. Open Monday from 1 to 6pm, Tuesday to Saturday 11am to 6pm, and on the first Sunday of the month 1 to 6pm.

Galerie Carla Koch. Prinsengracht 510. ☎ **020/639-0198.** Tram: 1, 2, or 5 to Prinsengracht.

For ceramics and glassware, this gallery employs some of the raciest design talent in Amsterdam, meaning that their products are always different and always interesting, if inevitably not to everyone's taste. Open Monday to Saturday noon to 6pm.

Italiaander Galleries. Prinsengracht 526. ☎ **020/625-0942.** Tram: 1, 2, or 5 to Prinsengracht.

There's a permanent exhibition of primitive art from around the world, particularly from Africa and Asia, and all sorts of ethnic jewelry. Open Wednesday to Saturday noon to 5:30pm.

BOOKS

✪ **American Book Center.** Kalverstraat 185. ☎ **020/625-5537.** Tram: 4, 9, 14, 16, 20, 24, or 25 to Muntplein.

You'll swear you never left the States when you see the array of best-sellers and paperbacks in the American Book Center on Kalverstraat near Muntplein, which claims to be the biggest U.S.-style book store on the European continent. Plus, there are magazines (risqué and otherwise) and hardcover editions, hot off the presses. Prices are higher than you'd pay at home, but the selection beats any airport or hotel gift store, with categories ranging from ancient civilizations, astrology, and baby care to science, science fiction, and war. If you think you'll buy a lot of books, you can buy a 1-year discount card for Dfl 15 ($6.40) that allows 10% off; also, students and teachers can get 10% off simply by showing a school ID. Open Monday to Wednesday and Friday and Saturday 10am to 8pm, Thursday 10am to 10pm, and Sunday 11am to 6pm.

Athenaeum Booksellers. Spui 14–16. ☎ **020/622-6248.** Tram: 1, 2, or 5 to Spui.

You can't miss this place. It's always crowded with book lovers, students, and scholars. The Athenaeum is best known for its nonfiction collection and has books in a number of different languages. There are magazine stands on the sidewalk. The store is open Monday to Wednesday and Saturday 9:30am to 6pm; Thursday from 9:30am to 9pm; Sunday noon to 5:30pm.

De Slegte. Kalverstraat 48–52. ☎ **020/622-5933.** Tram: 4, 9, 14, 16, 20, 24, or 25 to the Dam.

You won't find too many books in English here—most are in Dutch or other languages—but you find some, and if you collect books as a hobby, you might run across a real gem. It's probably one of the biggest, most-often-visited bookstores in Amsterdam. Open Monday 11am to 6pm, Tuesday to Friday 9:30am to 6pm, and Saturday 8am to 6pm.

English Bookshop. Lauriergracht 71. ☎ **020/626-4230.** Tram: 7, 10, 17, or 20 to Elandsgracht.

On the edge of the Jordaan, this small bookstore has a wonderful selection of books in English, mainly fiction and biography, and a small selection of British magazines. Occasionally, you can find a great book at a discount. Open Tuesday to Friday 1 to 6pm and Saturday 11am to 5pm.

Evenaar. Singel 348. ☎ **020/624-6289.** Tram: 1, 2, or 5 to Spui.

Since you are traveling, you may be in the mood for travel literature. Evenaar, which is close to Spui, sells not only travel guides but also a wide range of travel literature and large-format photo books on travel and anthropology, and secondhand and antique travel books. Open Monday to Friday noon to 6pm, Saturday 11am to 5pm.

Waterstone's Booksellers. Kalverstraat 152. ☎ **020/638-3821.** Tram: 1, 2, 4, 5, 14, 16, 17, 20, 24, or 25 to Spui.

Waterstone's is a British chain that has a large stock of fiction and nonfiction titles. You'll probably be able to find almost anything you're looking for on one of the three floors here. Open Monday 11am to 6pm, Tuesday, Wednesday, and Friday 9am to 6pm, Thursday 9am to 9pm, Saturday 9am to 7pm, and Sunday 11am to 5pm.

CARS

Ten Cate Fiat. Weesperzijds 143. ☎ **020/668-6373.** Tram: 12 to Amstel Station.

Ah, the Fiat 500! What the T-Bird was to the States, the diminutive Cinquecento was to Europe. No matter that when you wanted to overtake you found it easier to get out, pick the car up under your arm, and run with it. You could park one anywhere, and Italians always did. Henk ten Cate and his team are Fiat 500 enthusiasts, and they will sell or lease you an exceedingly little piece of lovingly restored automotive history. You might even be able to take it home in your hand-baggage. Their showroom is worth visiting just for the sight of dozens of Cinquecentos lined up side by side. Open Monday to Friday 9am to 5pm, Saturday 11am to 3pm.

CIGARS, PIPES & SMOKING ARTICLES

Holland is one of the cigar-producing centers of the world. Serious smokers know that Dutch cigars are different, and drier, than Cuban or American smokes. It's partly because of the Indonesian tobacco and partly because of the way the cigar is made, but whatever the reason, Dutch cigars can be a pleasant change for American tobacco enthusiasts.

P. G. C. Hajenius. Rokin 92–96. ☎ **020/623-7494.** Tram: 4, 9, 14, 16, 20, 24, or 25 to Spui.

This store has been Amsterdam's leading purveyor of cigars and smoking articles since 1826, first with a store on the Dam and then since 1915 in its present elegant headquarters. Cigars are the house specialty and the stock includes a room full of Havanas. Hajenius sells the long, uniquely Dutch, handmade clay pipes you see in old paintings and that are a good gift idea, and ceramic pipes, some painted in the blue-and-white Chinese-inspired patterns of Delftware. You also find lighters, cigarette holders, clippers, and flasks. Open Monday to Wednesday and Friday and Saturday 9:30am to 6pm, Thursday 9:30am to 9pm, Sunday noon to 5pm.

Smokiana & Pijpenkabinet. Prinsengracht 488. ☎ **020/421-1179.** Tram: 1, 2, or 5 to Prinsengracht.

This place stocks a vast range of pipes from the antique, to the exotic, to the downright weird. It's where to buy that unique pipe, into which the tobacco can be tamped with an air of deliberate insouciance, and the resulting fug flaunted in the faces of nonsmokers everywhere. Open Wednesday to Saturday noon to 6pm.

CLOCKS

Victoria Gifts. Prins Hendrikkade 47 (opposite Centraal Station). ☎ **020/427-2051.** Tram: 1, 2, 4, 5, 9, 13, 16, 17, 20, 24, or 25 to Centraal Station.

Dutch clockmakers turn out timepieces with soft-toned chimes in exquisite Old Dutch–style handcrafted cases covered with tiny figures and mottoes, insets of hand-painted porcelain, and hand-painted Dutch scenes. This small store is a happy hunting ground for these treasures. It also has a good stock of Delftware, embroidered flags, chocolates, and other quality gifts at reasonable prices. Open in Summer Monday to Saturday 9am to 8pm; in winter Monday to Saturday 9am to 8pm.

CRAFTS & CURIOS

✪ **Blue Gold Fish.** Rozengracht 17 (opposite Westerkerk). ☎ **020/623-3134.** Tram: 13, 14, 17, or 20 to Westermarkt.

"Dive into the pool of fantasy," say the owners of this colorful store and gallery. There's no real rhyme or reason to the items for sale. They cover a wide range of ceramics, jewelry, household items (including colorful lamps in the "Aladdin's Corner"), textiles, and all of them running the stylistic gamut from kitsch to chic. Still, there's unity in diversity in the more-or-less fantastic design sensibility that goes into each piece. Open Monday to Saturday 11:30am to 6:30pm.

Cortina Papier. Reestraat 22 (between Prinsengracht and Keizersgracht). ☎ **020/ 623-6676.** Tram: 13, 14, 17, or 20 to Westermarkt.

If you'd like the kind of personal journal that would look have looked good in *The English Patient* and *Dances with Wolves,* this is the place for you. Cortina does fancy notebooks, agendas and address books, and nice lines in writing paper, envelopes, and other such products. Open Monday 1 to 6pm, Tuesday to Friday 11am to 6pm, and Saturday 11am to 5pm.

E. Kramer Candle Shop. Reestraat 20 (between Prinsengracht and Keizersgracht). ☎ **020/626-5274.** Tram: 13, 14, 17, or 20 to Westermarkt.

This place provides illumination for everything from a romantic candlelit dinner to a wake, while filling all kinds of temporary and mobile lighting requirements in between. Some of the candles are little melting works of art and some are outrageously kitschy, but all will shed some light on your activities. The store also sells scented oils and incense, and even repairs dolls. Open Monday to Friday 10am to 6pm, Saturday 10am to 5pm.

La Savonnerie. Prinsengracht 294 (corner of Elandsgracht). ☎ **020/428-1139.** Tram: 7, 10, 17, or 20 to Elandsgracht.

This is the kind of clean-living store that a raffish place like Amsterdam can't get enough of. You can buy artisanal soap in all kinds of shapes and sizes. How about a soap chess set, soap alphabet blocks, and soap animal shapes? You can buy personalized soap and even make your own soap. Open Tuesday to Friday 10am to 6pm (8pm on Thursday in summer), Saturday 10am to 5pm.

Nieuws Innovations. Prinsengracht 297 (at Westermarkt). ☎ **020/627-9540.** Tram: 13, 14, 17, or 20 to Westermarkt.

This store is a source for all kinds of offbeat souvenirs, such as pens in the shape of fish, lipsticks, and (perhaps too near the bone for Amsterdam) syringes; washcloths in the form of hand-glove puppets; spherical dice; finger massage sets; and many other hard-to-define but colorful little bits and pieces. Open Monday 1:30 to 6:30pm; Tuesday, Wednesday, and Friday 10am to 6:30pm, Thursday 10am to 9pm, Saturday and Sunday 11am to 6pm.

Pakhuis Amerika. Prinsengracht 541 (at Runstraat). ☎ **020/639-2583.** Tram: 1, 2, or 5 to Prinsengracht.

All kinds of American souvenirs and antiques, imported from the United States, and just waiting to be paid for, wrapped, and brought straight back home again—and all for much more than you would have paid for them in the States! If nothing else, it's a kind of museum—your heritage (as Europeans see it) all together in one place. Open Monday to Saturday 11am to 8pm.

't Winkeltje. Prinsengracht 228 (at Leliegracht). ☎ **020/625-1352.** Tram: 13, 14, 17, or 20 to Westermarkt.

This place sells knickknacks such as colored bottles and glasses; modern versions of old tin cars and other children's toys from the 1950s and earlier; big plastic butterflies; lamps shaped like bananas; and many other such useful things. A little bit of this and a little bit of that. Open Monday 1 to 5:30pm, Tuesday to Friday 10am to 5:30pm, and Saturday 10am to 5pm.

DELFTWARE

Focke & Meltzer. P. C. Hooftstraat 65–67. ☎ **020/664-2311.** Tram: 2, 3, 5, 12, or 20 to Van Baerlestraat.

This main branch of a popular chain is the best one-stop store you'll find for authentic Delftware and Makkumware, Hummel figurines, Leerdam crystal, and a world of other fine china, porcelain, silver, glass, and crystal products. Open Monday to Friday 9:30am to 5:30pm and Saturday 9:30am to 5pm.

Heinen. Prinsengracht 440 (at Leidsestraat). ☎ **020/627-8299.** Tram: 1, 2, or 5, to Prinsengracht. Spiegelgracht 13. ☎ **020/421-8360.** Tram: 6, 7, or 10 to Spiegelgracht.

You can save considerably on hand-painted pottery and have the fun of seeing the product made at these stores, owned by a father-and-son team who sit inside their canal-house windows, quietly painting the days away. You get quality and a good selection of useful, well-priced items. Jaap (father) and Jorrit (son) both paint in five techniques: blue and white (Delft), polychrome (Makkum), Japanese Imari, Kwartjes (a modern-looking Delft with blue, red, and gold), and Sepia (brown and red). They are official dealers of De Porcelyne Fles and Tichelaars and have a third store, in Volendam, at Haven 92. Open Monday to Saturday 9:30am to 6pm.

DEPARTMENT STORES

De Bijenkorf. Dam 1. ☎ **020/621-8080.** Tram: 4, 9, 14, 16, 20, 24, or 25 to the Dam.

De Bijenkorf is Amsterdam's best-known department store, and the one with the best variety of goods. A recent renovation changed this once-frumpy little dry-goods emporium into Amsterdam's answer to New York's Bloomingdale's. On the ground floor, you find the usual ranks of cosmetic counters in the center section, plus a men's department and odds and ends such as socks and stockings, handbags and belts, costume jewelry, and stationery. And umbrellas—plenty of umbrellas! On upper floors there's everything from ladies' fashions to *dekbedden* (down comforters), plus a bookstore, several eating spots, and even a luggage section where you can pick up an extra suitcase or tote bag to take home your purchases. Records, color TVs, shoes, clothing, personal effects, appliances—it's all here. Open Monday 11am to 6pm; Tuesday, Wednesday, and Friday 9:30am to 6pm; Thursday 9:30am to 9pm; and Saturday 9am to 6pm.

Hema. Kalvertoren Shopping Center, Kalverstraat. ☎ **020/626-8720.** Tram: 4, 14, 16, 20, 24, or 25 to Muntplein.

Hema is the Woolworth's of Amsterdam, selling things like socks, toothbrushes, chocolate, cookies, and cheeses. If you can't figure out where to find something, your best bet is to look here. Open Monday 11am to 6pm, Tuesday to Friday 9:30am to 6pm, and Saturday 9am to 6pm.

Magna Plaza. Spuistraat 168 (behind the Dam's Royal Palace). ☎ **020/626-9199.** Tram: 1, 2, 5, 13, 14, 17, or 20 to the Dam.

Magna Plaza is not actually a department store, but a shopping mall, located amid the extravagant Gothic architecture of the former central Post Office. The Plaza's floors are filled with shops of all kinds and yet it's small enough to function as a kind of department store. The biggest, and certainly noisiest, store is the Free Records Superstore in the basement.

Marks & Spencer. Kalverstraat 66–72. ☎ **020/531-2468.** Tram: 4, 5, 9, 14, 16, 20, 24, or 25 to the Dam.

This is a branch of the popular British store chain, whose specialties are clothes of good quality in their class, even if they are not always very imaginative—the underwear is particularly good! It also has a food hall with a reputation for quality, freshness and convenience. Open Monday 11am to 6pm, Tuesday, Wednesday and Friday 10am to 6pm, Thursday from 10am to 9pm, Saturday 9:30am to 6pm and Sunday noon to 6pm.

Metz & Co. Keizersgracht 455 (at Leidsestraat). ☎ **020/520-7020.** Tram: 1, 2, or 5 to Keizersgracht.

This dramatic store, founded in 1740, is now owned by Liberty of London. It sells furniture, fabrics, kitchenware, and other traditional department-store items. The cupola and cafe are worth stopping for. Open Monday 11am to 6pm and Tuesday to Saturday 9:30am to 6pm.

Vroom & Dreesman. Kalverstraat 201–221 and 212–224 (near the Muntplein). ☎ **020/622-0171.** Tram: 4, 9, 14, 16, 20, 24, or 25 to Muntplein.

Less polished and pretentious than Metz & Co., and highly successful as a result, this is the Amsterdam branch of Vroom & Dreesman, a Dutch chain of department stores that pop up in key shopping locations all over Holland. It's a no-nonsense sort of store with a wide range of middle-of-the-road goods and prices and services to match. Open Monday to Saturday 9am to 6pm.

DIAMONDS

The following shops are members of the **Diamond Foundation Amsterdam.** They offer diamond-cutting and polishing tours, and sales of the finished product: **Amsterdam Diamond Center,** Rokin 1 (☎ 020/624-5787), open Friday to Wednesday 10am to 6pm, Thursday 10am to 6pm and 7 to 8:30pm; **Coster Diamonds,** Paulus Potterstraat 2–4 (☎ 020/676-2222), open daily 9am to 5pm; **Gassan Diamonds,** Nieuwe Uilenburgerstraat 173–175 (☎ 020/622-5333), open daily 9am to 5pm; **Stoeltie Diamonds,** Wagenstraat 13–17 (☎ 020/623-7601), open daily 9am to 5pm; and **Van Moppes Diamonds,** Albert Cuypstraat 2–6 (☎ 020/676-1242), open daily 9am to 5pm.

FASHIONS
WOMEN'S

Paris may set the styles, but young Dutch women—and some of their mothers—often know better than the French how to make them work. Whatever the current European fashion rage is, you can expect to see it in store windows all over Amsterdam, and in all price ranges. Some boutique faithfuls claim that they buy Paris designer fashions in Amsterdam at lower-than-Paris prices, but one quick check will tell you that designer wear is still expensive, whether you pay in guilders, francs, or hard-earned dollars.

It's more fun to ferret out the new, young crop of Dutch designers who regularly open shops in unpredictable locations all over town. Boutiques and their designers change rapidly with the tides of fashion, but the current top names and locations along the Rokin are: **Carla V., Sheila de Vries, Jan Jansen** (shoes), **Agnès B** (women's fashions), and **Puck & Hans,** whose pseudo-Japanese look catches the eye as you walk along.

Also stop by **The Madhatter,** Van der Helsplein 4 (☎ 020/664-7748), for handmade hats; **Mô,** Overtoom 336 (☎ 020/689-4369), for leather apparel (menswear also); and **Eva Damave,** Tweede Laurierdwarsstraat 51c (☎ 020/627-7325), for knitwear.

Maison de Bonneterie. Rokin 140–142. ☎ **020/626-2162.** Tram: 4, 9, 14, 16, 20, 24, or 25 to Rokin.

Here you find exclusive women's fashions, and Gucci bags and Fieldcrest towels and a star-studded cast of brand names on household goods and personal items. Open Monday 1 to 5:30pm and Tuesday to Saturday 10am to 5:30pm.

Peek and Cloppenburg. Dam 20. ☎ **020/623-2637.** Tram: 4, 9, 14, 16, 20, 24, or 25 to the Dam.

Peek and Cloppenburg is a different sort of department store—or perhaps a better description is that P&C is an overgrown clothing store. Open Monday noon to 6pm and Tuesday to Saturday 9:30am to 6pm.

MEN'S

In addition to the department stores listed above, you can find men's fashions at **Tie Rack,** Heiligeweg 7 (☎ 020/627-2978), and **Guus de Winter,** Linnaeusstraat 197 (☎ **020/694-0252**). If you're into fancy, colorful sweaters, check out those of former cabaret performers Greg and Gary Christmas, at their boutique **Backstage,** Utrechtsedwarsstraat 67 (☎ **020/622-3638**).

CHILDREN'S

Children's clothing stores are everywhere. Among them are **'t Schooltje,** Overtoom 87 (☎ 020/683-0444), which carries expensive but cute clothes for babies and children (well into the teen years); and the more affordable **Spetter Children's Fashion,** Van den Helstraat 53 1e (☎ 020/671-6249).

FOOD & DRINK

De Waterwinkel. Roelof Hartstraat 10. ☎ **020/675-5932.** Tram: 3, 5, 12, 20, or 24 to Roelof Hartplein.

Quality, purity, and beauty are the watchwords at the tastefully designed Water Shop. More than 100 varieties of mineral water from all over the world are on sale, ranging from ordinary, everyday water to designer water. Some of the bottles are miniature works of art in themselves. This is a store whose liquid assets are its stock-in-trade. Open Monday to Wednesday, Friday, and Saturday 9am to 6pm, Thursday 9am to 9pm.

✪ **H. Keijzer.** Prinsengracht 180. ☎ **020/624-0823.** Tram: 13, 14, 17, or 20 to Westermarkt.

H. Keijzer, which was founded in 1839, specializes in tea and coffee. It offers 90 different kinds of tea and 22 coffees; they generally range from Dfl 4 ($1.70) to Dfl 17.50 ($7.45) per 100 grams, depending on the market. Consider taking home several 100-gram packets of teas from different parts of the tea-growing world: Ceylon Melange (or Delmar Melange), an English-style blend from Sri Lanka; Darjeeling First Flush, from India; Yunnan, from China; and Java O.P. (Orange Pekoe), from Indonesia. All of these teas are popular with the Dutch. For a nice gift, select from an assortment of tea boxes; the small box with a picture of the store and other buildings costs Dfl 5 ($2.15). Open Monday to Friday 8:30am to 5:30pm and Saturday 8:30am to 5pm.

H. P. de Vreng en Zonen. Nieuwendijk 75. ☎ **020/624-4581.** Tram: 1, 2, 5, 13, 17, or 20 to Martelaarsgracht.

This traditional distillery creates Dutch liqueurs and gins according to the old-fashioned methods, sans additives. Try the Old Amsterdam jenever or some of the more flamboyantly colored liquids, like the bright green plum liqueur *Pruimpje prik in.* Some supposedly have aphrodisiac power. A chance to see the collection of 15,000 miniature bottles alone makes a visit worthwhile. Open Monday to Saturday 10am to 5pm.

Jacob Hooy & Co. Kloveniersburgwal 10–12. ☎ **020/624-3041.** Metro: Nieuwmarkt.

You feel you've stepped back into history if you visit Jacob Hooy & Co. This store, opened in 1743 and operated for the past 130 years by the same family, is a wonderland of fragrant smells that offers more than 500 different herbs and spices and 30 different teas, all sold loose, by weight. Health foods, homeopathic products, and natural cosmetics are also on sale. Everything is stored in wooden drawers and wooden barrels with the names of the contents hand scripted in gold. Across the counter are fishbowl jars in racks containing 30 or more different types of *dropjes* (drops or lozenges) that range in taste from sweet to sour to salty. Open Monday noon to 6pm, Tuesday to Friday 8am to 6pm, and Saturday 8am to 5pm.

Patisserie Pompadour. Huidenstraat 12. ☎ **020/623-9554.** Tram: 1, 2, or 5 to Spui.

The counter display here is amazing. There are close to 50 luscious pastries that can be enjoyed in this exquisite Louis XVI tearoom or wrapped to go. Open Tuesday to Friday 9:30am to 5:45pm and Saturday 9am to 5:30pm.

GAY

Mr. B. Warmoesstraat 89 (Red Light District). ☎ **020/422-0003.** Tram: 1, 2, 4, 5, 9, 13, 14, 16, 17, 20, 24, or 25 to Centraal Station.

This airy store is world famous for high-quality leather goods, from basic trousers and chaps to more revealing and fetish wear. The shop window's display of accessories for the S/M, leather and rubber guys, regular exhibitions of erotic art, and a great selection of piercing jewelry, ensures many a gaping tourist. Visiting tattoo and piercing artists from around the world make guest appearances for the real connoisseurs. There are cards and postcards to greet the friends you left behind. Open Monday to Friday 10am to 6:30pm (Thursday to 9pm), Saturday 11am to 6pm.

HABERDASHERY

H. J. van de Kerkhof. Wolvenstraat 9–11. ☎ **020/623-4666.** Tram: 1, 2, or 5 to Spui.

The walls of this store are lined with spools of ribbon and cord, and its notebooks are filled with examples of patches and appliqués. There are key tassels and tiebacks in all sizes, including very large "canal house" size. Open Monday to Friday 9am to 6pm and Saturday 10am to 5pm.

Knopen Winkel. Wolvenstraat 14. ☎ **020/624-0479.** Tram: 1, 2, or 5 to Spui.

"The Button Shop," an amusing store in the canal area, stocks over 8,000 different kinds of buttons. Buttons in this tiny store are sorted by color and displayed in specially designed cases. Prices range from Dfl 0.20 to Dfl 20 (10¢ to $8.50) per button. There's a special section of children's buttons, and sections for buttons of wood, leather, glass and metal, and pearl. Open Monday from 1 to 6pm, Tuesday to Friday 11am to 6pm, and Saturday 11am to 5pm.

HOUSEHOLD

Kitsch Kitchens. Eerste Bloemdwarsstraat 21. ☎ **020/428-4969.** Tram: 13, 14, 17, or 20 to Westermarkt.

The name just about says it all. You'll probably want to put on your shades before entering the world of glaringly bright colors that characterize Kitsch Kitchens' utensils and fittings in plastic, enamel, and papier-mâché. Kitsch Kitchens has extended its market by opening a second store, **Kitsch Kitchens Kids,** Rozengracht 183 (☎ **020/622-8261**), aimed at children. Open Monday to Friday 10:30am to 6pm, Saturday 10am to 6pm.

JEWELRY

BLGK Edelsmeden. Hartenstraat 28. ☎ **020/624-8154.** Tram: 13, 14, 17, or 20 to Westermarkt.

This store is run by a group of jewelry designers who produce and sell affordable jewelry with character. Each designer has his or her own slant on things. Some of their pieces represent a new and fresh spin on classic forms, while others are more innovative and imaginative. Open Tuesday to Friday 11am to 6pm, Saturday 11am to 5pm.

Galerie Ra. Vijzelstraat 90. ☎ **020/626-5100.** Tram: 16, 24, or 25 to Keizersgracht.

Marvelous contemporary designs and materials turn jewelry into an art form here. Owner Paul Derrez specializes in stunning modern jewelry in gold and silver, and goes a bit further, turning feathers, rubber, foam, and other materials into pieces that he describes as "playful." Open Tuesday to Friday 10am to 6pm, Saturday 10am to 5pm.

MARKETS

Amsterdammers are traders to the tips of their fingers, as you quickly see if you visit a street market. It's not that the Dutch will bargain for hours like a Moroccan in his souk or follow you around a square pulling bigger and brighter samples from beneath a poncho, like a bowler-hatted Ecuadorian. No, the Dutch street merchants exhibit their enthusiasm for trade in a more stolid way—simply by being permanent. Many of Amsterdam's open-air salesmen are at their stalls, vans, tents, and barges of the city's 26 markets 6 days a week, 52 weeks a year. In all, there are more than 50 outdoor markets every week in Amsterdam and its outlying neighborhoods, and on any given day, except Sunday, you have a choice of several.

   Besides the markets listed below, you may also enjoy visiting the **Textile Market** (at Noordermarkt, on Prinsengracht), held on Monday morning; the **Garden Market** (at Amstelveld, on Prinsengracht near Vijzelstraat), also on Monday; the **Stamp Market** (at the post office), held on Wednesday and Saturday afternoons; and the **Bird Market** (at Noordermarkt, on Prinsengracht), which displays a selection of caged birds on Saturday morning.

✪ **Albert Cuyp Markt.** Albert Cuypstraat. Tram: 16, 24, or 25 to Albert Cuypstraat; 4 or 20 to Stadhouderskade.

You find just about anything and everything your imagination can conjure up at this kilometer-long market—different types of foods, clothing, flowers, plants, and textiles. The market houses 350 different stalls and is open Monday to Saturday 10am to 4pm.

Bookmarket. Spui. Tram: 1, 2, or 5 to Spui.

Every Friday there's a book market held on the Spui. Usually, there are about 25 different booths that offer secondhand books. Often you can find some great deals (even for books in English)—perhaps even a rare book or two. Just about any subject is available, both fiction and nonfiction. The market is open Friday 10am to 4pm.

Farmer's Market (Boerenmarkt). Noordermarkt. Tram: 3 or 10 to Marnixplein.

This market, also known as the Bio Market, caters to Amsterdam's growing infatuation with health foods and natural products. It takes place every Saturday 8am to 2pm.

✪ **Floating Flower Market.** Singel at Muntplein. Tram: 1, 2, or 5 to Koningsplein; 4, 9, 14, 16, 20, 24, or 25 to Muntplein.

A row of barges has permanently parked here to sell a selection of fresh-cut flowers, bright- and healthy-looking plants, ready-to-travel packets of tulip bulbs, and all the necessary accessories for home gardening. Tulips here cost a few pennies less than at the flower stands around town—10 tulips go for Dfl 7.50 to Dfl 12 ($3.20 to $5.10). The prices definitely beat the cost of fresh flowers at home. Should you be invited to the home of an Amsterdammer, buy flowers here to take along with you—that's what the natives themselves do. The market is open from Monday to Saturday 10am to 6pm.

Kunst- & Antiekcentrum de Looier.

See "Antiques," above.

Thorbecke Sunday Art Market. Thorbeckeplein. ☎ **075/670-3030.** Tram: 4, 9, 14, or 20 to Rembrandtplein.

This market runs from March to December. Local artists come and show off their wares. You find sculptures, ceramics, paintings, graphics, jewelry, and mixed-media pieces. Picking your way through the artists' tables is a fine way to spend a sunny Sunday afternoon. From 11am to 6pm.

✪ **Waterlooplein Flea Market.** Waterlooplein. Tram: 9, 14, or 20 to Waterlooplein.

Waterlooplein is the classic market of Amsterdam, and perhaps of all Europe. It's often said that in the market's glory days before World War II, you could find amazing antiques among the junk and possibly even a proverbial dusty Rembrandt. Today your luck is more apt to run in the opposite direction, but Dfl 10 ($4.25) isn't a bad price for an old record album, and Dfl 100 ($42.55) will buy a leather jacket to keep you warm if there's a change in the weather. Most of the merchants now work out of tents, and some sell *patates frites met mayonnaise* (french fries, eaten Dutch style, with mayonnaise) from vans that are a long way from the pushcarts of yesteryear; but you still find cooking pots, mariner's telescopes, coal scuttles, bargain watches, nuts and bolts, and decent prints of Dutch cities. On Sunday in the summer (late May to the end of September), the junk goes away for a day and the antiques and books come in. The market is open daily 9am to 5pm.

MUSIC
Free Record Shop. Kalverstraat 230. ☎ **020/625-7378.** Tram: 4, 9, 14, 16, 16, 24, or 25 to Muntplein.

The records themselves aren't free, sadly, but the large ground floor and basement of this store hold an incredible number of cassettes, compact discs, and videos at competitive prices. Open daily from 9am to 6pm (9am to 9pm on Thursday).

SEX
Amsterdam's free-and-easy—you could even say laid-back—attitude to the mysteries of the flesh has spawned a vast range of shops devoted to satisfying customers' needs, whether real or pure fantasy. Many of these shops are down-and-dirty, sleazeball kinds of places, but not all. Here are a couple with a sense of style.

Absolute Danny. Oudezijds Achterburgwal 78. ☎ **020/421-0915.** Tram: 4, 9, 14, 16, 20, 24, or 25 to the Dam.

The name comes from its owner, Danny Linden, a graduate of the Fashion Academy and the Academy of Fine Arts, who brings her artistic sensibilities to bear on the erotic lifestyle her store supports. You find everything from sexy tableware (if you can imagine such a thing) to S/M clothing and accessories, with the main lines covering sexy lingerie and erotic clothing in leather and latex. Open Monday to Saturday 11am to 9pm.

Condomerie Het Gulden Vlies. Warmoesstraat 141. ☎ **020/627-4174.** Tram: 4, 9, 14, 16, 20, 24, or 25 to the Dam.

The Golden Fleece condom shop stocks a vast range of these items, in all shapes, sizes, and flavors, from regular brand labels to flashy designer fittings, all but guaranteeing your apparel of choice. The store claims to be the world's first specialized condom store—the start of a whole new protection racket. There is probably no significance whatsoever in the fact that the store is located on the edge of the Red Light District. Open Monday to Wednesday, Friday and Saturday noon to 6pm, Thursday noon to 8pm.

TOYS

Some museum shops are good sources for toys and other children's knickknacks. Try the shops at the **Scheepvaartmuseum (Maritime Museum),** Kattenburgerplein 1 (☎ **020/624-6601**), for model ships; the **Theatermuseum,** Herengracht 168 (☎ **020/623-5104**), for masks, costumes, and minitheaters; **newMetropolis,** Oosterdok 2 (☎ **020/531-3233**), for all kinds of scientific toys and gadgets; and the **Tropenmuseum,** Linnaeusstraat 2 (☎ **020/568-8215**), and **Artis Zoo,** Plantage Kerklaan 38–40 (☎ **020/523-3400**), for model animals and ecological stuff.

Ever wished that your kids would take an interest in the sweet, wholesome kinds of things that children ought to like—instead of getting their kicks from zapping aliens, surfing the Web, and watching MTV? Try taking them to the stores below.

Bell Tree. Spiegelgracht 10–12. ☎ **020/625-8830.** Tram: 6, 7, or 10 to Spiegelgracht.

Bell Tree is the place to find treasures for kids. The toys here don't blink, bleep, or run out of battery juice—many of them are actually made from wood! And they're not just modern versions of the kind of playthings that Grandma and Grandpa knew and loved, but real up-to-the-minute gear. Open Monday from 1 to 6pm, Tuesday to Saturday 10am to 6pm.

Kinderfeestwinkel. 1e van der Helststraat 15. ☎ **020/470-4791.** Tram: 16, 24, or 25 to Albert Cuypstraat.

The name means "Children's Party Shop," and that's just what it is. Everything that a child could possibly want for celebrating the big moments in life, such as birthdays. Open Tuesday to Saturday 10am to 6pm.

Amsterdam After Dark

Nightlife in Amsterdam, like an Indonesian *rijsttafel,* is a bit of this and a bit of that. The cultural calendar is full, but not jammed. There's a strong jazz scene, good music clubs, and enjoyable English-language shows at the little cabarets and theaters along the canals. The club and bar scene can be entertaining if not outrageous; the dance clubs may indeed seem quiet and small to anyone used to the flash of clubs in New York, L.A., or London. However, the brown cafes—the typical Amsterdam pubs—have never been better. And there's always the movies. Amsterdam is one of the few cities on the European continent where you can see first-run blockbuster hits from the United States with their English-language soundtracks intact.

ENTERTAINMENT ORIENTATION

INFORMATION   Your best source of information on nightlife and cultural events is *What's On in Amsterdam,* the VVV Tourist Office's monthly program guide in English, which costs Dfl 4 ($1.70). It provides a complete cultural guide to Amsterdam, day by day, with listings for concerts and recitals, theater, cabaret, opera, dance performances, rock concerts, art films, film festivals, special museum and art gallery exhibitions, and lots more. Many hotels have copies available for guests, in some cases for free, or you can get one at the VVV offices (see chapter 3 for addresses and hours). There is also the free monthly, newspaper-style *Uitkrant,* in Dutch, which can be picked up at many performance venues.

MAIN NIGHTLIFE AREAS   Leidseplein, hot and cool at the same time, is the center of Amsterdam's nightlife, with some of the city's most popular restaurants, bars, and nightspots all within dancing distance of each other. Leidseplein never really closes, so you can greet the dawn and start again. **Rembrandtplein** is a brash and brassy square that really comes alive at night, when it's awash with neon. Although it has a more downmarket reputation than Leidseplein, this area often seems even more intent on having fun, and there are enough cool and sophisticated places to go around. These two areas are connected by Reguliersdwarsstraat, which has some good cafes, including a few gay cafes, and also several fine clubs and restaurants. The **Rosse Buurt (Red Light District)** serves up its own unique brand of nightlife, and adjoining this is **Nieuwmarkt,** which is rapidly becoming a popular, if somewhat alternative, hangout.

TICKETS If you want to attend any of Amsterdam's theatrical or musical events (including rock concerts), make it your first task on arrival to get tickets. Box office information is given below. **Amsterdam Uit Buro (AUB) Ticketshop,** Leidseplein 26 (☎ 020/621-1211), can book tickets for almost every venue in town; it also handles advance booking from abroad. The VVV Amsterdam Tourist Office (see chapter 3 for addresses and hours) can also book tickets, and charges Dfl 5 ($2.15) for the service. Most upmarket and many mid-level hotels will book tickets as well.

HOURS & PERFORMANCE TIMES Concert, theater, opera, and dance performances generally begin at 8:15pm; jazz concerts begin at 11 or 11:30pm. Jazz clubs and music spots are usually open 10pm to 2am, and as late as 4am on weekends. Dance clubs open at 10 or 11pm and close at 4am on weeknights and 5am on weekends.

DRINK PRICES With the exception of the dance clubs, nightclubs, and other high-ticket nightspots in Amsterdam, you can expect to pay Dfl 3 to Dfl 6 ($1.30 to $2.55) for a beer or a Coke and Dfl 3 to Dfl 6 ($1.30 to $2.55) for *jenever* (Dutch gin, the national drink; try it at least once, *without* ice). To order your favorite whisky and water will probably cost you at least Dfl 7.50 ($3.20), and a mixed cocktail can be as much as Dfl 20 ($8.50). But, remember, these are average prices around town; the cost at a brown cafe (pub) could be less and a hotel bar could charge more.

DRESS CODE If you intend to go to the opera, a classical music concert, or the theater, don't worry about what to wear, since Amsterdam has a very informal dress code—no code at all, really. Of course, you might want to dress up, and in fact many people do, but you'll never be turned away for being "improperly" dressed.

SAFETY Wherever you wander in Amsterdam after dark, it's wise to be mindful of your surroundings. Fortunately, Amsterdam's less desirable citizens tend to congregate in the less desirable neighborhoods, and none of the nightspots described here are in a problem area, though taxis are advised in a few cases.

For personal safety in the Red Light District, stick to the main streets and the crowds. It's asking for trouble to go off on your own at night down some of those very narrow and dark side streets and connecting lanes between the canals—some are so narrow that you literally have to squeeze past people. The main streets are usually busy and quite brightly lit (what with all those red lights and neon signs) and most clubs have their own security, since they have a vested interest in not having their customers mugged. Remember, though, that the kinds of industries active here tend to attract less savory types, including muggers, pickpockets, drug dealers, junkies, street prostitutes and their pimps, and weird folks in general. But there are also plenty of tour groups who seem to be having a great time, judging by all the laughing that goes on as they walk around.

1 The Performing Arts

CLASSICAL MUSIC

Amsterdam's top orchestra—indeed one of the world's top orchestras—is the famed **Royal Concertgebouw Orchestra,** which performs mainly in the Concertgebouw, but can also be found giving open-air concerts in the Vondelpark. The Concertgebouw Orchestra can produce any of the great classical pieces at the tap of a baton, yet it is also willing to go out on a limb occasionally with more modern and experimental works. The city's other full orchestra, the **Netherlands Philharmonic Orchestra,** fondly known as the NedPho, isn't far behind its illustrious cousin, if behind at all.

Arts Adventure

This is a cultural program designed to extend the regular flow of cultural events into the previously dormant months of July and August—precisely the time when most tourists visit the city. The program includes more offbeat and informal events across the full range of the arts than would be the case with the main (September to June) cultural program of opera, ballet, and classical music. Further information is available from VVV offices and the **Amsterdam Uit Buro** (☎ **020/621-1211**).

It also performs in the Concertgebouw and in its main venue, the Beurs van Berlage. The NedPho has found its niche in a somewhat more adventurous diet, often incorporating opera collaborations. In addition, at either of these venues you may well catch one of Holland's other top orchestras, such as The Hague's **Residentie Orchestra** and the **Rotterdam Philharmonic,** and visiting orchestras from abroad.

When it comes to chamber music, the **Netherlands Chamber Orchestra, Amsterdam Baroque Orchestra,** and **Orchestra of the Eighteenth Century** provide plenty of possibilities, often playing with authentic period instruments and ably supported by the **Netherlands Chamber Choir.** Students of the **Sweelinck Conservatorium** fit themselves in at all possible times and places. You often hear these outfits in the Recital Hall of the Concertgebouw, the Beurs van Berlage, or in one of Amsterdam's historic churches (for information on venues, see below).

OPERA

Productions by the **Netherlands Opera** dominate the schedule at the Muziektheater. Although less well known internationally than the Royal Concertgebouw Orchestra or either of Holland's major dance companies, the Netherlands Opera has its own well-known performers and a devoted following. In recent years, under the artistic direction of Pierre Audi, it staged a successful Monteverdi trilogy before moving confidently on to Wagner's *Ring* cycle.

DANCE

The Dutch take pride in the growing international popularity and prestige of their major dance companies. The **Dutch National Ballet,** home-based at Amsterdam's Muziektheater, has a repertoire of both classical and modern works, many by choreographers George Balanchine and Hans van Manen. The **Netherlands Dance Theater,** choreographed by Czech artistic director, Jiří Kylián, is based in The Hague but frequently comes to the Muziektheater. Both companies are generally accompanied by the specialized **Netherlands Ballet Orchestra.**

THEATER

Amsterdammers speak English so well that Broadway and London road shows and English-language touring companies sometimes make Amsterdam a stop on their European itineraries. It's even possible that you'll find a production of Shakespeare's *Hamlet* or Agatha Christie's *The Mouse Trap* here. However, many of the theater-going opportunities in Amsterdam are more experimental and avant-garde, and most of them are in Dutch.

MAJOR CONCERT HALLS & THEATERS

Beurs van Berlage. Damrak 243 (near the Dam). ☎ **020/627-0466.** Tickets Dfl 15–40 ($6.40–$17). Box office Tues–Fri 12:30–6pm, Sat 12:30–5pm, and 1¼ hours before performances begin. Tram: 4, 9, 14, 16, 20, 24, or 25 to the Dam.

The former home of the Amsterdam Beurs (Stock Exchange) now has the **Netherlands Philharmonic Orchestra (the NedPho)** and the **Netherlands Chamber Orchestra** under its roof. What was once the trading floor of the Exchange, built in 1903 by H. P. Berlage, has since 1988 been a concert venue with two halls—the 665-seat Yakult Zaal and the 200-seat AGA Zaal. Holland's **Concertzender** classical radio station is also based here.

Carré. Amstel 115–125. ☎ **020/622-5225.** Tickets Dfl 20–250 ($8.50–$106.40). Box office Mon–Sat 10am–7pm, Sun 1–7pm. Tram: 6, 7, 10, or 20 to Weesperplein.

This big, plush theater on the banks of the River Amstel used to be a full-time circus, but now the clowns and animals are infrequent visitors, though spectacles such as The Flying Karamazov Brothers fill some of the gaps. In addition to opera, dance and ballet, look out for Dutch-language productions of top Broadway and London musicals—*Les Misérables, The Phantom of the Opera, Miss Saigon, Evita, Cats,* and *42nd Street* have all been on the bill. Top names in the world of rock and pop perform here, but the biggest names now strut their stuff at Amsterdam ArenA (see below). Get your tickets as far in advance as possible because the hottest shows sell out quickly.

✪ **Concertgebouw.** Concertgebouwplein 2–6. ☎ **020/671-8345.** Tickets Dfl 25–200 ($10.65–$85.10); summer concerts (Aug) Dfl 25 ($10.65). Box office daily 9:30am–7pm, until 8pm for same-day tickets; phone orders 10am–3pm. Tram: 3, 5, 12, or 20 to Museumplein; 16 to Concertgebouwplein.

The Concertgebouw (Concert Building) is one of the most acoustically perfect concert halls in the world and home base of the Royal Concertgebouw Orchestra. Musical performances have a distinctive richness of tone that is as much a pleasure for the performer as for the audience. During the musical season (September to March) and the annual Holland Festival, the world's greatest orchestras, ensembles, conductors, and soloists regularly perform here. Concerts and recitals are scheduled every day and often there's a choice of two programs at the same time on the same evening: one in the Grote Zaal, or Great Hall, and the other in a smaller recital hall, the Kleine Zaal, or Little Hall. Don't worry about your location—every seat in the Grote Zaal has a clear view. It's even possible to sit on the stage, behind the performers; tonal quality is slightly altered there, however, so seats are cheaper.

There are free lunchtime concerts, usually given by local or visiting musical groups, at 12:30pm on Wednesday in the Concertgebouw. The program may feature chamber music, symphonic performances, or abbreviated previews of a full concert to be played to paying guests that same evening.

✪ **Muziektheater.** Waterlooplein 22 (beside the River Amstel). ☎ **020/625-5455.** Tickets Dfl 40–120 ($17–$51.05). Box office Mon–Sat 10am–6pm, Sun 11:30am–6pm. Tram: 9, 14, or 20 to Waterlooplein.

In the 1980s, the construction of this superbly equipped 1,600-seat auditorium sparked street riots that sent tear gas drifting across what is now the stage. Today, it's the performances that cause a stir. The Muziektheater is one of the city's stellar performance venues and home base of the highly regarded Netherlands Opera and Dutch National Ballet. There are "musical lunches" during the concert season—free 30-minute concerts on some Tuesdays at 12:30pm (doors open at 12:15pm).

Stadsschouwburg. Leidseplein 26. ☎ **020/624-2311.** Tickets Dfl 15–Dfl 80 ($6.40–$34.05). Tram: 1, 2, 5, 6, 7, 10, or 20 to Leidseplein.

Recently renovated, the plushly upholstered, 950-seat Municipal Theater is the city's main venue for mainstream Dutch theater. It also mounts Dutch, and occasionally English, productions of international plays, both classic and modern. You can also take in opera and ballet here. The baroque theater from 1894, stands on the site of earlier theaters that were destroyed by fire.

OTHER VENUES

In addition to the big four, there are plenty of other venues in Amsterdam. No fewer than 42 of the city's churches are equipped with organs, some of them historic works of art in their own right. Four churches in particular—the **Engelse Kerk,** Begijnhof 48 (☎ 020/624-9665); **Nieuwe Kerk,** the Dam (☎ 020/626-8168); **Oude Kerk,** Oudekerksplein 23 (☎ 020/625-8284); and **Waalse Kerk,** Walenpleintje 157 (☎ 020/623-2074)—are regularly in use for baroque chamber music and organ recitals; as is the **Sweelinck Conservatorium,** Van Baerlestraat 27 (☎ 020/666-7641).

Theaters, some of which occasionally feature performances in English, include **De Balie,** Kleine Gartmanplantsoen 10 (☎ 020/623-2904); **Bellevue Theater,** Leidsekade 90 (☎ 020/624-7248), which also hosts modern dance; **De Brakke Grond,** at the Vlaams Cultureel Centrum, Nes 43 (☎ 020/626-0044), which otherwise has mostly Flemish theater; **Felix Meritis,** Keizersgracht 324 (☎ 020/626-2321); **Frascati,** Nes 63 (☎ 020/626-6866), which focuses on modern theater; the multicultural **Melkweg** (see below); **Nieuwe de la Mar,** Marnixstraat 404 (☎ 020/623-3462); and the new **Westergasfabriek,** Haarlemmerweg 8–10 (☎ 020/581-0425), a multipurpose arts complex in an old gas works. **De Stalhouderij,** Eerste Bloemdwarsstraat 4 (☎ 020/626-2282), is a tiny place that puts on only English-language theater. For open-air theater in summer, there's the **Vondelpark Openluchttheater,** Vondelpark (☎ 020/673-1499).

A MULTIDIMENSIONAL VENUE

✪ **Melkweg.** Lijnbaansgracht 234a (near Leidseplein). ☎ 020/531-8181. Cover Dfl 10–35 ($4.25–$14.90) plus Dfl 5 ($2.15) monthly club membership. Box office Mon–Fri 1–5pm, Sat–Sun 4–6pm. Tram: 1, 2, 5, 6, 7, 10, or 20 to Leidseplein.

A sometime hippie haven in an old dairy factory, the Melkweg (Milky Way) constantly reinvents its multimedia persona. Inside, you find a reasonably priced international restaurant (Eat@Jo's), coffee shop, bar, art center, dance floor, cinema, theater, concert hall, photo gallery, and exhibition space. You need to take out temporary membership before they let you in, but it's worth it. International big-name groups perform here, and DJs spin a musical mix that ranges from ska to house. Friday night is club night for the Electric Circus, a multimedia music extravaganza. In June, the club hosts the World Roots Festival, a world music concert series that features Caribbean and African bands. The Melkweg's organizers have always embraced liberalism and experimentalism, and its theater tends to showcase new groups, both international, and local. You can take in comedy, multicultural, and gay and lesbian theater. The entire set-up is a throwback to Amsterdam's glory days in the '60s, but is big enough, and wise enough, to accommodate the latest trends as well.

A COMEDY THEATER

✪ **Boom Chicago.** Leidseplein Theater, Leidseplein 12. ☎ 020/530-7300. Dfl 29.50–34.50 ($12.55–$14.70). Box office daily noon–8:30pm. Tram: 1, 2, 5, 6, 7, 10, or 20 to Leidseplein.

For several years, Boom Chicago has been bringing delightful English-language improvisational comedy to Amsterdam. *Time* magazine compared it to Chicago's famous Second City comedy troupe. Dutch audiences don't have much problem with the English sketches; they often seem to get the point ahead of the native English speakers in attendance. Spectators are seated around candlelit tables for eight people and can have dinner and a drink while they enjoy the show. The restaurant is open at 7pm, and meals cost Dfl 25 to Dfl 30 ($10.65 to $12.75) per person.

2 The Club & Music Scene

CONTEMPORARY MUSIC

De Ijsbreker. Weesperzijde 23 (beside the Amstel River). ☎ **020/668-1805.** Cover Dfl 15–25 ($6.40– $10.65). Tram: 3 to Wibautstraat.

For the latest in high-tech, electronic music, and anything else that goes out on a musical limb, this is the place. A very good cafe, with a shaded terrace overlooking the Amstel, adds to the club's appeal.

JAZZ & BLUES

Jazz, Dixieland, and blues may be American musical forms, but Europeans—and certainly the Dutch—have adopted them with gusto. July is the best month of the year for a jazz lover to travel to Europe. That's when three major festivals are scheduled almost back-to-back in France, Switzerland, and Holland, including the 3-day **North Sea Jazz Festival,** P.O. Box 87840, 2508 DE, The Hague (☎ 070/350-1604), held each year at the Congresgebouw in The Hague. It's a convention of the biggest names in the international jazz world, with more than 100 concerts—involving more than 600 artists—scheduled in 10 halls in 3 days.

Described below are a few of the jazz hangouts that dot Amsterdam's cityscape.

Alto Jazz Café. Korte Leidsedwarsstraat 115 (off Leidseplein). ☎ **020/626-3249.** No cover. Tram: 1, 2, 5, 6, 7, 10, or 20 to Leidseplein.

A regular quartet plays jazz nightly to a diverse crowd in this small, comfortable cafe. There are also guest combos and occasionally blues as well—the music is always top-notch. On Wednesday evening, the noted saxophonist Hans Dulfer plays, sometimes accompanied by his equally noted daughter Candy.

✪ **Bimhuis.** Oudeschans 73–77 (near the Rembrandthuis). ☎ **020/623-3373.** No cover Mon–Wed, Thurs–Sun Dfl 20–35 ($8.50–$14.90). Tram: 9, 14, or 20 to Waterlooplein.

This has been the city's premier jazz and improvisational spot for the past 20 years. "Bim," as locals affectionately call it, regularly features top European and American artists in a relaxed but serious atmosphere. You won't feel that you can't have a conversation, but you won't have to struggle to hear the music either. Tuesday night is workshop night; Sunday, Monday, and Wednesday concerts are rare.

Bourbon Street. Leidsekruisstraat 6–8 (off Leidseplein). ☎ **020/623-3440.** No cover, except for special acts. Tram: 1, 2, 5, 6, 7, 10, or 20 to Leidseplein.

Bourbon Street, a wonderful little club for jazz, blues, and funk, hosts local talent and guests from the States and elsewhere. There's a cover charge for well-known jazz groups or musicians. The music, which tends toward Dixieland and mainstream jazz, plays well into the night.

Joseph Lam Jazz Club. Van Diemenstraat 8 (west of Centraal Station). ☎ **020/622-8086.** Cover Dfl 9 ($3.85) Sat only. Bus: 35 to Van Diemenstraat.

This jazz nook beside the harbor offers Dixieland and bebop performed by local and little-known touring ensembles. The crowds tend to be mixed, consisting of couples on dates, hard-core jazz cats in berets, musicians, and younger jazz fans. The free jazz jam sessions on Sunday, which feature more experimental fare and acid jazz, are especially popular.

✪ **Maloe Melo.** Lijnbaansgracht 163. ☎ **020/420-4592.** Cover Dfl 5 ($2.15). Tram: 7, 10, 17, or 20 to Elandsgracht.

This small club isn't the Mississippi Delta, but Amsterdam's "home of the blues" features live blues every night and is generally packed. The music's quality varies but a pleasantly intimate setting and an eager audience make for a good time.

ROCK & POP CONCERTS

Nothing changes faster in Holland—or exhibits more variety—than the pop music scene, whether the latest craze is rock, reggae, new wave, or whatever. Performers en route to (or from) world-class stardom always seem to turn up in Amsterdam, and few of their shows have difficulty selling out. Big stars and large-scale productions are occasionally featured at **Carré,** Amstel 115–125 (☎ **020/622-5225**), or, in the case of rock stars, at **Amsterdam ArenA,** Arena Boulevard, Amsterdam Zuid-Oost (☎ **020/311-1313**), the Ajax soccer club's new stadium in the southeastern suburbs, which has a sliding roof to keep out the ubiquitous Dutch rain (metro: Strandvliet/ArenA). For ticket information, contact **Ticketline** (☎ **0900/300-125**) or **Mojo Concerts** (☎ **015/212-1980**).

DANCE CLUBS

For local residents, the club scene in Amsterdam is generally a "members only" situation. But as a tourist, you can simply show up and, as long as your attire and behavior suit the sensibilities of the management, you shouldn't have any problems getting past the bouncer. Drinks can be expensive—a beer or Coke averages Dfl 10 ($4.25), and a whisky or cocktail, Dfl 15 ($6.40)—but you can nurse one drink while you dance your feet off, or down a quick beer and move on if the crowd or the music mix is not your style.

The places listed below are some of the most popular at press time, and in Amsterdam these things don't change very quickly. But don't hesitate to ask around for new places once you get here. Of course, you can always consult the trusty *What's On in Amsterdam* for listings. As for the music, it sometimes seems that techno is the only noise in town.

Akhnaton. Nieuwezijds Kolk 25 (near Centraal Station). ☎ **020/624-3396.** Cover Dfl 10–15 ($4.25–$6.40). Tram: 1, 2, 5, 13, 17, or 20 to Martelaarsgracht.

Jazz, African bands, and salsa are featured regularly at a spot that caters to a youthful, multiethnic, hash-smoking crowd of joyful dancers.

Amnesia. Oudezijds Voorburgwal 3 (near Nieuwmarkt). ☎ **020/638-1461.** Cover Dfl 10–15 ($4.25–$6.40). Metro: Nieuwmarkt.

Trance-house and hard-core may be part of the history of dancing by the time you read this, but if they aren't yet, this is the place to come to grips with them. This determinedly youth-oriented disco is in the Red Light District.

Bayside Beach Club. Halve Maansteeg 4–6 (near Rembrandtplein). ☎ **020/620-3769.** No cover. Tram: 4, 9, 14, or 20 to Rembrandtplein.

"Life's a beach," they say, at the Beach Parties in this Florida-style bar-restaurant-dance joint. The waitresses here in minimalist Stars-and-Stripes bikinis seem to have been specially chosen for, shall we say, aesthetic purposes; but lest the establishment be accused of sexism, let me hasten to add that the male staff also seems to have been selected from an International Male catalog. There's live music and DJs on two different levels. Sunday is ladies night (free cocktails and an all-male revue).

Caneçao. Lange Leidsedwarsstraat 68–70 (near Leidseplein). ☎ **020/638-0611.** No cover. Tram: 1, 2, 5, 6, 7, 10, or 20 to Leidseplein.

This club features a heavy emphasis on Brazilian music, but includes other styles of South American music as well. If your spirits could do with a taste of samba or salsa, this is the place to be. Monday and Wednesday are salsa evenings, and the others are for Brazilian music.

De Duivel. Reguliersdwarsstraat 87. ☎ **020/626-6184.** No cover. Tram: 16, 24, or 25 to Keizersgracht.

Other nightclubs in Amsterdam play some hip-hop, but De Duivel is the only one to serve up rap classics and contemporary hip-hop tunes to the baggy-jeans set nightly.

iT. Amstelstraat 24 (near Rembrandtplein). ☎ **020/625-0111.** Cover Dfl 12–20 ($5.10–$8.50). Mixed nights Thurs, Sun. Tram: 4, 9, 14, or 20 to Rembrandtplein.

This extravagantly gay disco-club also does mixed nights where everybody performs with gay abandon in a raunchy atmosphere. Anything can happen, and usually does. The crowd is young, and the music is young, with techno and house being especially popular. There are occasional drag shows, and there's a room that's quieter and more conducive to conversation, or whatever.

Mazzo. Rozengracht 114 (near Westermarkt). ☎ **020/626-7500.** Cover Dfl 10–25 ($4.25–$10.65). Tram: 13, 14, 17, or 20 to Westermarkt.

It sometimes seems that Mazzo has been around forever. Who knows? Maybe Rembrandt discoed here. Its longevity has a lot to do with keeping up with the latest trends while providing something for everyone—though not on the same night. You find just about every kind of club music style on offer here at some time or other.

✪ **Odeon.** Singel 460 (near Muntplein). ☎ **020/624-9711.** Cover Dfl 10–15 ($4.25–$6.40). Tram: 1, 2, or 5 to Koningsplein.

Your feet might not know what to do at first amid the graceful surroundings of this converted 17th-century canal house. The period ceiling paintings and stucco decor seem more suited to minuets than disco moves. You can dance to jazz, funk, house, techno, R&B, and classic disco here—all at the same time, as there are three different floors.

Paradiso. Weteringschans 6–8 (near Leidseplein). ☎ **020/626-4521.** Cover Dfl 15–45 ($6.40–$19.15). Tram: 1, 2, 5, 6, 7, 10, or 20 to Leidseplein.

An old church has been transformed to present an eclectic variety of music. A dark and somewhat forbidding exterior belies the bright inside. You might catch some great acts here before they become really famous, or some already established international stars. The majestic interior has lofty ceilings and a high balcony encircling the room, affording excellent views of the central dance floor. The club has extremely popular theme nights, which range from jazz to raves to disco. The stylish VIP Club on Friday night—cover Dfl 17.50 ($7.35)—is easier to get into than RoXY (see below), and arguably better too.

RoXY. Singel 465–467 (near Muntplein). ☎ **020/620-0354.** Cover Dfl 10–25 ($4.25–$10.65). Tram: 4, 9, 14, 16, 20, 24, or 25 to Muntplein.

You have to be smartly dressed—power-smart—for the RoXY (a painfully chic acronym for Radical outlet for the Xenomaniac in You), probably the hippest and trendiest place in Amsterdam. The membership and dress policy is extremely strict (you don't have a prayer in sneakers, torn jeans, or T-shirts). In fact, it's just about impossible to get in—legend has it that Prince (when he was still The Artist Formerly

Known As . . .) is just one of the poor slobs who didn't make it past the heavyweight help at the door. RoXY was the first club in Amsterdam to play house music, and it has gained and maintained a reputation for being the place to be. The decor changes every month. Wednesday is Gay Night and Sunday is the women-only Pussy Lounge.

✪ **Sinners in Heaven.** Wagenstraat 3–7 (off Rembrandtplein). ☎ **020/620-1375.** Cover Dfl 15 ($6.40), after midnight Dfl 18 ($7.65). Tram: 4, 9, 14, or 20 to Rembrandtplein.

This is a seriously trendy disco-club, part of which looks like an S&M theme park, if you can imagine such a thing. The great and the good of the Dutch film, theater, and TV scene like to see and be seen here (especially the latter). It's on three floors, one of which is decked out like a castle, one like a church, and one like a dungeon. Every second Sunday of the month you can dance here to R&B, hip hop, and swing.

Soul Kitchen. Amstelstraat 32 (off Rembrandtplein). ☎ **020/620-2333.** Cover Dfl 10–15 ($4.25–$6.40). Tram: 4, 9, 14, or 20 to Rembrandtplein.

The Soul Kitchen cooks up some of the best musical soul food around for an over-25 crowd with a limitless appetite for hip-shaking funk and soul. Along with soul you can hoof it to '60s and '70s music. This place is best approached late, *very* late, because the action doesn't really heat up until after 3am.

3 The Bar Scene

BROWN CAFES

Anyone who's sipped a frothy Heineken knows the Dutch can brew beer. But you haven't really tasted Dutch beer until you've tasted it in Holland, served Dutch style in a real *bruine kroeg,* or brown cafe. These Dutch institutions are unpretentious, unpolished, and filled with camaraderie, somewhat like pubs in London or neighborhood bars in the United States. In a brown cafe, pouring another beer is much more important than dusting off the back bottles on the bar. In fact, the Dutch beer-pouring process itself is part of the charm of these places; it's a remarkable ritual of drawing a beer to get as much foam as possible and then using a wet knife to shave the head between a series of final fill-ups.

Even if you're not a beer lover, venturing into a brown cafe in Amsterdam will give you a peek into the everyday life of the city. You find brown cafes on almost every corner in the old neighborhoods of the city, and you can't miss them. Most have lacy curtains on the bottom half of the window, and perhaps a cat sleeping in the sun on the ledge. In winter the front door will be hung with a thick drape to keep out drafts; you may still find it there long into spring. Once you're inside, you find the smoky, mustard brownness that's unique to an Amsterdam brown cafe, the result of years—no, centuries—of thick smoke and warm conversation.

There may be booths or little tables sprinkled around the place, but the only spots of color and light will be the shining metal of the beer tap and, perhaps, a touch of red still showing in the Persian rugs thrown across the tables (that practice is typically Dutch, if you recall the old paintings) to catch sandwich crumbs and soak up beer foam. You feel the centuries of conviviality the minute you walk in the door of a really old, really *brown* brown cafe. Some have been on their corners since Rembrandt's time, haunted by the ghosts of drinkers past. The best of them are on the Prinsengracht, below Westermarkt, at the Dam, at Leidseplein, on Spui, or with a bit of looking, on tiny streets between the canals.

Café Chris. Bloemstraat 42 (near Westermarkt). ☎ **020/624-5942.** Tram: 13, 14, 17, or 20 to Westermarkt.

Lost Art?

Today's Amsterdammers are no more than a pale shadow of their esteemed ancestors when it comes to quaffing beer. In 1613 there were 518 taverns in the city, one for every 200 or so inhabitants. Today the ratio has slipped to one per 725. It seems that the 17th century was a golden age in more senses than one.

Café Chris opened in 1624 and has been going strong ever since. It's said to be the place where the builders of Westerkerk were paid every week or two. There are a lot of curious old features to this bar that keep drawing people year after year, including the quirky toilet in the bathroom, which, oddly, flushes from outside the door. On Sunday night loud opera music engulfs the bar, attracting a cultured bohemian crowd.

De Druif. Rapenburg 83 (behind the Eastern Dock). ☎ **020/624-4530.** Bus: 22 to Prins Hendrikkade.

This is one of those places that not too many people know about. De Druif ("The Grape") is located on the waterfront and is mainly frequented by a friendly local crowd. The bar's mythology has it that the Dutch naval hero, Piet Heyn, was a frequent patron (he lived nearby); however, as happens so often when good beer is at hand, this seems to be a tall tale come of wishful thinking—the bar opened in 1631 and Heyn died in 1629.

De Karpershoek. Martelaarsgracht 2 (facing Centraal Station). ☎ **020/624-7886.** Tram: 1, 2, 5, 13, 17, or 20 to Martelaarsgracht.

Opened in 1629, this bar was once a favorite hangout of sailors and seamen. The floor is covered with sand, as it was in the 17th century.

✪ **De Vergulde Gaper.** Prinsenstraat 30 (at Prinsengracht). ☎ **020/624-8975.** Tram: 1, 2, 5, 13, 17, or 20 to Martelaarsgracht.

This place is a double delight. In bad weather you can retreat into the warm, cozy brown cafe atmosphere indoors, and in good weather you can sit on a terrace beside the Prinsengracht—if you can get a seat. There's an unseemly dash whenever a table becomes free.

Gollem. Raamsteeg 4 (off Spui). ☎ **020/626-6645.** Tram: 1, 2, or 5 to Spui.

More than 200 different beers are on sale in this ever-popular brown cafe near Spui. Many of them are international, and in particular, Belgian favorites, but look for some weird-and-wonderful brews from around the world.

Hoppe. Spui 18–20. ☎ **020/420-4420.** Tram: 1, 2, or 5 to Spui.

"Standing Room Only" is often the space situation here and the crowds sometimes even overflow onto the street. It seems that, quite by accident, Hoppe has become a tourist attraction. Locals love this spot, which dates from 1670, and often pass through for a drink on their way home. It's worth stopping by just to see it.

In de Wildeman. Kolksteeg 3 (off Nieuwezijds Voorburgwal). ☎ **020/638-2348.** Tram: 1, 2, 5, 13, 17, or 20 to Nieuwezijds Kolk.

Tucked away in a medieval alley, this wood-paneled *bier-proeflokaal* (beer tasting house) dates from 1690. The tile floor and rows of bottles and jars behind the counters are remnants of its earlier days, when it functioned as a distillery. Today it serves 17 draught and 200 bottled beers from around the world. There is a separate room for nonsmokers.

Reijnders. Leidseplein 6. ☎ **020/623-4419.** Tram: 1, 2, 5, 6, 7, 10, or 20 to Leidseplein.

It would be hard for a cafe in this prime location not to be something of a tourist trap—but Reijnders has only barely succumbed to this temptation and can perhaps be forgiven. This is a brown cafe with a long and noble tradition, outstanding looks, and a glassed-in front porch that offers a great vantage point for viewing the comings and goings of Leidseplein.

't Loosje. Nieuwmarkt 32–34. ☎ **020/627-2635.** Metro: Nieuwmarkt.

This is a friendly place in the up-and-coming Nieuwmarkt area, popular with students, artists—and guidebook writers. It was built around 1900 and was originally used as a waiting room for the horse-drawn tram. The walls are still ornamented with tiles from that period and a painting of the South Holland Beer Brewery. There are lots of beers on tap.

✪ **'t Smalle.** Egelantiersgracht 12 (at Prinsengracht). ☎ **020/623-9617.** Tram: 13, 14, or 17 to Westermarkt.

Café 't Smalle is a wonderfully cozy spot where you're highly unlikely to get a seat, or even see one. It was opened by Pieter Hoppe in 1786 as a liquor distillery and *proeflokaal* (tasting house). If you really want an authentic brown cafe experience, you should at least try to stop by. 't Smalle has expanded its area of operations to the water's edge, with a fine terrace on the Egelantiersgracht, and to the water itself, on a boat moored alongside.

BONUS PICKS

As brown cafes are such an important part of the Amsterdam experience, in addition to my 10 favorites described above, here are 10 other great choices: **Bern,** Nieuwmarkt 9 (☎ **020/622-0034**); **Eijlders,** Korte Leidsedwarsstraat 47 (☎ **020/624-2704**); **De Eland,** Prinsengracht 296 (☎ **020/623-7654**); **De Engelbewaarder,** Kloveniersburgwal 59 (☎ **020/625-3772**); **Het Molenpad,** Prinsengracht 653 (☎ **020/625-9680**); **Kalkhoven,** Prinsengracht 283 (☎ **020/624-9649**); **Oranjerie,** Binnen Oranjestraat 15 (☎ **020/623-4611**); **Papeneiland,** Prinsengracht 2 (☎ **020/624-1989**); **De Reiger,** Nieuwe Leliestraat 34 (☎ **020/624-7426**); and **Tabac,** Brouwersgracht 101 (☎ **020/622-4413**).

TASTING HOUSES

There are only three major differences between a brown cafe and a *proeflokaal,* or tasting house: what you customarily drink, how you drink it, and who owns the place. The decor will still be basically brown and typically Old Dutch—and the age of the establishment may be even more impressive than that of its beer-swilling neighbors—but in a tasting house you traditionally order jenever (Dutch gin, taken "neat," without ice) or another product of the distillery that owns the place. Then, to drink your choice of libation, custom and ritual decree that you lean over the bar, with your hands behind your back, to take the first sip from your well-filled *borreltje* (small drinking glass).

Brouwerij 't IJ. Funenkade 7 (at Zeeburgerstraat). ☎ **020/684-0552.** Tram: 6 or 10 to Mauritskade.

In addition to the usual features, this proeflokaal has a fascinating location—it's situated in an unused windmill in the city's old harbor area—and a small brewery. You can take guided tours of the beer-making facilities (Friday at 4pm), and then taste the

Message in the Bottle

The process of conversing with the locals in a bar is smoothed if you can bandy about some Dutch drinking terminology. The most common word for a glass of *jenever* (Dutch gin) is a *"borrel"* (*bo*-rel) or the diminutive *"borreltje"* (*bo*-rel-che), though other terms such as *"hassebassie"* (*hass*-uh-bassie), *"keiltje"* (*kyle*-che), *"piketanussie"* (*pik*-et-an-oossee), *"recht op neer"* (rekht op near), and *"slokkie"* (*slok*-ee) are also used. Avant-garde imbibers may ask for an "uppercut" to prove their international credentials. A glass of *jenever* filled to the brim, as tradition mandates that it must be, is called a *"kamelenrug"* (cam-*ay*-len-rookh), meaning "camel's back," or an *"over het IJ-kijkertje"* (over het eye *kyk*-erche), meaning "view over the River IJ."

Jenever is often ordered with a beer chaser. The barkeep will then place the *"kopstoot"* (*cop*-stoat), meaning "knock on the head," of a *"stelletje"* (*stel*-etche), meaning "couple," on the bar. Beer or *"Pils"* (pilss) in a small glass is called a *"colaatje pils"* (*co*-la-che pilss); *"kabouter pils"* (ka-*bou*-ter pilss), meaning "dwarf beer"; or a *"lampie licht"* (*lam*-pee likht), meaning "little lamp." Ale in a large glass is known as a *"bakkie"* (*bak*-ee) or a *"vaas,"* which means jar or vase.

So if you breeze into a brown cafe, park yourself at the bar, and call for a "Recht op neer borrel, make sure it's a proper over het IJ-kijkertje, put a kopstoot with it, a colaatje if you please, and set up a bakkie for later while you're at it," you should get on swimmingly (of course, they might also send for the men in white coats).

brewery's Pilzen (5% alcohol by volume), Mug Bitter (5%), Pasij (7%), or Zatte (8%) brews. One popular new Brouwerij 't IJ concoction is Columbus, a hearty wheat beer that's reddish, flavorful, strong (almost 10% alcohol by volume), and the new brew of choice among many Amsterdam barflies.

D'Admiraal. Herengracht 319 (along the canal near Oude Spiegelstraat). ☎ **020/625-4334.** Tram: 1, 2, or 5 to Spui.

This tasting house has a small and pleasant outdoor cafe patio. There are also sofas and big comfortable armchairs inside—oh yes, and 15 different *jenevers* and 55 liqueurs, plus a fair Dutch dinner and snacks menu.

✪ **De Drie Fleschjes.** Gravenstraat 18 (off the Dam, behind the Nieuwe Kerk). ☎ **020/624-8443.** Tram: 1, 2, 4, 5, 9, 14, 16, 20, 24, or 25 to the Dam.

Not much has changed in this tidy and charming tasting house ("The Three Little Bottles") since it opened in 1650, except that in 1816 Heindrik Bootz liqueurs took over and have been tasted here ever since. There are 52 wooden casks along the wall facing the bar. Open Monday to Saturday noon to 8:30pm, Sunday 3 to 8pm.

De Ooievaar. Sint Olofspoort 1 (at the Zeedijk). ☎ **020/625-7360.** Tram: 1, 2, 4, 5, 9, 13, 16, 17, 20, 24, or 25 to Centraal Station.

This tiny place, the smallest proeflokaal in Holland, sells jenevers and Oudhollandse liqueurs. It's a pleasant place, with a bright bar area to offset the brown walls and wooden casks.

't Doktertje. Rozenboomsteeg 4 (off Spui). ☎ **020/626-4427.** Tram: 1, 2, 4, 5, 9, 14, 16, 20, 24, or 25 to Spui.

This antique-filled tasting house is near Spui, the main square of the Student Quarter. Ask to sample the homemade *boeren jongen* and *boeren meisjes,* the brandied fruits—raisins and apricots—that are traditional introductions to "spirits" for Dutch *jongen* and *meisjes,* boys and girls.

✪ **Wynand Fockink.** Pijlsteeg 31 (off the Dam). ☎ **020/639-2695.** Tram: 4, 9, 14, 16, 20, 24, or 25 to the Dam.

Don't waste your breath—regulars here know all about the little English pronunciation bomb hidden in the Dutch name. This popular *proeflokaal* dates from 1679. Aficionados of the 50 varieties of Dutch jenever and 70 traditional liqueurs on display often have to maneuver for elbow room to raise their glasses. One of the attractions here that wows visitors is the collection of liqueur bottles on which are painted portraits of every mayor of Amsterdam since 1591. That ought to set your pulse racing. Open daily 3 to 9pm. The attached *lunchlokaal* is, as its name implies, open for lunch.

TRENDY CAFES

Amsterdam has many contemporary cafes that are neither brown cafes nor your friendly neighborhood watering holes (many examples of both categories being acceptably trendy in themselves). You may hear some contemporary cafes described as "white cafes," as distinct from brown cafes. You may also hear talk of the "coke-trail circuit," though that's a bit passé nowadays.

Besides the cafes listed below, you might want to check out Amsterdam's "Grand Cafes," reviewed in chapter 5: Café Dulac, Café de Jaren, Café Luxembourg, De Balie, Grand Café L'Opera, Het Land van Walem, ✪ Oibibio, Ovidius, and ✪ Royal Café de Kroon.

Café Dante. Spuistrat 320 (at Spui). ☎ **020/638-8839.** Tram: 1, 2 or 5 to Spui.

This is art gallery chic. The owners cover the walls with a different exhibition of modern art every month. Some displays may leave you wanting to throw up everything and adopt a bohemian lifestyle, and others wanting just to throw up. Feel free to wander in and around.

✪ **Café Schiller.** Rembrandtplein 36. ☎ **020/624-9864.** Tram: 4, 9, 14, or 20 to Rembrandtplein.

It may be a little unfair to include Schiller in this designation, with its implication of trendiness. Schiller's style seems timeless. A bright glassed-in terrace on the square and a finely carved art deco interior make a good setting for the friendly, laid-back atmosphere, good food, and lively crowd of artistic and literary types.

Frascati. Nes 59 (behind Rokin). ☎ **020/624-1324.** Tram: 4, 9, 14, 16, 20, 24, or 25 to Spui.

Frascati belongs to a category similar to Schiller's, except that in this case its own good looks are complemented by a theatrical bent. The surrounding neighborhood is rife with alternative theater, and Frascati is a major player in this minor league.

Seymour Likely. Nieuwezijds Voorburgwal 250 (near Amsterdam Historical Museum). ☎ **020/627-1427.** Tram: 1, 2, 5, 13, 17, or 20 to Nieuwezijds Voorburgwal.

Woe unto you if you enter here wearing out-of-date duds. And it's no use wailing that they were the latest and hippest thing only yesterday—that's the whole point. The lips of all those beautiful young things inside that aren't curled around a glass, or each other, will be curled into a sneer. Cruel it may be, but you can always withdraw and try your luck across the road at Seymour Likely's offspring, Seymour Likely 2, which attracts a slightly older crowd.

West Pacific. Haarlemmerweg 8–10 (west of Centraal Station). ☎ **020/597-4458.** Tram: 10 to Van Halstraat.

This cavernous place, located in the unlikely setting of a disused gas works, the Westergasfabriek, has become an instant hit with the youthful in-crowd. And thereby lies the problem—getting in after about 11pm, especially on weekends, can be as hard as getting past St. Peter at the Pearly Gates, except that St. Peter is sure to be pleasanter than the cranially challenged pug uglies at West Pacific's door. Get there early to experience the delights of the inner sanctum.

ENGLISH, IRISH & SCOTTISH PUBS

Balmoral. In the Balmoral Hotel, Nieuwe Doelenstraat 26. ☎ **020/622-0722.** Tram: 4, 9, 14, 16, 20, 24, or 25 to Muntplein.

This pub specializes in hunting lodge atmosphere, tartanry, and malt whisky—of which it has 50 varieties. You almost expect to see a kilted piper sinking a wee dram at the bar while drawing a bead on a pheasant with a silver-chased fowling piece.

De Leydtse Herberghe. Leidseplein 2. ☎ **020/428-0428.** Tram: 1, 2, 5, 6, 7, 10, or 20 to Leidseplein.

Despite the Dutch name, this is an English-style pub on the first two floors, with lots of snug corners for conversation about Shakespeare or Manchester United over pints of warm ale (they have cold beers too). The Chesterfield Internet lounge is on the second floor, and the New York Steakhouse on the third floor.

Mulligans Irish Music Bar. Amstel 100 (off Rembrandtplein). ☎ **020/622-1330.** Tram: 4, 9, 14, or 20 to Rembrandtplein.

Both the Irish music and the *craic* (pronounced like crack—Irish crack is fast wit and good conversation, not that other stuff) here have been pretty good since it opened in 1988. Bring an instrument and you may be allowed to play.

JORDAAN CAFES

The Jordaan is Amsterdam's iconoclastic working-class district. It has suffered from the depredations of gentrifiers, demolition experts, and cleaner-up-ers, but still retains its distinctive style and preoccupation with its own collective navel. Cafes here are old style, colorful, and working class (a bit like London's Cockney pubs). You might even get a singsong of incredibly schmaltzy old Dutch songs about stolen kisses behind the windmill.

Café Nol. Westerstraat 109 (near Noordermarkt). ☎ **020/624-5380.** Tram: 3 or 10 to Marnixplein.

A bit younger and cooler than your average Jordaan cafe, but the young folks like to sing along as well, you know.

Café Rooie Nellis. Laurierstraat 101 (off Prinsengracht). ☎ **020/624-4167.** Tram: 13, 14, 17, or 20 to Westermarkt.

The decor here has to be seen to be believed—and even then you might not. This place has been owned by the same family for generations; it's real down-home Jordaan.

De Twee Zwaantjes. Prinsengracht 114 (at Egelantiersgracht). ☎ **020/625-2729.** Tram: 13, 14, 17, or 20 to Westermarkt.

The two swans of the cafe's name would find it hard going to spread their wings here, but in this intimate little place you're brought face-to-face with the Jordaanese in all their glory.

Smoking Coffeeshops

Tourists often get confused about "smoking" coffeeshops and how they differ from "no-smoking" ones. Well, to begin with, *smoking* and *no-smoking* don't refer to cigarettes—they refer to cannabis. Furthermore, the smoking shops are easily identified. Almost always, a smoking establishment is a "coffeeshop"—the Dutch spell it as one word. For coffee and a snack go to a "coffee shop"—two words. (Actually, there are not many places called "coffee shops" in Amsterdam; most regular cafes are called *cafes* or *eetcafes.*)

Coffeeshops not only sell cannabis, frequently in the form of hashish, but also provide a place where patrons can sit and smoke it all day if they so choose. Not too long ago, before there was a small crackdown on soft drugs in Amsterdam, smoking coffeeshops advertised their wares with a marijuana leaf sign. Though the practice of buying and smoking hashish in the coffeeshops is still tolerated, the marijuana leaf advertisements are now illegal.

In recent years Holland has given in to pressure from surrounding countries regarding its drug policy and has tightened the rules for coffeeshops. You used to be allowed to buy and retain 30 grams of soft drugs for personal use; now, however, you can technically buy only 5 grams at a time, though you're still allowed ("tolerated" is a better word) to be in possession of a total of 30 grams of soft drugs for personal use. In addition, each local authority can decide to impose stricter rules. The current mayor of Amsterdam is campaigning against "immorality" in the city and wants to close many coffeeshops and subject the remainder to strict rules. Nonetheless, Amsterdam is still a mecca for the marijuana smoker and seems likely to remain that way.

Each coffeeshop has a menu listing the different types of cannabis it sells. Hashish comes in two varieties: white and black. The black hash is usually more powerful. Connoisseurs say the best stuff has a stronger smell and is soft and sticky. Bags cost between Dfl 10 and Dfl 25 ($4.25 and $10.65), depending on the quality. Coffeeshops also have hashish joints (*stickie*) for sale, rolled with tobacco. Officially, coffeeshops are not allowed to sell alcohol, so they sell coffee, tea, and fruit juices. You won't be able to get any food in these, so don't expect to grab a quick breakfast, lunch, or dessert. Usually, however, the coffee is surprisingly good, considering that it's only an excuse for selling something else. You're even allowed to smoke your own stuff in the coffeeshop, so long as you buy a drink.

Some of the most popular smoking coffeeshops are **The Rookies,** Korte Leidsedwarsstraat 145–147 (☎ **020/694-2353**); **Borderline,** Amstelstraat 37 (☎ **020/622-0540**); and the shops of **Bulldog** chain, which has branches around the city (the **Bulldog Palace** is at Leidseplein 15; ☎ **020/627-1908**).

Tokers' tips: Don't buy on the street. You stand a fair chance of being ripped off, quality will be dubious, and there may be unpleasant additives. The coffeeshops are controlled, even if only in a notional way, and are much more reliable. For more details, including coffeeshop reviews, pick up a copy of the English-language *Mellow Pages* for Dfl 17.50 ($7.45) from many bookshops.

COCKTAILS WITH A VIEW

Ciel Blue Bar. In the Hotel Okura Amsterdam, Ferdinand Bolstraat 175. ☎ **020/678-7111.**
Tram: 25 to Ferdinand Bolstraat.

Even a low-rise city like Amsterdam has a high-rise hotel with a rooftop cocktail
lounge. This one is located on the 23rd floor. The drink prices are a little higher than
what you'd find at ground level, but the view is probably worth the cost. From a
comfortable vantage point in Amsterdam South, the sweeping panorama takes in the
city's residential neighborhoods, the river, and the harbor. Ciel Blue is a particularly
enchanting place to be in the evening, when the sun is setting and the lights are
beginning to twinkle on in the houses near the hotel.

GAY & LESBIAN BARS

The gay scene in Amsterdam is strong, and there is no lack of gay bars and night
spots in town. Below are listings of some of the most popular spots for gay men. For
lesbians, the scene is a little more difficult to uncover. Places that are hot now might
not be later, so you might want to call or visit **COC,** Rozenstraat 14 (☎ **020/
623-4079**), the office/cafe headquarters of the Organization of Homosexuals in the
Netherlands. The office and telephone lines are open daily from 10am to 5pm. More
information should be available from the **Gay and Lesbian Switchboard** (☎ **020/
623-6565**).

Most of the city's gay bars are in well-defined areas. For frivolous, old-style camp,
look along the Amstel near Muntplein and on Halvemaansteeg. You find trendier
places along Reguliersdwarsstraat. Casual locals head for Kerkstraat, on both sides of
Leidsestraat.

Lesbian bars are more thinly spread, from the longstanding Vive-la-Vie near
Rembrandtplein, to the brown-cafe atmosphere of Saarein in the Jordaan, to the
hipper Getto, a mixed bar and restaurant on Warmoesstraat (see listings below for
details).

Amstel Taveerne. Amstel 54 (off Rembrandtplein). ☎ **020/623-4254.** Tram: 4, 9, 14, or
20 to Rembrandtplein.

One of the city's oldest and most traditional gay bars, this is the kind of place where
about an hour after happy hour everyone starts singing popular songs. Although the
songs are in Dutch, the crowd welcomes visitors from other countries, so don't be
afraid to sing along.

Café April. Reguliersdwarsstraat 37 (near the Flower Market). ☎ **020/625-9572.** Tram: 1,
2, or 5 to Koningsplein.

It's said that every gay visitor to Amsterdam goes here at least once, so you're likely to
make friends that hail from around the world. A light menu is served. **April's Exit,** an
affiliated dance club at Reguliersdwarsstraat 42 (☎ **020/625-8788**), is close by, and
many people from the Café April head over after happy hour.

Cockring. Warmoesstraat 96 (Red Light District). ☎ **020/623-9604.** Tram: 4, 9, 14, 16,
20, 24, or 25 to the Dam.

The most popular gay disco in town generally lays down no-nonsense, hard-core, high-decibel dance and techno music on the dance floor. More relaxed beats in the sociable upstairs bar make a welcome break.

Getto. Warmoesstraat 51 (Red Light District). ☎ **020/421-5151.** Tram: 1, 2, 4, 5, 9, 13, 14, 16, 17, 20, 24, or 25 to Centraal Station.

This 3-year-old bar and restaurant attracts an equal mix of boys and girls with its hip interior and such events as "Club Fu" karaoke (first Monday of every month) and bingo (every Thursday). There is an eclectic dinner menu inspired by food from around the world, whether vegetarian or a Cajun crocodile steak, and the kitchen stays open until 11pm. Open Wednesday, Thursday, and Sunday 5pm to 1am, Friday and Saturday 5pm to 2am.

Saarein. Elandstraat 119 (Jordaan). ☎ **020/623-4901.** Tram 7, 10, 17, or 20 to Marnixstraat.

Once a female-only enclave with a feisty atmosphere, the bar is now open to both genders and has livened up a bit. Attractions include pool, darts, and pinball. The recent change in atmosphere has included the addition of food, with a well-priced dinner menu of continental fare 6pm to 9:30pm. Open Sunday to Thursday 5pm to 1am, Friday and Saturday 5pm to 2am.

Spijker. Kerkstraat 4 (corner with Leidsegracht). ☎ **020/620-5919.** Tram: 1, 2, or 5 to Prinsengracht.

This longstanding neighborhood bar attracts a casual crowd that extends a friendly welcome to visitors. The pinball machine and pool table are sociable focal points, and side-by-side video screens show an amusing juxtaposition of cartoons and erotica. Lively bar staffers keep the atmosphere relaxed with a varied selection of music and stiff drinks, and happy "hour" draws the crowds in daily from 5 to 7pm. Open Sunday to Thursday 1pm to 1am, Friday and Saturday 1pm to 3am.

Vive-la-Vie. Amstelstraat 7 (off Rembrandtplein). ☎ **020/624-0114.** Tram: 4, 9, 14, or 20 to Rembrandtplein.

This lesbian bar celebrated its 20th anniversary in 2000. The place attracts a young, lively crowd before club-hopping time, and lipstick isn't forbidden. The sidewalk terrace offers excellent summertime relaxation and a fine view of the flocks of tourists in neighboring Rembrandtplein. Open Sunday to Thursday 2:30pm to 1am, Friday and Saturday 3pm to 3am.

Web. St. Jakobsstraat 6 (at Nieuwendijk). ☎ **020/623-6758.** Tram: 1, 2, 5, 13, 17, or 20 to Nieuwezijds Kolk.

Behind its corrugated metal facade, this popular after-work drinks venue has a raunchy atmosphere and plenty of walk space. Tuesday is "beer bust" and Wednesday evening is prize-draw night. On Sunday evening at 7pm you can line up for a food buffet. Open Sunday to Thursday 2pm to 1am, Friday and Saturday 2pm to 2am.

For Women Only

Amsterdam is very much a center of women's activism, and there are many women's centers around the city. **Vrouwenhuis (Women's House),** at Nieuwe Herengracht 95 (☎ **020/625-2066**), has a cafe that opens on Wednesday noon to 5pm and Thursday noon to 9pm.

4 The Red Light District

Even if you don't want to play, this is a place you may want to see at night, when the red lights reflect from the inky surface of the canals. Lots of visitors come here out of curiosity or just for fun. There's no problem with wandering around, and you don't need to worry much about crime as long as you stick to the busier streets—and keep an eye out for pickpockets. While you can josh with the girls behind the windows, taking pictures of them is strictly forbidden; very large, very observant men are always on the lookout and will have no qualms about throwing your camera (and maybe you) into the canal. Women going around in groups of two or more won't be noticed any more than anyone else, but a single female could be subject to harassment.

The Red Light District, known in Dutch as the *Wallen* or *Rosse Buurt*, isn't very big. The easiest way in is on Damstraat, beside the Krasnapolsky Hotel on the Dam. Then stick to the main drag on Oudezijds Voorburgwal, as far north as the Oude Kerk, the venerable Old Church, which stands watch over this passable representation of Sodom and Gomorrah. If you don't mind the weird-looking, sad-sack males and the "heroin whores" hanging around on the bridges, you can go further in, to the parallel canal, Oudezijds Achterburgwal, and the cluster of good bars and restaurants, many of the latter Chinese, at Nieuwmarkt.

You pass lots of red-fringed window parlors populated by women, few of them Dutch, who favor a minimalist dress style; peep-show joints with private cabins; dark and noisy bars; theaters offering a popular form of performance art; bookshops filled with the illustrated works of specialists in a wide range of interpersonal relationships; video libraries; and dedicated apparel and appliance shops.

Without going into detail about the services on offer in the Red Light District, here are a couple of places that have shown an enduring popularity with visitors.

Bananenbar. Oudezijds Achterburgwal 37. ☎ **020/622-4670.** Tram: 1, 2, 4, 5, 9, 13, 16, 17, 20, 24, or 25 to Centraal Station.

Bananas are an essential prop in the nightly drama here, and audience participation is encouraged. Needless to say, the show is mainly of interest to males on temporary vegetarian diets. Let your sense of taste be your guide.

Casa Rosso. Oudezijds Achterburgwal 106–108. ☎ **020/627-8943.** Tram: 4, 9, 13, 14, 16, 20, 24, or 25 to the Dam.

In its own words, Casa Rosso puts on "one of the most superior erotic shows in the world, with a tremendous choreography and a high-level cast." Not everyone would describe it in those exact words, perhaps, but this is the local market leader in live shows.

5 More Evening Entertainment

EVENING CANAL-BOAT RIDES

Even if you took the daytime canal-boat ride, come back for cocktails or dinner. Special 2-hour candlelit wine-and-cheese cruises operate nightly year-round, except for December 31. Wine and cheese are served as you glide through the canal district, which is quiet and calm at night. It's a leisurely, convivial, and romantic way to spend an evening in Amsterdam. You can also join the 3-hour dinner cruise, which runs nightly from April to November, and on Tuesday and Friday nights in the winter. Boats depart from the Holland International Pier at Prins Hendrikkade 33a, opposite Centraal Station. Operators are **Holland International** (☎ **020/622-7788**);

Through a Glass, Clearly

A simple evening pleasure in Amsterdam, one totally free of charge, is walking along the canals and looking into the houses as you pass. You may think I'm making the shocking suggestion that you spy on people, but in Amsterdam it's not spying, or even peeking. The Dutch live their lives as open books and take great pride in their homes; they keep their curtains open in the evening because they want you to see how tidy and *gezellig* (cozy, homey, warm, and inviting) their living quarters are. This doesn't mean that you're meant to linger on the sidewalk staring through the windows, but a leisurely stroll past an Amsterdam canal house and a peek inside at the decor is quite all right. If you're hesitant about engaging in this Dutch national sport, settle for looking up to admire the elegant gables (illuminated from 30 minutes after sundown to 11:30pm) or looking down to watch the flickering reflections of the street lamps on the canals. The evening hours are a magic time in Amsterdam; if nothing else has brought you around, a sparkling ripple on the water can make you fall hopelessly in love with the city.

Rederij Lovers (☎ 020/622-2181); and **Key Tours** (☎ 020/624-7304). The 2-hour cruise costs Dfl 45 ($19.15); the 2½-hour, five-course dinner cruise costs Dfl 140 ($59.55). Reservations are required.

CINEMA

In most European cities it's either difficult or impossible to find a theater showing undubbed American and British films, but in Amsterdam you'll find a dozen or more first-run features in English, most of them Hollywood's finest. Program information is available in English in the free weekly *Film Agenda* brochure, which you can pick up at movie theaters, hotels, and cafes, and in Dutch in the bimonthly magazine *Preview* and the monthly newspaper-style *Filmkrant*, both of which are available at the cinemas. Admission prices are from Dfl 10 to Dfl 15 ($4.25 to $6.40), depending on the day, the time, and the movie, and tickets can be reserved in advance for a small charge. Don't worry if you're a few minutes late getting to your seat: A long string of commercials and trailers always precedes the feature (except at the art-house cinemas).

The following are the major movie theaters of Amsterdam, which mostly show first-run Hollywood films: **Bellevue Cinerama,** Marnixstraat 400 (☎ 020/620-8417); **Calypso 1-2,** Marnixstraat 402 (☎ 020/620-8417); **Cinecenter,** Lijnbaansgracht 236 (☎ 020/623-6615); **Cinema 1-2,** August Allebéplein 4 (☎ 020/615-1243); **City 1-2-3-4-5-6-7,** Kleine Gartmanplantsoen 13–25 (☎ 020/623-4570); and ✪ **Tuschinski 1-2-3-4-5-6,** Reguliersbreestraat 26–28 (☎ 020/626-2637). The Tuschinski is well worth visiting for its extravagant art deco style; on the upper balconies you can sit on plush chairs and sip champagne during the movie.

Note: If all of a sudden there's a break in the film, don't fret; it will last about 15 minutes, and it's called a *pauze*. If you aren't used to intermissions in the middle of movies, it can be incredibly annoying, especially as it seems always to come at an arresting moment on screen, but at least it gives you time to visit the toilet, buy an ice cream, or—if you must—grab a smoke.

Art house, international, and lesser-known films are often shown at **Desmet,** Plantage Middenlaan 4a (☎ **020/627-3434**); **Kriterion 1-2,** Roetersstraat 170 (☎ **020/623-1708**); **The Movies 1-2-3-4,** Haarlemmerdijk 161 (☎ **020/ 638-6016**); **Nederlands Film Museum,** Vondelpark 3 (☎ **020/589-1400**); **Rialto,** Ceintuurbaan 338 (☎ **020/675-3994**); and **De Uitkijk,** Prinsengracht 452 (☎ **020/623-7460**).

CASINOS

The Holland Casinos group operates the only legal casinos in Holland. Amsterdam's is the **Holland Casino Amsterdam,** in the Lido, Max Euweplein 62 (☎ **020/ 521-1111**), near Leidseplein. There are casinos in other towns as well, including the beach resort of Zandvoort (30 minutes by car or by train from Centraal Station). This is European gambling, with emphasis on the quiet games of roulette, baccarat, and blackjack, though there are abundant one-armed bandits, which the Dutch call "fruit machines," and blackjack, poker, and bingo machines (start saving your guilder coins!). You need correct attire to get into a casino in Holland (jacket and tie or turtleneck for men), and you also have to bring your passport to register at the door. The minimum age to gamble is 18. Admission costs Dfl 5 ($2.15). Casinos are open 1:30pm to 2am.

10

Side Trips from Amsterdam

Amsterdam is the brightest star of a small galaxy of cities and towns that together form what the Dutch call the Randstad (Rim City), a budding megalopolis. Stretching from Amsterdam to Rotterdam, the Randstad contains these two cities plus The Hague, Utrecht, Haarlem, Leiden, and Delft, and two-thirds of the country's more than 15 million people.

The area offers a number of interesting possibilities for a day outside the city. It won't be a day in the country, exactly, but you don't have to go far from Amsterdam to see tulips, windmills, and cheese markets. You can climb tall towers, visit interesting museums, ride a steam train, tour the world's largest harbor, and see giant locks and tiny canals. If you're historically minded, you'll want to explore sites associated with the Pilgrims (who lived in Holland for years before sailing to the New World on the *Mayflower*).

EXCURSIONS ORIENTATION

BUS TOURS   The major Amsterdam-based sightseeing companies—all of which offer a similar selection of tours at essentially the same prices—are: **Best of Holland Excursions,** Damrak 34 (☎ 020/623-1539); **Holland International Excursions,** Damrak 90 (☎ 020/551-2800); **Keytours,** Dam 19 (☎ 020/624-7304); and **Lindbergh Excursions,** Damrak 26 (☎ 020/622-2766). They provide a variety of half- and full-day tours into the surrounding area, particularly between April and October; in addition, there are special excursions at tulip time and at the height of the summer season (see the following pages for information on most destinations named here). Prices for half-day tours are Dfl 37.50 to Dfl 52.50 ($15.95 to $22.35), and for full-day tours, Dfl 72.50 to Dfl 92.50 ($30.85 to $39.35); children ages 4 to 13 are charged half fare, and children under 4 travel free.

Two tours offered year-round are the "Grand Holland Tour," an 8-hour drive that includes the Aalsmeer flower auction, The Hague and Scheveningen, Delft, and Rotterdam; and "Volendam and Marken," a 6½-hour trip to see the costumed villagers and their decorated houses, with a stop at a cheese farm along the way. An additional tour, generally available during tulip time (early April to mid-May), is "Holland in Bloom," a 4-hour drive through the bulb-growing district, with a stop at Keukenhof Gardens.

Other tours, generally available only between April and October (though some are year-round), include "Delft, The Hague, and

Side Trips: The Randstad

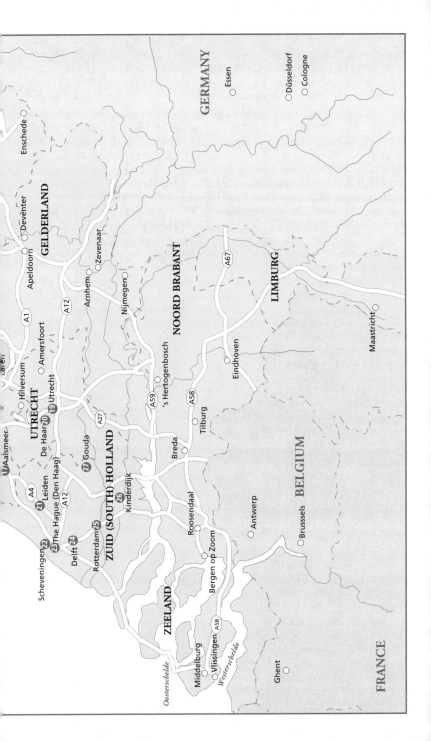

219

Scheveningen," a 9-hour trip; "Afsluitdijk and the IJsselmeer," an 8-hour drive across the Enclosing Dike and around the IJsselmeer (IJssel Lake, formerly the Zuiderzee, an inland sea); "Zaanse Schans and Edam," a 3½-hour tour via the windmills of Zaanse Schans to Edam (a cheese town, with no market); and "Alkmaar and Hoorn" (Friday only), a 5-hour trip to visit the cheese market and the 17th-century port of Hoorn.

CAR & CAMPER RENTAL   To rent a car for an excursion outside Amsterdam, you can expect to pay Dfl 75 to Dfl 100 ($31.90 to $42.55) per day, which will get you unlimited mileage in a no-frills car with a stick shift, such as a Honda Civic, Fiat Primo, or something similar. You pay as much as Dfl 360 ($153.20) per day for a fully equipped luxury car such as a BMW. And that's not counting gas, insurance, and a whopping tax of 18.5%. Gas costs around Dfl 11.80 ($5) per U.S. gallon for Super (leaded) and Dfl 10.25 ($4.35) for Euro (unleaded).

Unlimited-mileage rates represent a savings if you plan to do extensive wandering or want to keep the car long enough to make several successive excursions from Amsterdam; some car-rental companies offer this option only with a minimum rental of 7 days or more. During the winter season some Amsterdam firms offer special short-term unlimited-mileage plans.

Rates vary among companies, as do the makes of their cars, the rental plans available, and extra services (some companies, for example, have free car delivery to your hotel). Call around until you find the car, and the deal, that best suits your plans.

The major car-rental firms with offices in Amsterdam and with car pickup and return desks at Amsterdam's Schiphol Airport are **Avis,** Hogehilweg 7 (☎ **020/ 430-9611**); **Budget,** Overtoom 121 (☎ **020/612-6066**); **Europcar Interrent,** Overtoom 51–53 (☎ **020/683-2123**); and **Hertz,** Overtoom 333 (☎ **020/612-2441**). Some good local companies are **Adams,** Nassaukade 345–346 (☎ **020/685-0111**); **Amcar,** Jacob Obrechtplein 13–15 (☎ **020/662-4214**); **Baas Ouke,** van Ostadestraat 366 (☎ **020/679-4842**); and **KAV Autoverhuur,** Klokkenbergweg 17 (☎ **020/311-9811**).

For chauffeur-driven luxury cars and limousines, go to **Amsterdam Limousine Service,** P. Ghijsenlaan 3, Zaandam (☎ **020/664-1178**); or **CS Limousine Services,** Emmastraat 32 (☎ **020/673-7888**). To rent a camper, if that idea appeals to you, call **Braitman & Woudenberg,** Droogbak 4a (☎ **020/622-1168**), or **A-Point,** Kollenbergweg 11 (☎ **020/696-4964**).

TRAIN SERVICES   With a few exceptions, you can easily travel by train to the cities and towns described in this chapter and, once there, walk or take public transportation to the major sights. Dutch cities are not large and train stations are located within a few blocks of the center of town, with buses or trams parked out front. Trains run frequently throughout the day and night from Amsterdam Centraal Station to many of the cities mentioned in the following pages. There are, for example, trains departing at least every half hour to Alkmaar, to Rotterdam and points in between, and to Haarlem. Travel times are short (Rotterdam, the farthest train destination in this chapter, is just an hour away from Amsterdam Centraal Station; Zaandam, the nearest, just 8 minutes by train).

Fares, too, are reasonable. For example a *dagretour* (1-day round-trip ticket at about 10% to 20% savings) to Haarlem is just Dfl 17.25 ($7.35) in first class and Dfl 11.50 ($4.90) in second class; to Leiden, Dfl 35.75 ($15.25) in first class and Dfl 27.25 ($11.60) in second class; and to Rotterdam, Dfl 60.35 ($25.70) in first class and Dfl 48.50 ($20.65) in second class. Ask, too, about other options, such as the Zomertoer (Summer Tour) ticket, which permits travel for two persons throughout the entire rail network for a complete day, on 3 days during a 10-day period in July and August, for Dfl 105 ($44.70) for a one-person ticket and Dfl 135 ($57.45) for a two-person ticket.

The information office of **Nederlandse Spoorwegen (Netherland Railways)** (☎ **0900/9292**) is open Monday to Friday 7am to 11pm and Saturday, Sunday, and holidays 8am to 11pm. *Note:* Be sure to ask the time of the late trains back to Amsterdam; service is limited after midnight.

If you're trying to get information on Netherlands Railways before you leave home, call your nearest Netherlands Board of Tourism office (see "Visitor Information, Entry Requirements & Customs," in chapter 2).

BICYCLE   Holland has 15.5 million people and 11 million bicycles, so you better believe that the Dutch are all but born in the saddle. To fully engage in the Dutch experience, you positively have to climb aboard a bicycle and head out into the wide green yonder. You can hire bikes at many train stations around the country to tour the local highlights (and at many places in Amsterdam—see "Getting Around" in chapter 3). The tourism authorities have marked out many cycling tour routes and have published descriptive booklets and maps, available from VVV offices. A great suggestion for a longer tour is to cycle around the IJsselmeer, the big lake north of Amsterdam (see "Cycling Along the IJsselmeer Shore," below). This tour is perhaps the perfect Dutch experience, following a narrow track between the polders and the lake.

Cycling in Holland is safe, easy, and pleasant. Almost all roads have designated cycle paths, often separated from the road by a screen of trees or bushes, and there are separate traffic lights and signs for cyclists. (Mopeds, called *brommers* in Holland, and motor-scooters also use the cycle tracks.) One thing that can prove an unpleasant surprise for those who think that the absence of hills will make for easy riding is that in a totally flat landscape there is nothing to block the wind—which is fine when the wind is behind you, and not so fine when it's blowing in your face.

A company that offers great out-of-town (and in-town) cycling excursions is **Yellow Bike,** Nieuwezijds Kolk 29, off Nieuwezijds Voorburgwal (☎ **020/620-6940**).

TOURIST INFORMATION   Anywhere you travel in the Netherlands you can expect to find a local **VVV Tourist Information Office,** usually either near the train station or at the town's main square. If you're driving, you'll see blue-and-white *vvv* signs posted along major routes into town to direct you to the office. VVV offices are open during regular business hours, including Saturday in many places; hours are sometimes extended in larger cities and towns, and during the busy spring and summer seasons.

1 Haarlem

18km (11 miles) W of Amsterdam

If you have only 1 day to travel beyond Amsterdam, spend it in Haarlem. This city of music and art is just a 20-minute train journey from Centraal Station. It's the gateway to the reclaimed Haarlemmermeer polder land, near the beaches and the bulb fields, in the heart of an area dotted with elegant manor houses and picturesque villages. Haarlem is home to two of Holland's finest museums. A trip to Haarlem can easily be combined with one to nearby Zandvoort, which is on the same railway line (see below).

ESSENTIALS

GETTING THERE   There are trains departing at least every half hour from Amsterdam Centraal Station to Haarlem; journey time is 20 minutes. Buses depart every 15 minutes or so from outside Amsterdam Centraal Station to Haarlem, but they take longer than the train and there seems no benefit in using them. By car from Amsterdam, take N5/A5.

VISITOR INFORMATION   **VVV Haarlem** is at Stationsplein 1 (☎ **0900/ 616-1600;** fax 023/534-0537), just outside the train station.

WHAT TO SEE & DO

Traditionally, Haarlem is the little sister city of Amsterdam. It was where Frans Hals, Jacob van Ruysdael, and Pieter Saenredam were living and painting their famous portraits, landscapes, and church interiors during the same years that Rembrandt was living and working in Amsterdam. The finest attraction in the city is the ✪ **Frans Halsmuseum,** Groot Heiligland 62 (☎ **023/516-4200**), which may well be a high point of your trip to Holland. The galleries here are the halls and furnished chambers of a former home, and the famous paintings by the masters of the Haarlem school hang in settings that look like the 17th-century houses they were intended to adorn. Among other pieces is a superb dollhouse from around 1750, though "doll-house" seems an inadequate description for an exquisitely detailed miniature replica of an Amsterdam merchant's canal house. This is a beautiful place to spend an hour or two at any time. The museum is open Monday to Saturday from 11am to 5pm and Sunday from 1 to 5pm. Admission is Dfl 10 ($4.25) for adults, Dfl 5 ($2.15) for children 10 to 17, and free for children under 10.

Handel and Mozart both made special visits to Haarlem just to play the magnificent, soaring Christian Müller organ of St. Bavo Cathedral, the **Grote Kerk,** Oude Groenmarkt 23 (☎ **023/532-4399**). Walking to the town center from Haarlem station, you catch only glimpses of the church, but the moment you reach the market square it's revealed in all its splendor. Finished in 1520 after a relatively short building period (130 years), it has a rare unity of structure and proportion. The elegant wooden tower is covered with lead sheets and adorned with gilt spheres. The interior is light and airy, with whitewashed walls and sandstone pillars. Look for the tombstone of painter Frans Hals, and for a cannonball that has been embedded in the wall ever since it came flying through a window during the siege of Haarlem in 1572–73.

And, of course, don't miss the church's famous **Christian Müller Organ,** built in 1738. You can hear it at one of the free concerts given on Tuesday and Thursday from April to October. It has 5,068 pipes and is nearly 98 feet tall, and when it's going flat out it will blow your socks off. The woodwork was done by Jan van Logteren. Mozart played the organ in 1766 when he was just 10 years old. When you see it, you may be dumbstruck at the thought of little Wolfie reaching for one of its 68 stops. St. Bavo's is open Monday to Saturday 10am to 4pm. Admission is Dfl 3 ($1.30) for adults and Dfl 2 (85¢) for children under 14.

From St. Bavo's, it's an easy walk to the oldest and perhaps the most unusual museum in Holland, the **Teylers Museum,** Spaarne 16 (☎ **023/531-9010**). Here you find a curiously diverse collection of displays: drawings by Michelangelo, Raphael, and Rembrandt (which are shown on a rotating basis); fossils, minerals, and skeletons; and instruments of physics and an odd assortment of inventions, including the largest electrostatic generator in the world (built in 1784) and a 19th-century radarscope. The museum is open Tuesday to Saturday 10am to 5pm and Sunday 1 to 5pm. Admission is Dfl 10 ($4.25) for adults and Dfl 5 ($2.15) for students, seniors, and children 15 and under.

As in Amsterdam, an ideal way to see the city is by canal boat. These are operated by **Woltheus Cruises,** whose jetty is on the River Spaarne at the Gravensteenbrug (☎ **023/535-7723**). Boats leave every hour for a cruise around the canals.

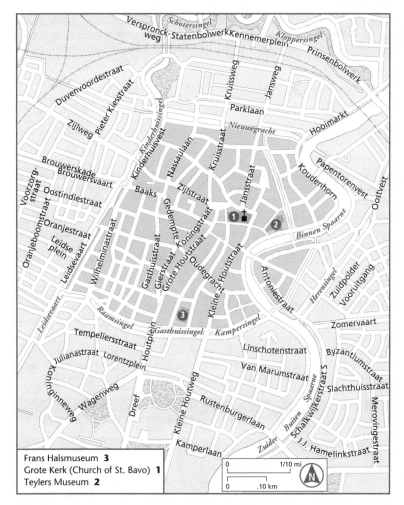

Frans Halsmuseum **3**
Grote Kerk (Church of St. Bavo) **1**
Teylers Museum **2**

NEARBY SIGHTS

The little village of **Spaarndam,** north of Haarlem, and reached by bus from outside Haarlem train station, is picturesque enough to warrant a visit just for the scenery, but its main claim to fame is a monument to a fictional character who has become an everlasting symbol of Holland and the Dutch people. You remember, of course, Young Pieter (of *Hans Brinker of The Silver Skates* by Mary Mapes Dodge, 1865), who saved Haarlem from disaster when he plugged a hole in the dike with his finger and steadfastly refused to leave until help came at the end of a long night. Because this fictional boy's heroic act so caught the imagination of people around the world, the Dutch government erected a **memorial** in 1950, dedicating it to the courage of Dutch youth.

Other attractions near Haarlem include the graciously restored 18th-century manor house and country estate, **Beeckestijn,** in the town of Velsen-Zuid near IJmuiden (open Wednesday to Sunday from noon to 5pm); the **Museum de Cruquius,** a steam-driven water mill and land-reclamation museum at Heemstede (open March to

October, Monday to Friday from 10am to 5pm, Saturday and Sunday from 11am to 5pm); and at IJmuiden, the three great locks of the **North Sea Canal.** For early birds, the **fish auctions** at IJmuiden, Halkade 4, are held Monday to Friday from 7 to 11am.

WHERE TO DINE

Café Mephisto. Grote Markt 29. ☎ **023/532-9742.** Main courses Dfl 14.50–22.50 ($6.15–$9.55); *broodjes* (sandwiches) Dfl 7.50–11.50 ($3.20–$4.90). No credit cards. Sun–Thurs 9am–2am, Fri–Sat 9am–3am (meals begin at noon daily). DUTCH/INTERNATIONAL.

You find reasonably priced meals at this comfortable brown cafe, where the decor is Jugendstil (Dutch art nouveau) and the music leans toward classic jazz. The kitchen turns out a respectable chicken saté and other soul food staples.

✪ **De Pêcherie Haarlem aan Zee.** Oude Groenmarkt 10. ☎ **023/531-4848.** Main courses Dfl 30–40 ($12.75–$17). MC, V. Mon–Sat noon–midnight, Sun 5pm–midnight. SEAFOOD.

You can just about smell the fresh breeze from the North Sea at this fine seafood restaurant facing Haarlem's Grote Kerk. You sit in wooden booths on chairs that have brightly colored canvas backings, like deck chairs. The menu features oysters, crab, prawns, and various fish dishes, all of which go well with the crisp house white wine.

Jacobus Pieck. Warmoesstraat 18. ☎ **023/532-6144.** Main courses Dfl 15–28 ($6.40–$11.90); snacks from Dfl 6.50 ($2.75). AE, MC, V. Mon–Sat 10am–11pm, Sun noon–11pm. DUTCH/INTERNATIONAL.

This popular café-restaurant has a lovely shaded terrace in the garden for fine-weather days, while inside it's bustling and stylish. Outside or in, you find excellent food for reasonable prices and friendly, efficient service. At lunchtime they serve generous sandwiches and burgers, and their salads are particularly good. Main dinner courses range from pastas and Middle Eastern dishes to wholesome Dutch standards.

2 Zandvoort

26km (16 miles) W of Amsterdam

If you feel like drawing a breath of fresh sea air and you don't have much time for it, do what most Amsterdammers do: Head for Zandvoort. On the North Sea coast just west of Haarlem, Zandvoort is brash and brassy in summer, though it often looks forlorn in the off-season. Yet even in winter it's a longstanding Amsterdam tradition to take the train here, walk up and down along the shore for an hour or so, then, head for one of the town's cafes. If you're in quick-look mode, Zandvoort can easily be combined with Haarlem as a day trip, as both are on the same railway line from Amsterdam.

ESSENTIALS

GETTING THERE You get to Zandvoort easiest by train from Amsterdam Central Station. Trains leave every hour; transfer at Haarlem (where the Zandvoort train is usually waiting on the adjacent platform); during summer extra trains go direct from Centraal Station. In either case, journey time is 30 minutes. Busses leave every 30 minutes from outside Centraal Station to Zandvoort, but they take longer than the train. By car go via Haarlem, on N5/A5/N200, but beware of frequent long traffic lines in summer.

VISITOR INFORMATION VVV Zandvoort is at Schoolplein 1 (☎ **023/ 571-7947;** fax 023/571-7003; www.vvvzk.nl), opposite the bus station in the center of town.

Hot Jets

For a fast-moving kind of excursion, try a ride to the seaside on a Russian-built jet-foil operated by the dramatically named **Fast Flying Ferries** (☎ 020/ 639-2247). Just as Russian helicopters look a bit ponderous and clunky compared to sleek Western choppers, so do Russian jet-foils look oddly different, but they get the job done. FFF runs a scheduled service through the North Sea Canal between Amsterdam and IJmuiden on the North Sea coast. The jet-foils leave from Landing Stage 7 behind Centraal Station at half-hourly intervals 7am to 10am and 4am to 7:30pm, and at hourly intervals 10am to 4pm; the journey to IJmuiden takes 30 minutes. Tickets cost Dfl 8.50 ($3.60) one way and Dfl 14.50 ($6.15) round-trip for adults, and Dfl 5 ($2.15) one way and Dfl 8.50 ($3.60) round-trip for children age 4 to 11, free for children under 4.

WHAT TO SEE & DO

There is not much more to Zandvoort than its **beach,** but what a beach! In summer, this seemingly endless stretch of smooth sand is lined with dozens of temporary beach cafe-restaurants and discos. Holland's prurient picture magazines publish seasonal articles about the antics of the *Jongens van Zandvoort* (Kids of Zandvoort), which are not much more than an excuse to show as many topless girls as possible. Besides the mainstream beaches, there are gay and naturist beaches, where the shocking sight of a clothed or even partially clothed individual can generate considerable moral outrage.

Windsurfing is pretty good at Zandvoort, which hosts international competitions in this sport, and in catamaran sailing.

At its northern end, beyond the suburb of Bloemendaal aan Zee, the beach runs into industrial IJmuiden, easily identified by the smokestacks of the Hoogovens steel plant. Water quality in this stretch of the North Sea probably leaves something to be desired, and sand in suspension gives it a muddy look.

Circuit Park Zandvoort, Burg van Alphenstraat 63 (☎ 023/574-0740), in the north of the town a short distance from the beach, used to be the venue for the Dutch Formula One Grand Prix motor race (and negotiations are taking place that may bring the race back), but for now it hosts only smaller events. If you come on a summer weekend, you might find a Formula Three training session or a Porsche meeting under way.

Equally racy, though less noisy, is **Holland Casino Zandvoort,** Badhuisplein 7 (☎ 023/574-0574), in the center behind the seafront promenade. This is one of only 10 legal casinos in Holland, with roulette, blackjack, and more. The dress code here is "correct" (collar and tie for men), and the minimum age is 18. You need your passport to get in. Casino Zandvoort is open daily from 1:30pm to 2am. Entry costs Dfl 6 ($2.55).

More tranquil pursuits can be found by walking through the extensive sand dunes of the **Kennemer Duinen** and **Amsterdamse Waterleiding Duinen** around the town. Reinforced by native vegetation, the dunes play an important part in the sea defense system and have been designated nature reserves. You can have an active fresh-air experience here, strolling along pathways through the woods on the landward side and westward across the dunes toward the sea. A variety of flora occupies this relatively small area, and the beach is never far away if the call of the sea proves too strong.

In town, there are casual shopping, eating and drinking possibilities.

3 The IJsselmeer

Only in Holland could you say, "This used to be a sea." The IJsselmeer, the big lake on Amsterdam's doorstep, actually was once a sea, called the Zuiderzee (as in the words of the song, "by the side of the Zuiderzee . . ."), until the Dutch decided they didn't want it to be one any longer, because it was always threatening to flood Amsterdam (remember that Amsterdammers don't like water in their *jenever*). So in the 1930s, workers blocked off the mouth of the Zuiderzee with a massive dike, the Afsluitdijk, running from North Holland to Friesland, and that was that. Nowadays, in the sea's place, there is a well-behaved freshwater lake called the IJsselmeer (pronounced *Eye*-sselmeer). You'll find the lake's long shoreline to be a scenic and popular escape from Amsterdam.

VOLENDAM, MARKEN & MONNICKENDAM
18km (11 miles), 16km (10 miles), and 12km (7½ miles) NE of Amsterdam

There are differences between Volendam and Marken—one is Catholic, the other Protestant; one is on the mainland, the other on a former island; one has women wearing white caps with wings, the other has women wearing caps with ribbons—but Volendam and Marken have been combined on bus-tour itineraries for so long that they seem to have contributed a new compound word to the Dutch language. Unfortunately, *volendammarken* will probably come to mean "tourist trap," or perhaps, "packaged Holland and costumes to go." Nonetheless, it's possible to have a delightful day in the bracing air of these waterside communities, where residents go about their daily business in traditional dress.

ESSENTIALS
GETTING THERE   You get to Volendam and Monnickendam by separate buses every hour from outside Amsterdam Centraal Station; the Monnickendam bus continues to Marken. Journey time to Volendam is 35 minutes; to Monnickendam 30 minutes; to Marken 45 minutes. When driving to Marken, which was once an island, you cross a 2-mile-long causeway from Monnickendam. You need to leave your car in the parking lot outside before entering the narrow streets.

VISITOR INFORMATION   VVV **Volendam** is at Zeestraat 37 (☎ **0299/363-747;** fax 0299/368-484; www.vvvvolendam.nl), beside the harbor; and **VVV Monnickendam/Marken** is at Nieuwpoort 15, Monnickendam (☎ **0299/651-998**). Opening times for both are Monday to Friday 9am to 5pm, Saturday 9am to 4pm.

WHAT TO SEE & DO
Volendam is geared for tourism in a big way, with lots of souvenir shops, boutiques, gift shops, and restaurants in full swing during summer months. Still, its boat-filled harbor, tiny streets, and traditional houses have an undeniable charm. If you simply must have a snapshot of yourself surrounded by fishermen in little caps and balloon-legged pants, this is the place to visit. Volendammers will gladly pose. You'll enjoy the day as long as you realize what the villagers understand quite well: Dutch costumes are a tradition worth preserving, as is the economy of a small town that lost most of its fishing industry when the enclosure of the Zuiderzee cut it off from the North Sea. Tourism isn't a bad alternative, they figure—it brings lots of people to town to see such attractions as the **fish auction,** the **diamond cutter,** the **clog maker,** and the **house** with a room entirely wallpapered in cigar bands.

  ✪ **Marken** used to be an island until a narrow causeway was built connecting it with the mainland, and it remains as insular as ever. This is a tiny green village of houses on stilts grouped around an equally tiny harbor. It's smaller and quieter than Volendam, and more rural, with clusters of farmhouses dotted around the polders and a candy-striped **lighthouse** on the IJsselmeer shore. This town does not go all over gushy for the tourists; it merely feeds and waters them, and allows them to wander around its pretty streets. Occupants of Marken's green-and-white houses wear traditional dress, as much to preserve the custom as for the tourists who pour in daily. There's a typical **house** open as a sort of museum and a **clog maker,** who usually works in the parking lot in summer.

In case you feel a bit uncomfortable gawking at the picturesque locals as they go about their daily routine of hanging out laundry, washing windows, and shopping for groceries, take comfort from knowing that your visit is not crass exploitation. This is a village that lost its livelihood when access to the open sea was cut off (some of the fishing boats that now sail the IJsselmeer hoist dark-brown sails as a sign of mourning for their lost sea fishing), and tourism has become an alternative industry, with a tax levied on every tour, which goes directly into the village coffers. Gawking saved Marken's life.

Monnickendam, in contrast to its two neighbors, doesn't pay much attention to tourists at all, but gets on with its own life as a boating center and with what's left of its fishing industry, as you can see in its busy **harbor.** Visit the **Town Hall,** at Noordeinde 5, which began life as a private residence in 1746, and step inside to admire the elaborately decorated ceiling. Then take a walk through streets lined with gabled houses and make a stop to admire the 15th-century late Gothic **Sint-Nicolaaskerk,** at Zarken 2.

WHERE TO STAY

If you want to overnight in Volendam or Monnickendam in traditional style, ask at their VVV offices about staying on one of the old wooden IJsselmeer *boters* and *skûtsjes* (sailing ships) moored in the harbor (this option is generally not available in Marken). It makes for a romantic, if somewhat cramped, way to spend the night. Another good bet is the:

Hotel Spaander. Haven 15–19 (north end of the harbor), 1131 EP Volendam. ☎ **0299/ 363-595.** Fax 0299/369-615. 84 units. TV TEL. Dfl 140–160 ($59.55–$68.10) double. Rates include breakfast. AE, DC, MC, V.

This old-fashioned hotel has a real harbor flavor to go with its waterfront location. The public spaces have an Old Dutch interior look; the rooms, however, are modern, brightly furnished, comfortable, and attractive. There's a heated indoor pool and a fitness center. The hotel's two dining rooms and outside terrace cafe are excellent restaurant choices. Meals average Dfl 45 ($19.15), without wine.

WHERE TO DINE

De Taanderij. Havenbuurt 1, Marken. ☎ **0299/601-364.** Main courses Dfl 15–25 ($6.40–$10.65), snacks Dfl 5–12.50 ($2.15–$5.30). No credit cards. Apr–Sept, daily 10am–10pm; Oct–Mar, Tues–Sat 10am–10pm, Sun 6–10pm. DUTCH/FRENCH.

This little *eethuis* at the end of the harbor is great for lunch or a traditional Dutch treat of *koffie en appelgebak met slagroom* (coffee with apple pie and cream) or *poffertjes* (small fried pancake "puffs" coated with confectioners' sugar and filled with syrup or liqueur). Seafood dishes are also served. The inside is an elegant and cozy interpretation of old Marken style. When the weather is good, a terrace will be spread onto the harborside, where you can absorb the sunshine, the tranquil view over the Gouwzee, and of course the luscious goodies on the menu.

HOORN

32km (20 miles) NE of Amsterdam

Hoorn is the home of Willem Cornelis Schouten, who in 1616 rounded South America's southernmost tip, which he promptly dubbed Kap Hoorn (Cape Horn). Trains depart at least every hour from Amsterdam Centraal Station to Hoorn; journey time is 1 hour. There are buses every hour or so leaving from outside Amsterdam Centraal Station, but they take much longer than the train. By car from Amsterdam, take the E22 north. The **VVV Hoorn** is at Veemarkt 4 (☎ **0900/403-1055;** fax 0229/315-023), between Hoorn train station and the town center. It can furnish information on Hoorn's many historic buildings and interesting houses, and a delightful "Walking in Hoorn" booklet.

WHAT TO SEE & DO

While in Hoorn (pronounced *Hoarn*) visit the **Westfries Museum,** Rode Steen 1 (☎ **0229/280-028**). This beautiful 1632 building holds 17th-century artifacts brought from Indonesia by the East India Company, armor, weapons, paper cuttings, costumes, toys, naive paintings (which embody a style that is deliberately "childlike"), coins, medals, jewels, civic guards' paintings, porcelain, and a second-floor exhibit that details the town's maritime history. There are also tapestries and 17th- and 18th-century period rooms. A collection of Bronze Age relics is exhibited in the basement. The museum is open April to September, Monday to Friday 11am to 5pm, Saturday 2 to 5pm, Sunday noon to 5pm; October to March, Monday to Friday 11am to 5pm, Saturday and Sunday 2 to 5pm. Admission is Dfl 7.50 ($3.20) for adults, Dfl 4 ($1.70) for seniors and children 16 and under.

During July there's an interesting craft market in the marketplace every Wednesday, with demonstrations and items for sale; and during the summer an **antique steam train** (☎ **0229/214-862**) takes tourists from Hoorn to Medemblik, a small IJsselmeer town nearby. Tickets cost Dfl 27.50 ($11.70) round-trip for adults, Dfl 17.50 ($7.45) for children 4 to 11, and are free for children under 4. The 8th-century **Radboud Castle** (☎ **0227/541-960**) in Medemblik, which was fortified in 1288 against possible rebellion from those troublesome Frisians, has been restored to its original state and is well worth a visit. The castle is open May 15 to September 15, Monday to Saturday 10 am to 5pm, Sunday 2 to 5pm. It is open every day from June to August, and on Sunday afternoons during other months. Admission is Dfl 5 ($2.15) for adults, Dfl 2.50 ($1.05) for children 5 to 13, and free for children under 5.

WHERE TO DINE

✪ **De Hoofdtoren.** Hoofd 2. ☎ **0229/215-487.** Main courses Dfl 19.50–55.50 ($8.30–$23.60); snacks from Dfl 7 ($2.75). AE, DC, MC, V. Daily 10am–10pm. DUTCH.

Boat-lovers will want to sit on the terrace of this cafe-restaurant in an old defense tower, in the midst of the busy harbor, surrounded by traditional IJsselmeer sailing ships and by pleasure boats large and small. The tower, which dates from about 1500, protected the harbor entrance and its interior retains many antique features. Traditional Dutch fare and grilled specialties, both meat and fish, are served at dinner. During the day there is a lunch and snacks menu.

De Waag. Rode Steen 8. ☎ **0229/215-195.** Main courses Dfl 17.50–32.50 ($7.45–$13.85); snacks from Dfl 7 ($2.75). MC, V. Daily 10am–1am. DUTCH.

This grand cafe in the monumental Weigh House from 1609 is open all day, for breakfast, lunch, and dinner. It stands on a square that is among the most beautiful in

Cycling Along the IJsselmeer Shore

It's possible to cycle to Hoorn and return to Amsterdam by train in a day, providing you're fit and healthy and ready for some vigorous exercise. Watch out for the wind—you may prefer to choose another day if it's blowing strongly in your face when you're ready to set out. You can turn back at various logical places on the route, but once you're beyond the halfway point, you're really committed to going all the way to Hoorn.

Still with me? Okay, board the IJ ferry at the pier behind Centraal Station and cross to Amsterdam North. Take Durgerdammerdijk, the road that runs east alongside the lakeshore, to **Durgerdam,** a lakeside village huddling below water level behind its protective dike, with its roofs sticking up over the top. You can either pedal beside the houses or venture up onto the dike-top path, past **Uitdam,** with a fine view over the polders to your left and the lake studded with the sails of old-style IJsselmeer sailing ships, *boters* and *skûtsjes,* to your right.

Beyond Uitdam, turn right onto the causeway that leads to **Marken.** You could turn left toward Monnickendam instead, which bypasses Marken and means less cycling. In summer you can take a boat, the *Marken Express,* from Marken harbor across to Volendam, a half-hour trip, with boats leaving every hour. This, in turn, means bypassing **Monnickendam.** Or, retrace your route back across the causeway from Marken and stay on the lakeside road to Monnickendam. Pass through Monnickendam, keeping to the shore, then on through **Katwoude** to **Volendam.** If you've had enough, this is a good place to take a break before cycling back to Amsterdam.

If you're still with the program, go inland a short way from the lakeside dike to **Edam,** famed for its Edammer cheese (see "The Cheese Towns," later in this chapter for more details). Turn right at the canal bridge at Damplein in Edam, and back along the canal to regain the IJsselmeer shore.

Ahead of you is a straight run north on the lakeside road through the polders. The villages of **Warder, Eteresheim,** and **Scharwoude** are your "checkpoints" on the way to **Hoorn.** You may be ready to flop aboard a train going anywhere by now, but should you have some puff left, visit Hoorn's beautiful inner harbor, the Binnenhaven. Then follow the green-painted signs, pointing first to the VVV office, then to the station, for the train ride back to Amsterdam.

the country, surrounded by 17th-century buildings from the town's heyday. You can still see the antique weighing scales in the wood-beamed interior.

ENKHUIZEN

44km (27½ miles) NE of Amsterdam

A great herring fleet of some 400 boats once sailed out of Enkhuizen harbor, and then came the Enclosing Dike, closing off the North Sea. Now Enkhuizen looks to tourism and pleasure boating for its livelihood, and its population has declined from 30,000 in its 17th-century heyday to a mere 13,000 today. Enkhuizen has no train station, but there are buses every hour or so from Hoorn train station. By car from Amsterdam, drive via Hoorn. The **VVV Enkhuizen** is at Tussen Twee Havens 1 (☎ **0228/313-164;** fax 0228/315-531; www.enkhuizen.nl), at the harbor.

WHAT TO SEE & DO

From the Enkhuizen–Lelystad dike parking area you can take a ferry over to the open-air ✪ **Zuiderzeemuseum,** Wierdijk 12–22 (☎ **0228/318-260**), where old farmhouses, public buildings, shops, and a church from around the Zuiderzee have been brought together to form a cobblestone-street village. The museum is open April to October, daily 10am to 5pm, and admission is Dfl 18,50 ($8.50) for adults, Dfl 16 ($6.80) for seniors, Dfl 13 ($5.10) for children 3 to 18, and free for children under 3.

4 The Zaanstreek

16km (10 miles) NW of Amsterdam

Much of this district is now taken up with shipping and industry, but nestled in its midst is the charm of the Zaanse Schans, a planned replica village made up of houses moved to the site when industrialization leveled their original locations. Although most of these houses are inhabited by the sort of Amsterdam expatriates who can afford and appreciate their historic timbers (and have the patience for the pedestrian traffic from the tour buses), a few can be visited as museums. It may all look familiar because you have seen pictures of the windmills and green wooden houses in many a Holland brochure; but it's hard to believe that until a century or two ago, not even the ground on which everything stands existed.

ESSENTIALS

GETTING THERE   There are trains and buses every 20 minutes or so to Zaandam from Amsterdam Centraal Station. By car from Amsterdam, take A8 north.

VISITOR INFORMATION   VVV **Zaanstreek/Waterland** is at Gedempte Gracht 76, Zaandam (☎ **075/616-2221;** fax 075/670-5381; www.vvvzaanstreek), on the main shopping street, between the train station and the town center. The office is open Monday to Friday 9am to 5:30pm, Saturday 9am to 4pm.

WHAT TO SEE & DO

To the pleasure of just walking through the **Zaanse Schans,** add a visit to four different kinds of **windmills:** One for lumber, one for paint, one for vegetable oil, and one for the renowned Zaanse mustard. At one time the industrious people of the Zaanstreek had almost 500 windmills working for them. Only 12 have survived, including these 4. A short tour of one shows you just how these wind machines worked; they're open for visitors at varying hours from late March to October. Stop at the **18th-century grocery** that was the beginning of Holland's largest supermarket chain (Albert Heijn) and the old-style **bakery,** visit the **clog shop** to see how the wooden shoes called *klompen* are made, and take a **minicruise** on the River Zaan. Most individual museums are open daily 10am to 5pm (tour buses full of visitors turn up all the time on organized day-trips). Admission varies from Dfl 4 to Dfl 5 ($1.70 to $2.15).

Several other points in the Zaanstreek are worth a visit. At **Koog-aan-de-Zaan** there's a 1751 windmill museum, **Het Pink.** At **Zaandijk** you can explore an 18th-century **merchant's home** furnished in the old Zaanse style.

Nearby **Zaandam,** the main town of the district, was an important shipbuilding center in the 17th century. In 1697 Peter the Great of Russia worked incognito for a few days at a Zaandam shipyard, studying shipbuilding methods with craftsmen whom he, an avid nautical student, considered the world's best. He stayed at the humble timber home of a local blacksmith, Gerrit Kist. The **Czar Peter House** (Czaar

Get Your Clogs On

Clogs are still a fixture in many farming areas, where they're much more effective against wet and cold than leather shoes or boots. They're also, of course, a tourist staple, and if you plan to buy a pair, Zaanse Schans is a good place to do it. Traditionally, those with pointed toes are for women and rounded toes are for men. All must be worn with heavy socks, so when buying, add the width of one finger when measuring for size.

Peterhuisje), Krimp 23, enclosed in a brick shelter contributed by Czar Nicholas II in 1895, contains souvenirs of Peter's stay, including an exhibition on his life and the small bed into which the 2.1-meter-tall Czar of All the Russias squeezed himself. Peter visited Zaandam again in 1698 and twice in 1717, each time paying Kist a visit. A **statue** of the czar at work on a boat stands in Damplein, the town's main square.

WHERE TO DINE

✪ **De Hoop op d' Swarte Walvis.** Kalverringdijk 15. ☎ **075/616-5629.** Lunch Dfl 70 ($29.80); 5-course dinner Dfl 97.50 ($41.50). AE, DC, MC, V. Mon–Sat midday–2:30pm, 6–10pm. DUTCH/INTERNATIONAL.

This gourmet restaurant with a mouthful of a name sits amid the green-painted Zaanse Schans houses, with a glass pavilion and terrace overlooking the River Zaan and the waterside villas on the opposite bank. You can expect an unforgettable treat, with subtle mixtures of superior produce (it is owned by the same company as the Netherlands' biggest supermarket chain) cooked and prepared to perfection.

5 The Flower Centers

The first tulip bulbs were brought to Holland in 1592 by the botanist Carolus Clusius, who planted them at the Hortus Botanicus in Leiden, but never got to see the first plants flower—they were stolen by rivals. Tulips soon became highly popular, especially among the aristocracy. Trading in bulbs was a lucrative business and prices soared to ridiculous heights. During the 17th-century's "Tulip Mania," a single bulb could be worth as much as a canal house complete with garden and coach house. Today, the bulbs are more affordable, but competition to produce new strains is still fierce. The place to see them in their full glory is the Keukenhof Gardens at Lisse, where vast numbers of tulips and other flowers create dazzling patches of color. Combine your visit with a trip through the bulb fields between Leiden and Haarlem, for which VVV offices provide a detailed "Bulb Route."

If you are interested in the original plants, a specialized tulip garden in Limmen, 30km (18 miles) northwest of Amsterdam, has re-created some of the older varieties. Here you can see the flowers that are so prominent in the floral displays painted by 17th-century artists—fancifully shaded in flaming patterns and with names like Semper Augustus or Bruin Anvers. You find the garden, the **Hortus Bulborum,** at Zuidkerkerlaan 23 in Limmen. It's open in April and May.

BULB FIELDS

The largest bulb growers are in the northern corner of the South Holland province and the southern part of North Holland, with the heaviest concentration along the 25-mile Haarlem–Leiden drive. The organized Dutch make finding the different growers easy, with a signposted **Bolenstreek (Bulb District)** route that covers about

60km (37½ miles). They suggest that you plan to drive it during weekdays, when stalls along the roads sell flower garlands (do as the natives do and buy one for yourself, another for the car).

The bulb fields stretch roughly from Haarlem southward to just north of Leiden. To get there from Amsterdam, you can either drive first to Haarlem, then south on N208, through Hillegom, Lisse, and Sassenheim; or drive south on A4 (E19) past Schiphol Airport to the Nieuw-Vennep junction, and then northeast on N207.

KEUKENHOF GARDENS

Flowers at their peak and the Keukenhof Gardens at Lisse (☎ 0252/465-555) both have short seasons, but if you're here in the spring, you'll never forget a visit to this park. It's a meandering 70-acre wooded green in the heart of the bulb-producing region, planted each fall by the major Dutch growers (each plants his own plot or establishes his own greenhouse display). Then, come spring, the bulbs burst forth and produce not hundreds of flowers, or even thousands, but millions (almost 8 million at last count) of tulips and narcissi, daffodils and hyacinths, bluebells, crocuses, lilies, amaryllis, and many others. The blaze of color is everywhere in the park and in the greenhouses, beside the brooks and shady ponds, along the paths and in the neighboring fields, in neat little plots and helter-skelter on the lawns. Keukenhof Gardens claims to be the greatest flower show on earth—and it's Holland's annual spring gift to the world.

The park is open late March to mid-May only, daily from 8am to 7:30pm. There are special train/bus connections via Haarlem and the nearby town of Leiden. Admission is Dfl 17 ($7.45) for adults, Dfl 15 ($6.40) for seniors, and Dfl 8.50 ($3.70) for children 4 to 12. There are four cafes where you can grab a quick lunch so that you don't have to go running around looking for a place to eat when you'd rather be enjoying the flowers.

FRANS ROOZEN NURSERY

Just one of many bulb growers, the **Frans Roozen Nursery,** Vogelenzangseweg 49, Vogelenzang (☎ 023/584-7245), a few miles south of Haarlem on the N206, provides excellent guided tours that illuminate the ins and outs of growing tulips and getting them to market. Their **Tulip Show** is open daily from late March to late May 8am to 7:30pm, and their **Summer Show** from July until early October, Monday to Friday 9am to 5pm. Admission is free, but your hosts have no objection whatsoever to you buying some of their products.

AALSMEER FLOWER AUCTION

Growing flowers is a year-round business that nets more than a half-billion dollars a year at the **Aalsmeer Flower Auction** (☎ 0297/393-939), held in the lakeside community of Aalsmeer, near Schiphol Airport. Every year, the auction sells 3 billion flowers and 400 million plants, coming from 8,000 nurseries. Get there early to see the biggest array of flowers in the distribution rooms and to have as much time as possible to watch the computerized auctioning process, which works basically like the old "Beat the Clock" game on television—the first one to press the button gets the posies. In keeping with a Dutch auctioneering philosophy that demands quick handling for perishable goods, the bidding on flowers goes from high to low instead of proceeding in the usual direction of bidding—up. Mammoth bidding clocks are numbered from 100 to 1. The buyers, many of whom are buying for the French and German markets, sit in rows in the four auditorium-style auction halls; they have microphones to ask questions and buttons to push to register their bids in the central computer (which takes care of all the paperwork). As the bunches of tulips or daffodils go by the stand on carts, they are auctioned in a matter of seconds. The first bid, which is the first one to stop the clock as it works down from 100 to 1, is the only bid. Around 600 lots change hands every hour. Whether or not its tactics are really for the sake of the freshness of the flowers, the Aalsmeer Flower Auction is smart Dutch business.

The auction is held Monday to Friday 7:30 to 11am. The entrance fee to the auction is Dfl 5 ($2.15) for adults, free for children 12 and under. Aalsmeer lies some 10 miles (16km) south of Amsterdam, close to Schiphol Airport. To drive there it is best to take the A4 (E19) south to the Hoofddorp junction, then go southeast on the N201. Bus 172 will take you there from Amsterdam Centraal Station.

6 The Cheese Towns

ALKMAAR
30km (19 miles) NW of Amsterdam

Every Friday morning during the long Dutch summer season there's a steady parade of tourists leaving Amsterdam to visit the ✪ **Alkmaar Cheese Market** in the small city of Alkmaar, northwest of Amsterdam, and it's quite a show they're on their way to see.

Trains depart at least every hour from Amsterdam Centraal Station to Alkmaar, and buses every half hour or so. By car from Amsterdam, take the A8 and A9 north, via Zaanstad. **VVV Alkmaar,** Waagplein 2–3 (☎ **072/511-4284;** fax 072/511-7513; www.peninsulaholland.com) in the town center, is open Monday 10am to 5:30pm, Tuesday and Wednesday 9am to 5:30pm, Thursday 9am to 9pm, Friday 9am to 6pm, and Saturday 9:30am to 5pm.

Cheeses are piled high on the cobblestone square and the carillon in the **Weigh House** tower drowns the countryside in Dutch folk music. Around the square dart the white-clad cheese carriers whose lacquered straw hats tell you which of four sections of their medieval guild they belong to: red, blue, yellow, or green. Carriers are so proud of their standards that every week they post on a "shame board" the name of any carrier who has indulged in profanity or has been late arriving at the auction. The square is filled with sightseers, barrel organs, souvenir stalls, and a tangible excitement.

The bidding process is carried on in the traditional Dutch manner of hand clapping to bid the price up or down, and a good solid hand clap to seal the deal. Then, once a buyer has accumulated his lot of cheeses, teams of guild members move in with their shiny, shallow barrows, and, using slings that hang from their shoulders, carry the golden wheels and balls of cheese to the Weigh House for the final tally of the bill. The market takes place from mid-April to mid-September, Friday from 10am to noon.

While you're in Alkmaar, there are a few other attractions you may want to see, including the **Old Craft Market** (also held on Friday from 10am to noon); the **House with the Cannonball,** a souvenir of the Spanish siege; and the **Remonstraat Church,** a clandestine church in a former granary.

EDAM
18km (11 miles) NE of Amsterdam

A short way inland from the IJsselmeer and about 5km (3 miles) north of Volendam, Edam has given its name to one of Holland's most famous cheeses. Don't expect to find it in the familiar red skin, though—that's for export. In Holland the skin is yellow. This pretty little town (pronounced *Ay*-dam) is centered around canals you cross by way of drawbridges, with views on either side of lovely canal houses, beautiful gardens, and canal-side teahouses.

ESSENTIALS

GETTING THERE Edam has no train station, but buses depart every hour or so from Amsterdam Centraal Station.

By car from Amsterdam, drive via Volendam (see "The IJsselmeer," above).

VISITOR INFORMATION VVV Edam is at the Stadhuis (Town Hall), Damplein 1 (☎ **0299/371-727;** fax 0299/374-236) in the town center.

WHAT TO SEE & DO

This was once a port of some prominence, and a visit to the **Captain's House,** just opposite the Town Hall, gives you a peek not only at its history but also at some of its most illustrious citizens of past centuries (look for the portrait of Pieter Dirksz, one-time mayor and proud possessor of what is probably the longest beard on record anywhere). Take a look at the lovely "wedding room" in the Town Hall, and if you visit during summer months, don't miss the cheese-making display at the **Kaaswaag (Weigh House).** The **Speeltoren (carillon tower)** tilts a bit and was very nearly lost when the church to which it belonged was destroyed. The carillon dates from 1561.

GOUDA

40km (25 miles) S of Amsterdam

Try to come here on a Thursday morning between 9am and noon during July and August, when the lively Gouda (pronounced *How*-dah, with a guttural *h*) cheese market brings farmers driving farm wagons painted with bright designs and piled high with round cheeses in orange skins. It's an altogether different scene from the market in Alkmaar.

ESSENTIALS

GETTING THERE There is train service every hour from Amsterdam via Leiden or Rotterdam to Gouda.

By car from Amsterdam, take A4 and N207 south.

VISITOR INFORMATION VVV Gouda, Markt 27 (☎ **0900/468-3288;** fax 0182/583-210), is open Monday to Saturday from 9am to 5pm.

WHAT TO SEE & DO

If you arrive on ✪ **cheese market day,** walk to the back of the **Stadhuis (Town Hall),** where you can sample the famous Gouda cheese. This gray stone building, with stepped gables and red shutters, is reputed to be Holland's oldest Town Hall, and parts of its Gothic facade date from 1449.

Gouda has been the center of a thriving **clay pipe industry** since the 17th century. One local style of pipe has a pattern on the bowl that's invisible when the pipe is new and only appears as the pipe is smoked and darkens; it's called a "mystery pipe," because the designs vary and the buyer never knows what the design will be. Gouda is also noted for its **candles.** Every year, from the middle of December, the market and the Town Hall are lit by candles.

Adrie Moerings Pottenbakkerij & Pijpenmakerij (Pottery and Pipemaker). Peperstraat 76. ☎ **0182/512-842.** Free admission. Mon–Fri 9am–5pm, Sat 11am–5pm.

This interesting factory, just a 5-minute walk from Markt, presents fascinating demonstrations of the centuries-old craft of making beautiful pottery and clay pipes.

You can watch the work going on and visit the pottery exposition and viewing room. This is a good place to pick up a uniquely Dutch memento of your visit.

Catharina Gasthuis Museum. Oosthaven 10. ☎ **0182/588-440.** Admission Dfl 5 ($2.15), ticket also valid in De Moriaan Museum. Mon–Sat 10am–5pm, Sun noon–5pm.

Gouda's municipal museum is in a 1665 mansion and former hospital. The jewel of its collections is a gold chalice that Countess Jacqueline of Bavaria presented to the Society of Archers in 1465. Its whereabouts were unknown for more than a century before it was recovered in the Town Hall's attic and brought here. There are also colorful guild relics, antique furniture, and a terra-cotta plaque whose Latin inscription proclaims that the humanist Erasmus may have been born in Rotterdam but was conceived in Gouda.

De Moriaan Museum. Westhaven 29. ☎ **0182/588-440.** Admission Dfl 5 ($2.15), ticket valid in the Catharina Gasthuis Museum. Mon–Fri 10am–5pm, Sat 10am–12:30pm and 1:30–5pm, Sun and holidays noon–5pm.

During the 18th century, this was the home of a Gouda merchant who sold spices, tobacco, coffee, and tea. The interior of his shop remained unchanged over the centuries. Going through to the back rooms, you find a large pipe collection. Upstairs is a beautiful display of *plateel,* a colorful local pottery that is Gouda's answer to Delftware.

Molen De Roode Leeuw (Red Lion Windmill). Vest 65 (west of Markt). ☎ **0182/522-041.** Admission Dfl 3 ($1.30). Thurs 9am–2pm and Sat 9am–4pm.

Completely renovated, this 1727 grain mill is again grinding away happily. You can go out on the platform and watch the vanes swish past, while inside, the huge wooden cogwheels and beams work the millstones. You can buy flour ground in the mill.

✪ **Sint-Janskerk (Church of St John).** Achter de Kerk 16 (south of Markt). ☎ **0182/512-684.** Admission Dfl 4 ($1.70). Mar–Oct, Mon–Sat 9am–5pm; Nov–Feb, Mon–Sat 10am–4pm.

Holland's longest church and one of its most majestic holds 64 beautiful stained-glass windows, with 2,412 panels. Some date back as far as the mid-1500s. To see the contrast between that stained-glass art of long ago and the work being carried out today, take a look at the most recent window, no. 28A, commemorating the World War II years in Holland.

✪ **Waag (Weighing House).** Markt 35–36. ☎ **0182/529-996.** Admission Dfl 6 ($2.55) for adults, Dfl 4 ($1.70) for children under 12, free admission for children weighing less than 40 pounds. Apr–Oct, Tues–Sun 1–5pm, Thurs 10am–5pm.

The monumental Weighing House, from 1668, is Gouda's pride. An exhibition inside uses interactive audiovisual media to tell the story of cheese. You get to know all about the manufacturing process, from grass through cow through milk to cheese, and have a chance to taste the finished product. The museum also explains Gouda's importance as a center of Dutch dairy production.

WHERE TO DINE

Mallemolen. Oosthaven 72. ☎ **0182/515-430.** Reservations recommended. Main courses from Dfl 37.50 ($15.95); 3-course fixed-price dinner Dfl 55 ($23.40). AE, DC, MC, V. Tues–Fri midday–2pm; Tues–Sun 5pm–midnight. CLASSIC FRENCH.

This excellent traditional restaurant is on what's known as "Rembrandt's corner." There's an ancient windmill on the same street. The restaurant has an Old Dutch look, though the cuisine is chiefly French. Dishes include tournedos with goose liver in a red-wine sauce.

7 Den Helder: Gateway to Texel Island

64km (40 miles) N of Amsterdam

Den Helder, at the tip of North Holland Province, is Holland's most important naval base and the site of its Royal Naval College. It has the dubious distinction of being possibly the only port in the world that ever lost a fleet to a company of horsemen. That happened back in January 1794, when the Dutch fleet found itself stuck in the frozen waters between Den Helder and Texel Island. French cavalry simply rode out to the ships and captured them all. The embarrassing defeat was quite a fall from the heights of glory the navy had known a century earlier when Admirals de Ruyter and Tromp led Dutch ships to victory over a combined English and French fleet off this same coast in 1673.

ESSENTIALS

GETTING THERE   There are trains departing at least every hour from Amsterdam Centraal Station to Haarlem, via Alkmaar. There are buses every half hour or so leaving from outside Alkmaar train station. By car from Amsterdam, take the A9 and N9 North, via Alkmaar.

Walking on the Wadden Sea

At low tide, the Wadden Sea, between the northern coast of Holland and the **Wadden Islands,** virtually disappears. The muddy seabed becomes visible, and seabirds feast on mollusks in the sand. At times like these, the Wadden Islands seem even closer to the mainland, and if you feel like walking the mudflats, you can join a *Wadlopen* (Wadden Walking) trip and plow your way across to one of the islands. **Don't attempt this without an official guide (there is a very real danger of being caught by the fast incoming tide); with one it is perfectly safe.**

Several companies, both in Groningen and Friesland, organize guided trips from May to early October. These range from a relatively easy round-trip on the flats to more difficult walks to the islands. Wear shorts and close-fitting ankle-high shoes or boots. The trips are very popular; groups are often as large as 75 to 100 people, with about seven guides to look after you. Weather permitting, you start walking at ebb tide, which can be at the crack of dawn. Soon the safe mainland looks far away, and you may feel lost in the middle of a salty mire trying to suck your feet in deeper with every step. But you get used to it, and your attention will be drawn to the unusual landscape as you realize that this is actually the bottom of a sea that you're walking on, and that in a few hours all this will have disappeared under water again. If you're lucky, you might encounter some seals gallivanting in pools left by the retreating tide or sunbathing on the flats. When you finally reach the island, you have to wait for high tide to be able to go back by boat.

Advance booking is necessary, and prices range from around Dfl 15 to Dfl 50 ($6.40 to $21.30) per person. Longer trips can take about eight hours (including the wait for the boat). For information and reservations, contact the **Wadloopcentrum Pieterburen** (☎ **0595/528-300**) in Pieterburen (Groningen) or **Wadloopcentrum Friesland** (☎ **0518/451-491**) in Holwerd (Friesland).

VISITOR INFORMATION   VVV Den Helder, Bernhardplein 18 (☎ 0223/
625-544; fax 0223/614-888; vvv.denhelder@trif.nl), next to the train station, is open
Monday 1 to 6pm, Tuesday to Friday 9:30am to 6pm, and Saturday 9:30am to 5pm.

WHAT TO SEE & DO

You can visit the **Den Helder Navy Museum** (Helders Marinemuseum), Hoofdgracht
3 (☎ **0223/657-534**), which holds exhibits illustrating the Dutch Royal Navy's
history, and take a look at the state shipyards. Among the ships on display is the
warship *De Schorpioen,* an impressive sight to behold. It was built in France for
the Dutch Navy in 1868. Although it's now safely chained to the quayside, this
steam-driven vessel was once a warship to be reckoned with. Its secret weapon was a
ram below the water line that could deal fatal blows to enemy ships. The steam engine
still works, and you can visit the restored captain's cabin and crew's quarters. While
you're in naval mode, visit the **Dorus Rijkers Lifeboat Museum** (Reddingmuseum
Dorus Rijkers), Bernhardplein 3 (☎ **0223/618-320**), which chronicles the history of
the service. The National Fleet Festival is held at Den Helder for 3 days during July.

AFSLUITDIJK (ENCLOSING DIKE)

It's impossible to grasp just what a monumental work this great barrier that begins
18km (11 miles) east of Den Helder and separates the Waddenzee from the IJsselmeer
is until you've driven its 30km (19-mile) length. Dr. Cornelis Lely came up with
the plans in 1891, but work was delayed for 25 years as he tried to convince the
government to allocate funds for its construction.

Massive effort and backbreaking labor went into this 300-foot-wide dike that stands
a full 21 feet above mean water level, keeps back the sea, and converted the salty
Zuiderzee into the freshwater IJsselmeer. Midway along its length, at the point
where the dike was completed in 1932, there's a **monument** to the men who put their
backs to the task and a memorial to Dr. Lely. Stop for a light snack at the cafe in
the monument's base and pick up an illustrated booklet that explains the dike's
construction. Nondrivers will find both a biking path and a pedestrian path along
the dike.

TEXEL

66km (41 miles) N of Amsterdam

During the summer months, it's a great idea to take the 20-minute ferry trip from Den
Helder to Texel (pronounced *Tess*-uhl), a quiet, family-oriented resort island in the
Waddenzee. Texel is the biggest and most populated of the Wadden Islands—with a
permanent population of less than 14,000, that's not saying much—and the only one
that can be reached directly from North Holland Province (though a tourist ferry
operates between the north of Texel and neighboring Vlieland island from May to
September). It has the serenity intrinsic to islands, even allowing for the many visitors
who pour in during summer. Beaches, boating, cycling, and bird-watching are the big
attractions here, yet eating, drinking, and partying have their place too.

ESSENTIALS

GETTING THERE   The TESO company's car ferries *Molengat* and *Schulpengat* sail
every hour at peak times from Den Helder to 't Horntje on Texel—a half-hour trip—
from 6:35am (8:35am on Sunday and public holidays) to 9:35pm. Reservations are
not accepted. There is a connecting bus service every hour from Den Helder railroad
station to the ferry terminal.

VISITOR INFORMATION   VVV Texel is at Emmalaan 66, Den Burg (☎ **0222/312-847;** fax 0222/314-129; www.texel.net), just off N501, the main road into town, is open Monday to Friday 9am to 6pm, and Saturday 9am to 5:30pm.

WHAT TO SEE & DO

Unlike some of the Wadden Islands, cars are allowed on Texel, but there's no doubt that the best way to get around and to respect the island's environment is to go by bicycle. Bikes can be brought over free on the ferry, or rented from dozens of outlets in the island's "capital," **Den Burg,** and from the other villages dotted around the coast.

Some 300 bird species have been observed on Texel, of which around 100 breed here. A short list of the star performers includes oystercatchers, Bewicks swans, spoonbills, Brent geese, avocets, marsh harriers, snow buntings, ringed plovers, kestrels, short-eared owls, and bar-tailed godwits. They can be seen in one of the three protected **nature reserves** that are open to the public: the **Schorren, Bol,** and **Dijkmanshuizen** reserves. Visitors must enter on guided tours organized by the **Natuurmonumenten,** Polderweg 2, De Waal (☎ **022/318-757**); call evenings only.

Nature trails through areas belonging to the **Staatsbosbeheer (State Forest Authority)** abound in the dunes and wooded areas, and can be freely visited as long as you stick to the marked paths. Guided tours of some of these areas are organized by ✪ **Ecomare,** Ruyslaan 92, De Koog (☎ **0222/317-741**). Ecomare's vistor center is also a seal rehabilitation facility—the waters around Texel used to be rich in seals until their numbers were greatly reduced by a virus in 1988. Ecomare assists with their recovery by caring for weak and injured seals until they are strong enough to be returned to the sea. A bird rehabilitation scheme does the same for avian life threatened by pollution and other hazards. Ecomare also offers temporary exhibitions.

8 Castle Country

MUIDEN

13km (8 miles) E of Amsterdam

The perfect starting point for a lovely day in the Middle Ages is the **Rijksmuseum Muiderslot,** near the small town of Muiden at Herengracht 1 (☎ **0294/261-325**). This is a turreted, fairy-tale-princess sort of castle—complete with moat—that perches on the far bank of the river Vecht, just 13km (8 miles) east of Amsterdam. Go there to see where Count Floris V was living when he granted toll privileges and thereby officially recognized the small, new community of "Aemstelledamme" in 1275, and where he was murdered just 20 years later. By car from Amsterdam, take the Muiden junction of the A1 (E231) east of Amsterdam. There is no VVV office in Muiden.

Muiderslot is where poet P. C. Hooft found both a home and employment—and, I suppose, inspiration for romantic images and lofty phraseology—when he served as castle steward and local bailiff for 40 years in the early 17th century. The castle is furnished essentially as Hooft and his artistic circle of friends (known in Dutch literary history as the Muiden Circle) knew it, with plenty of examples of the distinctly Dutch carved cupboard beds, heavy chests, fireside benches, and mantelpieces. The castle is open April to September, Monday to Friday 10am to 5pm and Sunday 1 to 5pm (last tour at 4pm); from October to March, Saturday and Sunday only 1 to 4pm (last tour 3pm). Admission is Dfl 10 ($4.25) for adults, Dfl 7.50 ($3.20) for seniors and children 4 to 12, and free for children under 4.

NAARDEN
19km (12 miles) E of Amsterdam

Just beyond Muiderslot is the still-fortified small town of Naarden, where, much in the spirit of locking the barn door after the horse was gone, the local inhabitants erected their beautiful star-shaped double fortifications after the town was brutally sacked by Don Frederick of Toledo and his boys in the late 16th century. Beneath the Turfpoort Bastion, you can visit the casemates (the artillery vaults) at the **Nederlands Vestingmuseum (Dutch Fortifications Museum),** Westwalstraat 6 (☎ **035/694-5459**), open from Easter to October, Tuesday to Friday (Monday also in summer) 10:30am to 5pm and Saturday, Sunday, and holidays noon to 5pm; November to Easter Sunday noon to 5pm. Admission is Dfl 10 ($4.25) for adults, Dfl 7.50 ($3.20) for children 5 to 16, and free for children under 5.

Also see the 15th-century **Grote Kerk,** on Marktstraat (☎ **035/694-9873**), renowned for its fine acoustics and annual performances of Bach's *St. Matthew Passion.* The Grote Kerk is open June to September daily 1 to 4pm.

There are trains every hour or so to Naarden from Amsterdam Centraal Station. By car from Amsterdam, take the A1 (E231) east. The **VVV Naarden (Gooi and Vechtsreek)** is at Adriaan Dortsmanplein 1B (☎ **035/694-2836;** fax 035/694-3424), inside the walls of the old town.

DE HAAR
29km (18 miles) SE of Amsterdam

One of the more richly furnished castles you can visit in Holland—and one that's still owner-occupied part of the year—is **Kasteel de Haar,** Kasteellaan 1 (☎ **030/677-1275**), at Haarzuilens near Utrecht. Like most castles, De Haar has had its ups and downs—fires and ransackings and the like—over the centuries, but thanks to an infusion of Rothschild money in the early 1900s, it now sits in all its 15th-century moated splendor in the middle of a gracious Versailles-like formal garden. Its walls are hung with fine paintings and precious Gobelin tapestries of the 14th and 15th centuries; its floors are softened with Persian rugs; and its chambers are furnished in the styles of Louis XIV, XV, and XVI of France. The castle is open March 1 to August 19 and October 12 to November 15, Monday to Friday 11am to 4pm and Sunday and public holidays 1 to 4pm (these dates and times are subject to constant change, so phone before going). Admission is Dfl 16 ($6.80) for adults, Dfl 10 ($4.25) for children 5 to 12, and free for children under 5. The castle is a few miles south, then west, from the Maarssen Junction of the A2 (E35) Amsterdam-Utrecht expressway.

9 The Hague & Scheveningen
63km (43 miles) SW of Amsterdam

Amsterdam may be the capital of the Netherlands, but The Hague ('s-Gravenhage, or more commonly Den Haag, in Dutch) has always been the seat of government and the official residence of the Dutch monarchs, whether or not they chose to live there (Juliana, when she was queen, preferred to live near Utrecht, whereas Queen Beatrix has chosen Huis ten Bosch in The Hague Woods as her home). In 1998 the city celebrated its 750th anniversary—it was in 1248 that Count William II of Holland was crowned king of the Romans in the German city of Aachen, but he chose to live at the Binnenhof Palace in what is now The Hague.

The Hague, only 43 miles from Amsterdam, is a beautiful and sophisticated city full of parks and elegant homes, with an 18th-century French look that suits its role as the diplomatic center of the Dutch nation and the site of the International Court of Justice (housed in the famous Peace Palace). Among the city's attractions are a number of fine antiques shops and a weekly antiques and curios market May to September, on Thursday and Sunday 10am to 5pm; October to May, on Thursday noon to 6pm. (An ironic counterpoint to The Hague's genteel image is that it has the worst reputation in Holland for soccer-related hooliganism—some supporters of FC Den Haag behave like Visigoths on match days.)

The beach resort and fishing port of Scheveningen is so close it seems to be part of the same city. Scheveningen exhibits a curious combination of costumed fishermen's wives (they only dress up in their traditional Dutch garb for special events, such as *Vlaggetjesdag*—Flag Day—in mid-May when the first of the new season's herring are landed) near the harbor and tuxedoed croupiers from the casino across from the beautifully restored 19th-century **Kurhaus Hotel.** This is probably the most chic seaside resort in Holland (though as with seaside resorts the world over, that is not necessarily saying much), with the usual cast of international-name boutiques and upscale restaurants.

ESSENTIALS

GETTING THERE   The Hague makes an easy day trip from Amsterdam, with frequent train and bus service. Be advised that The Hague has two major train stations, Centraal and Hollands Spoor; most of the sights are closer to Centraal Station, but some trains only stop at Hollands Spoor. A "Schiphol Line" offers fast rail service (30 minutes) to Amsterdam's airport. When driving from Amsterdam, take the A4.

Scheveningen is about 3 miles from The Hague. Take tram lines 1 and 9 from Den Haag Centraal Station to Gevers Deynootplein, or drive via A44 and follow the signs.

VISITOR INFORMATION   Tourist information is available from **The Hague Visitors & Convention Bureau,** Nassaulaan 25 (☎ **070/361-8820;** fax 070/361-5459), and from **VVV Den Haag,** Koningin Julianaplein (☎ **0900/ 340-3505;** fax 070/347-2102; www.denhaag.nl), in front of Centraal Station; open September to June Monday to Saturday 9am to 5:30pm; July and August Monday to Saturday 9am to 5:30pm, Sunday 11am to 5pm.

WHAT TO SEE & DO IN THE HAGUE

Perhaps the most notable attraction of The Hague is the impressive **Binnenhof,** or Inner Court, a complex of Parliament buildings located at Binnenhof 8a (open Monday to Saturday from 10am to 4pm). You can join a tour to visit the lofty, medieval **Ridderzaal (Hall of the Knights),** in which the queen delivers a speech from the throne each year. If you're in Holland on the third Tuesday in September, be sure to be there to see her arrive and depart in her real golden coach—like Cinderella—drawn by high-stepping royal horses; it's quite a spectacle. Depending on the volume and urgency of governmental business, you can tour one or the other of the two chambers of the **States General,** the Dutch Parliament. The last guided tour starts at 3:45pm and the cost is Dfl 5 or Dfl 6 ($2.15 or $2.55) for adults, Dfl 4 or Dfl 5 ($1.70 or $2.15) for seniors and children 13 and under, depending on the exact tour being offered at the time. It's requested that you book in advance by telephone (☎ **070/364-6144**) if you intend to take the guided tour—call ahead in any case to make sure tours are being given on the day you intend to visit. Admission to the Parliament exhibition in the reception room of the Hall of Knights is free.

Adjacent to the Binnenhof Parliament complex is the elegant Italian Renaissance-style ✪ **Mauritshuis,** Korte Vijverberg 8 (☎ **070/302-3435**), which was built in 1644 as the architecturally innovative home of a young court dandy and cousin of the

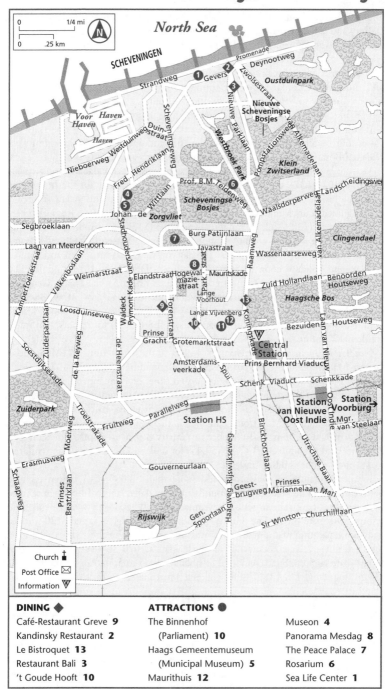

The Hague & Scheveningen

North Sea

SCHEVENINGEN

Voor Haven
Haven

DINING ◆
Café-Restaurant Greve **9**
Kandinsky Restaurant **2**
Le Bistroquet **13**
Restaurant Bali **3**
't Goude Hooft **10**

ATTRACTIONS ●
The Binnenhof
(Parliament) **10**
Haags Gemeentemuseum
(Municipal Museum) **5**
Mauritshuis **12**

Museon **4**
Panorama Mesdag **8**
The Peace Palace **7**
Rosarium **6**
Sea Life Center **1**

Church
Post Office
Information

Orange-Nassaus. Today this small palace is officially known as the **Royal Picture Gallery** and is the permanent home of an impressive art collection given to the Dutch nation by King Willem I in 1816. Highlights include 13 Rembrandts, three Frans Hals, and three Vermeers (including the famous *View of Delft*), plus hundreds of other famous works by such painters as Breughel, Rubens, Steen, and Holbein (including his famous portrait of Jane Seymour, third wife of Henry VIII of England). The gallery is open Tuesday to Saturday 10am to 5pm and Sunday 11am to 5pm. Admission is Dfl 13.50 ($5.75) for adults, Dfl 7.50 ($3.20) for seniors and children 18 and under.

If you have an interest in royalty and palaces, take a ride on bus no. 4; its route passes four Dutch palaces built during the 16th and 17th centuries, including Palace Huis ten Bosch, the home of Queen Beatrix (no visits are permitted).

Venture beyond the city center to visit the famous **Peace Palace,** Carnegieplein 2 (☎ **070/302-4137**), donated by Andrew Carnegie as a home for the International Court of Justice and the Permanent Court of Arbitration. The palace is open for hourly guided tours Monday to Friday 10am to 4pm (10am to 3pm from October to May). Tours cost Dfl 6 ($2.55) for adults and Dfl 3 ($1.30) for children 12 and under. Also stop at the impressive center of popular sciences, **Museon,** Stadhouderslaan 41 (☎ **070/338-1305**), which is open Tuesday to Friday 10am to 5pm and Saturday, Sunday, and holidays noon to 5pm. Admission is Dfl 12 ($5.10) for adults, Dfl 8 ($3.40) for children 5 to 12, and free for children under 5. The **Haags Gemeente-museum (Municipal Art Museum),** Stadhouderslaan 41 (☎ **070/338-1111**), designed by Hendrik Petrus Berlage (1927–34), is open Tuesday to Sunday 11am to 5pm. Admission is Dfl 12 ($5.10) for adults, Dfl 8 ($3.40) for seniors, and free for children 12 and under.

Not far away in the Scheveningen Woods is the enchanting ✪ **Madurodam,** George Maduroplein 1 (☎ **070/355-3900**), a miniature village in 1-to-25 scale that represents the Dutch nation in actual proportions of farmland to urban areas. It presents many of the country's most historic buildings in miniature, with lights that actually work, bells that ring, and trains that run efficiently—as all do in Holland. It's open daily March to May from 9am to 10pm, June to August 9am to 11pm, in September 9am to 9pm, and October to January 3 9am to 6pm. Admission is Dfl 22.50 ($9.55) for adults, Dfl 17.50 ($7.45) for seniors, Dfl 15 ($6.40) for children 4 to 11, and free for children under 4.

In the **Rosarium** in Westbroekpark, more than 20,000 roses bloom each year between July and September. The grounds are open daily 9am to 1 hour before sunset.

If you don't have time to visit Scheveningen from The Hague, you can still see the resort town, sort of, at The Hague's **Panorama Mesdag,** a superb 120-yard-long panoramic painting of the resort as it was in 1880, done in the style of The Hague school. It can be seen at Zeestraat 65 in The Hague (☎ **070/364-4544**) Monday to Saturday 10am to 5pm, Sunday and public holidays noon to 5pm. Admission is Dfl 7.50 ($3.20) for adults, Dfl 4 ($1.70) for children 3 to 13, and free for children under 3.

WHAT TO SEE & DO IN SCHEVENINGEN

The attractions of **Scheveningen** are no longer limited to bicycling on the dunes, deep-sea fishing in the North Sea, and splashing in the waves at the beach or in a wave pool (an indoor/outdoor heated swimming pool that has mechanically produced surf). The city's indoor amusements, which have long included blackjack and roulette at the **Holland Casino Scheveningen,** Kurhausweg 1 (☎ **070/306-7777**), opposite the Kurhaus Hotel, have been supplemented by video games and pinball machines at the beautiful old Scheveningen Pier jutting out into the North Sea, shopping and noshing at the Palace Promenade shopping mall, and, of course, fish dinners at the restaurants around the harbor (where you just might catch a glimpse of a fisherman's wife wearing the traditional costume of Scheveningen). The beach and bathing zone is called Scheveningen Bad—but it looks pretty good to the Dutch.

Tourist information is available from **VVV Scheveningen,** Gevers Deynootweg 1134 (☎ **0900/340-3505;** fax 070/361-5495; www.denhaag.com), at the Palace Promenade shopping mall.

The **Sea Life Center,** Strandweg (aka the Boulevard) 13 (☎ **070/354-2100**), takes you under the sea in an aquarium with a walk-through underwater tunnel, from where you can see the denizens of the deep, including sharks, swimming around above your head. The center is open daily 10am to 6pm (10am to 8pm in July and August) and costs Dfl 16 ($6.80) for adults, Dfl 12 ($5.10) for seniors, Dfl 10 ($4.25) for children 4 to 11, and is free for children under 4.

WHERE TO DINE

Café-Restaurant Greve. Torenstraat 138. ☎ **070/360-3919.** Main courses Dfl 25–32 ($10.65–$13.60); 3-course dinner Dfl 45 ($19.15). AE, DC, MC, V. Cafe, daily 10am–1am; restaurant, Mon–Sat 6–11pm, Sun 6–10pm. MEDITERRANEAN.

What was once a car showroom is now a popular cafe-restaurant. The large windows of the cafe look out on the lively Torenstraat; the restaurant is more intimate with its low ceiling, candlelight, and wooden tables. There's a small à la carte menu, but together with the list of daily specials it's very difficult to make a choice. You can choose a dish either as a starter or as a main course, which is an ideal solution for small appetites (or when you just want a taste from every dish on the menu!). Fish and lamb dishes, like bouillabaisse or lamb cutlets with feta cheese and ouzo sauce, are popular.

✪ **Kandinsky Restaurant.** In the Steigenberger Kurhaus Hotel, Gevers Deynootplein 30. ☎ **070/416-2634.** Main courses Dfl 45–75 ($19.15–$31.90); 5-course menu du chef Dfl 105 ($44.70). AE, DC, MC, V. Mon–Fri noon–2pm; daily 6–10:30pm. No lunches served July–Aug. FRENCH/MEDITERRANEAN.

Save your most special Scheveningen meal for this small, exquisite restaurant, officially opened by Mme Claude Pompidou, widow of the late French president. Beside the beach, the dining room overlooks the sea and its decor features signed lithographs by abstract artist Wassily Kandinsky. The cuisine here is classic French plus some Italian and other Mediterranean variations, and you can order vintage wines by the glass. The Kurhaus serves a lavish buffet daily for Dfl 45 ($19.15) for lunch and Dfl 52.50 to Dfl 62.50 ($22.35 to $26.60) for dinner, both spread in the gorgeous Kurzaal area, where dancing is added to dinner on Friday and Saturday nights at only slightly elevated prices.

Le Bistroquet. Lange Voorhout 98. ☎ **070/360-1170.** Reservations required. Main courses Dfl 39.50–57.50 ($16.80–$24.45). AE, DC, MC, V. Mon–Fri noon–2pm; Mon–Sat 6–10:30pm. FRENCH.

This small and very popular restaurant in the city center is one of The Hague's best. The quietly elegant dining room features lovely table settings. The menu is mostly French and includes lamb, fish, and fresh vegetables.

Restaurant Bali. Badhuisweg 1. ☎ **070/350-2434.** Reservations required. Rijsttafel from Dfl 57.50 ($24.45). AE, DC, MC, V. Mon–Sat 5–10pm, Sun 4–10pm. INDONESIAN.

Since 1946, the Bali has been serving a superb rijsttafel, and over the years, it has become widely recognized as the best in the region. An Indonesian staff in native dress brings you the beautifully prepared, spicy dishes. In the adjoining Bali bar, international cocktails are served with expertise. Try the Bali Mystery after dinner—and don't ask me its ingredients; all I know is that it's great. The restaurant is a short walk from the sea.

✪ **'t Goude Hooft.** Groenmarkt 13. ☎ **070/346-9713.** Main courses Dfl 27.50–39.50 ($11.70–$16.80); fixed-price 3-course lunch Dfl 35 ($14.90); fixed-price 3–6 course dinner Dfl 39.50–85 ($16.80–$36.15). AE, DC, MC, V. Mon–Sat 10am–midnight, Sun 11am–midnight. DUTCH.

There's a definite old Dutch flavor to this wonderful, large, happy restaurant overlooking the Market Square, yet its 1600s exterior cloaks a 1938 interior installed after a disastrous fire. The wooden beams, brass chandeliers, and rustic chairs and tables blend harmoniously with the stained-glass windows. There's a large terrace cafe overlooking the "Green Market" square, pleasant on sunny days, and the long menu covers everything from snacks to light lunches to full dinners, and the budget-priced tourist menu. This is a good place to drop by for just a beer or coffee. Highly recommended.

10 Rotterdam

75km (51 miles) S of Amsterdam

For a change from the thick blanket of history in and around Amsterdam, consider a visit to this modern Dutch city. Here, instead of the usual Dutch web of little streets and alleyways, there's a spacious and elegant shopping mall; and instead of Amsterdam's miles of winding canals, there's the biggest and busiest ocean harbor in the world.

Rotterdam is a fascinating place to see and experience, particularly when you consider that this city was a living monument to Holland's Golden Age until it was bombed to rubble during World War II. At the war's end, rather than try to re-create the old, Rotterdammers looked on their misfortune as an opportunity and approached their city as a clean slate. They relished the chance—unique in Holland—to create an efficient, elegant, and workable modern city and the results are a testimony to their ability to find impressive solutions to their problems. (Rotterdammers are said to be born with their sleeves already rolled up.)

By the time the workers had finished, they had dredged a long deep-water channel and filled in the shallow banks of the estuary that connected the city with the North Sea to create a 20-mile-long harbor called the **Europoort** (pronounced the same as "port" in English) that now handles more cargo and more ships every year than any other port in the world (250 million tons of cargo annually). You may think that visiting a harbor is boring business on a vacation, but Rotterdam's makes any other harbor you've ever seen look like a Fisher-Price toy! One of the most memorable sights in Holland is the ship-jammed channel of Rotterdam harbor. Container ships, bulk carriers, tankers, sleek greyhounds of the sea, and careworn tramps, all are waited on by a vast retinue of machines and humans. Trucks, trains, and barges, each carrying its little piece of the action, hurry outward from the hub only to be drawn back again as if by gravity. Rotterdam is the pump that replenishes Europe's commercial arteries.

ESSENTIALS

GETTING THERE   Two trains run each hour around the clock from Amsterdam to Rotterdam's Centraal Station; the trip takes 50 minutes. Buses from Amsterdam arrive at Centraal Station. When driving from Amsterdam, take A4 to The Hague, then A13 to Rotterdam.

VISITOR INFORMATION   VVV Rotterdam, Coolsingel 67 (☎ **0900/ 403-4065;** fax 010/413-0124; www.vvv.rotterdam.nl), on the corner of Stadhuisplein, is reached by tram no. 1, or the Stadhuis stop of the Metro. The office is open Monday to Thursday 9:30am to 6pm, Friday 9:30am to 9pm, Saturday 9:30am to 5pm, and Sunday (April to September) noon to 5pm.

WHAT TO SEE & DO

The first thing to do in Rotterdam is to take a **Spido Harbor Trip** (via Metro to Leuvehaven station; ☎ 010/413-5400). Departures are every 30 to 45 minutes 9:30am to 5pm, April to September; two to four times per day, October to March. The season of the year will determine how much of the vast Europoort you'll be able to see, but it's an unforgettable experience to board a boat that seems large in comparison to the canal launches of Amsterdam—two tiers of indoor seating and open decks—and then feel dwarfed by the hulking oil tankers and container ships that glide like giant whales into their berths along the miles of docks. The basic harbor trip, offered year-round, is a 75-minute tour of the city's waterfront; between April and September, it's possible to take an extended (2¼-hour) trip daily at 10am and 12:30pm; and on a limited schedule in July and August, you can make all-day excursions to the sluices of the Delta Works and along the full length of the Europoort. Prices vary according to the trip, but run from Dfl 16.50 to Dfl 49.50 ($7 to $21.05) for adults and Dfl 8 to Dfl 25 ($3.40 to $10.65) for children 3 to 11. There's a music/dinner cruise offered from April to November that costs Dfl 99.50 ($42.35), which includes the cruise, a welcome cocktail, a four-course meal, two glasses of wine, and coffee. A reservation is absolutely necessary.

Back on dry land, the nearby **Boymans-van Beuningen Museum,** Museumpark 18–20 (☎ 010/441-9400), is another of Holland's treasure troves of fine art. In this case, however, Dutch painters share wall space with an international contingent that includes Salvador Dalí and Man Ray, Titian and Tintoretto, Degas and Daumier. Plus, there are fine collections of porcelain, silver, glass, and Delftware. The museum houses a gift shop and a restaurant where you can have a quick lunch. It's open Tuesday to Saturday 10am to 5pm and Sunday and holidays 11am to 5pm (closed New Year's Day and April 30). Admission is Dfl 8 ($3.40) for adults, Dfl 6 ($2.55) for children 4 to 16.

Not all of Rotterdam is spanking new. One of the neighborhoods spared by the German bombers is the tiny harbor area known as **Delfshaven (Harbor of Delft),** where the Puritan Separatists known as the Pilgrims embarked on the first leg of their trip to Massachusetts. This is a pleasant place to spend an afternoon. You can wander into the church in which the Pilgrims prayed before departure, peek into antiques shops and galleries, and check on the progress of housing renovations in this historic area.

Two interesting places to visit in Delfshaven are the **Sack Carriers' Guild House,** Voorstraat 13–15 (☎ 010/477-2664), where artisans demonstrate the art of pewter casting, and the adjoining warehouses that make up **De Dubbelde Palm-Boom (Double Palm Tree Historical Museum),** Voorhaven 12 (☎ 010/476-1533), which displays objects unearthed during the excavations of Rotterdam. Both are open Tuesday to Friday 10am to 5pm, Saturday, Sunday, and public holidays 11am to 5pm (closed New Year's Day and April 30).

WHERE TO DINE

✪ **Henkes' Brasserie.** Voorhaven 17 (in old Delfshaven). ☎ **010/425-5596.** Main courses Dfl 31.50–36.50 ($13.40–$15.55); fixed-price 3-course dinner Dfl 47.50 ($20.20). AE, DC, MC, V. Daily 11:30am–midnight;kitchen closes at 10pm. CONTINENTAL.

Henkes' Brasserie is an ideal place to appreciate the special atmosphere of old Delfshaven. The waterside terrace invites you to while away a sunny afternoon, interrupted only by a leisurely stroll down the harbor, then to return for dinner. Inside,the old Henkes' jenever (Dutch gin) distillery has been completely transformed; the interior now features the furnishings of a 19th-century Belgian insurance bank.

Rotterdam

HOLLAND

Rotterdam

The warm woodwork and brass chandeliers create a dining room on a grand scale. You can enjoy seafood and meat dishes, or seasonal specialties like venison with a chocolate-port sauce.

Restaurant Engels. Stationsplein 45 (next to Centraal Station in the huge *Groothandelsgebouw,* or Business Center). ☎ **010/411-9550.** Main courses Dfl 25.50–39.50 ($10.85–$16.80); fixed-price 3-course dinner in Don Quijote and Tokaj and Sun brunch in Brasserie Engels Dfl 39.50 ($16.80); Carvery buffet in the Beefeater Dfl 29.50–45 ($12.55–$19.15). AE, DC, MC, V. Daily 8am–1am. INTERNATIONAL/LIGHT FARE.

This marvelous eatery is actually a complex of four restaurants, each dedicated to a different international cuisine: Don Quijote (Spanish), Tokaj (Hungarian), The Beefeater (British), and Brasserie Engels (Dutch/Continental). Tokaj and Don Quijote offer live music. There's an à la carte menu (full dinners, light meals, sandwiches, omelettes, snacks) and a vegetarian menu.

THE WINDMILLS OF KINDERDIJK

There are three things that stir the soul of a true Hollander: the Dutch flag, the Dutch anthem, and the sight of windmill sails spinning in the breeze. There are 19 water-pumping windmills at Kinderdijk, a tiny community between Rotterdam and Dordrecht; that means 76 mill sails, each with a 14-yard span, all revolving on a summer day. It's a spectacular sight and one of the must-sees of Holland. The mills are in operation on Saturday afternoon in July and August 2:30 to 5:30pm; the visitor's mill is open April to September, Monday to Saturday 9:30am to 5:30pm.

To get there, board a train from Rotterdam's Centraal Station to Rotterdam's Lombardijen Station; from there, take Bus 154 to Kinderdijk. If you're driving, take the N207 toward Bergambacht and then board the ferry across the river Lek. On the other side, turn right and follow the road along the river toward Kinderdijk.

11 Utrecht

42km (26 miles) SE of Amsterdam

When the Dutch Republic was established in the late 16th century, Utrecht was one of its more powerful political centers, having been an important bishopric since the earliest centuries of Christianity in Holland. As a result, this is a city of churches; there are more restored medieval religious structures here than in any other city in Europe. Most are in the old heart of town, including the beautiful Domkerk and its adjacent Domtoren, or Dom Tower, the tallest in Holland (and worth a climb). Two other church buildings, the St. Agnes and Catherine Convents, now house two of Utrecht's many fine museums; for centuries these structures filled a variety of roles (orphanages, hospitals, and so on) during the period of Protestant influence in the Netherlands.

Also unique to Utrecht is its bilevel wharf along the Oude Gracht Canal through the Center, where restaurants, shops, and summer cafes have replaced the hustle and bustle of the commercial activity of former times, when Utrecht was a major port along the Rhine.

Commerce continues to be the city's major focus, as you quickly realize if you arrive by train. Centraal Station is in the Hoog Catherijne (High Catherine)—a vast, multitiered, indoor shopping mall that spreads over a 6-block area and traverses both a multilane highway and the web of railway tracks. Another part of the complex is Jaarbeursplein, which holds a 40-room exhibition hall built especially to house the annual Utrecht Trade Fair, at which Dutch industry has presented its best products every year since 1916.

Auberge De Hoefslag **3**
Bisschopes Hof
   (The Bishop's Garden) **5**
Centraal Museum **7**
Domplein **6**
Het Catharijneconvent **8**
Rijksmuseum van Spielklok
   tot Pierement **4**
Stadskasteel Oudaen **1**
't Hoogt **2**

ESSENTIALS

GETTING THERE   Trains depart at least every half hour from Amsterdam Centraal Station to Utrecht. By car from Amsterdam, take the A2 south.

VISITOR INFORMATION   **VVV Utrecht,** Vredenburg 90 (☎ **0900/414-1414;** fax 030/233-1417; info@vvvutrecht.nl), is open Monday to Friday 9am to 6pm, and Saturday 9am to 5pm.

WHAT TO SEE & DO

Don't let Utrecht's modern face dampen your interest in visiting this well-preserved 2,000-year-old city. To tour the city, take a **canal-boat ride,** with Rederij Lovers (☎ **030/231-6468**) or Rederij Schuttevaer (☎ **030/272-0111**), who leave from Nieuwekade; rides are offered Monday to Sunday every hour on the hour 11am to 5pm. At the end of the trip, visit **'t Hoogt,** Hoogt 4, at the corner of Slachstraat. This 17th-century burgher's house is now an art cinema. It's open Monday to Sunday noon to 1am, and admission is Dfl 10 ($4.25) per screening.

   The major attraction in Utrecht is the **Domplein,** where, if you have the stamina and the inclination, you can climb the 465 steps to the top of the **Domtoren,** or Dom Tower (☎ **030/286-4540**). Guided tours take place every hour from May to September daily 10am to 5pm; October to April on weekends only noon to 5pm. Admission is Dfl 6 ($2.55) for adults, Dfl 4 ($1.70) for children 11 and under.

Also, visit the **Domkerk** cathedral (☎ **030/231-0403**), which took almost 3 centuries to build, from 1254 to 1517. The original Romanesque structure was replaced bit by bit; first the choir, then the tower, and finally the nave and transepts. The nave collapsed during a violent storm in 1674 and was never rebuilt; the choir and transepts survived and remain disconnected from the tower. Standing in the cloisters and looking up at the church, you get some impression of how imposing this cathedral must have been. The interior bears traces of the fierce wave of iconoclasm that spread over Holland in the second half of the 16th century. There's a battered altarpiece in one of the side chapels, and a sandstone Holy Sepulcher, dated 1501, shows a defaced Christ in a tomb under a badly damaged Gothic arch. The Domkerk is open every Sunday 2 to 4pm, Monday to Saturday 10am to 5pm May to September, and Monday to Saturday 11am to 4pm October to April. Admission is free.

Other worthwhile sights nearby are the **Bisschopes Hof,** or Bishop's Garden (open daily 11am to 5pm), and the **Dom Kloostergang,** a cloister arcade built in the 15th century, with magnificent stained-glass windows depicting scenes from the legend of St. Martin. Information on any of the sights on or near the Domplein can be obtained by calling ☎ **030/231-0403.**

In another medieval church, visit the merry **National Museum from Music Box to Street Organ** (Rijksmuseum van Spielklok tot Pierement), Buurkerkhof 10 (☎ **030/231-2789**), where you can hear and see 600 different music makers. There are hourly tours Tuesday to Saturday 10am to 5pm and Sunday and holidays noon to 5pm. Admission is Dfl 10 ($4.25) for adults, Dfl 5 ($2.15) for children 4 to 12, and free for children under 4.

Also, be sure to see the exceptional collection of medieval religious art at **Het Catharijneconvent,** Nieuwegracht 63 (☎ **030/231-3835**); it's open Saturday and Sunday 11am to 5pm. The **Centraal Museum,** Agnietenstraat 1 (☎ **030/236-2362**), has a ship from Utrecht that dates from 1200, a number of paintings of the Utrecht artistic school of the 16th century, and a dollhouse that dates from 1680. There's an impressive collection of Dutch modern art and Dutch 20th-century applied art—the De Stijl group—displayed in the former artillery mews on the grounds of the museum. An important item in the Centraal Museum collection is the **Rietveld-Schroder House,** Prins Hendriklaan 50, built in 1924 and designed by Gerrit Rietveld according to the ideas of the De Stijl group. The Rietveld-Schroder House is open Wednesday to Saturday 11am to 5pm and Sunday noon to 5pm, or by appointment. The museum itself is open Tuesday to Saturday 10am to 5pm and Sunday and holidays noon to 5pm. Admission is Dfl 6 ($2.55) for adults and Dfl 3 ($1.30) for children 13 and under.

WHERE TO DINE

✪ **Auberge de Hoefslag.** Vossenlaan 28, Bosch en Duin. ☎ **030/225-1051.** Fixed-price dinner Dfl 95 ($40.45) for 3 courses, Dfl 130 ($55.30) for 4 courses. AE, DC, MC, V. Mon–Sat noon–2:30pm and 5:30–9:30pm. SEAFOOD/GAME/FRENCH.

This beautiful dining spot, located on wooded grounds just a little northeast of Utrecht, is considered by many to be Holland's top restaurant. Amsterdammers think nothing of driving the 30 miles down here for dinner. There's a Victorian garden feel to the lounge, while the dining room is reminiscent of an upscale hunting lodge, with lots of dark wood, an open hearth, and ceiling-to-floor doors opening to the terrace. The de Hoefslag changes its menu daily, setting specials after the chef has returned from the market. The seafood is superb, as are pork, lamb, and game dishes.

Stadskasteel Oudaen. Oudegracht 99. ☎ **030/231-1864.** Main courses Dfl 35–45 ($14.90–$19.15); fixed-price 3-course meals Dfl 52.50 ($22.35); fixed-price 4-course Dfl 72.50 ($30.85); fixed-price 5-course meals Dfl 77.50 ($33). AE, DC, MC, V. Cafe, daily 10am–2am; restaurant, Mon–Sat 5:30–9pm. CONTINENTAL.

This medieval town castle has been transformed into a culinary palace. Downstairs, in what once was the main hall, you can sit in the cafe and savor beer brewed on the premises, according to medieval recipes. Upstairs is the restaurant "Tussen hemel en aarde" ("Between heaven and earth"), with its original fireplace still intact and a rustic tile floor. The menu changes weekly, according to what is freshest and in season.

12 Three Historic Art Towns: Delft, Leiden & Laren

DELFT

54km (34 miles) SW of Amsterdam

Yes, this is the home of the famous blue-and-white porcelain, and you can visit the factory of De Porceleyne Fles where it is produced, but don't let Delftware be your only reason to visit. The small, handsome city is quiet and intimate, with flowers in its flower boxes and linden trees bending over gracious canals. The cradle of the Dutch Republic, Delft is still the burial place of the royal family, and the birthplace and inspiration of artist Jan Vermeer, the 17th-century master of light and subtle emotion.

ESSENTIALS

GETTING THERE   There are frequent rail and bus connections to Delft from Amsterdam and Rotterdam. Delft is connected to The Hague by tram. By car, Delft is just off A13, the main Rotterdam–The Hague motorway.

VISITOR INFORMATION   VVV Delft, Markt 83–85 (☎ **015/212-6100;** fax 015/215-8695; www.vvvdelft.nl), in the center of town, is open Monday to Friday 9am to 5:30pm, and Saturday 9am to 5pm.

WHAT TO SEE & DO

The house where Vermeer was born, lived, and painted is long gone from Delft, as are his paintings. The artist's burial place, the **Oude Kerk,** Roland Holstlaan 753 (☎ **015/212-3015**), a church also noted for its 27 stained-glass windows by Joep Nicolas, is closed for restoration until 2001. You might, however, want to visit the **Nieuwe Kerk,** on the Markt (☎ **015/212-3025**), where Prince William of Orange and all other members of the House of Orange-Nassau are buried. It's open April to October, Monday to Saturday 9am to 6pm; November to March, Monday to Saturday 11am to 4pm. Admission is Dfl 4 ($1.70) for adults, Dfl 2 (85¢) for children 3 to 12, and free for children under 3.

The **Prinsenhof Museum,** St. Agathaplein 1 (☎ **015/260-2358**), on the nearby Oude Delft Canal, is where William I of Orange (William the Silent) lived and had his headquarters in the years when he helped found the Dutch Republic. This is where he was assassinated in 1584 (you can still see the bullet holes in the stairwell). Today the Prinsenhof is a museum of paintings, tapestries, silverware, and pottery, and is the site of the annual Delft Art and Antiques Fair, held in late October or early November. It's open year-round Tuesday to Saturday 10am to 5pm and Sunday 1 to 5pm; June to August, also on Monday 1 to 5pm. Admission is Dfl 6 ($2.55) for adults, Dfl 3 ($1.30) for children under 13.

In the same neighborhood you can see a fine collection of old Delft tiles displayed in the wood-paneled setting of a 19th-century mansion museum called **Lambert van**

Meerten, located at Oude Delft 199 and open Tuesday to Saturday 10am to 5pm and Sunday 1 to 5pm. Or to see brand-new Delftware, and one of the daily demonstrations of the art of hand-painting Delftware, visit the showroom of ✪ **Koninklijke Porceleyne Fles,** Rotterdamseweg 196 (☎ **015/256-9214**). The showroom is open for guided tours January to March and October to December, Monday to Saturday 9am to 5pm; April to September, Monday to Saturday 9am to 5pm, Saturday and Sunday 9:30am to 5pm. Admission is Dfl 6 ($2.55) for adults, free for children 12 and under.

WHERE TO DINE

✪ **Spijshuis de Dis.** Beestenmarkt 36. ☎ **015/213-1782.** Main courses Dfl 19.50–37.50 ($8.30–$15.95); 4-course menu Dfl 52.50 ($22.35). AE, DC, MC, V. Thurs–Tues 5–9:30pm. DUTCH.

Some of the best Dutch cooking in the country is dished up at this atmospheric restaurant east of the market. Look out for traditional plates presented in modern variations. These include *Bakke pot*—a stew made from three kinds of meat (beef, chicken, and rabbit) in beer sauce, served in the pan; VOC mussels (named after the Dutch initials for the East India Company), prepared with garlic and spices such as ginger and curry; and asparagus in season (May–June). Steaks and lamb fillet are other specialties. If you're feeling especially decadent, opt for a luscious dessert of vanilla ice cream with hot cherries, whipped cream, and cherry brandy.

LEIDEN

36km (22½ miles) SW of Amsterdam

Historians may know that the Pilgrim Fathers lived here for 11 years before sailing for North America on the *Mayflower*. Leiden's proudest homegrown moment came in 1574, when it was the only Dutch town to withstand a Spanish siege. This was the birthplace of the Dutch tulip trade in 1594, and of the painters Rembrandt and Jan Steen, and it is the home of the oldest university in the Netherlands. Finally, with 14 museums, covering subjects ranging from antiquities, natural history, and anatomy to clay pipes and coins, Leiden seems perfectly justified in calling itself "Museum City."

ESSENTIALS

GETTING THERE   There are frequent trains from Amsterdam; the station is northwest of the town center (about a 10-minute walk). By car, take A4.

VISITOR INFORMATION   VVV **Leiden** is just opposite the train station at Stationsplein 210 (☎ **0900/222-2333;** fax 071/512-5318). The office is open Monday to Friday 9am to 5:30pm, Saturday 10am to 2pm.

Roots of a Love Affair

In the spring of 1594, a highly respected yet perennially disgruntled botanist, Carolus Clusius, strode purposefully into the Hortus Botanicus, his research garden at the University of Leiden. He stopped beside a flower bed where an experiment begun the year before was coming to fruition, and cast a critical eye over some little splashes of color nodding their heads in the spring breeze. Clusius was no great admirer of humanity, but flowers were something else, so we may suppose that his dyspeptic disposition softened for a moment as he paused to admire the first tulips ever grown in Holland. A nation's love affair with a flower had begun.

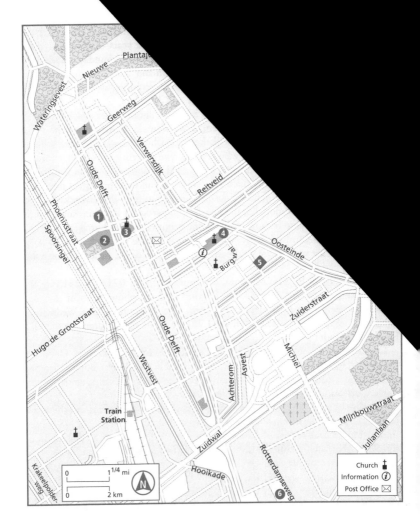

WHAT TO SEE & DO

Probably the best way to tour the town is to cruise its canals or follow one of four special city **walking tours.** One tour, called "The Pilgrim Fathers" (see below), makes a large circle around the old center of the city; the others —"Town Full of Monuments," "In the Footsteps of Young Rembrandt," and "Along Leiden's Almshouses"—make shorter circuits that can easily be combined to give you a comprehensive look at the sights near the university. The tours are organized by the VVV and cost between Dfl 4 and Dfl 10 ($1.70 and $4.25).

The ✪ **National Museum of Antiquities** (Rijksmuseum van Oudheden), Rapenburg 28 (☎ **071/516-3163**), which houses the 1st century A.D. Temple of Taffeh, presented by the Egyptian government as a gift to the Dutch nation for its assistance in saving monuments before the construction of the Aswan High Dam. The museum is open Tuesday to Friday 10am to 5pm, Saturday and Sunday noon to 5pm. Admission is Dfl 8 ($3.40) for adults, Dfl 6 ($2.55) for seniors and children 6 to 18, and free for children under 6.

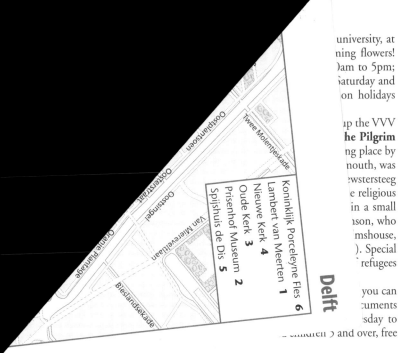

Oosterplantsoen · Twee Molentjeskade · Oosterstraat · Oostsingel · Van Miereveltlaan · Oranje Plantage · Bieslandsekade

Koninklijk Porceleyne Fles **6**
Lambert van Meerten **1**
Nieuwe Kerk **4**
Oude Kerk **3**
Prisenhof Museum **2**
Spijshuis de Dis **5**

Delft

university, at
ning flowers!
]am to 5pm;
Saturday and
on holidays

up the VVV
he Pilgrim
ng place by
nouth, was
wstersteeg
e religious
in a small
son, who
mshouse,
). Special
refugees

you can
cuments
sday to
children 5 and over, free

On the other side of town, visit the **Stedelijk Museum de Lakenhal,** Oude Singel 28–32 (☎ 071/516-5360), to view works by local heroes Rembrandt and Jan Steen, and others, plus period rooms from the 17th to 19th centuries, and temporary modern art exhibitions. Also on parade is Leiden's pride and joy: a copper stew pot said to have been retrieved by a small boy who crawled through a chink in the city wall just minutes after the lifting of the Spanish siege. He found this very pot full of boiling stew in the enemy's camp and brought it back to feed the starving inhabitants. Ever since, stew has been a national dish and is still traditionally prepared for the Leiden city holiday, October 3, which is the anniversary of its liberation; every year on this day *haring en witte brood* (herring and white bread) are distributed, just as they were in 1574. The museum is open Tuesday to Friday 10am to 5pm, and Saturday, Sunday, and holidays (except Christmas and New Year's Day) noon to 5pm. Admission is Dfl 6 ($2.55) for adults and Dfl 3 ($1.30) for children 6 to 18.

A windmill, **De Valk,** sticks up like a sore thumb on Molenwerf in the middle of town, and a 13th-century citadel, **De Burcht,** still stands on a mound of land in the center between two branches of the river Rhine, Oude and Nieuwe, providing a great view of the rooftops around.

WHERE TO DINE

Annie's Verjaardag. Oude Rijn 1a. ☎ **071/512-6358.** Main courses Dfl 18.50–33.50 ($7.85–$14.25). No credit cards. Sun–Thurs 10am–1am, Fri–Sat 10am–2am. DUTCH/CONTINENTAL.

This lively restaurant at water level has vaulted cellars that are a favorite eating spot for both students and locals, who spill out onto the canal-side terrace in fine weather. When the canals are frozen, the view is enchanting, as skaters practice their turns. The dinner menu is simple but wholesome and during the day you can enjoy sandwiches or tapas.

Botanical Gardens of the University **4**
Leiden American Pilgram Museum **5**
National Museum of Antiquities **3**
Stadscafé Van der Werff **1**
Stedelijk Museum de Lakenhal **2**

☼ **Stadscafé van der Werff.** Steenstraat 2. ☎ **071/513-0335.** Main courses Dfl 19.50–36.50 ($8.30–$15.55). AE, DC, MC, V. Daily 10:30am–5pm and 6–10pm. CONTINENTAL.

A relaxed cafe-restaurant in a grand 1930s villa on the edge of the old town, that is popular with the town's students and ordinary citizens alike. Even if you're not having dinner, and enjoying dishes like a basic Indonesian saté, or their surf-and-turf *kalfsbiefstukje met gebakken gambas en een kreeftensaus* (beefsteak with fried prawns in a lobster sauce), you can still while away your evening just having a drink and reading a paper. The cafe is open until 1am.

LAREN

26km (16 miles) SE of Amsterdam

ESSENTIALS

GETTING THERE   There are trains every hour or so from Amsterdam Centraal Station to Hilversum, from where buses leave every half hour or so to Laren. By car from Amsterdam, take A1 (E231) east.

VISITOR INFORMATION   **VVV Gooi and Vechtstreek,** Adriaan Dortsmanplein 1B, Naarden (☎ **035/694-2836;** fax 035/694-3424), is open Monday to Friday from 9am to 5pm, Saturday from 10am to 5pm.

What to See & Do

The Dutch legacy of impressive art was not a one-shot, Golden Age phenomenon, nor were the later 19th-century contributions solely the work of Vincent van Gogh. Visit the pretty little suburban town of Laren, 24 km (15 miles) east of Amsterdam in the district of Het Gooi, and you discover a less well-known Dutch art center, where a number of important painters chose to live and work at the turn of the century. Among the town's star residents were Anton Mauve, the Dutch impressionist who attracted other members of The Hague School, and the American painter, William Henry Singer, Jr., who chose to live and paint in the clear light of Holland rather than follow his family's traditional path to fame and fortune via the steel mills of Pittsburgh.

Today Laren's principal attraction is Singer's former home, once called the Wild Swans, and now the **Singer Museum,** Oude Drift 1 (☎ **035/531-5656**). It houses both the works of the former occupant and also his collection of some 500 works by American, Dutch, French, and Norwegian painters. Open Tuesday to Saturday from 11am to 5pm and Sundays and holidays from noon to 5pm (closed January 1, April 30, and December 25). Admission changes depending on the exhibition. To reach the museum by public transportation from Amsterdam, take bus 136, which departs from Amstel Bus Station every half hour and takes you directly to the museum stop in Laren.

Appendix A: Amsterdam in Depth

If your knowledge of Dutch history is confined to Peter Minuit buying Manhattan Island and Peter Stuyvesant as governor of Nieuw Amsterdam, read on. A working knowledge of the history of Amsterdam adds interesting dimensions to your visit.

HOLLAND'S BEGINNINGS

It's ironic, in view of Holland's preference for peaceful international relations, that the Dutch first made their appearance on history's stage amid a welter of violence and blood, defending their homeland against those iron-fisted conquerors, the Romans. The earliest inhabitants of what is now the Netherlands were three tribes that settled the marshy deltas of the "lowlands" sometime in the dawn of recorded history. They were the Belgae of the southern regions; the Batavi, who settled in the area of the Great Rivers; and the fiercely independent Frisians, who took up residence along the northern coast. Each tribe posed a challenge to Julius Caesar when he came calling in the first century B.C., but he nevertheless managed, after prolonged and effective objections from the locals, to get both the Belgae and the Batavi to knuckle under.

By Caesar's own account the Batavi made a fair job of defending the "good meadowland" of ancient Batavia. They were, he said, the fiercest fighters his legions had ever encountered. In their swampy, tide-washed homeland, between the Roman devil and the deep gray sea, the Batavians struggled to avoid going under, continuing their resistance until 12 B.C. against the general Nero Claudius Drusus. They later became allies of Rome, and the dashing Batavian cavalry took on a romantic aura not unlike that of Jeb Stuart's. An elite unit of Batavians formed the Emperor Augustus's personal bodyguard. Not all Romans admired their martial virtues. The poet Martial mocked the "slow-witted" Batavians—though presumably not to their faces—saying they were as foolish as they were fierce.

Roman legionary bases, one of which grew into the city of Novio Magus (Nijmegen), were used as jumping-off points for invasions of Friesland to the north and Germany to the east. Rome never did have its way with the Frisians, however. In A.D. 47, Emperor Claudius gave up the costly attempt to acquire the marshy northlands (to an Italian they must have seemed like worthless real estate anyway), settling for

Dateline

- **12th century** Fishermen establish a coastal settlement at the mouth of the Amstel River.
- **1204** Gijsbrecht van Aemstel builds a castle at the village.
- **1270** The Amstel River is dammed in an effort to control water flow over the land; the settlement is dubbed "Aemstelledamme."
- **1275** Count Floris V grants Aemstelledamme freedom from tolls on travel and trade, in the first documented recognition of the settlement.
- **1300** Bishop of Utrecht grants Amsterdam its town charter.
- **1323** Amsterdam declared a toll center for imported beer.
- **1334** Oude Kerk mentioned in contemporary city records as the first parish church.
- **1345** "Miracle of the Host" increases the city's religious standing and attracts Catholic pilgrims from around Europe.
- **1350** Amsterdam becomes transit point for grain, gaining status as an important trade center.
- **1400** Population swells to almost 5,000.
- **1452** Fire destroys the mostly timber city.
- **1489** Hapsburg Emperor Maximilian of Austria grants Amsterdam the right to use the imperial crown on its coat of arms.
- **1514** Amsterdam is the largest town in Holland, with a population of 12,000.
- **1517** Martin Luther, at Wittenberg, Germany, issues his condemnation of the Catholic Church, sparking the Protestant Reformation.
- **1530** Anabaptists, a radical Protestant sect, develop a significant following in the city.

continues

the Rhine as the northern frontier of the Roman Empire. Having seen off the Romans, the Frisians in the 5th century did even better against the next would-be conquerors—hordes of Saxons and Franks, who overran the by now enfeebled Romano-Batavians to the south. Not until the late 8th century did the Frisians surrender their independence, when the mighty Charlemagne, king of the Franks and emperor of the West, forced them to give up their pagan gods in exchange for Christianity. Yet even Charlemagne was obliged to promise that the Frisians would remain free "so long as the wind blows out of the clouds and the world stands."

AMSTERDAM'S ORIGINS

Amsterdam was founded at the place where two fishermen and a seasick dog jumped ashore from a small boat to escape a storm in the Zuiderzee. The dog threw up, thus marking the spot. Sound like a shaggy dog story? Well, the city's original coat of arms backs up the tale, and you can see representations of it on the facade of the Beurs van Berlage (Old Stock Exchange) and the Munttoren (Mint Tower), and above the Mayor's fireplace in the old Town Hall (now the Royal Palace) on the Dam.

At any rate, it seems that fishermen, with or without dogs, did play the decisive role in founding Amsterdam. Early in the 12th century, some fishermen realized that the area at the mouth of the Amstel River allowed their wooden cog ships easy access to the lucrative fishing in both the IJ inlet and the Zuiderzee. They built huts there, probably on raised mounds of earth called *terps,* examples of which still abound in coastal Friesland. The low-lying marshy terrain left these early settlers at the mercy of tides and storms, and many must have died or lost their homes as a result of flooding. Traders followed the fishing families, distributing the catch to the more developed surrounding towns and villages.

Archaeological remains show that by 1204, local big wheels were moving in on what the peasants had created. The lord of Aemstel, Gijsbrecht II, made the first power play, building a castle at the settlement and lording it over the locals. Gijsbrecht had to watch his back, though, where the count of Holland, supported by the bishop of Utrecht, was maneuvering for position.

Around 1270 the fishermen dammed the Amstel, at the point where today's square called the Dam stands, in an effort to control water flow over the land. This is the source of the city's original name, Aemstelledamme. To this day you can watch the sluices on either side of where the old dam stood being opened by hand when the canals get their nightly flushing.

There are few records of the village of Aemstelledamme before 1275, when Count Floris V of Holland granted privileges that allowed locals to trade anywhere in Holland or Zeeland without having to pay tolls along the way. This is the settlement's first official documentary record, and the year is considered to be the city's foundation date. Gijsbrecht IV of Aemstel resented Floris's efforts to win friends and influence people on his patch, and in 1296 he murdered Floris in his castle at Muiden.

Gijsbrecht didn't have long to enjoy his victory. Two years later Floris's brother, Guy of Hainaut, defeated Gijsbrecht in battle and hauled him up in front of the bishop of Utrecht for judgment; his land was confiscated and he was imprisoned and later exiled. In 1300, the bishop granted Aemstelledamme its town charter and in 1317 ceded the town formally to the counts of Holland.

INCREASING PROSPERITY

During the 14th and 15th centuries, Holland's position at the mouths of the great European rivers made it a focal point in the many shifts of feudal power. After numerous small-scale struggles for control, the House of Burgundy became the first major feudal power in the Low Countries, consolidating its hold on the region by acquiring fiefdoms one by one through various means—marriage, inheritance, and military force. Its day soon passed, however, as the Austrian Habsburg emperor Maximilian I acquired the Low Countries from the Burgundians by much the same means.

As these political and dynastic struggles raged beyond the rim of the broad Dutch horizon, Amsterdammers were quietly making themselves wealthy. Always skillful merchants, they began to establish strong guilds of craftsmen and to put ships to sea for herring (an industry that took a big leap forward in 1385, when Willem Beukelszoon discovered a way to cure herring at sea), wool, grain, salt and timber. They opened up lucrative trade with the Baltic by joining the powerful Hanseatic League.

Amsterdam began its rise to commercial prosperity in 1323, when Count Floris VI established the city as one of two toll points for

- **1535** Anabaptists seize Town Hall; the uprising fails and its leaders are executed.
- **1550** Education of public grows.
- **1560** Calvinism is a growing force in the city's affairs.
- **1566** First Protestant services held in public; Catholic churches sacked in the *Beeldenstorm* (Iconoclastic Fury).
- **1578** Amsterdam abandons the Spanish, and Catholic, cause; Calvinists take over in what is called the *Alteratie*.
- **1589** First correctional facility for men opens.
- **1596** First correctional facility for women opens.
- **1600** Population reaches 50,000.
- **1602** United East India Company (V.O.C.) established.
- **1609** Amsterdam Exchange Bank opens.
- **1611** Amsterdam Stock Exchange opens.
- **1613** Construction begins on Canal Belt: Herengracht, Keizersgracht, and Prinsengracht.
- **1626** Peter Minuit buys Manhattan Island from the Manhattoes Indians; founds Nieuw Amsterdam colony (later renamed New York).
- **1632** Opening of Athenaeum Illustre, precursor to the city's first university.
- **1634** "Tulip mania" begins; price of bulbs soars to insane heights.
- **1637** Great Tulip Crash.
- **1642** Rembrandt paints *The Night Watch*.
- **1665** Portuguese Synagogue opens.
- **1669** Building of timber houses is forbidden due to the risk of fire.
- **1696** Undertakers riot.
- **1697** Russia's Czar Peter the Great stays at Zaandam, near Amsterdam, to work

continues

incognito in a shipyard and study Dutch shipbuilding methods.

- **1745** Three schools for needy children open.
- **1784** Society for the Welfare of the Community established.
- **1787** King of Prussia occupies Low Countries.
- **1791** United East India Company (V.O.C.) is liquidated.
- **1795** Velvet Revolution. French forces occupy Amsterdam and the Batavian Republic is established; William V flees to England.
- **1806–10** Louis Bonaparte, Napoléon's brother, reigns as king of the Netherlands, with Amsterdam his capital and the former Town Hall on the Dam his palace.
- **1815** After Napoléon's defeat at Waterloo, Amsterdam becomes capital of the independent Kingdom of the Netherlands.
- **1839** Amsterdam-Haarlem railway line opens.
- **1854** Poor Law created.
- **1870** Diamond industry grows.
- **1876** Opening of North Sea Canal.
- **1877** Municipal Sanitation Department set up.
- **1885** Rijksmuseum opens.
- **1889** Centraal Station opens.
- **1890** City government assumes control of privately owned utilities.
- **1894** Social Democratic Labor Party formed.
- **1897** July 21: First automobile arrives in the city.
- **1902** Socialist wins first seat on the city council.
- **1910** Flushable water system set up.
- **1917** Despite Dutch neutrality in World War I, Holland suffers food shortages, causing public riots.
- **1928** Amsterdam Olympics.

continues

the import of beer. At that time beer was essential for health. Drinking water was a risky, germ-laden activity, particularly in overcrowded towns whose rivers were both reservoir and toilet. Drinking beer, on the other hand, had no undesirable side effects—aside from an occasional headache—and cast a warm glow over what must often have been a miserable life. Later, Amsterdam was granted toll rights on exported ale. Beer thus became a major component of its prosperity, and remains important to this day, as anyone who visits the city's Heineken Reception Center will see.

The city's merchants, growing rich on the contents of the warehouses they built along the canals, trampled on the toes of other Hanseatic League cities in the competition for trade and came out ahead.

PILGRIM CITY

During the Middle Ages, the Netherlands was a bastion of Catholicism, with powerful bishops in the cities of Utrecht and Maastricht and a holy shrine in the upstart town of Aemstelledamme, which attracted its own share of pilgrims during the age of the Crusades. No one is sure when Amsterdam became an independent parish, but it is thought to have been around 1334, when the Oude Kerk (Old Church) is first mentioned in the city's records, though a small timber chapel on the spot dates from around 1300.

In 1342, Floris VI granted Amsterdam another charter, giving it more independence and definitive boundaries. As the town became more of a city and grew in prosperity, churches, monasteries, nunneries, and cloisters called *begijnhofs* (beguinages) began to spring up. Eventually there were 18 begijnhofs, which functioned as social welfare agencies, providing care to the sick, orphaned, or poor and hospitality to travelers and pilgrims. You can tour the main Begijnhof (see "Sights of Religious Significance" in chapter 6). The many religious institutions helped attract people to the city.

A few years later, a major event, referred to as the "Miracle of the Host," increased the city's religious standing. It is said that on the Tuesday before Palm Sunday in 1345, a dying man sent for a priest to administer last rites. He was given the Host; a few hours later he vomited on the fire, and the next day they found the unburnt Host amid the embers. Soon afterward, it was placed in a shrine built to commemorate this miracle; twice it was removed and taken to another place of worship, but each time it returned itself to the original shrine.

During a procession to the Oude Kerk involving the same Host, many miracles were said to have happened. The bishop erected a chapel in place of the dying man's house. Within a few years the place came to be known as the *Heilige Stede* (Holy Place), and, though the Host disappeared during the Protestant ascendancy in Amsterdam (when Catholics were forbidden to worship openly), an annual pilgrimage, De Stille Omgang, still recalls the miracle.

The Host might not have burned, but the city did—twice. In contrast to the solid structures you see today, early canal houses were made from timber, had thatched roofs, and stood on wood pilings that reached down through the soft upper soil to a firmer layer of sand beneath. In 1421, they went up in smoke in the city's first great fire, a performance repeated in 1452. At that point the city fathers put an end to building with wood; today, only two timber houses remain in the old city: the 15th-century Het Huyten Huis in the Begijnhof and the 16th-century 't Aepje, a former seaman's hostel, at Zeedijk 1.

THE REFORMATION

The 16th century was a time when religion was often truly inseparable from power and politics, when kings still routinely considered themselves their kingdom's link with the divine. This century also witnessed the Reformation, which began in 1517 with Martin Luther nailing his *Ninety-five Theses* to the door of the Catholic Church in Wittenberg, Germany, and the eventual spread of Protestantism throughout the Christian world. It was a time of tremendous religious ferment.

Nations throughout Europe wrestled with the notion of religious diversity. In Holland, ironically, the anti-Catholic, iconoclastic ideas of Protestantism took root in the Dutch psyche at the same time as the Dutch provinces officially came under the rule of Charles V, the intensely Catholic Habsburg emperor and king of Spain. Holland, and Amsterdam in particular, became a pressure point and fulcrum for the shifting political scene that the Reformation occasioned everywhere in Europe. It was the rigorous doctrines of John Calvin and his firm belief in the separation of church and state that began to take root in Amsterdam.

- **1932** Enclosing Dike completed; Zuiderzee becomes the IJsselmeer, a freshwater lake.
- **1934** Great Depression leads to shortages and riots; the government uses the army to keep order.
- **1940** German troops invade and occupy Holland.
- **1941** "February Strike" against persecution of the Jews.
- **1944–45** "Hunger Winter," as Nazi occupation forces blockade western Holland.
- **1945** May 7: Canadian troops liberate the city.
- **1947** *The Diary of Anne Frank* is published.
- **1951** *The Dockworker* statue commemorating the 1941 February Strike is unveiled.
- **1952** Completion of the Amsterdam-Rhine Canal.
- **1966** Protests against Princess Beatrix's marriage to German Claus von Amsberg, a soldier in the World War II German army.
- **1973** Van Gogh Museum opens.
- **1975** Amsterdam's 700th anniversary. Dutch Guyana gains independence as Surinam; influx of immigrants to Amsterdam. Cannabis use is decriminalized.
- **1978** First squatters occupy the old Handelsblad newspaper offices.
- **1980** Sixteen people squat at 72 Vondelstraat. Police remove them, but they return and violent confrontation takes place.
- **1986** "Stop the Stopera" campaign fails, and the combined new *Stadhuis* (Town Hall) and *Opera* (Muziektheater) open at Waterlooplein.
- **1987** *Homomonument* to the world's persecuted gays and lesbians is unveiled.

continues

- **1990** Vincent van Gogh Centenary. A million people visit the commemorative exhibition at the Van Gogh Museum.
- **1992** Amsterdammers vote to restrict vehicle use in the city center. An El Al Boeing 747 cargo plane, carrying chemical warfare agents, takes off from Schiphol Airport and crashes into apartment blocks in the Bijlmermeer housing project, killing around 50 people.
- **1995** Amsterdam celebrates its canals, river, and harbor with the 6-month festival "City on the Water."
- **1997** Treaty of Amsterdam confirms European Monetary Union and the euro as the common European currency from 1999.
- **1998–99** Museumplein redeveloped; a landscaped garden is added and an extension to the Van Gogh Museum.
- **2000** Amsterdam is one of the host cities of the Euro 2000 European Championship soccer tournament. Passenger Terminal Amsterdam for cruise ships opens.

Among the more radical Protestant sects were the Anabaptists, some of whom had left Germany in 1530 in hopes of finding a more tolerant climate in Amsterdam. The Anabaptists rejected the Catholic celebration of saints' days and infant baptism, favoring adult baptism instead, and did not believe in the Trinity. For the most part, they gained their following among the poor. In general, the city's Catholics tolerated the presence of Anabaptists in their midst—until 1535, when a group of them seized the Town Hall in anticipation of the Second Coming. The Anabaptists found the city unwilling to go along and the leaders of the uprising were executed.

Despite the reprisals, the Anabaptists continued their agitation. On February 11, 1535, a so-called prophet, Hendrick Hendrickszoon, was preaching to a small group of men and women when he suddenly told them that the Lord had spoken to him and that all present were damned to Hell. The congregation asked for forgiveness, which was immediately granted, but then Hendrickszoon ripped off his clothes, threw them on the fire, and bade the others to do the same—which they did. Then they all ran naked through the city, including the landlady of the building in which they had been holding their meeting. These zealots have been referred to as the "Naked Runners"—Amsterdam's original streakers—ever since. The men were all executed, and the landlady was hanged in the doorway of her building as an example to the public. In this, Amsterdam became like many communities in Europe, abandoning religious toleration in favor of religious repression.

Not all events had religious fanaticism as their motive force. A big step forward in our knowledge of Amsterdam at this time took place in 1538, when Cornelis Anthoniszoon created a painted woodcut map, giving a bird's-eye view of the city that clearly showed landmarks such as the Dam, the Oude Kerk and the harbor. Anthoniszoon's woodcut began a long and illustrious tradition of mapmaking in the city, and if you can find a reproduction of it you can compare both the similarities with today and the changes that almost 5 centuries have wrought.

About 20 years later a series of events changed the course of history in Holland and Amsterdam, turning the country toward a path that would make it

A High-Placed Friend

The Holy Roman Emperor Maximilian I took a shine to the city after he was cured of an illness by the miraculous Host and because it supported his *Kabeljauwen* (Codfish) faction against the rival *Hoeken* (Hooks) in local power struggles. In 1489, the emperor allowed the city to use his imperial emblem on its coat of arms.

a world-renowned symbol of religious, political, and intellectual tolerance. In 1555, Philip II, a great-grandson of Emperor Maximilian I, became king of Spain. An ardent Catholic, he was determined to defeat the Reformation and set out to hunt heretics everywhere throughout his empire. The Dutch resented Philip's intrusion into their affairs and began a resistance movement. Within 10 years a League of Protestant Nobles had been formed in the Netherlands by the taciturn but tactful William of Orange, count of Holland, known also as William the Silent. Philip's response was to send the vicious duke of Alba to Holland. He was to function as an overseer, with specific instructions to establish a Council of Blood to enforce the policy of "death to heretics."

The Dutch nobles fought back, though they had no army, no money to raise one, and little support from the Dutch cities, including Catholic Amsterdam, which was interested mostly in maintaining its prosperous trade. William of Orange and his brother John of Nassau managed to wage war on Spain despite all this, their only ally a ragtag "navy" of Protestant pirates called the Sea Beggars. They were helped when Spain levied a new tax on its Dutch "colony," an action so unpopular as to rally the majority of Dutch people— Protestant and Catholic alike—to the anti-Spanish cause.

A few towns, including Amsterdam, declined to join the fight against Alba, deeming resistance bad for business. These communities were spared destruction when the Spanish invaded. The Spanish armies marched inexorably through Holland, besting the defenses of each city to which they laid siege, with few exceptions. In an ingenious if desperate move, William of Orange saved the city of Leiden by flooding the province, allowing the Sea Beggars to sail their galleons right up to the city's walls. The attack surprised the Spaniards in the middle of dinner; they were promptly routed. A stew pot left behind became a national symbol of freedom for Holland, and its contents inspired the traditional Dutch dish called *hutspot*.

This victory galvanized the Dutch in fighting for their independence. The Calvinist merchants of Amsterdam turned out their Catholic city council in 1578 in a revolution called the *Alteratie* (Changeover), and the city abandoned the pro-Catholic Spanish cause. As the Protestant Reformation took hold, the city's many Catholics were forbidden to hold public office or to worship openly, a situation that continued for more than a century. The Dutch nobles strengthened their commitment to each other in 1579 by signing the Union of Utrecht, in which they agreed to fight together in a united front. Although the union was devised solely to prosecute the battle against Spain, consolidation inevitably occurred, and by the turn of the 17th century what had once been the Spanish Netherlands became the Seven United Provinces—Zeeland, Friesland, Utrecht, Gelderland, Groningen (Overijssel), North Holland, and South Holland. The struggle with Spain would continue through the first half of the 17th century, but Holland's strength was growing and a new, prosperous era was about to begin.

THE GOLDEN AGE
Over the first 50 to 75 years of the 17th century, the legendary Dutch entrepreneurial gift would come into its own. These years have since become known as the Golden Age—it seemed that every business venture the Dutch initiated during this time turned a profit and that each of their many expeditions to the unknown places of the world resulted in a new jewel in the Dutch trading empire. Colonies and brisk trade were established to provide the luxury-hungry merchants at home with new delights, such as fresh ginger from Java, foxtails from America, fine porcelain from China, and flower bulbs from

Turkey that produced big, bright, waxy flowers and grew quite readily in Holland's sandy soil—tulips. Holland was rich and Amsterdam was growing.

Until the late 16th century Amsterdam had always lagged behind neighboring cities in economic terms, despite having extended its trade routes to Russia, Scandinavia, and the Baltic. But in 1589 Amsterdam's biggest commercial rival, the Belgian port of Antwerp, was taken over by the Spanish, prompting many industrious Protestant and Jewish craftspeople to flee to Amsterdam. Of the Jewish influx, the jurist Hugo Grotius wrote in 1614: "Plainly God desires them to live somewhere. Why not here rather than elsewhere?" These immigrants brought with them their merchant skills and their businesses—including the diamond industry, which has remained a famous and central part of the city's commerce.

Over the next 65 years Amsterdam grew into one of the world's great cities. In 1602, traders from each of the major cities in the Republic of the Seven Provinces set up the Verenigde Oostindische Compagnie (V.O.C.), the United East India Company, which was granted a monopoly on trade in the East. Printed shares in the V.O.C. were traded at the world's oldest stock exchange, founded that same year in the Oudezijds Kapel. The company's purpose was to mount safe, cost-effective, exploratory voyages and trading ventures to the East Indies, and it was wildly successful. The East India Company established the Dutch presence in the Spice Islands (Indonesia), Goa, South Africa, and China. You can see a full-size replica of an East India Company sailing ship, the *Amsterdam,* tied to the wharf outside the Netherlands Maritime Museum.

Great wealth flowed back to Amsterdam, and the merchants used it to build the canals and the impressive 17th-century architecture along the Golden Bend on the Herengracht. In 1613 work on the three major canals (Herengracht, Keizersgracht, and Prinsengracht) was begun. City planners designed a system in which the large canals were connected by smaller transverse canals to make travel by water more convenient throughout Amsterdam. They decided that the wealthy would live facing the major canals, while the connecting canals were set aside for the middle and lower classes.

The growing city bustled in many other ways: A variety of churches and other houses of worship was built during this time, traders and craftspeople of all sorts began setting up protectionist guilds, and there was an increase in interest in the arts and sciences. Artists, including Rembrandt, were working overtime, cranking out paintings commissioned by newly affluent merchants who had become obsessed with portraying themselves and surrounding themselves with beautiful images. It is thought that most affluent Dutch homes had at least four paintings in them at that time.

Crazy About Tulips

With profits from global trade flooding into Amsterdam, the burgeoning merchant class needed some visible sign of their vast disposable income to flaunt in the faces of friends and rivals. Astonishingly, these straitlaced Calvinists, whose financial rectitude—not to say parsimony—was proverbial, went overboard for tulips.

The price of bulbs skyrocketed from virtually nothing in 1620, to finally top out at 30,000 florins for three bulbs in 1637. This was serious money—the going rate for the most prestigious houses on Amsterdam's most illustrious canalsides, with garden and coach house thrown in. When the bubble of "Tulip Mania" burst soon afterward, more than a few fortunes vaporized with it.

Let's clear up some matters of nomenclature. *Dutch* is the result of a 15th-century ethnological misunderstanding on the part of the English, who couldn't distinguish too clearly between the people of the northern Low Countries and the various German peoples. So, to describe the former, they simply corrupted the German "Deutsch" to Dutch.

The term *Holland* is a bit of a misnomer, since, strictly speaking, it refers only to the provinces of North Holland and South Holland and not to the whole country. The Dutch themselves call their country *Nederland* (the Netherlands) and themselves *Nederlanders.* But they recognize that *Dutch* and *Holland* are popular internationally and are here to stay, so, being a practical people, they make use of them.

Golden Age Amsterdam can be compared to Renaissance Florence and Periclean Athens for the great flowering that transformed society. "There is perhaps no other example of a complete and highly original civilization springing up in so short a time in so small a territory," wrote the historian Simon Schama in *The Embarrassment of Riches* (1987). Learning flourished. Amsterdam's first school of higher education, the Athenaeum Illustre, was established in 1632. The Athenaeum Illustre was not a university, but it did raise the city's educational possibilities above the level offered before. The Guild of Surgeons began giving anatomy demonstrations to both interested doctors and laypeople. As a symbol of the city's civic pride and wealth, the new Stadhuis (Town Hall) on the Dam, completed in 1665 to replace an earlier one that was destroyed by fire, is hard to beat—so lavishly appointed is it that it was later taken over by royalty and became the Royal Palace.

The long war with Spain finally ended in 1648 after 80 years, and though the Nieuw Amsterdam colony (present-day New York City) in North America was lost to the English in 1664, the Dutch continued to grow wealthy from their Spice Islands holdings. The descendants of William of Orange had by then established a de facto monarchy, which was further strengthened when William III married into the English royal family. The ascension of William III and his wife, Mary, to the English throne in 1688 may have been the beginning of the end for the Dutch Republic, however. Wars, commercial failures, misguided political decisions, and low morale were the hallmarks of the next century of Dutch history, which ended with the House of Orange in exile.

DECLINE & FALL

In the final reckoning, a Golden Age is a nostalgic concept, a looking back wistfully to a "better age" that can exist only in the past. Gold is the color of a late afternoon in autumn: The light of spring may shine once again, but first must come the long night of winter. Anyone who had given the matter much thought—and there is not much sign that anyone did—might have concluded that Holland's golden moment would likely fade away gently into the mists of time. In reality, it came to an end with all the unexpected suddenness of a crash of blue-sky thunder.

The Dutch call 1672 the *Rampjaar* (Year of Disaster). France, under Louis XIV, invaded the United Provinces by land and the English attacked by sea. This war (1672–78) and the later War of the Spanish Succession (1701–13) drained the country's wealth and morale. The buccaneering, can-do, go anywhere spirit of traders, artists and writers ebbed, replaced by conservatism and closed horizons.

A long period of decline set in during the 18th century. At the Museum Willet-Holthuysen and Museum Van Loon you get an idea of the decadent, French-influenced style in which wealthy Amsterdam families lived during the Golden Age's fading afterglow. In 1748 the city's taxpayers signaled they had as much as they could stomach of watching the rich get richer, the poor get poorer, and civic leaders blatantly help themselves from the public purse, by going on a rampage. Tax collectors' houses and the fine canal-side mansions of the merchants and bankers, particularly favored targets of the mob's anger, were stormed and looted. The riot was suppressed and its ringleaders hanged.

By the second half of the century, Amsterdam was a hotbed of intrigue by pro-French, antiroyalist democrats called the Patriots, who seized control of the city on April 27, 1787. An army of Prussian troops soon came to the rescue of the House of Orange, tramping into the city on October 10 to put down the rebellion. In 1791 the United East India Company was liquidated, in a key indicator of the nation's steep commercial decline.

THE 19TH CENTURY

Revolutionary France invaded Holland in 1794, capturing Amsterdam and establishing the Batavian Republic in 1795, headed by the pro-French Dutch Patriots. Napoléon brought the short-lived republic to an end in 1806 by turning the town hall of Amsterdam into a palace and setting up his brother, Louis Napoléon, as king of the Netherlands. Louis did a good job of representing the interests of his new subjects—by, for instance, permitting them to trade surreptitiously with Britain, which was at war with Napoléon and under French blockade. So good, in fact, that Napoleon deposed him in 1810 and brought the Netherlands into the empire.

The French reign was short lived, but the taste of royalty proved sweet. When the Dutch recalled the House of Orange in 1815, it was to fill the role of king in a constitutional monarchy. The monarch was yet another William of Orange; however, because his reign was to be a fresh start for the republic, the Dutch started numbering their Williams all over again (which makes for a very confusing history).

In the 1860s Amsterdam's economy grew strong again as the city worked to equip itself for modern trade. The first improvement was the building of a railway line between Haarlem and Amsterdam in 1839. The North Sea Canal, which ran from Amsterdam to IJmuiden and gave Amsterdam a better crack at German industrial trade, was built in 1876. Another major boon to the city was the building of the Suez Canal in 1869, which made travel to Asia easier.

For about 2 centuries after Amsterdam's Golden Age the city's population remained at a quarter of a million. Between 1850 and 1900, however, it jumped to half a million. As did most major cities during the Industrial Revolution, Amsterdam began to face issues of overpopulation. Housing was in short supply, the canals were increasingly befouled with sewage, and for many life in the city became increasingly nasty, brutish, and short.

Rabbit King

At his 1806 inauguration, King Louis Napoléon deployed his rusty (but not trusty) Dutch to inform his mystified subjects, "Ik ben uw Konijn" (I am your Rabbit). What he had meant to say, of course, was, "Ik ben uw Koning" (I am your King).

Holland maintained strict neutrality during World War I, but the war still had an impact on Amsterdam. While the wealthy exploited the situation by selling arms and other supplies, the city suffered from acute food shortages, and the poor were constantly faced with starvation. In 1917 there were food riots; Amsterdam answered with soup kitchens and rationing. In the 1920s Amsterdam shared in the wealth as Europe's condition improved, but conditions were very bad during the 1930s, when the widespread unemployment brought on by the Great Depression caused the government to use the army in 1934 to control the unruly masses. During this time many poor Dutch families were forced to move to Germany, where jobs were easier to come by.

Amsterdam was just beginning to recover from the Depression when the Germans invaded on May 10, 1940. The overmatched Dutch army resisted bravely, but with Rotterdam blitzed into ruins and a similar fate threatened for Amsterdam and other cities, the end came quickly. Queen Wilhelmina—probably the most popular Dutch ruler since William the Silent, a tiny woman whom Churchill once called "the only man in the Dutch government"—fled to England, where she stayed until 1945. An Austrian Nazi, Arthur Seyss-Inquart, was put in charge of the occupied Netherlands.

As he did in most other cities he conquered, Hitler managed to gain a following in Amsterdam. However, there was resistance by the citizens to Nazi treatment of Jews, Gypsies, and homosexuals. In February 1941 city workers organized a strike to protest the deportation of Jews. Today, in the Old Jewish Quarter, where many Jews lived until the war, you can see the statue *The Dockworker,* a tribute to the February Strike (Amsterdam was the first city in the world to have a memorial to the quarter-million gays and lesbians killed by Nazis during World War II—it's called the *Homomonument*). Unfortunately, the strike did little good; by 1942 the Nazis had forced all Dutch Jews to move to three isolated areas in Amsterdam. Between July 1942 and September 1943 most of Amsterdam's Jews were sent to death camps. Of the 60,000 Jews in Amsterdam, only 6,000 survived (the figures for the Netherlands as a whole were 140,000 and 16,000 respectively). Among the murdered was a teenage girl who has come to symbolize the many victims of the Holocaust—Anne Frank.

In September 1944 the people of Amsterdam hoped for liberation, as the German armies were on the run after their defeat in Normandy and Allied troops had crossed into Holland from Belgium. On September 17, the greatest airborne assault in history, Operation Market Garden, was launched. Paratroops of the U.S. 101st and 82nd Airborne Divisions landed near Eindhoven and Nijmegen, and after bitter fighting, captured the cities and their river bridges. Farther north, the British 1st Airborne Division landed at Arnhem to take the vital bridge over the Rhine—the gateway to Hitler's Germany and the key to hopes of ending the war in 1944. It was, in a phrase that has gone down in history, "a bridge too far." The British division was destroyed after landing virtually on top of the German 2nd SS Panzer Corps.

Amsterdam's citizens were then faced with what is known as the Hunger Winter. Food supplies were practically nonexistent, and many people were forced to steal or buy provisions on the black market. Those who ventured into the country in hopes of getting milk and eggs were in danger of not getting back to the city before curfew. On May 5, 1945, the grim ordeal came to an end, as the Dutch celebrated the Allies' liberation of the Netherlands. Canadian troops reached Amsterdam first, on May 7—a short way behind that intrepid war correspondent and later popular television news anchorman, Walter Cronkite. A few diehard Nazis opened fire on jubilant crowds at the Dam, killing 22 people.

POSTWAR TURBULENCE

After World War II, Amsterdam began to grow and prosper again. In the 1960s the city was just as much a hotbed of political and cultural radicalism as San Francisco. Hippies trailing clouds of marijuana smoke took over the Dam for their downtown pied à terre and camped out in Vondelpark and in front of Centraal Station. Radical political activity, which began with "happenings" staged by the small group known as the Provos—from *provocatie* (provocation)—continued and intensified in the 1970s. In 1966 the Provos were behind the protests that marred the wedding of Princess Beatrix to German Claus von Amsberg; smoke bombs were thrown and fighting broke out between protesters and police. The Provos formally disbanded in 1967, but much of their program was adopted by the Green Gnomes, or *Kabouters*. This group won several seats on the municipal council, but it too eventually faded.

Some radicals joined neighborhood groups to protest specific local government plans. The scheme that provoked the greatest ire was a plan to build a subway through the Nieuwmarkt area. Demonstrations to defend the housing that had been condemned to make way for the subway were launched in 1975, with the most dramatic confrontation between the police and the human barricades taking place on Blue Monday, March 24. Thirty people were wounded and 47 arrested in a battle of tear gas and water cannons against paint cans and powder bombs. Despite the protests, the subway was built and opened in 1980.

With the influx of immigrants from newly independent Surinam and other countries, the shortage of decent affordable housing has continued to be a major issue; in fact, it was to spark the squatting movement that came to dominate the late 1970s and '80s. Squatting, or *kraaken* in Dutch, is the occupation by homeless people of empty or temporarily unoccupied properties. In a city with such a severe shortage of housing, it has been, and to some extent remains, a viable option, particularly for the young. The squatting movement is well organized, but its associations with anarchist, antisocial, and antiauthoritarian groups and its disregard for private property rights make it an unsavory phenomenon to many, though there is some public sympathy for the *squatters'* plight. In 1978 the first squatters occupied the old *Handelsblad* newspaper office building, but it took a series of squatter initiatives to unify the squatters into a movement. The biggest confrontations came in 1980, first at the Vondelstraat squat in the heart of the museum area, where 500 police with armored vehicles evicted squatters. Riots followed, and 50 people were wounded and much damage was sustained. The second and larger disturbance occurred on Beatrix Coronation Day, when 200 buildings were occupied in 26

Tell *That* to the Marines

Off-duty Dutch Marines, one of whose girlfriends had allegedly been insulted by a hippie outside Centraal Station, went into battle in 1967 against the long-haired menace. They swept the hippies from the station environs, "scalping" any who lingered long enough to be captured. In 1970, those few good Dutchmen were at it again, storming the hippie encampment at the Dam and chasing its denizens over the horizon.

cities, and in Amsterdam itself protesters battled the police and totally disrupted the festivities. Other squatting incidents followed, but slowly both sides developed a more constructive dialogue that has managed to avert further violent confrontations.

Protests similar to those that had been started against the subway were launched against the proposals to build a new Stadhuis (Town Hall) and Opera (Muziektheater) side by side on Waterlooplein, a complex that became known as the Stopera. Despite an energetic and at times violent campaign to "Stop the Stopera," both buildings were completed in 1986, and the Muziektheater is now a star in the city's cultural firmament.

The Provos and Green Gnomes had long advocated specific environmental programs, such as the prohibition of all motor vehicles from the city. At one point, they actually persuaded the city authorities to provide 20,000 white-painted bicycles free for citizens' use—sadly, this admirable scheme was abandoned when most of the bicycles were stolen, no doubt to reappear in freshly painted colors as "private" property. Some of their ideas came to fruition in 1992, however, when the populace voted to create a traffic-free zone in the city center.

Although the turbulent events of the 1970s and '80s seem distant today, the independent spirit and social conscience that fueled them remains, and Amsterdam is still one of the most socially advanced cities in Europe. New priorities are emerging, however, with the general aim of boosting Amsterdam's position as a global business center and the location of choice for foreign multinationals' European headquarters, and of consolidating its role as one of Europe's most important transport and distribution hubs. These aims are aided by an ongoing effort to change the city's hippie-paradise image to one more in tune with the needs of commerce.

AMSTERDAM TODAY

Not so long ago Amsterdam was a simple, homogeneous city, notable for its hundreds of arching bridges, thousands of historic gabled houses, and many canals—more than Venice, in fact. The city seemed to have survived intact from its moment of glory in the 17th century. It was a quiet, unhurried, provincial sort of town, and it was very, very clean. But, beginning with its recovery from World War II, Amsterdam started to grow and change. Today it's a sophisticated international city with a busy harbor and an abundance of industrial towers, multistory apartment communities, and elevated highways—all the hallmarks of a modern urban center. The modernization process has had its pluses and minuses. Much tranquillity has been lost along the way, though replaced with an increased vibrancy. But Amsterdam still remains a kind of big village, retaining a human scale that at least affords the illusion of simplicity.

More and more people from Holland, Europe, and farther afield are making tracks toward the city. Footloose young Hollanders seem to have no other ambition than to live here—and who can blame them when you consider the "excitement" of growing up in a squeaky clean Dutch village? Young Americans and Europeans still see Amsterdam as a kind of mecca of youth rebellion to which a pilgrimage must be made (though Prague has stolen some of Amsterdam's allure in that respect). Immigrants find social support systems and a relative absence of the discrimination they face in many other European cities, though areas like Amsterdam East and the Bijlmermeer, with a high percentage of immigrants, are experiencing growing social problems.

What other place in the world could you choose where all of life's comforts, and all novelties that man could want are so easy to obtain as here and where you can enjoy such a feeling of freedom.

—René Descartes, French philosopher (1628)

Amsterdam will at least give one's regular habits of thought the stimulus of a little confusion.

—Henry James, American novelist (1875)

Shopkeepers here still keep their portals tidy, and a few homemakers still wash their steps each morning, but graffiti, miscellaneous grime, and other problems of city life inhabit Amsterdam as much as any other urban center. (The ubiquitous mounds of dog poop on the sidewalks, for instance, have become something of a symbol of the city.)

Fortunately, it's easy to overlook these shortcomings. The historic heart of the city is still there to charm you with its tree-lined canals, gabled houses, and graceful bridges. The Dutch National Monument Care Office (Monumentenzorg) has exercised great foresight in working to preserve the feel of the 17th century along the canals. There are still traces of yesteryear in the street life, too: You see barrel organs and bicycles, antiques shops and herring stands. In addition to the palpable sense of history a trip to Amsterdam will occasion, there are other lures—great museums, fine dining, and a diverse nightlife scene.

You'll have no problem finding the legacy of the city's Golden Age, nearly 400 years ago, in the new Amsterdam. Fuming traffic, power drills, telephone boxes, bicycles, tour boats, and souvenir shops have dulled some of the luster, but the moment always comes when a window in time opens and Amsterdam's heritage asserts itself.

2 Below Sea Level

Amsterdam is the major city of the Netherlands, a tiny country that's barely half the size of the state of Maine, in the United States. A burst of vigorous driving will get you from one corner of the Netherlands to the other in a morning, and you can travel by train from Amsterdam to the farthest point of the railway network in an afternoon. The nation's 41,865 square kilometers (16,325 square miles) are the most densely populated in the world, holding 15.5 million people, or approximately 1,000 per square mile.

Holland is the great river delta of northwest Europe, tucked into a corner between Germany and Belgium. It's a marshy country—there are 7,925 square kilometers (3,090 square miles) of water within Holland's borders in the form of lakes, rivers, and canals—with a dense, sandy, and peatlike soil that tends to settle over time. The country sinks an average of 1 meter, or 39 inches, every 1,000 years. As a result, approximately 50% of Holland, an area that holds about two-thirds of its people, now lies *below* sea level, protected from flooding only by sand dunes, dikes, and Dutch engineering ingenuity.

If the sea has given Holland so much throughout its history, it has threatened much, too. An aircraft descending towards Amsterdam's Schiphol Airport has to descend a little further than would be the case for an airport in most other places on earth, because the runway is 7m (7½ ft.) below sea level. That it is not 7m beneath the sea is due to Dutch engineering skill, which has kept the country's collective head above water for the last thousand years.

The Dutch have always had an intimate relationship with the sea. Two thousand years of living in its wake, listening to the waves beating against the walls raised against its clear and present danger, has driven the sea into the national psyche. Holland without water is as unimaginable as Arabia without sand. But that the solid, timeless buildings of Amsterdam, and its 725,000 inhabitants, stand where waves should by all rights be lapping is a difficult concept for foreigners to grasp.

While visiting Holland in 1859, Matthew Arnold was so amazed at what he saw that he wrote home, "The country has no business to be there at all." Maybe so, but the Dutch have a ready answer: "God made the earth," they tell you, "and the Dutch made Holland." That they did, and they did a fine job of it. Some 2,600 square kilometers (1,000 square miles) of the country was under water just 100 years ago. The A1/A6 highway out of Amsterdam runs north-east for 20km (12½ miles), across a narrow stretch of water to Flevoland, the Netherland's newest province. There is something convincing about Flevoland as evidence of reclamation: Its main towns, Almere and Lelystad, are so new that the paint on the buildings has scarcely had time to dry. The land itself has an unshaped feel, despite forests that have been planted and the tractors you can see ploughing the fields and harvesting crops.

The "Great Rivers"—the Rhine, the Waal, and the Maas (or Meuse, as it is known in Belgium and France, where its headwaters lie)—divide the country along geographic and spiritual lines. The Dutch living in the lower land "above," or north of, the rivers have long been predominantly Calvinist, whereas the population of the higher lands "below," or south of, the rivers has been traditionally Catholic. (Interestingly, the southerners, whose spiritual capital is Maastricht, lump Amsterdammers together with the "cold-blooded" northerners as people too straitlaced to know how to enjoy themselves.)

Natural regions are formed by the mountains—well, hills—of the southeast; the forest in the center of the country (the provinces of Utrecht and Gelderland); the islands and former islands along the coast of the North Sea (the province of Zeeland in the southwest and a string of sandbar islands off the coast of the province of Friesland in the north); the polders, or reclaimed land, of the former Zuiderzee (now a freshwater lake called the IJsselmeer); and the flat farmland of the rest of the country (some of which is actually old and well-established polder land).

The Netherlands is a WYSIWYG kind of country: What you see is what you get. There are no dramatic canyons or towering peaks. The nation's highest point wouldn't top the roof of a New York City skyscraper, and its average altitude is just 37 feet above sea level. This makes for few panoramic vantage points; you can't see most of the lakes and canals until you're about to fall into them. Are the views therefore boring? The answer is a flat no. As the famous Dutch landscape painters of the 17th century showed the world, vistas in Holland are among the most beautiful anywhere: wide-angle views of green pastures and floating clouds, with tiny houses, church spires, and grazing cattle silhouetted against the horizon.

If the coastal dikes that protect Holland from the North Sea should ever be overwhelmed, most of Amsterdam would vanish beneath the waves (did you check that insurance policy?). In the passage between City Hall and the Muziektheater at Waterlooplein you can view the Normaal Amsterdams Peil (NAP), the Standard Amsterdam Level. This bronze plate forms a fixed point against which measurements of height above and depth below sea level are made throughout western Europe—you need to look upward to see the sea level.

A graphic cross-section of the topography between the North Sea and Amsterdam, which you can buy printed on postcards and posters, shows that the Vondelpark would become a lake, the Metro system would be well and truly drowned and the trams would float away, but that if you contrived to be on the Oude Kerk tower you wouldn't even get your feet wet.

3 Dutch Character & Language

CHARACTER

It's not Holland that's extraordinary, it's the Dutch. Can you imagine Americans, for example, having the patience to retake acres and acres of land from the sea, seemingly by spoonfuls, knowing at the outset that the project might take centuries to complete? (And it did.) Or can you imagine Germans, sharing as they might the Dutch love of precision, devoting 7 years to the building of a perpetually moving planetarium in a living room simply to educate their neighbors, as one Dutchman did in the 18th century? And who but the Dutch would have the ingenuity and audacity to tell rivers when and where to flow and birds where to fly, to turn inland cities into world ports, and to risk a fortune on a project whose margin for error was so small that misplacing any of a series of massive, deep-water pilings spread out over a 3-mile span by as little as 10 inches would have resulted in failure?

But these are collective traits and national accomplishments. You want to know what to expect from the person in the street and behind the shop counter. The most honest thing to say about the Dutch is that they can be both the most infuriating and the most endearing people in the world. One minute they treat you like a naughty child (surely you've heard the expression about someone talking to you like a Dutch uncle) and the next they're ready for a laugh and a beer. They can be rude or cordial (it may depend on the weather), domineering or ever ready to please (it may depend on you). In a shop, they may get annoyed with you if you don't accept what they have, or get mad at themselves if they don't have what you want.

Dutch people have a passion for detail that would boggle the mind of a statistician—and a sense of order and propriety that sends them into a tailspin if you mess things up. They organize everything (people, land, flower beds), and they love to make schedules and stick to them. They may allow you to indulge an occasional whim, though they haven't a clue what it means to "play it by ear." They do love to quote homilies ("While the cat's away, the mice will play"; "Everybody talks about my drinking, but no one knows about my thirst"; "In the concert of life, no one gets a program"), including a number that tend to suffer in translation ("Try to find it out with a wet thumb"; "It fits like a hand shoe").

The Dutch aren't particularly emotional or hotheaded, but then they aren't shy about speaking their minds either. They are fiercely independent and yet so tolerant of other people's problems and attitudes that their country nearly equals the United States as a traditional haven for the world's exiles and émigrés. (You find in the telephone book Italian, Spanish, and French names that belong to centuries-old Dutch families as respectable as the Van Dijks and Van Delfts.)

For centuries Amsterdam has been a magnet for the oppressed and persecuted, particularly in the 17th century, when it became a haven for Jews and

The 17th-century Dutch got right up the noses of the English by competing against them aggressively and successfully for maritime trade and, in 1667, by sailing boldly up the Medway near London and trashing the English fleet. So the English added verbal abuse to their counterattack arsenal. That's why we have *Dutch courage*—alcohol-induced courage; *Dutch treat*—you pay for yourself; *going Dutch*—everybody pays their share; and *double Dutch*—gibberish. Americans were kinder to their Revolutionary War supporters, speaking of *beating the Dutch*—doing something remarkable.

Huguenots driven from France and other Catholic countries (though, paradoxically, Catholics in Holland were not allowed to practice their faith openly). That tradition has continued into the 20th century.

The uniquely Dutch combination of tolerance and individualism has from time to time allowed scandalous eyesores to develop: the nightly spectacle of hippies sleeping on the Dam in the 1960s; the riots that occurred within earshot of the pomp and pageantry of Beatrix's investiture as queen of the Netherlands; and the dubious decision of prominent Dutch cabinet ministers to pose nude in the chambers of Parliament for publication in the Dutch edition of *Playboy* magazine.

LANGUAGE

You may speak English in Amsterdam almost as freely as you do at home, particularly to anyone in the business of providing tourist services, whether cab driver, hotel receptionist, waitperson, or shop assistant. English is Holland's second language and it is taught in the schools from the early grades, with the result that nearly everyone speaks it fluently. Most Dutch today are also conversant in French or German, or both, and some speak Spanish as well.

If foreign languages interest you, however, Dutch should prove a fascinating study. It's a Germanic tongue that at first sounds like a close cousin to German because of the guttural, rolled "s" and "sch" sounds, and the abundance of the letters *k, v,* and *b;* but after a couple of days, English speakers may begin to hear words that sound familiar. In fact, Dutch is a bridge language between German and English; in the northern province of Friesland one can hear a Dutch regional language that's supposedly the closest cousin to Old English.

4 Art & Architecture

ART

THE GOLDEN AGE   Although there were earlier Dutch artists, Dutch art came into its own during the 17th century, benefiting, like so many other aspects of Dutch society, from the wealth of the Golden Age. During this busy time, artists were blessed with wealthy patrons whose support allowed them to give free reign to their talents. Art held a cherished place in the hearts of average Dutch citizens too, as the Englishman Peter Mundy, who traveled to Amsterdam in 1640, observed: "Many times blacksmiths and cobblers will have some picture or other by their forge and in their stall. Such is the general notion, inclination, and delight that these county natives have to paintings." The Dutch were particularly fond of pictures that depicted their world: landscapes, seascapes, domestic scenes, portraits, and still lifes. The art of this period remains some of the greatest ever created in Holland, and Amsterdam was (and still is) a major art center.

The roots of 17th-century Dutch realism are clearly found in the work of Belgian **Jan van Eyck** (1395–1441). Another influence was the new "realism of light and dark," or *chiaroscuro,* that had first been introduced into art by **Caravaggio** (1573–1610). Early 17th-century Utrecht artist **Gerrit van Honthorst** (1590–1656), who had studied in Rome with Caravaggio, brought the technique to Holland, where he influenced such Dutch artists as the young Rembrandt. Best known for lively company scenes such as *The Supper Party* (ca. 1620; Uffizi, Florence), which depicted ordinary people against a plain background and set a style that continued in Dutch art for many years, Honthorst often used multiple hidden light sources to heighten the dramatic contrast of lights and darks. Among the great landscape artists of this period, **Jacob van Ruisdael** (1628–82), an art dealer's son, stands out. In his paintings, human figures either do not appear at all or are shown as almost insignificantly small; vast skies filled with moody clouds often cover two-thirds of the canvas. His *Windmill at Wijk bij Duurstede* (ca.1665), which you can view in the city's Rijksmuseum, combines many characteristic elements of his style: The windmill stands in a somber landscape, containing a few small human figures, with a cloud-laden sky and a foreground of agitated water and reeds.

Frans Hals (1581–1666), the undisputed leader of the Haarlem school (schools differed from city to city), was a great portrait painter whose relaxed, informal, and naturalistic portraits contrast strikingly with the traditional formal masks of Renaissance portraits. His light brush strokes help convey immediacy and intimacy, making his works perceptive psychological portraits. He had a genius for comic characters, showing men and women as they are and a little less than they are, as in *Malle Babbe* (1650). As a stage designer of group portraits, Hals's skill is almost unmatched—only Rembrandt is superior. Although he carefully arranged and posed each group, balancing the directions of gesture and glance, his *alla prima* brushwork (direct laying down of pigment) makes these public images—such as *The Archers of St. Aidan* (1633)—seem spontaneous. It's worth taking a day trip to Haarlem just to visit the Frans Halsmuseum and view such works as his *Officers of the Militia Company of St. George* (ca.1627).

The great genius of the period was **Rembrandt van Rijn** (1606–69). One of his accomplishments was pushing the art of chiaroscuro to unprecedented heights. In his paintings the values of light and dark gradually and softly blend together; this may have diffused some of the drama of chiaroscuro, but it achieved a more truthful appearance. Rembrandt's art seemed capable of revealing the soul and inner life of his subjects, and to view his series of 60 self-portraits is to see a remarkable documentation of his own psychological evolution. The *Self-Portrait with Saskia* (in the Museum Het Rembrandthuis) shows him with his wife at a prosperous time when he was being commissioned to do portraits of many wealthy merchants. Later self-portraits are more psychologically complex, often depicting a careworn old man whose gaze is nonetheless sharp, compassionate, and wise.

Rembrandt's series of religious paintings and prints is intensely spiritual, but the figures are treated in very human terms; these works project a sense of contemplative stillness. His religious prints brought him much renown and were a major source of income. At the Museum Het Rembrandthuis in Amsterdam—which has been restored to much the way it was when the master

An estimated 20 million paintings were produced in Amsterdam during the Golden Age.

lived and worked there—you can see many of his self-portraits along with some 250 etchings.

In his group portraits—such as *The Night Watch* (1642) and *The Syndics of the Cloth Guild* (1662), both on view in the Rijksmuseum—each individual portrait is done with care. Although art historians do not know how he proceeded, a long studio sitting may have been required of each man. The unrivaled harmony of light, color, and movement of these works is a marvel to be appreciated. Compare, too, these robust, masculine works with the tender *The Jewish Bride* (ca. 1665), also in the Rijksmuseum.

In his later years Rembrandt was at the height of his artistic powers, but his work was judged too personal and eccentric by his contemporaries. Some considered him a tasteless painter who was obsessed with the ugly and ignorant of color; this opinion prevailed until the 19th century, when Rembrandt's genius was reevaluated.

Jan Vermeer (1632–75) of Delft is perhaps the best known of the "little Dutch masters" who specialized in one genre of painting, such as portraiture. Although they confined their artistry within a narrow scope, these painters rendered their subjects with an exquisite care and faithfulness to their actual appearances.

Vermeer's work centers on the simple pleasures and activities of domestic life—a woman pouring milk or reading a letter, for example—and all of his simple figures positively glow with color and light. Vermeer placed the figure (usually just one, but sometimes two or more) at the center of his paintings against a background in which furnishings often provided the horizontal and vertical balance, giving the composition a feeling of stability and serenity. Art historians have determined that Vermeer used mirrors and the *camera obscura,* an early camera, as compositional aids. A master at lighting interior scenes and rendering true colors, Vermeer was able to create an illusion of three-dimensionality in works such as *The Love Letter* (ca. 1670), in Amsterdam's Rijksmuseum. As light—usually afternoon sunshine pouring in from an open window—moves across the picture plane, it caresses and modifies all the colors.

Jan Steen (1626–79) is another artist who painted marvelous interior scenes, often satirical and didactic in their intent. The allusions on which much of the satire depends may escape most of us today, but any viewer can appreciate the fine drawing, subtle color shading, and warm light that pervades such paintings as *Woman at Her Toilet* and *The Feast of St. Nicholas* (both in the Rijksmuseum).

REVIVAL   It took until well into the 19th century before Dutch art regained some of the vitality of the 17th century. Artists of the Amsterdam and The Hague schools were at the forefront. **George Hendrik Breitner** (1857–1923) painted powerful scenes of everyday life on Amsterdam's streets and canals.

If **Vincent van Gogh** (1853–90) had not failed as a missionary in the mining region of Belgium, he might not have turned to painting and become the greatest Dutch artist of the 19th century. *The Potato Eaters* (1885) was the anxious and sensitive first masterpiece of van Gogh. Dark and crudely painted, it depicts a group of peasants gathered around the table for their evening meal after a long day of manual labor. The viewer is powerfully impressed with a sense of the hard, rough conditions of their lives. Gone are the beauty and serenity of traditional Dutch genre painting.

After the death of his father, Vincent traveled first to Antwerp and then to Paris to join his favorite brother, Theo. In Paris, he discovered and adopted the brilliant color palette of the impressionists. Theo, an art dealer, introduced him to Gauguin, and the two artists had many conversations on the expressive power of pure color. Van Gogh developed a thick, highly textured style of brushwork that complemented his intense color schemes.

In 1888 van Gogh traveled to Arles in Provence. He was dazzled by the Mediterranean sun, and his favorite color, yellow (it signified love to him), dominated such landscapes as *Wheatfield with a Reaper* (1889). Until his death 2 years later, van Gogh remained in the south of France painting at a frenetic pace, in between bouts of madness. In *The Night Café* (1888), the red walls and green ceiling of a billiard hall combine with a sickly yellow lamplight to charge the scene with an oppressive, almost nightmarish, air. (With red and green, Vincent wrote, he tried to represent "those terrible things, men's passions.") We see the halos around the lights swirl as if we, like some of the patrons slumped over their tables, have had too much to drink.

The Vincent van Gogh Museum in Amsterdam has more than 200 of his paintings—including all of those mentioned here, and *The Sunflowers*—presented to Holland by Theo's wife and son with the provision that the canvases not leave Vincent's native land.

Before **Piet Mondrian** (1872–1944) became a master/originator of De Stijl (also called neoplasticism), he was a painter of windmills, cows, and meadows. He painted his expressionistic masterpiece, *The Red Tree* (1909)—which looks as though it's bursting into flame against a background of blue—at age 41, and it marks a turning point in his career as a contemporary painter. He had always said that when he had discovered his true personality, he would drop one of the two *a*'s in his last name (originally Mondriaan)—it is this canvas that he first signed as Mondrian.

In 1917, with his friend Theo van Doesburg, Mondrian began a magazine entitled *De Stijl* (The Style), in which he expounded the principles of neoplasticism—a simplification of forms, reducing what is represented to a limited number of signs, or in other words, purified abstraction. In large part this movement was an outgrowth of and a reaction against the cubist work of Picasso and Braque, which Mondrian had seen while he lived in Paris from 1912 to 1914. To Mondrian and the poets, sculptors, and architects associated with De Stijl, abstraction was a moral necessity; to simplify vision would simplify life, and a universal plastic language would bring about a better world. For these reasons, the geometric painters of the De Stijl school attempted a "controllable precision." Their basic form was the rectangle—with horizontal and vertical accents at right angles. Their basic colors were the primaries—red, blue, and yellow—along with black and white. In works such as *Composition in Blue, Yellow, and Black* (1936), on view in the Haags Gemeentemuseum in The Hague, no part of the picture plane is more important than any other; with its design, Mondrian achieves an equilibrium but does not succumb to a mechanical uniformity.

Mondrian suppressed the use of curves and the color green in his later work because, he said, it reminded him of nature. Ironically, Mondrian's principal source of income for much of his life was painting flowers on porcelain. In 1940 Mondrian moved to New York City, which he loved, to escape the war in Europe. In the evenings he would take walks around the art deco

Rockefeller Center; the geometry of the lighted windows reminded him of his paintings. Mondrian's last paintings were lively abstract representations of New York: *Broadway Boogie Woogie* (1942) and *Victory Boogie Woogie* (1943), which you can view at the Haags Gemeentemuseum.

In the late 1940s **Karel Appel** (b. 1921), a Dutch abstract painter, sculptor, and graphic artist who helped found the experimental Cobra group, came on the scene. His work, including *Child and Beast II* (1951), has a childlike quality, employing bright colors and abstract shapes. He once said, "I paint like a barbarian in a barbarous age." He worked in Amsterdam for some time, and in order to pay debts to the city, he painted a mural in what used to be the Amsterdam Town Hall (now the Grand Amsterdam Hotel)—for years the mural was considered so revolting it was covered up. If you go to Café Roux (the cafe at the Grand Amsterdam), you can see it preserved behind glass.

ARCHITECTURE

If you're interested in architecture, Amsterdam is a great place. You might think the canal houses in Amsterdam all look similar (they do for the most part, in terms of shape). However, if you look a little more closely you find that Amsterdam's buildings demonstrate a wonderful mix of architectural detail ranging from classical to Renaissance to modern.

EARLY AMSTERDAM   Amsterdam's very first houses were built of wood and had thatched roofs, for practical reasons: Wood was lighter than stone or brick, and therefore a timber house was less likely to sink into the marshy, constantly shifting ground. Even today, though foundations are much stronger than they were in the beginning, you see canal houses leaning precariously against each other as a result of the ground movement. (You might also see that the streets and sidewalks of Amsterdam are constantly being torn up, straightened out, and relaid for the same reason.) Houses were narrow but very deep and fairly tall. The gables were made of wood, and on each floor the gable projected out farther than the one below for drainage purposes.

In 1452 about three-quarters of Amsterdam was destroyed by fire. The side walls of new houses were thereafter made of brick to prevent the spread of fire from one house to its very near neighbor. At the beginning of the 16th century (again to counter the threat of fire), thatched roofs began to disappear beneath a covering of clay and were eventually replaced with tiles. The houses, though now made of brick, looked exactly like the wood ones that came before.

In the 16th and 17th centuries the *strap and scroll* ornament became quite popular. A fluid form, the strap and scroll frames the top part of the facade and resembles curled leather. The *step gable,* a nonclassical element resembling a small staircase (with varying numbers of steps and varying step heights), was used on many of the buildings you see as you walk along the canals today. Often you find step gables of this period augmented by Renaissance features, such as vases and masks.

Hendrik de Keyser (1565–1621), an architect who worked in Amsterdam at the height of the Renaissance, is known for using decorative, playful elements in a way that was practical to the structure. For instance, he combined hard yellow or white sandstone decorative features (like volutes, keystones, and masks) with soft red brick, creating a visually stimulating multicolored facade, while utilizing the sandstone as protection for the brick from rain erosion. **Philip** and **Justus Vingboons** were architects and brothers who worked in the Renaissance style, and if you walk along the Herengracht, Keizersgracht, and Prinsengracht, you see many of the buildings they designed. With them the medieval stepped gable gave way to a more ornate one with scrolled sides, decorative finials, and other features.

Many other buildings from the 17th century have typically classical elements, such as pilasters, entablatures, and pediments. These details give a sense of order and balance to their facades and move away from de Keyser's playful Renaissance style. The classical pediment, often used as a protective element against the rain, was typically used to shield windows and to cap gable ends. It was during this time that a harder, brown brick came to be used as a replacement for the red brick used in the 16th century.

Because classical elements tend to have straight lines and don't flow like the Renaissance elements did, the focus on the facade shifted to a more boxed-in, central location that eventually grew into the raised-neck gable (a tall, narrow, rectangular gable). It was during this classical period that fruits and flowers were used as ornamentation in the scrolls. Soon, the raised-neck gable gave way to the neck gable (which looks relatively the same, only shorter) with human and animal figures carved into the scrolls. **Jacob van Campen** (1595–1657), who built the elaborate **Town Hall** at the Dam, now the Royal Palace, was probably the single most important architect of the classical period in Amsterdam architecture.

Around 1665, **Adriaan Dortsman** (1625–82), best known as an architect of the classic restrained Dutch style, began building homes with balconies and attics, leaving off the pilasters and festoons that had adorned facades earlier in the century. The emphasis had once again shifted, this time from ornamentation and decoration to utility of space and harmony of the features with the basic structure.

THE 18TH & 19TH CENTURIES   During the 18th century Amsterdam's population did not increase, so new housing wasn't needed. However, many people rebuilt the facades of their homes and incorporated some new styles that architects had been studying. **Daniel Marot,** a French architect who lived in Amsterdam from 1705 to 1717, is credited with introducing the "Louis" styles to Amsterdam, and they are common to buildings of the 18th century.

The heavy baroque Louis XIV style was suitable for the neck gable, but the asymmetrical, rococo Louis XV style was better executed on a new gable type—the bell gable. Its name is description enough, though you might at first confuse it with the neck gable because if you look only at the outer lines of the top of the structure, you frequently see the same basic triangular shape (due to the ornamentation of the neck gables); however, the bell gable is very clearly shaped like a bell.

During this period much of Amsterdam's architecture underwent a reversion to classicism, albeit in a more ornate manner. Many of the more ornate gables were replaced with straight cornices. However, in 1876, **Petrus Josephus Herbertus Cuypers** (1827–1921) came on the scene, quickly establishing himself as the most influential architect of the time. Perhaps best known for designing Centraal Station and the Rijksmuseum, he worked in a neo-Gothic style using steep roofs and dormers and is considered to be the "grandfather of modern architecture." He ascribed to a theory known as structural rationalism, which is Gothic in principle, and believed in utilizing ornamentation that is natural and organic to the basic form of the structure.

At the end of the century this heavily ornamented look was simplified by, among others, **Willem Kromhout** (1864–1940), who designed the American Hotel. **Hendrik Petrus Berlage** (1856–1934), said to be the "father of modern architecture," followed, and his Amsterdam Exchange and Diamond

Worker's Trade Union buildings are two examples of a more refined Dutch style. Kromhout's and Berlage's most important works were not built until the beginning of this century.

THE 20TH CENTURY   Between 1900 and 1940 many different styles of architecture were purveyed from the offices of various Amsterdam architects, but one style stands out above the others: the famous Amsterdam school, with **Ed. Cuypers** (nephew to P. J. H. Cuypers) at the helm. Architects **P. L. Kramer, M. de Klerk,** and **J. M. van der Mey** were employed by Cuypers at the beginning of the century and were all contributors to the Amsterdam school. Some of Amsterdam's most fantastic buildings were designed by its members; they succeeded in creating forms of brickwork that had existed only in the fantasies of earlier architects. These buildings are massive, but somehow fluid, and use such decorative features as stained glass, wrought iron, and corner towers.

Closer to the middle of the century, the decorative brickwork features used by the Amsterdam school were abandoned because architects were more interested in creating an absolutely functional space, placing a premium on eliminating architectural flourishes that cluttered and detracted from the utility of a space. Lines were clean, straight, and sharp—not rounded and free-form. Up sprang high-rises constructed with concrete, steel, and glass. After World War II, the focus on design shifted to suburban development and urban renewal. It was then that this "functionalism," just becoming popular before the war, really flourished. This architectural ideology is the basis for what we know as modern urban planning, with its sleek skyscrapers and high-rise office and apartment buildings.

5 Famous Amsterdammers

Karel Appel (b. 1921)   This controversial abstract expressionist painter in 1950 cofounded Cobra (Copenhagen, Brussels, and Amsterdam), a group of now-famous artists. In 1954 he won the UNESCO prize and in 1960 the Guggenheim prize. You can view a great deal of his work at the city's Stedelijk Museum; go to Café Roux in the Grand Amsterdam Hotel (formerly the Amsterdam City Hall) for a close-up view of a piece he did to pay a debt he owed the city. Apparently, the city hall staff were so repelled by the mural that they covered it up—now it's a site of artistic pilgrimage.

Hendrik Petrus Berlage (1856–1934)   Considered the father of modern Dutch architecture, he advocated a return to simplicity of form and clarity of line and structure. His theories can be seen most clearly at work in the Amsterdam Stock Exchange (1898–1903) and the Diamond Workers' Union Building (1899–1900). An admirer of Frank Lloyd Wright, Berlage greatly influenced the Amsterdam School of architecture, and modern urban planning.

Willem Jansz Blaeu (1571–1638)   A cartographer and printer, Blaeu founded a company in Amsterdam that was famous for marine publications, globes, and atlases, and for navigational and astronomical instruments. You can see examples of his work at the Amsterdams Historisch Museum and the Netherlands Maritime Museum. Blaeu's son, Jan, published in 1663 the 11-volume *Atlas Major*.

Johann Cruyff (b. 1947)   Cruyff himself might be astonished to find his name in such august company, but there are many who will testify to his supreme artistry, poetry, and skill as he captained Amsterdam's soccer club Ajax, proponents of a highly mobile, fluent, and deadly system of play called Total Football, to three successive European Cup triumphs (1971–73) and led Holland to the World Cup final in 1974.

Petrus Josephus Hubertus Cuypers (1827–1921)   One of the most important late 19th-century Dutch architects, a Catholic proponent of neo-Gothic, he designed mainly churches. His two major secular works in Amsterdam, the Rijksmuseum (1876–85) and Centraal Station (1881–89), both slip in neo-Gothic elements to an underlying Dutch Renaissance, gabled style in brick.

Eugène Dubois (1858–1940)   A geologist and anatomist, Dubois in 1891 discovered Java Man, the first known fossil of the early hominid species *Homo erectus*. He concluded it had walked upright and called it *Pithecanthropus erectus*. Dubois later became professor of geology at the University of Amsterdam.

Gabriel Daniel Fahrenheit (1686–1736)   Born in Danzig, Prussia (now Gdansk, Poland), he spent most of his life in Amsterdam, manufacturing weather instruments. He produced the first mercury thermometer in 1714 and invented the hygrometer (for measuring atmospheric humidity).

Anne Frank (1929–45)   Anne is famous the world over for her diary, a profoundly moving record of a Jewish teenager's struggle to cope with the horrific realities of war and the Nazi occupation. Anne and her family went into hiding when the Germans took Amsterdam. Cut off from other outlets for her energies, she began to keep a journal telling of her thoughts, feelings, and experiences. The last entry was on August 1, 1944, shortly before she and her family were discovered and deported to concentration camps. Anne and her sister were sent to Bergen-Belsen, where they died of typhus just a few days before Allied forces liberated the camp. Otto Frank, Anne's father, was the only survivor of the Frank family, and it was he who first had Anne's diary published.

Pieter Corneliszoon Hooft (1581–1647)   This leading Dutch Renaissance poet and playwright wrote the first pastoral play in Dutch, *Granida* (1605). He later turned his hand to history, in *Nederlandsche Historien* (*Dutch History*, 1642–54), about the Dutch Revolt against Spain.

Piet Mondrian (1872–1944)   Mondrian attended the academy in Amsterdam before moving on to Paris, and later, New York. A leader of the De Stijl group of artists, Mondrian developed a geometric art style he called neoplasticism, which influenced the later Bauhaus movement and international style of architecture.

Rembrandt van Rijn (1606–69)   This painter, whose works hang in places of honor in the world's great museums, may be *the* most famous Amsterdammer, to both outsiders and today's city residents. Born in Leiden, Rembrandt moved to Amsterdam in 1632, earning acclaim as a highly sought portraitist. Later, however, as he refused to compromise his artistic ideas, he began to lose popularity. In 1639 he bought a home (now the Museum Het Rembrandthuis) on Jodenbreestraat in the Old Jewish Quarter, but soon began to have financial difficulties. One of his most famous paintings today, *The Night Watch,* was refused by those who had commissioned it. In 1656 Rembrandt declared bankruptcy, a financial state from which he would never recover. He is buried in the Westerkerk.

Baruch Benedictus de Spinoza (1632–77)   A giant of philosophy, Spinoza devoted his life to writing compelling and far-reaching treatises, most of which were published after his death. *Ethica,* his best-known work, attempted to prove ethical theories using mathematics. His unorthodox ideas had him expelled in 1656 from the Portuguese Synagogue. Spinoza's day job—he worked as a lens grinder—financed his philosophizing and writing.

Jan Pieterszoon Sweelinck (1562–1621) A composer who for some 45 years was organist at the Oude Kerk. He was a prolific composer for organ and harpsichord, and wrote 250 choral works. Amsterdam's music school is called the Sweelinck Conservatorium.

Joost van den Vondel (1587–1679) Van den Vondel is one of the most famous Dutch poets and playwrights of Amsterdam's Golden Age. His best-known works are *Gijsbrecht van Aemstel* and *Lucifer*. Amsterdam's Vondelpark is named after him.

6 Recommended Reading

PHOTOGRAPHY

Morning mist on a canal; the remains of an abandoned bicycle; kids playing soccer in Vondelpark; feeding the pigeons at the Dam; explosions of merry-making on Queen's Day. The 143 pages of photographer Martin Kers's beautiful book, ***Amsterdam*** (Inmerc/Schipper Art Productions, 1991), dazzle with a mix not only of subjects, but also of vantages and camera angles, panorama and detail. A master of composition, Kers infuses even demolished buildings and library books with his visual magic. In parks and on bridges, on canals and terraces, he captures the atmosphere of the city and those in it as they pose for their picture, walk the dog, or mend a bike. With text by Dutch poet Willem Wilmink.

Jacob Olie's evocative images of 19th-century Amsterdam have only recently been rescued from oblivion—5,000 of his negatives resurfaced in 1960. A schoolteacher with a passion for photography, Olie shot most of his pictures during the 1860s, when photography was in its infancy, and during the 1890s, when development in technique permitted him to break new ground. Though strictly documentary, the 79 black-and-white photographs in ***De Verbeelding*** (Amsterdam, 1999), a small, landscape-shaped book, ooze nostalgia. They afford glimpses of recognition, showing people going about their business in a semirural, unhurried city where canals have not yet been filled in and where trams are powered by horses, carts by men, and trains by steam.

SOCIETY

Should you be turned off by the pun in the title of ***The UnDutchables*** (White-Boucke Publishing, 3rd edition 1993), don't read the book, for it goes on: On Gulden Pond, Modern Dutches and Duchesses, and more in that vein. And if you're ready to believe that all Dutch people are rude, their children undisciplined, and Dutch drivers abusive, then this isn't for you either. But if you're sufficiently skeptical to decide for yourself what to believe and you recognize caricatures when you read them, you may find yourself chuckling as you learn more about Dutch attitudes to home, money, children, transport, and much more besides. Colin White and Laurie Boucke, Anglo-American expatriates who first published this paperback in 1989, have their tongues firmly in their cheeks throughout, choosing first to amuse and only second to inform.

CUISINE

Heleen Halverhout's postcard-sized booklet ***The Netherlands Cookbook*** (also published as ***Dutch Cooking;*** De Driehoek, 1987), might be considered unambitious, but then the same is true of Dutch cooking—nourishing rather than rich, solid rather than subtle. What other cookbook would give recipes for boiled, mashed and fried potatoes? Winter favorites like pea soup, *hachée* (beef and onion stew), and *hotchpotch* are among those featured, alongside whimsical illustrations that play on Dutch stereotypes. Halverhout explains Dutch eating habits and devotes plenty of space to cakes and traditional desserts such as *Hague bluff* and *John-in-the-bag*.

HISTORY

You get inside the mind of Amsterdam's greatest period in Simon Schama's ***The Embarrassment of Riches: An Interpretation of Dutch Culture in the Golden Age*** (Alfred A. Knopf, 1987). Schama pulls off the difficult feat of being lighthearted and scholarly at the same time—a chapter headed "The Pretzel and the Puppy Dog" refers to a portrait of a child by Jacob Cuyp. Most of the 700 pages feature reproductions of works of art, which are explained in the text. Though Schama modestly describes his essays as "more eccentric than persuasive," there is no doubt that he has succeeded in his intention "to map out the moral geography of the Dutch mind, adrift between the fear of deluge and the hope of moral salvage."

If a single individual may be said to personify the Holocaust, that person must be Anne Frank. Anne's diary, compiled as a series of letters addressed to "dearest Kitty," and kept for more than 2 years until her arrest on August 4, 1944, has come to symbolize the plight of millions of Jews during the Nazi terror. This "definitive edition," ***The Diary of a Young Girl*** (Doubleday, New York/Viking, London, 1995/1997), includes a map of the secret annex of the house on Prinsengracht where Anne and her family hid and photos of its occupants. Her candid descriptions of the world of a teenage girl living in tragically restricted conditions, of her thoughts and dreams, hopes and fears, boredom and anguish, have moved millions.

Amsterdam, A Brief Life of the City (The Harvill Press, 1999), roves through 800 years in 300-some pages during which author Geert Mak lays bare the city's soul, linking tales about ordinary folk with historical fact. The journey from boggy, 12th-century settlement of fishermen and farmers to modern metropolis is populated with princes and painters, Calvinists and Catholics, "Provos" and rebels, and enlivened with black and white illustrations. Mak's combination of journalistic skill and historic insight amply fulfills his ambition to write a work of history you can read in your hotel room before going to bed.

ART

If you want to buy a book about Old Masters, make it ***The Glory of the Golden Age*** (Waanders, Zwolle, 2000), by Judikje Kiers and Fieke Tissink. Published to coincide with the bicentennial of Amsterdam's Rijksmuseum, this weighty tome comprehensively covers the painting, sculpture, and decorative art of Holland's Golden Age (1600–1700). Works by Rembrandt, Vermeer, Frans Hals, and Jacob van Ruisdael are presented along with that of lesser known artists. Roughly chronological, the book contains a wealth of description about the country's vibrant 17th-century art scene.

Lavish and comprehensive, the ***Van Gogh Museum*** (Waanders, Zwolle, 1997), by Ronald de Leeuw, a former director, presents the museum's collection in words and pictures. The Van Gogh has 200 paintings by the artist, seven sketchbooks and hundreds of drawings, as well as works by his contemporaries. Vincent's correspondence with his brother Theo helps place

Van Gogh in context, from the "official" 19th-century art to the fin de siècle. Chapters on Van Gogh in Holland, Paris, Arles, St. Rémy, and Auvers paint an easy-to-read chronological picture of Vincent's life and the way it was affected by his friends, most notably by Paul Gauguin and Emile Bernard.

For a more personal insight into Van Gogh's life and art, read Ken Wilkie's *The Van Gogh File: A Journey of Discovery* (Souvenir Press, 1990). What began as a routine magazine assignment in 1972 to coincide with the opening of the Van Gogh Museum, became exactly what the book's subtitle indicates, a journey that continued long after the article was published. Wilkie, a journalist and long-term resident of Amsterdam, followed Vincent's trail through the Netherlands, Belgium, England, and France. Along the way he met some of the last surviving people to have known or met the artist. In one of many dramatic discoveries, he finds an original Van Gogh drawing (authenticated by the Van Gogh Museum) while rummaging through a pile of old photographs in an English attic. The revelations from Vincent's private life, his search for love and family, are equally compelling.

Appendix B:
Useful Terms & Phrases

1 Basic Vocabulary

English	Dutch	Pronunciation
Hello	**Hallo**	*ha*-loh
How are you?	**Hoe gaat het met U?**	hoo *khaht* et met oo?
Very well	**Uitstekend**	out-*stayk*-end
Thank you	**Dank U**	*Dahnk* oo
Thank you very much	**Dank U wel**	*Dahnk* oo wel
Good-bye	**Dag**	dakh
Please	**Alstublieft**	*ahl*-stoo-bleeft
Yes	**Ja**	yah
No	**Neen**	Nay
Excuse me	**Pardon**	par-*dawn*
Give me . . .	**Geeft U mij . . .**	*khayft* oo may . . .
Where is . . .?	**Waar is . . . ?**	*vahr* iz . . . ?
he station	**het station**	het *stah* -ssyonh
a hotel	**een hotel**	ayn *ho* -tel
a restaurant	**een restaurant**	ayn res-to-*rahng*
the toilet	**het toilet**	het *twah* -let
To the right	**Rechts**	rekhts
To the left	**Links**	links
Straight ahead	**Rechtdoor**	rekht-*doar*
I would like . . .	**Ik zou graag . . .**	ik zow khrakh . . .
to eat	**eten**	*ay* -ten
a room for one night	**een kamer voor een nacht**	ayn *kah* -mer voor ayn nakht
How much is it?	**Hoe veel kost het?**	hoo fayl kawst het
The check	**De rekening**	duh *ray* -ken-ing
When?	**Wanneer?**	vah-*neer*
Yesterday	**Gisteren**	*khis* -ter-en
Today	**Vandaag**	van-*dahkh*
Tomorrow	**Morgen**	*mor* -khen
Breakfast	**Ontbijt**	*ohnt* -bayt
Lunch	**Lunch**	lunch
Dinner	**Diner**	*dee* -nay

NUMBERS

1	**een** (ayn)	15	**vijftien** (*vayf*-teen)
2	**twee** (tway)	16	**zestien** (*zes*-teen)
3	**drie** (dree)	17	**zeventien** (*zay*-vun-teen)
4	**vier** (veer)	18	**achtien** (*akh*-teen)
5	**vijf** (vayf)	19	**negentien** (*nay*-khun-teen)
6	**zes** (zes)	20	**twintig** (*twin*-tikh)
7	**zeven** (*zay*-vun)	30	**dertig** (*der*-tukh)
8	**acht** (akht)	40	**veertig** (*vayr*-tukh)
9	**negen** (*nay*-khen)	50	**vijftig** (*vayf*-tukh)
10	**tien** (teen)	60	**zestig** (*zes*-tukh)
11	**elf** (elf)	70	**zeventig** (*zay*-vun-tukh)
12	**twaalf** (tvahlf)	80	**tachtig** (*takh*-tukh)
13	**dertien** (*dayr*-teen)	90	**negentig** (*nay*-khen-tukh)
14	**veertien** (*vayr*-teen)	100	**honderd** (hon-dayrt)

DAYS OF THE WEEK

Monday	**Maandag** (*mahn*-dakh)	Friday	**Vrijdag** (*vray*-dakh)
Tuesday	**Dinsdag** (*deens*-dakh)	Saturday	**Zaterdag** (*zahter*-dakh)
Wednesday	**Woensdag** (*voohns*-dakh)	Sunday	**Zondag** (*zohn*-dakh)
Thursday	**Donderdag** (*donder*-dakh)		

MONTHS

January	**Januari** (*yahn*-oo-aree)	July	**Juli** (yoo-*lee*)
February	**Februari** (*fayhb*-roo-aree)	August	**August** (awh-*khoost*)
March	**Maart** (mahrt)	September	**September** (sep-*tem*-buhr)
April	**April** (ah-*pril*)	October	**Oktober** (oct-*oah*-buhr)
May	**Mai** (*mah*-eey)	November	**November** (noa-*vem*-buhr)
June	**Juni** (yoo-*nee*)	December	**December** (day-*sem*-buhr)

SEASONS

Spring	**Lente** (*Len*-tuh)	Fall/autumn	**Herfst** (Herfsst)
Summer	**Zomer** (*Zoh*-muhr)	Winter	**Winter** (*Vin*-tuhr)

2 Dutch Menu Savvy

BASICS

ontbijt breakfast	**jam** jam
lunch lunch	**kaas** cheese
diner dinner	**mosterd** mustard
boter butter	**peper** pepper
brood bread	**suiker** sugar
honing honey	**zout** salt

SOUPS (SOEPEN)

aardappelsoep potato soup	**kippensoep** chicken soup
bonensoep bean soup	**soep** soup
erwtensoep pea soup	**tomatensoep** tomato soup
groentensoep vegetable soup	**uiensoep** onion soup

EGGS (EIER)

eieren eggs	**roereieren** scrambled eggs
hardgekookte eieren hard-boiled eggs	**spiegeleieren** fried eggs
omelette omelette	**zachtgekookte eieren** boiled eggs

FISH (VIS)

forel trout
gerookte zalm smoked salmon
haring herring
kabeljauw cod
kreeft lobster

makreel mackerel
mosselen mussels
oesters oysters
sardienen sardines
zalm salmon

MEATS (VLEESWAREN)

biefstuk steak
haasbiefstuk filet steak
eend duck
gans goose
lamscotelet lamb chops
lever liver
ragout beef stew

kalkoen turkey
kip chicken
konijn rabbit
koude schotel cold cuts
runder bief beef
spek bacon
worst sausage

VEGETABLES/SALADS (GROENTEN/SLA)

aardappelen potatoes
asperges asparagus
augurken pickles
bonen beans
bieten beets
erwten peas
groenten vegetables
komkommersla cucumber salad
kool cabbage
patates frites french fries

prinsesseboonen green beans
purée mashed potatoes
radijsen radishes
rapen turnips
rijst rice
sla lettuce, salad
spinazie spinach
tomaten tomatoes
wortelen carrots
zuurkool sauerkraut

DESSERTS (NAGERECHTEN)

ananas pineapple
cake cake
compôte stewed fruits

ijs ice cream
nagerecht dessert

BEVERAGES (DRANKEN)

bier (or pils) beer
cognac brandy
koffie coffee
melk milk

rode wijn red wine
thee tea
water water
witte wijn white wine

COOKING TERMS

gebakken fried
gekookt cooked
geroosteerd boiled

goed doorgebakken well done
niet doorgebakken rare

Index

See also Accommodations and Restaurant indexes below.

RESTAURANTS

FROMMER'S® COMPLETE TRAVEL GUIDES

Alaska
Amsterdam
Arizona
Atlanta
Australia
Austria
Bahamas
Barcelona, Madrid &
    Seville
Beijing
Belgium, Holland &
    Luxembourg
Bermuda
Boston
British Columbia & the
    Canadian Rockies
Budapest & the Best of
    Hungary
California
Canada
Cancún, Cozumel &
    the Yucatán
Cape Cod, Nantucket &
    Martha's Vineyard
Caribbean
Caribbean Cruises & Ports
    of Call
Caribbean Ports of Call
Carolinas & Georgia
Chicago
China
Colorado
Costa Rica
Denmark
Denver, Boulder & Colorado
    Springs
England
Europe

European Cruises & Ports
    of Call
Florida
France
Germany
Greece
Greek Islands
Hawaii
Hong Kong
Honolulu, Waikiki & Oahu
Ireland
Israel
Italy
Jamaica
Japan
Las Vegas
London
Los Angeles
Maryland & Delaware
Maui
Mexico
Montana & Wyoming
Montréal & Québec City
Munich & the Bavarian
    Alps
Nashville & Memphis
Nepal
New England
New Mexico
New Orleans
New York City
New Zealand
Nova Scotia, New Brunswick
    & Prince Edward Island
Oregon
Paris
Philadelphia & the
    Amish Country

Portugal
Prague & the Best of the
    Czech Republic
Provence & the Riviera
Puerto Rico
Rome
San Antonio & Austin
San Diego
San Francisco
Santa Fe, Taos & Albuquerque
Scandinavia
Scotland
Seattle & Portland
Shanghai
Singapore & Malaysia
South Africa
Southeast Asia
South Florida
South Pacific
Spain
Sweden
Switzerland
Thailand
Tokyo
Toronto
Tuscany & Umbria
USA
Utah
Vancouver & Victoria
Vermont, New Hampshire
    & Maine
Vienna & the Danube Valley
Virgin Islands
Virginia
Walt Disney World &
    Orlando
Washington, D.C.
Washington State

FROMMER'S® DOLLAR-A-DAY GUIDES

Australia from $50 a Day
California from $60 a Day
Caribbean from $70 a Day
England from $70 a Day
Europe from $70 a Day

Florida from $70 a Day
Hawaii from $70 a Day
Ireland from $60 a Day
Italy from $70 a Day
London from $85 a Day

New York from $80 a Day
Paris from $80 a Day
San Francisco from $60 a Day
Washington, D.C.,
    from $70 a Day

FROMMER'S® PORTABLE GUIDES

Acapulco, Ixtapa &
    Zihuatanejo
Alaska Cruises & Ports of Call
Bahamas
Baja & Los Cabos
Berlin
California Wine Country
Charleston & Savannah
Chicago
Dublin

Hawaii: The Big Island
Las Vegas
London
Los Angeles
Maine Coast
Maui
Miami
New Orleans
New York City
Paris

Puerto Vallarta, Manzanillo
    & Guadalajara
San Diego
San Francisco
Sydney
Tampa & St. Petersburg
Venice
Washington, D.C.

FROMMER'S® NATIONAL PARK GUIDES

Family Vacations in the National Parks
Grand Canyon

National Parks of the American West
Rocky Mountain

Yellowstone & Grand Teton
Yosemite & Sequoia/ Kings Canyon
Zion & Bryce Canyon

FROMMER'S® MEMORABLE WALKS

Chicago
London

New York
Paris

San Francisco
Washington, D.C.

FROMMER'S® GREAT OUTDOOR GUIDES

New England
Northern California

Southern California & Baja
Southern New England

Washington & Oregon

FROMMER'S® BORN TO SHOP GUIDES

Born to Shop: France
Born to Shop: Italy

Born to Shop: London
Born to Shop: New York

Born to Shop: Paris

FROMMER'S® IRREVERENT GUIDES

Amsterdam
Boston
Chicago
Las Vegas

London
Los Angeles
Manhattan
New Orleans

Paris
San Francisco
Seattle & Portland
Vancouver

Walt Disney World
Washington, D.C.

FROMMER'S® BEST-LOVED DRIVING TOURS

America
Britain
California

Florida
France
Germany

Ireland
Italy
New England

Scotland
Spain
Western Europe

THE UNOFFICIAL GUIDES®

Bed & Breakfasts in California
Bed & Breakfasts in New England
Bed & Breakfasts in the Northwest
Bed & Breakfasts in Southeast
Beyond Disney
Branson, Missouri

California with Kids
Chicago
Cruises
Disneyland
Florida with Kids
Golf Vacations in the Eastern U.S.
The Great Smoky & Blue Ridge Mountains

Inside Disney
Hawaii
Las Vegas
London
Miami & the Keys
Mini Las Vegas
Mini-Mickey
New Orleans
New York City
Paris

San Francisco
Skiing in the West
Southeast with Kids
Walt Disney World
Walt Disney World for Grown-ups
Walt Disney World for Kids
Washington, D.C.

SPECIAL-INTEREST TITLES

Frommer's Britain's Best Bed & Breakfasts and Country Inns
Frommer's Britain's Best Bike Rides
The Civil War Trust's Official Guide to the Civil War Discovery Trail
Frommer's Caribbean Hideaways
Frommer's Adventure Guide to Central America
Frommer's Adventure Guide to South America
Frommer's Adventure Guide to Southeast Asia
Frommer's Food Lover's Companion to France
Frommer's Gay & Lesbian Europe
Frommer's Exploring America by RV
Hanging Out in Europe

Israel Past & Present
Mad Monks' Guide to California
Mad Monks' Guide to New York City
Frommer's The Moon
Frommer's New York City with Kids
The New York Times' Unforgettable Weekends
Places Rated Almanac
Retirement Places Rated
Frommer's Road Atlas Britain
Frommer's Road Atlas Europe
Frommer's Washington, D.C., with Kids
Frommer's What the Airlines Never Tell You